Schools in an Age of Mass Culture

PRENTICE-HALL INTERNATIONAL, INC., *London*
PRENTICE-HALL OF AUSTRALIA, PTY., LTD., *Sydney*
PRENTICE-HALL OF CANADA, LTD., *Toronto*
PRENTICE-HALL OF INDIA (PRIVATE), LTD., *New Delhi*
PRENTICE-HALL OF JAPAN, INC., *Tokyo*
PRENTICE-HALL DE MEXICO, S.A., *Mexico City*

Schools in an Age of Mass Culture

An Exploration of Selected Themes in the History of Twentieth-Century American Education

SOLOMON WILLIS RUDY
Professor of History, Fairleigh Dickinson University

PRENTICE-HALL, INC. ENGLEWOOD CLIFFS, N.J.

Prentice-Hall Education Series
John S. Brubacher, editor

To My Father

Library of Congress Catalog Number: 65-11035

Printed in the United States of America: C-79446

Preface

This book seeks to review in historical perspective certain selected themes of twentieth-century American education. It makes no pretence at being a comprehensive survey of every aspect of this subject. Material dealing with the development of colleges and universities has been omitted since these matters have been adequately reviewed elsewhere. For similar reasons, no systematic analysis of the evolution of educational philosophy or the progressive education movement has been attempted. Rather this study attempts to probe into a limited number of basic questions that have loomed large in recent history of American education. Because of this consideration, it has seemed advisable to the author to forego any attempt at a consecutive chronological narrative and to concentrate instead upon surveying certain main problem areas topically. Each of the themes selected for discussion, however, is related in one way or another to what has appeared to be the fundamental historical direction that American education has been taking: the complicated adjustment of an elaborate system of public schools at all levels of learning to the demands, not just of an enduring democratic tradition, but also of an all-inclusive mass culture. This overriding reality, it is believed, brings order and unity to the seeming chaos of modern American education.

Professor John S. Brubacher of the University of Michigan has been friend, consultant, and helpful critic at every stage of the preparation of this book. The library staffs of Clark College, the University of Illinois, Harvard University, the New York Public Library, and the

v

Worcester (Massachusetts) Public Library have aided me immeasurably by making the necessary sources available. My wife Dorothy L. Rudy has contributed more to this book than I am able to enumerate in a list of acknowledgments—not only by her typing, critical reading, and advising, but even more by her unwavering belief in the importance of the project.

Willis Rudy
Norwood, New Jersey

Table of Contents

Schools in an Age of Mass Culture

CHAPTER ONE

The Setting

In 1900 two fat volumes issued from the press of J. B. Lyon Company of Albany, New York. They had been edited by an enterprising and dynamic young Professor of Philosophy and Education at Columbia University, Nicholas Murray Butler, who soon afterwards became the university's President. His project brought together in book form a series of nineteen monographs, which collectively served as the contribution of the Department of Education of New York State to the United States educational exhibit at the Paris Exposition of 1900. The authors of the separate studies included some of the very best minds in the contemporary American educational world, men of the calibre of U.S. Education Commissioner William Torrey Harris, psychologist J. McKeen Cattell, Negro educator Booker T. Washington, and Dr. Butler himself. Here in these pages was a comprehensive summing up of America's achievements in education as the giant New World democracy stood on the threshold of a new century.[1]

And what is the picture that emerges from the fact-filled pages of this ambitious turn-of-the-century survey? Editor Butler, in his introductory remarks, calls our attention to what he believes is the keynote of American education in the year 1900. That keynote, above all else,

---

[1] Nicholas Murray Butler, ed., *Education in the United States*, 2 vols. (Albany, N.Y.: J. B. Lyon Company, 1900).

1

he declares, is spontaneity. Everything that was happening and had happened was the result of individual initiative and the will of local groups of people. Consequently, there was, in the European sense, no real American "system" of education. Here, says Butler, one finds the explanation for the seemingly anarchic and hodgepodge bent that the foreign observer frequently discerns in American education. "Its varied form," he writes, "its uneven progress, its lack of symmetry, its practical effectiveness, are all due to the fact that it has sprung, unbidden and unforced, from the needs and aspirations of the people." [2]

Speaking to the Twentieth Century Club in 1901, President Charles W. Eliot of Harvard University supplemented Butler's analysis by calling attention to the historical background of the present achievement. The American people, Eliot reminded his audience, had put forth a truly "stupendous" effort to build up their schools during the century and a quarter that had passed since their national independence was proclaimed. In so doing, they had been struggling with "a huge and novel problem." What was this problem? It was nothing less, said the Harvard president, than one of seeking to educate the *whole* people of the country, hoping thus "to prepare *all* American boys and girls for a life of unprecedented freedom." [3]

A review of the history of American education demonstrates the validity of President Eliot's argument. By the middle of the nineteenth century, the rise of Jacksonian Democracy and its accompanying "Educational Awakening" had established the "common school" as one of the generally accepted pillars of the American way of life. State after state had given support to the proposition that "a school common to all, teaching a body of materials considered necessary to all, was vital to the maintenance of a healthy republic." [4] This public sanction of a free, universal, nonsectarian school for all the people won the approbation of liberals and conservatives alike. Whatever their respective motivations and political goals, democratic education increasingly was viewed as the ideal solution, the problem resolver, the cure-all. It had become a settled part of the American democratic faith. Nor was this belief in the efficacy of widespread public education to preserve and stabilize a democratic society weakened in the decades following the

[2] *Ibid.*, I, vii-ix.

[3] Charles W. Eliot, "Survey of the Condition of American Education: Some Account of Its Successes and Failures," in *Twentieth Century Club* (University Lectures, 1901-1902 [Boston: J. P. Shults, 1901]), pp. 2-3.

[4] Lawrence A. Cremin, *The American Common School: An Historic Conception* (New York: Teachers College, Columbia University, 1951), pp. 219-21.

Civil War. "During the 1880's and 1890's," writes one student of the problem, "statesmen and professional educators alike looked to an expansion of the country's school systems to ensure national progress and safeguard republican institutions despite recurrent agrarian unrest, violent labor strife, the rise of the city and the political machine, and an unprecedented influx of immigrants." [5]

Returning now to President Eliot's Twentieth Century Club address, we find the Harvard president in the course of his remarks enumerating a number of general circumstances which confronted American schools and which, he maintained, made the task of educators one without precedent in the history of education. One of these, he said, was "the extraordinarily varied nature of the families to which their pupils belong." Another resulted from the fact that American schools were "trying to prepare their pupils for a subsequent life out in a world which has been shifting and changing with an unprecedented rapidity." The most significant of these changes in terms of its impact on the schools, Dr. Eliot declared, was "the transfer of the great majority of the population from the country to the city." [6]

Looking back over the more than three decades which had transpired since the end of the Civil War, Eliot believed that American education had scored "some substantial gains" during that period of time. One indication of progress he found in the rise of the kindergarten movement. Schools and colleges, he maintained, had "learnt much from kindergartens about the importance of dealing with the individual child rather than with large groups of children." [7] Susan E. Blow, one of the pioneer American proponents of pre-grade school training, noted in one of the monographs contributed to Butler's survey volumes that by 1900 the kindergarten movement had penetrated a number of the nation's larger school systems and had also gained recognition in a substantial group of teacher-training institutions.[8]

Turning his attention to the field of elementary education, Dr. Eliot declared that considerable improvement had been achieved there by 1900. He liked the fact that there were now more observational studies in the American elementary school program; less arithmetic and more geometry; less spelling and more literature; better teaching of subjects

[5] Rush Welter, *Popular Education and Democratic Thought in America* (New York: Columbia University Press, 1962), p. 143.
[6] Eliot, "Condition of American Education," pp. 3-4.
[7] *Ibid.*, p. 4.
[8] Susan E. Blow, "Kindergarten Education," in Butler, *Education in the United States.* **I**, pp. 56-70.

such as geography and history. The onetime chairman of the famous Committee of Ten on secondary school studies was happy to see the beginnings of a change which was close to his heart, namely, the systematic teaching of subjects of a secondary school character in the upper elementary grades (foreshadowing the later junior high school approach). Nevertheless, he felt that there remained an urgent need in these first eight grades for "greater attention to the individual." [9]

Commissioner W. T. Harris, surveying American elementary education for Butler's study, preferred to stress administrative trends and statistical growth. In 1897-98, he pointed out, universal education had reached a stage where some 15 million children, or 70 per cent of the American school age population between five and eighteen years of age, were in the public schools. In the nearly three decades since 1870, attendance at the nation's public schools had increased, more than proportionately to the growth in the country's population, from less than 7,000,000 to 15,000,000. An additional one- and one-half million children were enrolled in private and parochial schools. American expenditures for public education had increased even more rapidly than school enrollments. In 1870 they amounted to 63 million dollars annually, while in 1898 they had reached 199 million, an increase from $1.64 to $2.67 per capita. Harris declared that the chief reason for this increase was the appropriation of more money for professionally educated teachers and better methods of instruction.

As the country was being transformed by industry and railroad development from a rural to an urban way of life, public education benefited. Compulsory school attendance laws, the Commissioner observed, had now been put into effect in some 30 states. The traditional district school of the rural areas, with its often makeshift teacher, ungraded classroom, and shortened term, was on the run. Nearly one half of the American population was now within reach of graded public schools that remained in session from 180 to 200 days a year, and that uniformly employed professional teachers. The average period of time spent in school per inhabitant of the United States was 4.3 years, but in industrially advanced states like Massachusetts, it was 7 years. Democratic common schooling for all people was on the march, and Commissioner Harris remarked with satisfaction that it had already accomplished as its greatest good "the transformation of an illiterate population into a population that reads the daily newspaper, and perforce thinks on national and international interests." The Commissioner left the distinct

[9] Eliot, "Condition of American Education," p. 4.

impression that further railroad building and urbanization would gradually bring systematic, graded mass schooling to the nation's most remote rural areas.[10]

Devoting attention to the rapidly changing field of secondary education, all turn-of-the-century commentators agreed in stressing the significance of the growth of the public high school. Eliot told his Twentieth Century Club audience that a "remarkable increase" had taken place within the past 15 years in the proportion of American children attending secondary schools, and that "it would be difficult to imagine a greater educational gain for the whole country." [11] Nicholas Murray Butler directed attention to the fact that there were 5,315 public high schools in the United States in 1897-98, employing 17,941 teachers and enrolling 449,600 pupils (the census of 1900 revealed that the total number of high schools had mounted to 6,005). Butler was convinced that the increase in number of these schools, the flexibility of their courses of study, and the growing value of the training they offered were "among the most significant educational developments" of the last two decades.[12] Public high school enrollments still included only a small minority of the total number of American adolescents of secondary school age. Nevertheless, William T. Harris felt that the future was clear. He told an NEA audience in 1901 that the increase of wealth in America inevitably would enable the people to send their children to better schools and for longer periods of schooling. Back in 1860, Harris recalled, when there were in all about 40 public high schools, wise men had shaken their heads and expressed doubt that the constitution permitted the education of the people in free high schools. District schools might be all right, but the Founding Fathers never intended to furnish a liberal education to all children at the expense of the taxpayers. So ran the argument then, but in the twentieth century the "unprecedented increase of secondary and higher education" was likely to go on at an even faster rate than was true at present "because it is due to the growth of productive industry in the country" and the resultant increase of wealth in the community.[13]

President Eliot also referred in his address to the important changes which were under way in the American secondary school curriculum.

[10] William Torrey Harris, "Elementary Education," in Butler, *Education in the United States.* I, pp. 79-104.

[11] Eliot, "Condition of American Education," p. 5.

[12] Butler, "Introduction," in *Education in the United States.* I.

[13] William Torrey Harris, "Recent Growth of Public High Schools in the United States as Affecting the Attendance of Colleges," *NEA Proceedings* (1901), 175-79.

On the whole, he found these changes were for the better. A wider range of subjects was being taught in the high schools than previously, but fewer subjects were now required of the individual pupil. Eliot felt furthermore that "the postponement of the forking of the ways in all secondary schools, and the gradual introduction of the elective system into such schools [were] both valuable improvements." [14]

Reporting somewhat more fully on these curricular changes, Elmer Ellsworth Brown, Professor of Education in the University of California, noted in one of the monographs of the Butler series that the elective system, given a boost by the Committee of Ten Report of 1893, was making rapid progress in American high schools. This, he indicated, reflected a changing philosophy of the purposes of secondary education. Already the seeds of the uniquely American "comprehensive high school" of later days were noted by Brown.

> The conviction that the secondary schools should not be merely tributary to the colleges is gaining ground. What is good education in the high school, it is maintained, is good preparation for the higher schools. The independence of the secondary school carries with it independent responsibility for the supply of the actual educational needs of the youth attending such a school. And the students in the high schools are thought to have reached the stage of differentiation of educational needs. . . . The elementary schools, with their single course of study, are conservators of spiritual unity. The secondary schools can and ought to serve a different purpose. Their instruction should be adapted to the cultivation of the diverse talents of the youth enrolled in them. No two students have exactly the same aptitudes; so far as possible, every student should pursue a different course of instruction from every other student.[15]

Professor Brown proceeded to specify the ways in which American high schools were, in fact, diversifying their course offerings in accordance with this broadly conceived curricular philosophy, citing examples of particular high school programs to prove his point. Many had established "parallel" Classical, Literary (modern languages substituted for Latin and Greek), and English (noncollege preparatory) four-year programs. Commercial courses were being established in various schools, and there was even the beginning of a movement to set up separate *public* business or commercial high schools. With the rise of the manual training movement, a number of high schools oriented in that direction

---

[14] Eliot, "Condition of American Education," p. 4.

[15] Elmer Ellsworth Brown, "Secondary Education," in *Education in the United States*. I, p. 175.

had been established in large cities, although their founders disclaimed "any intention of establishing schools for the teaching of trades." A few evening high schools, offering "very elastic courses of study," had appeared in these big urban centers. Methods of instruction in the natural sciences were being revolutionized by the introduction of work in laboratories. All in all, a "differentiation" was appearing in American secondary education, which Brown asserted was "not limited to the diversifying of studies within the several schools." Statistics put out by the United States Office of Education for the years 1897-98 emphasized that the American public high school as it existed at that time, unlike most European secondary schools, was hardly a college preparatory institution exclusively. Of the total number of American children attending public and private high schools and academies in 1897-98, only 14.02 per cent, or 77,759, were listed as preparing for college, at least in terms of the actual courses taken. And of the total number graduating from such institutions in 1898, whatever the academic atmosphere maintained within them, only 30.60 per cent, or 19,940, were college preparatory students.[16]

Both Eliot and Brown noticed the rather considerable development in American high schools of a highly organized "student life," partially copying that of the colleges. Secondary schools in America, apparently, were not destined to be purely scholastic institutions. In his monograph Brown spoke of the "instinct of association" being strong in American high school youth and finding expression in the formation of all sorts of clubs, leagues, societies, fraternities, organizations, and publications. Class offices were "sought for with keen competition." Athletic associations and teams played games with rival high schools, calling forth the most "unbounded enthusiasm." [17] In Dr. Eliot's view, this whole interest in school sport was "greatly exaggerated," reflecting perhaps a "characteristic American intensity." Yet this was not all pure loss, he was forced to admit. Gymnasiums had been built and physical training developed. "Men and women who are to be devoted to the intellectual life," he declared, "especially need a sound physical training in youth and an inextinguishable liking for out-of-door exercise." [18]

Turning to the vital subject of the training of teachers for America's

---

[16] *Ibid.*, pp. 179-203. It should perhaps be noted, by way of clarifying the above statistics, that 40.42 per cent of all the *male* students graduating in 1898 were college preparatory, whereas the percentage for female graduates was much smaller, amounting to about 25 per cent.

[17] *Ibid.*, pp. 188-89.

[18] Eliot, "Condition of American Education," p. 5.

schools, Dr. Eliot gave his opinion that "on the average" teacher education had "greatly improved" by the end of the nineteenth century. It had been "a great gain," he stated, "to require for admission to the normal schools the previous accomplishment of a high school course of study." [19] B. A. Hinsdale, Professor of the Science and Art of Teaching in the University of Michigan, was not as happy with the situation as his Harvard contemporary. Hinsdale recalled in one of the Butler monographs that American teacher training was only 60 years old. He reminded his readers that the American commitment to universal schooling had made it "impossible to train teachers as fast as the schools required them; the need has constantly outrun the public ability, and still more, perhaps, the public purse." Under such circumstances, no people could have made supply equal demand. Furthermore, what John Stuart Mill once called "the fatal belief" of the American that "anybody is fit for anything" constantly weakened efforts to set genuinely professional standards of teacher competence. Still, Hinsdale averred, much had been accomplished. Normal schools were increasing in number and upgrading their standards. Teacher training was being undertaken by leading colleges and universities on a graduate as well as an undergraduate level. Summer schools for teachers were doing much to improve professional standards, as were teachers' institutes, reading circles, state certification requirements, and the like. According to the 1896-97 figures of the United States Office of Education, 1,487 institutions of learning reported that they gave courses designed for the professional training of teachers. Of these, 164 were public normal schools, 198 were private normal schools, 196 were colleges and universities, 507 were public high schools, and 422 were private high schools and academies. While foreign critics might deprecate this chaotic state of affairs, Hinsdale asserted that "however impossible our system might be in continental countries, in America it works much better than they can readily conceive." [20]

One final sign of American educational progress which Dr. Eliot chose to call to the attention of his audience at the Twentieth Century Club was the rise of professional educational administration. To him it was immensely gratifying that urban school systems were more and more employing "educational experts in . . . supervising and executive functions." It was also encouraging, he said, that "the former method of entrusting executive functions to small subcommittees of a large

[19] *Ibid.*, p. 4.
[20] B. A. Hinsdale, "The Training of Teachers," in *Education in the United States.*
I.

school committee is passing away." He hoped that such practices in school administration would "soon be extinct." [21] Andrew S. Draper, writing on educational administration for Butler's monograph series, documented a trend in American school management which, by the coming of the twentieth century, was very much in the direction of the kind of expert professionalism which Eliot believed to be desirable.[22]

Draper, Commissioner of Education of New York State in 1905, summarized for an NEA audience the over-all significance of the present American educational achievement as being ultimately based upon the country's dedication to democracy. Here, he felt, was a sharp contrast with English education. "The English purpose would have every English child read and write and work. . . . There is no educational mixing of classes and no articulation or continuity of work. The controlling influence in English politics is distinctly opposed to universalizing education, through fear of unsettling the status and letting loose the ambitions of the serving classes." So, too, it was in France, according to Draper. "The children of the masses are trained for service." But not so in America! Americans, said Draper, wanted more than mere industrial strength and military power.

> There is an essential and universal educational purpose in America which distinguishes our system from all others. We will have no classes in education. We are for the equal chance for all. Even more—much more: We are for moral greatness and it is the national belief that the true greatness of the nation and the welfare of mankind depend not only upon giving every one his chance, but in aiding and inspiring every one to seize his chance.[23]

Another distinguished American educator, President G. Stanley Hall of Clark University, summed up for the Twentieth Century Club the ways in which he believed American education in 1901 could stand proudly on its own, owing no excuses to the scholarly pundits of the Old World for doing so. America, he said, had no need of the European system of early separating of the sexes; of charging fees in state schools; of closely tying state schools to state churches; of feudal-type privileges and rewards of office for some educators and low salaries for others; of extreme centralization and total absence of local initiative. "We do

---

[21] Eliot, "Condition of American Education," p. 4.

[22] Andrew S. Draper, "Educational Organization and Administration," in *Education in the United States.* **I.**

[23] Andrew S. Draper, *The Nation's Educational Purpose* (Albany, N.Y.: State Department of Education, 1905).

not want the dormitory system of the Lycée;" Hall declared, "the high mental pressure and absence of physical exercise of the Gymnasium; the fagging system or the uniforms of the English schools." [24]

Two observers from abroad added their own kind words about the accomplishments of America's schools on the threshold of a new century. British historian G. P. Gooch praised "the universal recognition" in America of the importance of schooling, "the earnest study of its conditions, the ungrudging supply of money from public and private sources, its cheapness, and the mixture of classes which it involves." If there was any great lack, Gooch suggested that it had always been, as it was at the present time, one of a large enough "number of efficient teachers." [25] Gabriel Compayré, Rector of the University of Lyons, fairly rhapsodized in the *Revue Pedagogique* for April, 1901, on the favorable impression the American educational exhibit at the Paris World's Fair (1900) had made on French opinion. The French were sometimes inclined to laugh, he said, at American chauvinism and boastfulness. Let them not laugh too quickly at American education! "The public school of the United States is evidently passing through an era of prosperity. . . . Taken all in all, everything is satisfactory. The states have always shown themselves generous toward their schools, and private benefactors do not neglect them in the distribution of their gifts." "I do not believe," Monsieur Compayré concluded, "that in any other country, in any other time, the work of education has aroused so much effort, so much zeal. And what changes in a century!" [26]

In a volume of lectures and essays published in 1903, Charles W. Eliot took notice of a basic fact that characterized the attitude of Americans toward their schools and toward the other institutions of their evolving democratic society.[27] Essentially, this phenomenon might be summed up by saying that their reach, overambitious as it had been, had always exceeded their grasp. The founders of the Republic had expected miracles from prompt public enlightenment; later generations were disappointed that popular education had not banished all vice, crime, disorder, and folly. But it was not only in the field of public education that democratic hopes remained unrealized. Universal suf-

[24] G. Stanley Hall, "Comparison of American and Foreign Systems of Popular Education," in *Twentieth Century Club* (University Lectures, 1901-1902 [Boston: J. P. Shults, 1901]), p. 23.

[25] G. P. Gooch, "Some Notes on American Education," *Westminster Review*, 156 (September 1901) pp. 294-301.

[26] Gabriel Compayré, "Education in the United States," reprinted in *The School Journal* (June 1 and 8, 1901).

[27] See Chap. 9.

frage had not, *ipso facto*, produced good government. Political freedom had not automatically produced responsible public service. Intolerant of anything less than total success, the American took little heed of the unprecedented difficulties that were involved, nor did he take into account that "these difficulties have increased with every generation." [28]

Much of the restlessness and impatience of which Eliot spoke was coming to the surface of American life by 1900. The nation was poised on the brink of the profound renovation of social and political patterns that historians have called "the Progressive Era." The dominant precepts inherited from earlier, more "innocent" stages of American cultural development were being subjected to rigorous criticism.[29] A whole new school of American philosophers and social scientists, men like Charles Beard, Oliver Wendell Holmes, Jr., James Harvey Robinson, and Thorstein Veblen, all relativists of one sort or another, were transforming the American mind with concepts such as "instrumentalism, progressive education, legal realism, the economic interpretation of politics, the new history, institutional economics, and political liberalism." [30] In this atmosphere of ferment Americans were bound to turn a newly critical eye upon their schools. In 1899 Dewey published his enormously influential little volume *School and Society*. Before him Francis Wayland Parker, Joseph Mayer Rice, Felix Adler, and others had already sounded the tocsin for educational reform. In the years that were immediately ahead, Edward L. Thorndike, G. Stanley Hall, and a host of less well-known luminaries were to join Dewey in a progressive education crusade to make the schools less formalistic, less mechanical, less dominated by inefficiency and inanity. It was the hope of these bold innovators that American education could be made more socially responsive, more helpful in the meaningful reconstruction of the modern social order, more cognizant of the needs of the individual child, more solidly based on an objectively established science of learning.[31]

One of the major figures in the era of progressive education and in the development of child study in America, President Granville Stanley

[28] Charles W. Eliot, *More Money for the Public Schools* (Garden City, N.Y.: Doubleday & Company, Inc., 1903), pp. 56-63.

[29] Henry F. May, *The End of American Innocence* (New York: Alfred A. Knopf, Inc., 1959), esp. pp. 38-50.

[30] Morton G. White, *Social Thought in America: The Revolt Against Formalism* (New York: Viking Press, 1949).

[31] Lawrence A. Cremin, *Transformation of the School* (New York: Alfred A. Knopf, Inc., 1961).

Hall of Clark University, listed for his Twentieth Century Club audience a series of changes in American education that he felt would become increasingly necessary in the years to come. Among these he specified the following items:

> Professional training for all teachers, instead of the small percentage found in this country. . . . The requirement of at least a complete college education for all high school teachers, and of university training in upper classes. . . . More professional courses in colleges and universities for those intending to teach. . . . The abolition of lesson setting and recitation as now practiced and more instruction by the teacher, with fewer textbooks, possible only when teachers are more educated. . . . The emancipation of the high schools . . . from the excessive dominance of college entrance requirements. . . .[32]

Many of the goals proposed by Hall were endorsed by progressive educators of the early twentieth century. Many of these changes, indeed, were potential in the very stage of development reached by American education in 1901, the year in which the pioneer psychologist delivered his lecture. How many of these innovations, however, would actually be accomplished in the next half century? Only the future could disclose the answer.

[32] Hall, "Comparison of American and Foreign Systems of Popular Education," p. 24.

CHAPTER TWO

Child-Centered Schools

. . . . The home, like the state, has its problems of government and must give controlled scope to the spirit of liberty which animates the growing child. . . . The task of child care is not to force him into a predetermined pattern but to guide his growth. This developmental point of view does not mean indulgence. It means a constructive deference to the limitations of immaturity. . . .[1]

As evidenced by the above statement, it was obvious that by 1943 American education had moved decisively in the direction of a child-centered orientation. Schools were placing more emphasis than ever before upon the learner as a total personality and reacting organism and upon the learning mechanism itself rather than upon a set body of subject matter that was required to be learned. To this radical change of emphasis a number of factors had contributed. One was the increasing preoccupation with an expanding "science of education" and more particularly the burgeoning field of tests and measurements. Another was embodied in the idea of guidance, represented by the work of a growing army of school counselors, guidance specialists, and personnel workers. Closely connected with the foregoing developments was the controversial movement known in all its diverse phases as "progressive edu-

[1] Arnold Gesell and Frances L. Ilg, *Infant and Child in the Culture of Today* (New York: Harper & Row, Publishers, 1943), pp. 10-11.

cation." Each of these influences played its part in furthering and deepening a newly aroused concern for the individual pupil's personality, aptitudes, and psyche as the center of the school's work.

It is certainly not necessary at this point to make a detailed historical review of the progressive education movement in America; that has already been done thoroughly and perceptively.[2] The major consideration to be emphasized here is that, beginning with John Dewey, educators with a progressive orientation helped to foster a heightened concern for the individual child as the center of the educational process. It is true, of course, that we must guard against oversimplifying the history of twentieth-century progressivism in education. The movement was marked by a many-faceted pluralism which attempted to weave together many strands (some of them rather disparate). Actually the weaving process did not always proceed as smoothly as progressive proponents desired.[3] Be that as it may, one element in the tapestry that stood out from the very beginning was the outlook of the child-centered school.

Through the influence of two progressively minded educators, Harold Rugg and Ann Shumaker,[4] and under the guidance of pedagogues with a similar frame of reference, an approach to teaching emerged that was basically individualistic in orientation, permissive in methodological concept, and alertly responsive to the newer findings of the Freudian and other schools of contemporary psychology.[5] To be sure, we may find notable examples of child-centered thinking in the writings of earlier educational theorists such as Rousseau, Pestalozzi, and Froebel.[6] These men did not, however, claim as much of a "scientific" basis for their findings as did the progressive ideologists of the twentieth century, and, in any case, it was only in the latter period that such concepts began

[2] Lawrence A. Cremin, *Transformation of the School* (New York: Alfred A. Knopf, Inc., 1961).

[3] *Ibid.*; see also two articles by Cremin, "The Progressive Movement in American Education: A Perspective," *Harvard Educational Review*, XXVII (Fall, 1957), pp. 251-67; "The Origins of Progressive Education," *Educational Forum*, XXIV (January 1960), pp. 133-39. There is an interesting essay on Dewey in Merle E. Curti, *Social Ideas of American Educators* (Paterson, N.J.: Littlefield, Adams & Co., 1959).

[4] Harold Rugg and Ann Shumaker, *The Child-Centered School* (New York: Harcourt, Brace & World, Inc., 1928).

[5] See Stanwood Cobb, *The New Leaven* (New York: The John Day Company, Inc., 1928); also William H. Kilpatrick, *Foundations of Method* (New York: The Macmillan Company, 1925).

[6] Robert Ulich, *History of Educational Thought* (New York: American Book Company, 1945), esp. pp. 317-19.

to exert a really determinative influence upon actual procedures in American schools.[7]

Originating in the hopeful, pragmatic atmosphere of turn-of-the-century America, an America in the full throes of the Progressive Era in society and politics, the New Education's position was firmly based on certain fundamental psychological assumptions. The school, it was believed, must develop a better understanding of the individual child's motivations and impulses. This called for expert analysis, careful measurement, and scientific guidance. As Dewey himself later defined the newer education:

> If one attempts to formulate the philosophy of education implicit in the practices of the newer education, we may, I think, discover certain common principles amid the variety of progressive schools now existing. To imposition from above is opposed expression, and cultivation of individuality; to external discipline is opposed free activity; to learning from texts and teachers, learning through experience; to acquisition of isolated skills and techniques by drill is opposed acquisition of them as means of attaining ends which make direct vital appeal; to preparation for a more or less remote future is opposed making the most of the opportunities of present life; to static aims and materials is opposed acquaintance with a changing world.[8]

In addition to the obvious functional and instrumental emphasis in the above statement, there is an over-all bias in favor of what many progressives were calling the "child-centered" school. As Stow Persons has astutely noted, the older America—nineteenth-century America—had been primarily an adult's world. Its schools had been expected to mold youth in the image of its forebears. Progressive education rejected such paternalism as absolutistic and sought instead a school system that would accept the activities and interests of children as being just as important as those of adults. In such schools the teacher was to be friend and adviser rather than superior; differences between the generations would dissolve; and a child-centered program would encourage the pupil to grow and work by means of natural tasks and to develop the

[7] Classic statements of the new approach may be found in such influential works of John Dewey as *The School and Society* (Chicago: The University of Chicago Press, 1899); *The Child and the Curriculum* (Chicago: The University of Chicago Press, 1902); *Schools of Tomorrow* (New York, 1915); and *Democracy and Education* (New York: The Macmillan Company, 1916).

[8] John Dewey, *Experience and Education* (New York: The Macmillan Company, 1938), pp. 5-6.

capacity to solve problems and reconstruct experience meaningfully.[9] These changes in educational thinking coincided significantly with a fundamental change in the American social order—a shift from a well-knit, tradition-oriented, largely rural environment to a more diverse, complex, impersonal, and unsettled urban-industrial milieu. They also paralleled and were closely linked to a revolution in the average American parent's conceptions of appropriate child-rearing procedures. The more permissive attitudes, which Martha Wolfenstein has labeled "fun-morality," came increasingly to displace pre-existing Puritanical and authoritarian concepts in the child-training literature which shaped the viewpoint of millions of American parents on the all-important question of "bringing up Junior." For some parents the advanced attitudes developed into a species of "child worship." [10] And as it was in the home, so it more and more came to be in the school.

Counselors and Guidance Specialists

In 1909 a little book entitled *Choosing a Vocation* by Frank Parsons was published posthumously in Boston. This event is generally regarded as marking the beginning of the guidance movement in the United States. The close connection of educational and vocational counseling of this type and the child-centered viewpoint brought forward by John Dewey and other progressive educators is evident in the strong "personalistic" approach that characterized both. As one study of post-World War II personnel work put it, "Students are developing organisms demanding a personalized learning experience. . . ." [11] To best help the "whole" pupil, according to this concept, the findings of scientific psychology must be fully utilized and all available details

[9] Stow Persons, *American Minds, A History of Ideas* (New York: Holt, Rinehart & Winston, Inc., 1958), pp. 407-8. Other interesting analyses of the progressive education ideology may be found in David Riesman, *Constraint and Variety in American Education* (Garden City, N.Y.: Doubleday & Company, Inc., 1958), pp. 142-52; 172-74, and B. A. G. Fuller, "Pot-Shots at Present Pedagogy," *Philosophical Review*, L (March 1941), pp. 134-35.

[10] Martha Wolfenstein, "Fun-Mortality: An Analysis of Recent American Child-Training Literature," in Margaret Mead and Martha Wolfenstein, *Childhood in Contemporary Cultures* (Chicago: University of Chicago Press, 1955), pp. 169-75; see also Martha Weinman Lear, *The Child Worshipers* (New York: Crown Publishers, Inc., 1963).

[11] C. Gilbert Wrenn and Reginald Bell, *Student Personnel Problems* (New York: Holt, Rinehart & Winston, Inc., 1942), p. 8.

about the pupil's personality must be accumulated by the professional counselors and personnel workers.[12]

Guidance "as an informal function of adults is probably as old as civilization itself." [13] However, as an organized movement it appears to have made its first appearance in various American cities during the first decade of the twentieth century. By 1908 the Vocation Bureau in Boston (originated by Frank Parsons and continued by Meyer Bloomfield) and the Student Aid Committee in New York City (initiated by Eli Weaver and a group of local school teachers) had made their mark. These purely private and unofficial undertakings, with a strong emphasis on *vocational* guidance, soon stimulated similar programs in the public schools. As the country was speedily being transformed into an industrial giant, child labor laws and compulsory attendance regulations were put into operation. Consequently, pupils were remaining longer in school. In this context it seemed essential to the early pioneers of vocational guidance that youth be given expert counseling as to what vocations and careers would best meet its needs. Such guidance, they argued, should be established as a regular and continuous service of the public schools.[14]

The crusade for social justice, so characteristic of the climate of the Progressive Era, and the pioneer phase of the guidance movement are closely linked, as evidenced by the career of Frank Parsons, founder of the Boston Vocation Bureau. After varied employments, in both blue- and white-collared areas, he joined the faculty of the Law School of Boston University in 1891, at which time he began publishing works on banking, insurance, and trust law. His dissatisfaction with political and economic conditions in the country came to the fore when he ran for the office of mayor of Boston as the joint nominee of the Populist, Socialist, and Prohibition parties. Although the atmosphere was one of social unrest, his platform was unable to carry him to city hall. He retired from the political scene to Kansas State College where he remained for 4 years until his resignation, along with that of President Will and others, was forced, according to his charges, by the "railroad interests." [15]

[12] C. Gilbert Wrenn, "Guidance—An Overview," *NEA Journal* (January 1959), pp. 16-17.

[13] Mauritz Johnson, Jr., *et al.*, *Junior High School Guidance* (New York: Harper & Row, Publishers, 1961), p. 2.

[14] John M. Brewer, *History of Vocational Guidance* (New York: Harper & Row, Publishers, 1942), pp. 53 ff.

[15] Parson's mature views on the railroad question are to be found in his book,

Following his resignation, Parsons joined the faculties of Ruskin University and Boston University and gave numerous lectures throughout the country, speaking in favor of such progressive causes as direct election of senators, civil service reform, and proportional representation. Furthermore, his active career included the presidency of the National League for Promoting Public Ownership of Monopolies, the chairmanship of the lecture department of the Social Reform Union, and membership on the lecture committee for the National Direct Legislation League. He continued publishing his attacks on monopolies in the _Arena_ and other reformist-minded publications.

Parsons found time in his busy schedule to actively support the Civic Service House of Boston, a civic center established in 1901 through the combined efforts of Pauline Agassiz Shaw, Jane Addams, and Lillian Wald, and managed by Meyer Bloomfield and Philip Davis, themselves both of immigrant origin. Impressed with the need for an education program at the Civic Service House, Parsons, with the assistance of his close friend Ralph Albertson, helped in 1905 to found a vocational school there known as the Bread-winners' College.[16] The college was a result of his conviction that positive guidance of youth in the choosing of a career was a necessity in any modern school system because of the "miserable condition of the great masses enmeshed" in the industrial system. The lack of training available to many youths both before and after employment appalled him. The inefficient methods of preparing for a life work and the resultant waste of human effort he laid at the door of industry. As early as 1894 he had written:

> The training of a race-horse, and the care of sheep and chickens have been carried to the highest degree of perfection that intelligent planning can attain. But the education of a child, the choice of his employment, are left very largely to the ancient haphazard plan—the struggle for existence, and the survival of the fittest.
>
> Men work best when they are doing what nature has especially fitted them for. And the same laborers will achieve immensely fuller and richer results if they are spurred on by interest, or love, or patriotism than if these interests or emotions have no partnership in their actions. . . .[17]

The Heart of the Railroad Problem: The History of Railway Discrimination in the United States, the Chief Efforts at Control, and the Remedies Proposed, with Hints from Other Countries (Boston: Little, Brown & Co., 1906).

[16] _Ibid._; see also Percy W. Bidwell's sketch, "Frank Parsons," in the _Dictionary of American Biography_, XIV (New York: Charles Scribner's Sons, 1934), p. 266.

[17] Frank Parsons, _Our Country's Need_, as quoted in Brewer, _History of Vocational Guidance_, pp. 56-57.

These same ideas, which prompted him to organize the Bread-winners' College, also led him to secure financial backing from Mrs. Shaw in 1908 to underwrite the establishment of the Boston Vocation Bureau, which he was to serve as first director. These ideas, basic to his philosophy, are reflected in his pioneering posthumous book *Choosing a Vocation*, which appears indeed to contain the first coinage of the phrase "vocational guidance" and to define systematically the objectives and methodology of the new field.[18]

A vocational bias continued to dominate the thinking and operations of the early guidance counselors as they began to appear in various school systems during the World War I period and on into the 1920's. The mental and aptitude testing movement, which developed along somewhat parallel lines during these years, meanwhile helped forge many important tools for the use of school guidance personnel. As the nature and extent of individual differences became apparent, counseling programs were broadened to provide pupils not only with job information but also with somewhat more general advice on choosing studies and pursuing them successfully. Bolstered by the findings of such researchers as E. L. Thorndike, Donald G. Paterson, John M. Brewer, E. G. Williamson, and W. V. Bingham, the guidance field assumed more and more of the aspects of a distinct profession, becoming increasingly a combination of "educational guidance" and "vocational guidance." Helping students to select a career obviously required advice on the selection of a supporting school curriculum. Moreover, as counselors in the high schools worked on the more or less interrelated problems of jobs and courses, they became valuable assistants to school administrators in helping to maintain discipline and maximum possible school attendance.[19]

By the 1920's, too, the guidance movement began to come under the influence of yet another body of thought, namely, the rapidly developing field of mental health and "personality adjustment." Specialists in the latter area were uncovering findings which suggested that not all unhappiness among school children was due to unfortunate course selections or vocational choices. Reflecting this line of thought, Stewart Paton, a lecturer on Neurobiology at Princeton University, complained

[18] Frank Parsons, *Choosing a Vocation* (Boston: Houghton Mifflin Company, 1909); Bidwell, "Frank Parsons," p. 266.
[19] Johnson, *et al., Junior High School Guidance*, pp. 2-3; see Milton E. Hahn and Malcolm McLean, *Counseling Psychology* (New York: McGraw-Hill, Inc., 1955), pp. 1-4; Edmund G. Williamson, ed., *Trends in Student Personnel Work* (Minneapolis: University of Minnesota Press, 1949).

in 1920 that "little provision is made in our educational system today to assist the student to know himself, to size up the present situation, and to adjust life intelligently to meet the demands of the immediate circumstances." Paton reproached the existing academic outlook for being excessively limited.

> Educators as well as the public have been so thoroughly hypnotized by the academic conception of education that the failures, including graduates *summa cum laude*, from high schools and colleges who later appear in sanatoriums, hospitals for the insane, almshouses, reformatories, and prisons, or who develop the peculiar emotional unrest of the psychoneurotic, usually are not recognized as the products of the educational system. . . .[20]

Doctor Gesell and the Child-Study Movement

The new "personalistic" approach to pupil guidance owed much to the flourishing child-study movement which first appeared around the turn of the century. Originating among European Darwinians who began to study child development systematically by keeping detailed biographical records, this method attracted much attention in the United States through the promotional activities of G. Stanley Hall, President of Clark University. Hall's special technique was to collect information on child behavior by sending out a number of questionnaires. From 1894 to 1902 Hall and his associates at Clark sent out more than one hundred such forms, covering a wide range of topics such as crying and laughing, early sense of self, childhood fears, psychology of ownership, and feelings about old age and death. Although the validity of many of Hall's findings were questioned by other psychologists, it is clear that, almost singlehandedly, he popularized child study in America and launched it on its career.

Soon other research projects in this field were organized. The Worcester, Massachusetts, State Normal School, at Hall's suggestion, collected 35,000 records of observations of school children.[21] By 1930 the campaign had gotten into its full stride. Foundations were beginning to

[20] Stewart Paton, *Essentials of an Education* (New York: National Committee for Mental Hygiene, Inc., 1920).

[21] See Edwin G. Boring, *History of Experimental Psychology* (New York: Appleton-Century-Crofts, Inc., 1950), pp. 560-63; see also Florence L. Goodenough, *Mental Testing* (New York: Holt, Rinehart & Winston, Inc., 1949), pp. 27-32.

make grants to finance the establishment of child-research institutes. A White House conference was held on Child Health and Protection that summarized the growing body of knowledge in the new field as it existed up to that time. By the mid-thirties attention was turning to the problems of adolescence: a new series of studies was begun at the junior and senior high school level. Techniques of child study were now becoming "increasingly sophisticated, better developed, more adapted to the complexity of relevant factors, and more oriented toward theoretical systems." [22]

Best embodying the main currents of this era was Doctor Arnold Gesell, founder of the world-famed Gesell Institute of Child Development in New Haven, Connecticut. Born in 1880 in the then little two-street village of Alma, Wisconsin, along the banks of the Upper Mississippi, Gesell grew up a perceptive small-town boy in a tradition-dominated culture. Family life was close-knit; everyone knew everyone and the round of village tasks set the pattern of existence; nature was vividly present (Gesell recalled later how "hills, valley, water, and climate concurred to make the seasons distinct and intense"). Many deep and moving experiences left their impress upon him. "I saw death, funerals, devastating sickness," he remembered in later years. There were "ominous quarantines, accidents and drownings at close range. Acute and chronic alcoholism were common sights open to public view. Epileptic convulsions occurred on the street and sidewalk. A muttering 'crazy man' walked endlessly back and forth in his garden. A condemned murderer stared at us through the bars in the county prison. A watchdog was poisoned and a burglary committed in the blackness of night. Strange and sobering things kept happening as though they were part of the normal course of existence." These experiences of Gesell, the child, influenced the course of research of Gesell, the clinical psychologist. In an attempt to discover the meaning and direction of life, he concluded of his past, "None of these experiences was overpowering, but cumulatively they left a deposit of impressions which sensitized a background for my clinical studies in later life." [23]

Always interested in a teaching career, Gesell acquired the necessary certificate at the age of 19 and took a position teaching history, Ger-

---

[22] "Educational Measurements," *Review of Educational Research*, XXVII (June 1956), 281-82.
[23] See the obituary in *New York Times*, May 30, 1961, p. 17; also Helen Puner, "Gesell's Children Grow Up," *Harper's Magazine*, 212 (March 1956), pp. 37-43.

man, commercial geography, and accounting and coaching the football team at the Stevens Point High School. Continuing his studies at the University of Wisconsin, the young teacher received a Ph.B. degree in 1903. The following year his ambitions carried him eastward to Clark University, a center of graduate study in pedagogy and applied psychology then in its heyday under G. Stanley Hall. The move had a decisive effect on the young man's life. His interest in children, he later related, "came out of my environment at Clark under Hall." Hall, he declared, was "a true genius . . . a naturalist Darwin of the mind." In 1906 Gesell received his Doctor of Philosophy degree in psychology from Clark. Now his ideas for the future became more specialized—"I wanted to chart the whole span of child development." But he was uneasily aware of the fact that he didn't know enough anatomy and physiology to accomplish his objective. ("I couldn't be comfortable from a scientific point of view without medicine.") After returning to the teaching profession as a high school principal and as professor of psychology at the California State Normal School, Gesell's chance finally came to acquire the additional training he felt he needed. He was offered a part-time position at Yale as an Assistant Professor of Education with the understanding that he would also be free to attend the Yale School of Medicine. Gesell leaped at the opportunity and by 1915 had secured his M.D.

When Gesell inaugurated research in child development in the New Haven Dispensary in 1911, Yale had no department of child psychology. During the succeeding years Gesell was able to make the Yale Clinic of Child Development, as it came to be called, famous throughout the world. Doggedly, patiently, he built up a body of empirical data designed to picture the "total developmental" status of children and to serve as a basis for defining the "normative criteria" which could be used to appraise the normal, deviant, and defective behavior of children at various age levels. In 1918 he and his staff made a "mental survey" of the children in all the elementary schools of New Haven, concluding from this study that the public schools should institute "a consistent program of individual attention to individual children." The public school could afford no longer to deal indiscriminatingly, in crude wholesale fashion, with the people's children. It *must* become aware of mental hygiene; it *must* incorporate scientific procedures stemming from the findings of mental hygiene into its day-by-day routine; it *must* develop a continuous interest in child development from birth certificate to diploma, a point of view "which will regard the total and the continuing child and be primarily concerned with the healthy norms of his behavior." [24]

By 1923 Gesell had the knowledge and experience to publish his *Mental Growth of the Pre-School Child*, quickly hailed as the first systematic presentation of detailed clinical data showing how children's behavior develops. (It was not until two years later that the first national conference on child development convened.) In this monograph Gesell returned to the theme of the importance of developing a child-centered point of view in the nation's public school system. "Our vast aggregation of elementary schools," he wrote, "ought . . . to be regarded as our largest and, in a sense, most legitimate official child-welfare agency. Certainly the historic sanction and strategic position of the public school system in the American commonwealth make it the most promising instrument for the further development of public policies in behalf of a very large proportion of those exceptional children who, because of handicap or other circumstances, need a special measure of extra parental care during the years of their education." [25]

Dr. Gesell and his clinic were by now achieving acclaim. Grants began to pour in from the Rockefeller and Carnegie Foundations and from the General Education Board. Noted psychologists, physicians, and child-study specialists hastened to join the clinic's staff. In 1930, with the backing of a Rockefeller endowment, Gesell's organization was set up in a five-floor, Georgian building with a nursery school, clinical examination and observation rooms, infant out-patient service, and photographic division. The clinic also had now acquired the dignity of recognition as a full-fledged department of the Yale School of Medicine, the first child-development group to be so honored by an American university. [26]

With national prominence, perhaps inevitably, came criticism. Workers in the burgeoning child-development field who had a basically Freudian orientation accused Gesell of being too one-dimensional in his studies—too interested in the evolving *form* of child personality and not enough in its accompanying emotional *content*. He was condemned for ignoring the role of the "unconscious" mind. He was criti-

---

[24] Arnold Gesell, *Exceptional Children and Public School Policy* (New Haven: Yale University Press, 1921).

[25] Arnold Gesell, *The Pre-School Child* (Boston: Houghton Mifflin Company, 1923), pp. 85-86. See also "Mental Hygiene Service for Children" in Frankwood E. Williams, ed., *Social Aspects of Mental Hygiene* (New Haven: Yale University Press, 1925), pp. 102-107.

[26] *New York Times*, May 30, 1961, p. 17; Puner, "Gesell's Children Grow Up."

cized for refusing to attach psychiatrists or psychiatric social workers to the child-guidance clinics he founded, thus pretty much ignoring therapeutic functions. To all this, Gesell replied, "We have followed where experience seemed to lead. . . . We didn't try to conquer experience in advance," and continued tenaciously to collect empirical evidence. Thousands of children passed through his clinic; hundreds of thousands of feet of motion pictures were taken illustrating child behavior patterns. With two close co-workers, Dr. Frances L. Ilg and Dr. Louise Bates Ames, he prepared three widely influential books, summing up the fruits of the work of his clinic over more than three decades: *Infant and Child in the Culture of Today, The Child from Five to Ten,* and *Youth: The Years from Ten to Sixteen.*[27] Immediate best sellers, these volumes sold hundreds of thousands of copies at home and abroad, being translated into a number of foreign languages including Japanese, Korean, Finnish, and Hebrew.

American parents by the 1940's were talking about "Gesell babies" as a kind of national child-rearing norm. Much to Dr. Gesell's annoyance, the clinic's published summations were used without discrimination in an attempt to appraise the behavior of children at various age levels and stages of growth. The assumed predictability of childhood behavior patterns inspired one famous cartoon in the *New Yorker* magazine, which showed a child reading a Gesell book and exclaiming: "Gee, what a stinker I'm going to be next year!" Through it all, Gesell continued to work away at his task, establishing his own Child Development Institute when he retired from Yale in 1948. One conclusion that seemed to emerge from his findings, as they were interpreted by schoolmen with a thoroughgoing child-centered approach, was that "it is fruitless to try to hurry nature and to put pressure on children to excel at something they'll learn naturally when they're developmentally ripe." [28] Such an interpretation seemed to lend "scientific" weight, in their opinion, to the new trends in educational methodology and philosophy that had been supported by theoreticians such as Dewey and Kilpatrick.

Another important implication of work such as Gesell's in the new sciences of mental health and human relationships (fields which after World War II were entitled the "behavioral sciences") seemed to be that vocational and educational guidance in the public schools were not

[27] Arnold Gesell, Frances L. Ilg, *et al., Infant and Child in the Culture of Today* (New York: Harper & Row, Publishers, 1943); *The Child from Five to Ten* (New York: Harper & Row, Publishers, 1946); *Youth: The Years from Ten to Sixteen* (New York: Harper & Row, Publishers, 1956).

[28] Puner, "Gesell's Children Grow Up," p. 42.

enough. What also seemed to be requisite now, many felt, was something which increasingly came to be called "personal counseling." Up to 1930, however, not much progress had been made in differentiating this function from the pre-existing programs of vocational and educational guidance. After that date, more and more of a separation appeared as guidance workers in the high schools became aware of increasingly large numbers of students who were troubled by personal problems involving hostility to authority, sex relationships, unfortunate home situations, and financial stringencies.

As the field of guidance work and counseling evolved into an increasingly complex and highly specialized profession, there was a demand that it be accorded recognition as an integral part of the school's instructional program.[29] Proponents of the "home room" as a valuable guidance device in the modern secondary school called upon all teachers to perform guidance functions. The home room, argued one enthusiast, would do away with the excessively "artificial," intellectual emphasis of earlier times and give needed attention to the "all-around" needs and adjustment of the average pupil in the new era of mass education. As a result, the "average" pupil would then come to like school, instead of detesting it because of its barren academic content.[30] Other authors of treatises on guidance during the '30's and '40's came to reflect the point of view similar to that of proponents of a broader "life-adjustment" and child-centered approach to education. Thus Hugh M. Bell, in a work on personal counseling which appeared in 1939, flatly stated that "the goal of counseling is facilitation of student adjustment through personal contact between counselor and student." Such adjustment was to be impressively multifold in nature: it was to include "School Adjustment," "Health Adjustment," "Vocational and Occupational Adjustment," "Motor and Mechanical Adjustment," "Social Adjustment," "Home Adjustment," "Emotional Adjustment," and "Religious Adjustment." [31] Writing in a similar vein, Margaret Bennett and Harold C. Hand emphasized in 1938 that in order for group guidance in high schools to be effective it must deal with the "real life" adjustment problems of the

---

[29] Gordon Mackenzie, "Developing and Administering the Curriculum and Pupil Services," in Nelson B. Henry, ed., *Changing Conceptions in Educational Administration*, 45th Yearbook, Part II (Chicago: National Society for the Study of Education, University of Chicago Press, 1946), pp. 20-52.

[30] Harry C. McKown, *Home Room Guidance* (New York: McGraw-Hill, Inc., 1934), pp. 5-21.

[31] Hugh M. Bell, *Theory and Practice of Personal Counseling* (Stanford, Calif.: Stanford University Press, 1939), pp. 2-6.

"whole student." Otherwise, the authors solemnly warned, students might come to regard the "guidance hour" as just "so much well-intentioned but boring drivel." [32]

By the era of World War II, personal counselors in a number of school systems had been differentiated administratively from other guidance workers. By this time, too, research in the personal counseling field was beginning to advance "from highly subjective evaluation and description of process to a search for precise variables, operational definitions, and better controlled experimentation." [33] Not only in American high schools, but in colleges and universities, social welfare institutions, hospitals, industries, businesses, the armed services, and government agencies as well, a "personnel movement" of significant proportions had emerged. Personal counseling itself was becoming more highly specialized as it came to be influenced appreciably by developments in mental hygiene, psychiatry, psychiatric social work, psychoanalysis, rehabilitation work, and medically oriented clinical psychology. School counselors were being offered many valuable new tools, and many were refashioning their older ones to assimilate the new insights. Meanwhile, the professional separation between the educational, vocational, and personal guidance fields in and out of the public schools was reflected in such developments as the appearance of the parallel National Vocational Guidance Association (which by 1945 was issuing a professional certificate) and the American Personnel and Guidance Association. Also indicative of the trend was the fact that, in 1953, the Division of Counseling and Guidance of the American Psychological Association changed its name to the Division of Counseling Psychology. The Association had already given official recognition to counseling psychology five years before by making it one of the three areas in which diplomas were administered by the American Board of Examiners in Psychology.[34]

By mid-century the guidance and personal counseling fields had also received official recognition from the governments of the majority of American states, which had established standards for professional certification. In 1957 41 states required such certification for guidance

[32] Margaret Bennett and Harold C. Hand. *Group Guidance in High School* (New York: McGraw-Hill, Inc., 1938), pp. 3-5.
[33] Merle M. Ohlsen, Fred C. Proff, and Edward C. Roeber, "Counseling and Adjustment," *Review of Educational Research*, XXVI (June 1956).
[34] *Ibid.*; see also Hahn and MacLean, *Counseling Psychology*, pp. 2-5; Johnson, *Junior High School Guidance*; Williamson, *Trends in Student Personnel Work*; Louis Wirth, "The Social Sciences," in Merle E. Curti, *American Scholarship in the Twentieth Century* (Cambridge: Harvard University Press, 1953).

workers in schools. In addition, 12 states also demanded certification for school counselors or psychologists.[35] The expansion and diversification of the field had meanwhile been further reflected in a vast increase in the number of training programs provided for prospective guidance workers. A United States Office of Education survey found in 1959 that at least 223 American institutions of higher education were offering programs for guidance and student personnel workers at the graduate level. The greatest number of such courses were apparently to be found in state-supported institutions.[36]

Despite the many training programs provided, American schools in the Fifties and early Sixties faced serious shortages of guidance and counseling personnel. The Office of Education estimated in 1960 that the United States, which then had 9,000 full-time high school counselors at work and 19,000 part-timers, was at least 20,000 *short* of the number of full-time specialists needed. Forty per cent of American secondary schools had no guidance counselor at all. Furthermore, many working in the field were inadequately trained. And even when a school maintained a full-time guidance department with a properly trained specialist in charge, that counselor very often was overburdened with clerical duties. Sometimes he had to cope singlehandedly with as many as 1,500 students, and thus could not afford more than half an hour with each student during the entire school year. Such conditions were making many college graduates reluctant to go into counseling. Unquestionably, many were also discouraged by the prospect of "prolonged, often strained contacts with parents" and the necessity of "working after the last school bell rings, holding conferences . . . and attending numerous other meetings." Then, too, some undoubtedly agreed with the guidance specialist in the Baltimore school system who observed in 1959 that "school administrators have not assumed the leadership necessary to establish the proper meaning of guidance and the proper function of the counselor." The thorny question of guidance's appropriate status has not yet been satisfactorily resolved everywhere in the American school system.[37]

During the 1950's a series of research studies documented the im-

---

[35] Royce E. Brewster, *Guidance Workers Certification Requirements* (U.S. Office of Education Bulletin No. 22 [Washington, D.C., 1958]).

[36] Paul MacMinn and Roland G. Ross, *Status of Preparation Programs for Guidance and Student Personnel Workers* (U.S. Office of Education Bulletin No. 7 [Washington, D.C., 1959]).

[37] Robert C. Lloyd, "Guidance—In the Big-City School," *NEA Journal* (January 1959), pp. 20-22; Theodore Irwin, "We Need 20,000 Guidance Counselors," *Coronet* (October 1960), pp. 52-56.

portance of careful and intelligent counseling in reducing juvenile delinquency, cutting down the number of drop-outs from public secondary
schools, encouraging students to make honor grades, making it possible
for a larger proportion of high school students to be admitted to college,
and preventing young people from wasting or misdirecting their lives.[38]
Typical of the studies conducted is the following one reported by the
division of vocational high schools in the nation's largest city in 1955.
This report began by noting that: "With the chronological promotional
policy now in effect in the lower schools, some students now reach
secondary schools with the intelligence levels formerly considered not
sufficient to do adequate elementary school work. The average I.Q. of
students entering the vocational high schools in 1953 was 85.7." Under
such circumstances, by no means limited to this one example, it was
obvious that guidance counselors would have their work cut out for
them. The New York report continued:

> It is a serious question whether it is possible to make skilled workers
> out of individuals with intelligence scores lower than this average; yet
> one half of the entering pupils are in this group. If the demands made
> on the student by the shop or classroom teacher are too great for his
> comprehension, he is likely to rebel in some fashion. This may take the
> form of refusal to work, absence from school, or conduct that will dis-
> tract attention from his inadequacy. When pupils are grouped according
> to their abilities, they are not made conspicuous by their inferior perform-
> ance. They enjoy competition with their equals if the tasks are not be-
> yond them. Teachers in the vocational high schools long ago learned to
> modify the subject matter to keep within the abilities of the pupils, but
> they often fail to recognize that the difficulties of a troublesome pupil
> may be traced to his inability to understand the work of the class even
> at the lower level. Most vocational high schools make provisions for such
> pupils by means of low-ability tracks in both the academic and shop sub-
> jects. The guidance counselor is concerned with the organization of the
> special courses and the assignment of the proper pupils to them.[39]

As Theodora Carlson, the editor of *School Life*, put it, "that anyone
should suffer from lack of guidance" in a school system that was gen-

---

[38] Louis Kaplan, *Mental Health and Human Relations in Education* (New York:
Harper & Row, Publishers, 1959), pp. 32-35; Solomon O. Lichter, *et al.*, "Preven-
tion of School Drop-Outs," *School and Society* (April 7, 1962), pp. 159-68; David
Siegel, Frank E. Wellman, and Allen T. Hamilton, *An Approach to Individual
Analysis in Educational and Vocational Guidance* (U.S. Office of Education Bulletin
No. 1 [Washington, D.C., 1959]).

[39] *Guidance in Vocational High Schools* (Curriculum Bulletin, 1954-1955, Series
No. 2 [New York: Board of Education of the City of New York, 1955]).

erally recognized throughout the world for having developed guidance as one of its chief features was "on the surface unbelievable." Yet the facts were there and the existing shortages were grave. Congress took a giant step toward alleviating the situation when it included in the National Defense Education Act of 1958 an allotment of over $87,000,000, to be expended during the succeeding four years, to expand established guidance programs, improve testing services, and train guidance counselors. Title V of the Act gave the states matching grants on the basis of school-age population, first, to support testing programs that would identify outstanding students in secondary schools, and second, to develop counseling programs in those schools. Another section of the Act authorized contracts between the United States Office of Education and institutions of higher education to provide short-term or regular-session "institutes" for teachers who either were in the guidance field or hoped to enter it. Such persons would receive regular stipends while attending the "institutes." During the summer of 1960, Federal funds supported 84 such Counseling and Guidance Training Institutes at colleges and universities from coast to coast. Supplementing the federal effort, there now appeared local or regional programs such as that of the Board of Cooperative Educational Services in New York State. More than 90 B.C.E.S. units were put into operation in various parts of the state, providing roving guidance counselors as well as specialists in remedial reading and speech, and also making available the services of social workers, psychiatric consultants, and psychometrists to school systems that did not have their own counseling staff.[40]

By mid-century, then, guidance had obviously become vital to the successful functioning of the American system of mass education. Some observers were not sure, however, that this development and the child-centered-school attitude, which it helped to foster, was an entirely unmixed blessing. Sociologist David Riesman in 1956 bemoaned the fact that the attitude implanted in the minds of parents by some school guidance workers seemed to be that one should not "ask children to do anything which they regard as stuffy, tiresome, or unpleasant." He himself preferred the idea (perhaps "a cruel hangover from a patriarchal and puritanical past") that children "like the rest of us had to shoulder some of the burdens of transmitting the cultural heritage even if this

---

[40] Theodora E. Carlson and Catherine P. Williams, *Guide to the National Defense Education Act of 1958* (U.S. Office of Education Circular No. 553 [Washington, D.C., 1959]), pp. 13-15; Harrison Sasscer, "New Federal Programs Promote Testing and Guidance," *NEA Journal* (January 1959), p. 29.

meant a certain pressure on them to learn to read both words and music." [41] Similarly quizzical in attitude was former President Harold Taylor of Sarah Lawrence College, who warned that although the modern American child had been more thoroughly and self-consciously "understood" by parents, teachers, and guidance specialists, this comprehension did not necessarily help the child to grow into a meaningful maturity. It might rather create new problems for the individual by freeing him of personal responsibility and giving him nothing against which to rebel. Taylor reminded his readers,

> At every step members of the younger generation have been cautioned, watched and studied, treated as subjects for analysis. They are the children of understanding parents. They have learned to live with the handicap of being understood, and in the process have understood more than we have realized.

And what were the consequences? "We have then wondered why the young have been so silent, why they didn't show more initiative, why they seemed to settle for so much less than they could try for, why they sailed along with the tide and weren't interested in bucking it." The brutal fact, in Taylor's opinion, was that the youth of mid-century had been so effectively psychologized, guided, counseled, and "understood" that they found it difficult to discover what to rebel against. As one of this much "counseled" generation graphically put it: "Everyone was required to be well-rounded; well-rounded in the sense that all the sharp edges are rubbed off until one is perfectly round, like a tennis ball, with a little friendly fuzz on the top." [42]

Although the point made by critics such as Taylor had much validity, such seemed to be the price that the American nation felt it must pay because of its dedication to equalitarian socio-political objectives. In 1950 Dr. James Bryant Conant astutely pointed out that there was no need for a comprehensive guidance program in the more rigidly stratified societies of Europe or Asia. There the educational system helped to perpetuate the social system. The selection of future professional men and community leaders was made at a relatively early age, in some cases on the basis of family status and in others on the basis of exceptional native ability. Separate educational tracks were then provided for the

[41] David Riesman, *The Oral Tradition, The Written Word, and the Screen Image* (Yellow Springs, Ohio: Antioch Press, 1956), pp. 16-21; see also his *Individualism Reconsidered* (New York: Free Press of Glencoe, Inc., 1954), pp. 210-12.

[42] Harold Taylor, "The Understood Child," *Saturday Review of Literature*, 44 (May 20, 1961), pp. 46-49, 66.

different children as early as the age of ten, depending upon their social and professional destination. "Relatively few false hopes are awakened by too extensive an education of those who must later be content with manual labor; a far more intensive education than is possible in the United States can be provided for the future members of the professions."

Why, then, could not such a simple and logical system be followed in the United States? Mainly because the basic premise of the American social philosophy was different. Historical development had produced in the twentieth-century United States a democratic creed which maintained "that as a goal all careers are open to every young person before maturity and all careers are of equal importance to society and of equal social status." Americans wished to offer basic educational opportunity *equally* to *all* their youth, while at the same time providing special training for the gifted.[43] The only way to accomplish such a colossal task—one which never ceased to amaze or baffle European observers—was through the maintenance of the most extensive and best possible guidance program in every American public school system. Only in this way, Conant concluded, could the nation resolve successfully the educational dilemma which confronted it and provide *both* education for all and education for leadership.

Science in Education

"Whatever exists at all exists in some amount. To know it thoroughly involves knowing its quantity as well as its quality. . . . To measure a product well means to define its amount so that competent persons will know how large it is, with some precision, and that this knowledge may be recorded and used." [44] Edward L. Thorndike, writing in the 1918 Yearbook of the National Society for the Study of Education, advanced the above thesis as the credo of the twentieth-century movement for educational measurement, and it certainly was nowhere stated better or more cogently.

The idea of measuring quantity in the collection of facts about people, schools (or cattle, for that matter) was scarcely a new one. Again and

[43] James B. Conant, "Foreword," in John W. M. Rothney and Bert Roens, *Guidance of American Youth* (Cambridge: Harvard University Press, 1950), pp. xii-xv.

[44] Edward L. Thorndike, "The Nature, Purposes, and General Methods of Measurements of Educational Products," as quoted in Cremin, *Transformation of the School*, p. 185.

again in ancient times enumerations were made to measure the facts about land, population, armies, and tax receipts. The term "statistics" may have been employed as early as 1668 A.D. As for tests to measure educational achievement, these, too, seem to have been in use from very early times. In China, for example, as far back as the ninth century A.D., systematic and well-developed tests were given to determine admission to what might be called the "civil service" of that time. With the growth of powerful national states in Western Europe, the need for better statistical methods increased considerably. It was no mere coincidence that valuable new mathematical concepts such as the theory of probabilities (worked out in embryonic form by Pascal and Huygens in the seventeenth century) began to appear at this moment in history. In the eighteenth century the science of statistical measurement made further progress: among other things, Halley developed his series of mortality tables, de Witt worked out basic principles for annuity life insurance, and Malthus formulated his famous law of diminishing returns.[45]

The first specific applications of statistical methods to the study of educational problems were made in the latter half of the nineteenth century. Francis Galton, a grandson of Erasmus Darwin and cousin of Charles Darwin, initiated at this time a number of statistical studies of heredity, human populations, and individual abilities. Involving as they did the question of aptitude or intelligence—i.e., the capacity to acquire knowledge or skill of some type—these studies had important educational implications. Galton's first important book *Hereditary Genius*, published in 1869, sought to apply the law of "deviation from an average" to his studies on leading men in Great Britain.[46] Galton's researches into patterns of mental inheritance were influenced by the earlier work of the Belgian astronomer and statistician Adolphe Quetelet. In books such as *Sur l'homme et le developpement de ses facultés* (1835), the Belgian had shown that laws of probability could be applied to the measurement of human characteristics.[47] Galton, whose

---

[45] William W. Turnbull, "The Development of Modern Tests," *Conference on Testing* (Princeton, N.J.: Educational Testing Service, 1959); Jesse Sears, "Development of Tests and Measurements," in I. L. Kandel, ed., *Twenty-Five Years of American Education* (New York: The Macmillan Company, 1904), pp. 118-22.

[46] Francis Galton, *Hereditary Genius* (New York: Appleton-Century-Crofts, Inc., 1870).

[47] Lambert Adolphe Jacques Quetelet, *Sur l'homme et le developpement de ses facultés, ou essai de physique sociale* (Paris: Bachelier, 1835); *Instructions Populaires sur le calcul des probabilites* (Bruxelles: H. Tarlier, 1828); *Anthropometrie, ou, Mesure des differentes facultés de l'homme* (Paris: Bailliere, 1871); *Letters Addressed*

interest in the problem had been aroused by the observation that eminent men were likely to have eminent sons, spent close to 40 years studying human mental development and its relation to heredity.

As book after book issued from Galton's pen, his conclusions were subjected to heated criticism, like many other findings of the embattled Darwinians of that era. Undaunted, Galton continued his work and groomed a disciple, the mathematician Karl Pearson. In 1904 Galton, although eighty-two, was still mentally vigorous and active enough to endow a permanent fellowship at the University of London for the study of human inheritance (a field he had some years before labeled "eugenics").[48] The controversy he had aroused was not stilled after his death. Later commentators charged that a close affinity existed between Sir Francis's ideas and Social Darwinist concepts of inherent racial "superiority" which, in its most extreme form, fostered a garbled pre-Nazi pseudo-science of human biological determinism.[49]

Whatever the merits of such criticism, it is impossible to deny the significance of the methods Galton employed to investigate the subjects that interested him. Following in the footsteps of Quetelet, he worked doggedly to systematize his observations by statistical measures. In 1882 he opened his famous testing laboratory in South Kensington Museum for inventorying British abilities. Thus, though not actually an educational researcher, Galton was at an early stage employing tests and other precise quantitative measures to reach conclusions about heredity, psychology, and individual differences that had profound educational implications.[50]

to H.R.H. *The Grand Duke of Saxe Coburg and Gotha on the Theory of Probabilities* (London: C. Layton, 1849); Frank H. Hankins, *Adolphe Quetelet as Statistician* (New York: David McKay Co., Inc., 1908).

[48] Francis Galton, *English Men of Science, Their Nature and Nurture* (London: Macmillan & Co., Ltd., 1874); *Life History Album* (London: Macmillan & Co., Ltd., 1889); "The Possible Improvement of the Human Breed," *Smithsonian Institution Annual Report* (1901), pp. 523-38; *Noteworthy Families* (with E. Schuster), (London: J. John Murray, Publishers, Ltd., 1906); *Memories of My Life* (London: Methuen & Co., Ltd., 1908); see also Karl Pearson, *The Life, Letters and Labours of Francis Galton* (New York: Columbia University Press, 1914-1930).

[49] Jacques Barzun, *Darwin, Marx, Wagner: Critique of a Heritage* (Boston: Little, Brown & Co., 1941), pp. 106-9, 335-36, 382-83; Stow Persons, *American Minds: A History of Ideas* (New York: Holt, Rinehart & Winston, Inc., 1958), pp. 276-81; John Herman Randall, Jr., *The Making of the Modern Mind* (Boston: Houghton Mifflin Company, 1926), pp. 492-93; Richard Hofstadter, *Social Darwinism in American Thought* (Boston: Beacon Press, 1955), pp. 161-67.

[50] Edwin G. Boring, *A History of Experimental Psychology* (New York: Appleton-Century-Crofts, Inc., 1950), pp. 570-72; Florence L. Goodenough, *Mental Testing* (New York: Holt, Rinehart & Winston, Inc., 1949); Sears, "Development of Tests and Measurements," pp. 122-23.

The new interest in measuring individual differences soon spread to America. James McKeen Cattell, a young psychologist of the functionalist school who had studied at Leipzig under the redoubtable Wilhelm Wundt, sought to follow in Galton's footsteps by establishing in the late 1880's a psychological laboratory at the University of Pennsylvania for the measurement of abilities. In the course of his work there, Cattell devised a set of 50 tests that were given to students and also to those members of the general public who wished to have their abilities appraised. In 1890 he published an article entitled "Mental Tests and Measurements" which described these procedures.[51] This pioneering paper became a classic not only because it meant that American leadership was interested in the embryonic measurement movement, but also because it introduced the term "mental test" for the first time to psychological literature.[52]

By this time, experimental psychologists were becoming more actively concerned with mental testing. As Boring points out, this was a case where the *Zeitgeist* was clear. Almost immediately after Cattell's 1890 article was published, other American psychologists started to use his methods. One such man was Joseph Jastrow who in 1892 employed a similar series of mental tests with students at the University of Wisconsin, and who in 1893 set up a special exhibition of his procedures, modeled on Galton's London Laboratory, at the World's Columbian Exposition in Chicago.[53] Also active in furthering the progress made by Cattell was Joseph Mayer Rice, author of a controversial series of articles in *The Forum Magazine* in 1892 and 1893 showing the weaknesses in the American system of public education. Interested in measuring pupil achievement by means of a standard test, Rice devised such instruments for the fields of spelling, arithmetic, and languages.[54] He was most interested in measuring statistically the minimum time required for effective teaching of these subjects, hoping that more time would then be liberated for enrichment of the curriculum. Thousands of school

[51] "Mental Tests and Measurements," *Mind*, 15 (1890), pp. 373-79.

[52] Edward L. Thorndike, "Professor Cattell's Relation to the Study of Individual Differences," in *The Psychological Researches of James McKeen Cattell; A Review by Some of His Pupils* (New York: The Science Press, 1914); Boring, *Experimental Psychology*, pp. 570-71; Goodenough, *Mental Testing*, pp. 30-42.

[53] Joseph Jastrow and G. W. Moorehouse, "Some Anthropometric and Psychologic Tests of College Students," *American Journal of Psychology*, 4 (April 1892), pp. 420-28; Joseph Jastrow, "The Section of Psychology," in *World's Columbian Exposition, Official Catalogue, Part 12* (Chicago: W. B. Conkey Company, 1893).

[54] Joseph Mayer Rice, *The Public School System of the United States* (New York: Appleton-Century-Crofts, Inc., 1893).

children were tested. Although these tests were criticized by later workers as being crude and of doubtful validity, Rice's importance as a measurement pioneer cannot be denied.[55]

By the turn of the century, therefore, the measurement movement in America was beginning to take hold. It was at this point that Edward L. Thorndike, America's most important measurement specialist, made his appearance. While a student at Wesleyan University, Thorndike's interest had been caught by William James's opus, *Principles of Psychology*. In 1895 he transferred to Harvard to study directly under James, and there he remained for the next two years. Interested in the measurement of animal intelligence, young Thorndike undertook to incubate and hatch chickens in his rented room in Cambridge. His landlady, however interposed a veto, and Professor James tried to find space for the youthful experimenter in the Harvard laboratory or museum building. These efforts failing, the professor thereupon allowed Thorndike and his brood of chicks the use of the James's cellar, much to the amusement of the famous Harvard philosopher's children. Meanwhile, J. McKeen Cattell of Columbia heard of Thorndike's work and offered him a fellowship there. Thorndike, who was having a hard time supporting himself in Cambridge, gratefully accepted the offer.

Continuing his work on animal intelligence, Thorndike received a doctorate from Columbia in 1898. His thesis, based on a widely discussed experiment involving puzzle-boxes for cats, revealed much about trial-and-error patterns of learning. He then accepted a teaching position at Western Reserve University, where he continued his studies of animal learning. A year later Cattell convinced the Dean of the newly founded Teachers College at Columbia that a man "who had made a study of monkeys was worth trying out on humans," and the young man was brought to that institution as an instructor.[56] There then followed a notable scholarly career of 40 years during which Thorndike made important contributions to human and animal psychology, curriculum construction, educational administration, and the study of heredity, as well as to educational measurements and the testing movement.[57]

Jesse Sears maintains that Thorndike, in 1902 while a professor at Teachers College, Columbia University, offered the first true course in

---

[55] Walter W. Cook, "Achievement Tests," in W. S. Monroe, ed., *Encyclopedia of Educational Research* (New York: The Macmillan Company, 1950), pp. 1461-77.

[56] Boring, *Experimental Psychology*, pp. 561-64.

[57] Curti, *Social Ideas of American Educators*, pp. 459-98.

educational measurement to be given in the United States.[58] Scores of
students came to the college to study under him and to carry his teachings of scientific measurement back with them to school systems across
the land. Faithful disciples worked with him to develop precise scales
for measuring school achievement in various subjects. His endeavor to
inform the public was not primarily limited to the teaching profession.
He also launched a scholarly career, presenting in 1901 with the assistance of Woodworth a justly famous paper demolishing the traditional
transfer of training theory. Two years later appeared Thorndike's influential volume *Educational Psychology*.[59] And in 1904 he published his
Theory of Mental and Social Measurements, the first systematic work of
its kind.[60] There followed many other trail-blazing studies as the years
went by.[61]

In 1903 Thorndike declared that, "It is the vice or the misfortune of
thinkers about education to have chosen the methods of philosophy or
of popular thought instead of those of science." His long and busy
career represented a serious effort to convince American students of
education that, in order to attain meaningful results, they must base
their work upon careful statistical measurements and rigorously apply
the scientific method to all that they did.

While Thorndike and other Americans were seeking to develop an
educational science that would be solidly based upon quantitative measurement, their work, as before, was significantly affected by the findings
of European researchers. Most influential of all was the breakthrough
achieved by Alfred Binet, a conscientious Parisian investigator into the
fascinating workings of the human mind. Binet, in 1905 a professor at
the Sorbonne, is generally recognized as "France's greatest psychologist
of that generation." [62] A hard-working, imaginative experimentalist, he
joined with Henri Beaunis in 1889 in founding the first French psychological laboratory at the Sorbonne. Six years later Binet established

[58] Sears, "Development of Tests and Measurements," pp. 133-35.

[59] Edward L. Thorndike, *Educational Psychology* (New York: B. Westermann Co.,
Inc., 1903).

[60] Edward L. Thorndike, *An Introduction to the Theory of Mental and Social
Measurements* (Lancaster, Pa.: Science Press, 1904).

[61] For example, see his *Empirical Studies in the Theory of Measurement of Intelligence* (New York: Teachers College, Columbia University, 1927).

[62] Edith J. Varon, *Development of Alfred Binet's Psychology* (Princeton, N.J.:
Psychological Review Co., 1935); see also Beth Lucy Wellman and Boyd R.
McCandless, *Factors Associated with Binet IQ Changes of Pre-School Children*
(Washington, D.C.: American Psychological Association, 1946).

L'année psychologique, the first French journal of psychology.[63] Meanwhile he was publishing a notable series of studies of human mental processes. His first book on this subject *La psychologie du raisonnement* appeared as early as 1886. In 1891 he brought out a study entitled *Les alterations de la personalité,* and in 1894 he wrote an interesting review on great calculators and chess players. Many other special studies on mental phenomena were initiated during these years by the path-breaking Sorbonne professor.[64]

In 1903 Binet published a work entitled *L'étude expérimentale de l'intelligence.*[65] This monograph represented an advanced stage in the study of a problem that had long intrigued him, namely, the measurement of an individual's capacity to acquire knowledge or skill of some kind. For years Binet had been searching for an objective, reliable measure of such aptitude. It was the same problem that, in one form or another, had intrigued Galton, Cattell, Jastrow, Thorndike, and others. These early attempts to measure mental capacities were limited in effectiveness, however, because they tended to concentrate on some one specific trait or aspect, such as sensory discrimination, reaction time, or memory. Binet and his colleagues at the Sorbonne arrived at the conclusion, after years of testing school children, that tasks could be devised which would constitute adequate objective samples of the kind of abstract judgment and reasoning which one could expect to be characteristic of those who might be classified as "intelligent." To do this, however, the traditional approach of "faculty" psychology (which still exerted important influence) would have to be revised and "general" intelligence would have to be measured.[66]

In 1904 the opportunity arose which would enable Binet to test his thesis. His interest in the education of retarded children had long been known. In that year the French Ministry of Education appointed a commission to investigate this field, a commission which was soon in touch with Binet and others. When it was decided to set up special schools for the retarded, Binet was asked to suggest means for selecting

[63] Sears, "Development of Tests and Measurements, pp. 130-33; Turnbull, "Development of Modern Tests;" Goodenough, *Mental Testing,* pp. 34-39.

[64] See obituary notices and the list of principal works of Alfred Binet in *American Journal of Psychology,* 23 (January 1912), pp. 140-41.

[65] Alfred Binet, *L'étude expérimentale de l'intelligence* (Paris: Schleicher Frères, 1903).

[66] Irving Lorge, "Exploring Man's Intelligence," in Lyman Bryson, ed., *An Outline of Man's Knowledge* (Garden City, N.Y.: Doubleday & Company, Inc., 1960), pp. 123-26.

the children to attend these institutions. With Theodore Simon, a former student and now a close colleague, Binet set to work to devise a formal scale for measuring the intelligence of children. The approach differed in a number of ways from all previous attempts to measure mental aptitude. For one thing, it aimed at obtaining a general idea of a child's mental development by setting before him a wide variety of tasks, eschewing precise measures of single presumed faculties or abilities. Second, the scale required only a short time for its administration. Third, it made no attempt to measure all the supposed sensory, perceptual, and motor constituents of human "intelligence," but concentrated instead on what was considered to be the most essential factor, namely, the ability to make sound judgments. Finally, it was standardized by arranging test items in order of difficulty, rather than in terms of specific subject matter, this order being based upon the performances of 50 normal children and a number of retarded and subnormal children. A series of 30 tests, "ranging in difficulty from those suitable only for the classification of very low-grade idiots to those intended for children in the upper elementary grades," determined the scale. Not only higher mental processes, but also tasks calling for attention, motor coordination, and the ability to execute simple orders, to distinguish between objects, or to imitate certain gestures were included. On the basis of his tested achievement, any child could be classified as retarded, normal, or advanced for his age.[67]

The Binet-Simon scale of 1905 proved to be most useful in measuring the mental capacity of retarded children. But what of children of "normal" intelligence? More and more Binet became interested in constructing a measurement device that would apply to them. By 1908 it was ready. The new Binet-Simon scale was radically different in structure from the earlier one. A child's standing was no longer stated in terms of number of items passed but rather in terms of mental age. The 1908 scale assigned the 58 tests, to be administered in connection with it, to different age levels. The number of tests for each year varied from three to seven. Each test was assigned to a specific age level only after the French investigators had determined, by study of a control group, that at least *three-quarters* of the children of that age could handle it successfully.[68]

[67] Alfred Binet and Theodore Simon, *Les Enfants Anormaux: Guide pour l'admission des enfants anormaux dans les classes de perfectionnement* (Paris: Colin, 1907); Goodenough, *Mental Testing*, pp. 35-51.

[68] Alfred Binet and Theodore Simon, *The Development of Intelligence in Children* (Vineland, N.J.: Training School, Department of Research, 1916); Alfred Binet:

Shortly before Binet's untimely death in 1911, a second revision of his intelligence test scale appeared. This made no change in the fundamental principles of that of 1908, but it spelled out more exactly the mathematical formula for determining the precise mental age of any individual child taking the tests.[69] By this time, then, the concept of "mental age" as measurable by statistical methods had taken definite shape. Mental age and chronological age were now seen to be quite different things. Following up on Binet's findings, a German psychologist named Wilhelm Stern suggested in 1912 that a "mental quotient" be recognized as a more *constant* measure of the intellectuality of a given individual than "developing mental age." This would be calculated by dividing a child's mental age by his chronological age. As Irving Lorge points out, by this time "intelligence testing had moved from the rough appraisal of special and separate sensory functions to a far more precise measure of mental ability based on units of mental age and refined still further by the addition of the intelligence quotient. . . ." [70]

Binet's intelligence scales attracted considerable attention not only in Germany and France, but also in England, Russia, and—most notably —the United States. No people took more enthusiastically to the new concept of intelligence testing than the Americans. Henry H. Goddard, who had studied under G. Stanley Hall at Clark University and later was to make a widely discussed study of the feeble-minded Kallikak family, was greatly impressed by Binet's work. Indeed, so convinced was Goddard of its significance that he promptly set to work translating the 1905 tests into English (the first such translation) and putting them to actual use with American children. At the time he was working in a school for subnormal children at Vineland, New Jersey, and so had a wonderful field for experiment close at hand. After trying out the tests on the Vineland children, he utilized them with 2,000 normal children as well. The data gathered in this way served as the basis for a revision of the Binet-Simon scale which Goddard published in 1908. By this time school teachers were coming to summer session workshops at Vineland where, under the guidance of Goddard and his assistants, they eagerly absorbed the new gospel of tests and testing, returning to

---

Les idées modernes sur les enfants (Paris: E. Flammarion, 1909); Lorge, "Exploring Man's Intelligence," pp. 125-26.

[69] Alfred Binet and Theodore Simon, A *Method of Measuring the Development of the Intelligence of Young Children* (Authorized Translation) (Lincoln, Ill.: The Courier Co., 1912).

[70] Lorge, "Exploring Man's Intelligence," p. 126.

their school systems full of determination to employ these interesting new devices for the classification of pupils.[71]

Following in the footsteps of Goddard, other American psychologists began to attempt revisions of the Binet-Simon scale. The most influential studies were the ones formulated by Lewis M. Terman and his associates at Stanford University. In 1916 Terman, another one of Stanley Hall's pupils from Clark, published what promptly came to be known as the "Stanford Revision" of the Binet scales.[72] This extensive reworking of the original instrument included some 90 tests in all, six for each age level from three to ten, eight for age twelve, and six for age fourteen. Instructions for scoring and administering the tests were made more precise than they had hitherto been. Special care was taken to secure a representative sample of children for use in standardization. Terman included in his standardization group only those children who, at the time of being tested, were within two months of their birthdays and who were attending schools situated in so-called "average" American communities. Most important of all, however, the 1916 Stanford Revision introduced and popularized the concept of "I.Q." in American education. Perpetuating the suggestion for a numerical mental ratio advanced by Stern in 1911, Terman and his associates renamed it "intelligence quotient" and argued that it remained fairly constant through an individual's life. Terman used test results from both selected and unselected samplings of American children to establish the distribution of levels of intelligence in these age groups. He then proceeded to assign specific valuations to different intelligence quotient ranges. Thus, the top 1 per cent of 1,000 "I.Q.'s" in his sample was found to score 130 or above, and this group was held to range from "very superior intelligence" to "near genius or genius." On the other hand, the lowest

[71] See the following selections by Henry H. Goddard: "Four Hundred Feeble-Minded Children Classified by the Binet Method," *Pedagogical Seminary,* 17 (September 1910), pp. 387-97; "Two Thousand Normal Children Measured by the Binet Measuring Scale of Intelligence," *Pedagogical Seminary,* 18 (June 1911), pp. 232-59; *The Adaptation Board as a Measure of Intelligence* (Vineland, N.J.: The Training School, 1915); *Psychology and the Normal and Subnormal* (New York: Dodd, Mead & Co., 1919); *Human Efficiency and Levels of Intelligence* (Princeton, N.J.: Princeton University Press, 1920).

[72] See the following selections by Lewis M. Terman: "Genius and Stupidity: A Study of Some of the Intellectual Processes of Seven Bright and Seven Stupid Boys," (Ph.D. dissertation, Clark University) *Pedagogical Seminary,* 13 (1906), pp. 307-73; "Report of the Buffalo Conference on the Binet-Simon Tests of Intelligence," *Pedagogical Seminary,* 20 (1913), pp. 549-54; *The Measurement of Intelligence: An Explanation of and a Complete Guide for the Use of the Stanford Revision and Extension of the Binet-Simon Intelligence Scale* (Boston: Houghton Mifflin Company, 1916).

1 per cent which scored 70 or below was designated as varying from "borderline deficiency" down to "definite feeble-mindedness." [73]

The Stanford Revision rapidly became the most widely used American intelligence test, serving as a standard for all testing in the United States for more than two decades. Nevertheless, Terman was well aware of the deficiencies that remained in his 1916 scale. The extremities had not been as thoroughly standardized as the middle scale. Only a single form of test was available in each instance, making it difficult to assess the value of retests or check the accuracy of results. To remedy these and other defects, Terman's group worked diligently for more than ten years to produce an improved scale. A much broader standardization group was now employed, composed of over 3,000 individuals from all major areas, urban and rural, of the United States. To make certain that the sample would be representative of the entire American population, paternal occupations were ascertained and proportions were assigned to each occupational level as reported in the latest United States Census. Two forms of the new scales were prepared, each covering an age range from two years through adolescence and recognizing four levels of adult intelligence ("average," "somewhat superior," "decidedly superior," and "extremely superior").[74]

The testing movement received a decided stimulus from the impact of World War I. Up to this time very little had been done with group testing. When the nation entered the war, the American Psychological Association was asked to suggest what the science of psychology could do to help attain victory. In answer it proposed the preparation of a series of mental tests to enable the army to screen out those too incompetent to make adequate soldiers and to identify those who had leadership potential. The result was the development of two types of group tests. One of these, the Army Alpha, was verbal and designed for recruits who could read and comprehend English. The other, the Army Beta, was a nonverbal performance test intended for those who did not know English. Nearly two million "doughboys" took the Army

[73] Lewis M. Terman, Grace Lyman, George Ordahl, *et al, The Stanford Revision and Extension of the Binet-Simon Scale for Measuring Intelligence* (Baltimore: Warwick & York, Inc., 1917); Lewis M. Terman, *The Intelligence of School Children* (Boston: Houghton Mifflin Company, 1919); A. Delvaux, *Controle de la Stanford Revision de Terman (échelle Binet-Simon) sur des enfants de milieux sociaux differents* (Bruxelles: Lamartin, 1932).

[74] Lewis M. Terman, *Measuring Intelligence; A Guide to the Administration of the New Revised Stanford-Binet Tests of Intelligence* (Boston: Houghton Mifflin Company, 1937); Quinn McNemar, *The Revision of the Stanford-Binet Scale: An Analysis of the Standardization Data* (Boston: Houghton Mifflin Company, 1942).

Alpha. This was group testing with a vengeance, usually two or three hundred recruits being tested at a time. Mass production methods were therefore necessary to process such vast numbers.[75]

The Armistice in 1918 was signed before the American Army was able to derive much value from its ambitious testing program. The Alpha and Beta tests, however, had given enormous publicity to group intelligence testing and had demonstrated to many public school systems its practicability. Testing and applied psychology had gained acceptance. Increasingly, too, Americans began to dispute the meaning of the Army test results. Some people happily cited these findings as conclusive proof that the average American adult was no more capable mentally than a twelve-year-old child, that whites were more intelligent than Negroes, and that the great majority of Americans were uneducable beyond high school. Certain educators heatedly rejoined that conclusions such as these were based on a complete misinterpretation of the results of the wartime tests. In the course of the resulting uproar, the potential significance of standardized tests in American society made a notable impact on the public consciousness.

By the 1920's it was clear that the field of tests and measurements was beginning to come into its own. Only three universities had offered courses in the subject before World War I, but in the November, 1920, issue of the *Journal of Educational Research*, it was reported that most state universities, half the nonstate universities, and half the state normal schools of the country were offering courses in educational measurement. Research departments now appeared in most of the big city school systems, departments which employed tests and measurements to classify and grade children, investigate costs, evaluate teaching efficiency, and diagnose problem cases. Extensive surveys of school conditions were being made by various expert agencies. Here, again, the main reliance of the investigators came to be upon statistical appraisals.[76] One observer graphically described the vogue of the times as follows: " 'Mental ages' and 'I.Q.'s' obtained from half a dozen different group tests were joyfully computed and entered on children's permanent record cards by teachers and school principals with as much assurance as their grandfathers had placed in the skull maps drawn up by their favorite phrenologist. The decade of the 1920's was the heyday of the

[75] Boring, *Experimental Psychology*, p. 575.
[76] Lewis M. Terman, *et al. Intelligence Tests and School Reorganization* (New York: Harcourt, Brace & World Inc., 1923).

testing movement, the age of innocence when an I.Q. was an I.Q. and few ventured to doubt its omnipotence." [77]

As experience with group tests accumulated, it became increasingly evident that devices of a nonverbal type were badly needed in both the educational and business worlds to measure mental traits other than traditional literate "intelligence." In the Twenties and early Thirties, therefore, investigators turned their attention to the measurement of motor ability, aptitudes for various industrial occupations and trades, and traits that might be considered constituent elements in "personality." The most famous of the projective techniques developed to measure such characteristics was devised by Hermann Rorschach and put forward in a monograph with a very limited distribution, published in Switzerland in 1921. It was not long before a number of enthusiastic American disciples had introduced the Rorschach test in the United States and publicized its use in a number of fields.[78]

With the advancement of the science of educational measurement, it became clear that what was being measured under the heading of human "intelligence" was an immensely complicated phenomenon. It was furthermore doubtful whether or not this entity, whatever it was, remained fixed and immutable. One research study after another demonstrated that schooling influenced performance on intelligence tests. Other influences making for varying test results were shown to be home conditions, impact of the community, and socio-economic status. In an effort to break down the protean concept of intelligence into its constituent elements, a group of researchers in Britain and the United States developed an approach that came to be known as "factorial analysis." An American psychologist at the University of Chicago, L. L. Thurstone, collected his research findings, dating from 1924, in a summation volume entitled *Multiple-Factor Analysis*, which he published after World War II.[79]

---

[77] Goodenough, *Mental Testing*, pp. 77-78.

[78] "Educational Measurements," *Review of Educational Research*, XXVI (June 1956), pp. 270-79.

[79] Louis Leon Thurstone, *Multiple-Factor Analysis: A Development and Expansion of the Vectors of Mind* (Chicago: University of Chicago Press, 1947); see also the following selections by Thurstone: *The Nature of Intelligence* (New York: Harcourt, Brace & World, Inc., 1924); *The Reliability and Validity of Tests* (Ann Arbor, Mich.: J. W. Edwards Publishers, Inc., 1931); *The Theory of Multiple Factors* (Ann Arbor, Mich.: J. W. Edwards Publishers, Inc., 1933); *The Vectors of Mind: Multiple Factor Analysis for the Isolation of Primary Traits* (Chicago: University of Chicago Press, 1935).

From these and other investigations a more subtle, perspicacious picture of the nature of intelligence emerged. It was now known for certain that a great many factors existed which entered into many different types of combinations in specific skills. A few of these factors were discovered to be more generally involved than others in successful human activity, and these were designated as "primary" mental abilities. Thurstone distinguished seven such primary factors: number, word fluency, space, verbal meaning, memory, reasoning, and perceptual speed. These he arranged in a grid, with the first three qualities representing "content" and the next three "process." Specific tests and subtests were now devised to measure in specific individuals these main factors and even the interactions between "content" and "process." In short, it was now believed that there was not any *one* factor broad enough to be called "general ability." "Intelligence" began to be regarded as the sum of several independently variable abilities, all of them important, all useful, and all subject to a certain extent to environmental influences.

It was in this new context that the testing programs of the American Armed Forces in World War II were worked out. As a consequence, the several wartime test series of 1941-45 were much more complex and varied than the Army Alpha and Beta. The services continued to give a General Classification Test, but this miscellaneous approach was supplemented now by batteries of tests designed to measure eight different basic abilities. Great strides were made by the military services in the development and application of aptitude tests. The extensive psychological testing program of the Air Force alone was later documented in a series of 19 volumes! [80]

World War II played an even greater role in publicizing the tests and measurements movement than had World War I. Following 1945 industries, government agencies, colleges, universities, hospitals, social welfare agencies, and public school systems clamored for testing programs. Every possible skill, every potential mental factor or aptitude, every notable personality trait was now conscientiously weighed and measured. A bewildering variety of mental tests and rating scales were developed to meet the expanding demands of American society. A bibliography of the field published in 1945 listed no less than 5,294 such test items. In the nation's public school systems alone, some 108 *million* standardized tests were used in the year 1957. At a conference on testing held at Princeton University the following year, it was announced that 55 per cent of the above total was made up of achieve-

[80] *Review of Educational Research*, XXVI, pp. 270-71.

ment tests, 35 per cent of various types of intelligence and aptitude tests, and the remaining 10 per cent of personality tests. More than 1,000 published versions of tests were utilized in the schools that one year, with at least 20 test publishers feverishly working to meet the demand. Interestingly enough, it was the opinion of one expert at the Princeton conference that of all the tests used in American schools, at least 75 per cent were given *below* grade nine.[81] When we add to these rather overwhelming figures the total of nearly a million students taking various types of college entrance tests, college achievement tests, and merit scholarship tests, we can only conclude that the American student, entering the second half of the twentieth century, was probably the most tested youngster in history.

In conclusion, what was the significance of testing for twentieth-century American education? Two Australian observers noted in 1930 that the development of such techniques was important "as marking another stage in the candid recognition by the school of responsibility for aspects of the pupil's life other than the merely academic." These visitors added that every large Australian school should in their opinion aim at providing similar services.[82] These and other schoolmen from abroad correctly divined that the measurement movement, as it had taken shape in America, represented, at least implicitly, a reaction against the traditional concepts of education which derived from Western civilization's past. In place of such time-honored ideas, George S. Counts pointed out that "scientific measurement" had substituted the modes of thought and methods of work of modern science. Also significant as a motivation, he cited, was a kind of compulsive utilitarianism, a drive by the American people to make their schools more efficient.[83]

Not all observers of modern measurement, however, have viewed it with equanimity. As early as 1912, humanist-scholar Paul Shorey complained in the *School Review* that proponents of the scientific study of education, such as G. Stanley Hall, had "magnified their office and enlarged their claims beyond all reason." The upshot of their work, he charged, was to exalt sentiment above disciplined intelligence and emotional impressionability above accuracy.[84] Even more caustic in his com-

---

[81] Educational Testing Service, *Conference on Testing*, pp. 30-40, 56-59.

[82] K. S. Cunningham and G. E. Phillips, *Some Aspects of Education in the U.S.A.* (Melbourne, Australia: Melbourne University Press, 1930).

[83] George S. Counts, *The American Road to Culture* (New York: The John Day Company, Inc., 1930), pp. 168-72.

[84] Paul Shorey, "An Educational Culture—Bouillon," *School Review*, 20 (February 1912), pp. 75-78.

ments was the pitiless dissector of American foibles, H. L. Mencken. In an essay published in 1922, the sage of Baltimore thundered that schoolmen, facing an unmanageable task, were seeking "refuge from its essential impossibility in a Chinese maze of empty technic." In America, Mencken contended, "where all that is bombastic and mystical is most esteemed, the art of pedagogics becomes a sort of puerile magic, a thing of preposterous secrets, a grotesque compound of false premises and illogical conclusions . . . mathematical formulae are worked out for every emergency; there is no sure-cure so idiotic that some superintendent of schools will not swallow it." The trouble with all such "New Thought" in pedagogy, in Mencken's not too humble opinion, was that it was based on a false premise, namely, the democratic theory of education—"that is, by the theory that mere education can convert a peasant into an intellectual aristocrat, . . . in brief, that it is possible to make purses out of sow's ears." [85]

Measurement men might dismiss criticism such as this as representing the undocumented, distorted maunderings of a sensation-seeking journalist, but it was not as easy to overlook admonitions which issued from education's Olympus. In 1929 John Dewey set forth his views on the question in a monograph entitled *Sources of a Science of Education.* "Educational science," said Dewey, "cannot be constructed simply by borrowing the techniques of experiment and measurement found in physical science." Education, to Dewey, was ultimately an art rather than a science. It was too dynamic ever to be reduced to mathematical formulae. Measurement might be used as a technique "to guide the intelligence of teachers," but it should never be allowed to dictate rules of action. "There is no subject matter," Dewey insisted, "intrinsically marked off, earmarked so to say, as the content of educational science." [86]

Nor was Dewey the only well-known educator to express serious doubt about the sweeping claims that were being advanced on behalf of "scientific measurement." Abraham Flexner, founder of the Institute of Advanced Study at Princeton, noted that measurement "tells nothing of the background, temperament, creative powers, and outlook of the individual whose specific achievements it so carefully recorded." [87] His-

---

[85] H. L. Mencken, *Prejudices, Third Series* (New York: Alfred A. Knopf, Inc., 1922), pp. 238-53.
[86] John Dewey, *Sources of a Science of Education* (New York: Liveright Publishing Corporation, 1929), pp. 26-48.
[87] Abraham Flexner, *Henry Pritchett, A Biography* (New York: Columbia University Press, 1943), p. 127.

torian Merle Curti detected in the challenge to the transfer of training theory levied by measurement specialists a "scientific" rationalization for the modern emphasis upon narrow technical and vocational subjects at the expense of broader liberal studies. Curti saw the American enthusiasm for mental testing as being directed into conservative channels by those who favored the perpetuation of a stratified society.[88] Agreeing with this critique, philosopher Horace M. Kallen noted that with the "I.Q.," the school "becomes a caste-ing device, an instrument of classification and distribution of the generations of Americans in the national economy." Business enterprise, said Kallen, "leaped at the idea. . . . All over the land testing was taken for a trouble-and-money-saving device." Besides, he added, the test and measurement cult provided welcome relief from the headaches of coping with oversized classes, irrelevant curricula, mutually contradictory educational psychologies, and lack of any common assumptions on the purposes of teaching.[89]

George Counts found the reason for the popularity of scientific measurement in the fact that "the people of the United States almost never view education as a way of life or of personal culture. They rather look upon it as an external means for the attainment of some definite and desirable goal." [90] Educational "science" promised efficiency, results, and savings for the taxpayer. Administrators were quick to jump on the statistics bandwagon, argued one later student of the movement, because in this way they could impress businessmen and other "practical-minded people" with their tough-minded realism and "sound business principles." In this setting, intellectual goals based upon a scholarly tradition scarcely mattered.[91]

Following World War II, the value of the "I.Q." was increasingly called into question. In October of 1959, John M. Stalnaker, President of the National Merit Scholarship Corporation, told an educational conference that the "I.Q." was not as important as what a person accomplishes. The relationship between I.Q. and productivity even in scholarly fields, he asserted, was not as high as many people assumed. Motivation was equally important. The "I.Q.," in Stalnaker's opinion,

[88] Merle E. Curti, *The Growth of American Thought* (New York: Harper & Row, Publishers, 1943), p. 641.
[89] Horace M. Kallen, *The Education of Free Men* (New York: Farrar, Straus & Company, 1949), pp. 44-45, 166.
[90] Counts, *American Road to Culture*, pp. 170-71.
[91] Raymond E. Callahan, *Education and the Cult of Efficiency* (Chicago: University of Chicago Press, 1962).

"lacks a rigorous theoretical foundation and presents to the general public, parents, and students, a grossly oversimplified picture of mental organization." Other types of tests including college entrance examinations were also viewed rather narrowly now. In December, 1962, the director of admissions at Columbia College reported that a study of 72 students admitted to that institution with below-average verbal aptitude scores indicated that such scores were not necessarily an accurate measure of a young person's ability to do good work in college. Here, again, motivation rather than potential as recorded by test scores seemed to be the key to success.[92]

Probing even more deeply into the deficiencies of the testing movement was Martin L. Gross, who in 1962 published a searching critique of the use of tests in industry and schools. This work entitled *The Brain Watchers* warned against the slipshod or distorted use of such devices as a mass screening procedure in cases where findings were interpreted (or rather, misinterpreted) by insufficiently qualified teachers and guidance counselors. Many personality tests put a low premium on creative talent, he charged, while giving preference to conformity, conservativism, and lack of imagination.[93]

As the public controversy over the use and abuse of tests mounted, the Carnegie Corporation of New York sought to throw some objective light on the matter. In early June, 1962, it made a grant of $333,000 to the Russell Sage Foundation under the terms of which the latter was to engage in a three-year study of the "social consequences" of intelligence, aptitude, and achievement tests. One of the objectives of the project, it was announced, would be to discover whether people believed that varying achievement was due to intelligence or to hard work. Also the Russell Sage staff would seek to discover whether modern extensively tested pupils, with knowledge of their own intelligence and aptitudes in relation to classmates, were in danger from such knowledge. Finally, the investigators were interested in the impact of testing on teachers. Were parents disciplining their children according to the I.Q. standing? Were teachers who knew the test scores and I.Q.'s of their pupils tending to rate them in their class work in accordance with these scores?

Reviewing the history of "scientific measurement," particularly in its American aspect, one gains the impression that all too frequently the field was abused by its devoted disciples. They very often claimed too much for it or applied its results too sweepingly and dogmatically. Why

[92] *New York Times*, October 30, 1959, p. 23; December 3, 1962, p. 29.
[93] Martin L. Gross, *The Brain Watchers* (New York: Random House, Inc., 1962).

was this the case? For one thing, educational measurement was a relatively new discipline, striving hard for academic recognition. Some of its over-enthusiastic exponents undoubtedly felt that the best way of breaking into the charmed circle of the academic muses was to show large results. Then, too, the keynote of modern Western civilization was "science," and, therefore, if even the most puerile statistical finding could be accepted as possessing "scientific" validity, it would be likely to attain academic respectability. Furthermore, the intensive specialization and departmentalization of twentieth-century culture left a chaotic void into which measurement promised to bring unity. In a certain sense, educational measurement acquired for modern schoolmen an almost mystical quality. Here, in a mass education, "child-centered school" environment was the unshakeable authority of numbers, statistics, and quantitative yardsticks. These assuredly could conveniently transcend all embarrassing differences of educational philosophy and all controversial questions of values or ideology which might irritate powerful groups in the community. Here was a utilitarian, slide-rule approach which the average parent and payer of the school tax could appreciate, not only because it was "scientific," but also because it was efficient and "money-saving."

We are obliged to ask, finally, whether the results of the measurement movement may be set down as all unhappy ones. Can we accept such a negative conclusion when measurement as an active force in American education dates back no more than half a century. Certainly the ideal of the movement was neither mean nor unworthy. The ambitious dream that sought a "scientific" accuracy to be attained in American teaching through objective analyses, precise measuring sticks, and scrupulous quantitative standards would do no discredit to a latter-day Francis Bacon. The hope that teachers and school administrators would in time come to depend less on personal guesses and prejudices and more on concrete, demonstrable evidence was manifestly praiseworthy. How far statistical measurement would ultimately carry American education in the direction of these laudable goals only future history, the final "measurer" of human accomplishment, could reveal.

CHAPTER THREE

The School in the American Social Matrix

What Benjamin Disraeli termed "the microcosm of a public school" [1] has in all societies always been profoundly influenced by the total cultural setting. Since what we usually call "education" far exceeds the bounds of formal schooling, the stretched perimeter of influence of other cultural agencies has had a significant impact on the activities of teachers and on pedagogical thinking in the schools themselves. Circumstances were hardly different in twentieth-century America. There parent-teacher associations, philanthropic foundations, and special-interest groupings strove energetically to shape the development of the people's schools. The attitude of the prescriptorial culture was reflected vividly, too, in the outlook and policies of school boards and professional administrators, as well as in the social standing accorded to teachers.

PTA's and Their Expectations

The banquet hall of the Arlington Hotel in Washington, D.C., was jammed with two thousand seriously attentive, determined ladies on Wednesday morning, the 17th of February, 1897. Presiding at the

[1] *Vivian Grey: A Romance of Youth,* I (New York: M. Walter Dunne, 1904), p. 5.

rostrum was a luminary from Chevy Chase, Maryland, Mrs. Alice McClellan Birney, bearing the distinguished title of President of the First National Congress of Mothers. Her words of welcome to the assembled ladies (after emphasizing the importance of building more kindergartens so that prisons and insane asylums would not be necessary) concluded with this stirring exhortation:

> . . . . It has been truly said, "To cure was the voice of the past; to prevent, the divine whisper of today."
> May the whisper grow into a mighty shout throughout the land until all mankind takes it up as the battle cry for the closing years of the century. Let mothers, fathers, nurses, educators, ministers, legislators, and, mightiest of all in its swift, far-reaching influence, the press, make the child the watchword and ward of the day and hour; let all else be secondary, and coming generations will behold a new world and a new people.[2]

The applause was hearty as Mrs. Birney resumed her seat. Mrs. Mary Lowe Dickinson, President of the National Council of Women of New York City, followed with an address of gratitude for "such a royal welcome as has been given to us." Then the ladies adjourned to go to the White House, there to be received by Mrs. Grover Cleveland. Thus commenced the First National Congress of Mothers. And thus was born, with appropriate ceremony, the modern parent-teacher movement of the United States.

What were the events that led to this widely publicized meeting? Scattered Mothers' Clubs first appeared tentatively and locally as early as 1855, when the country was in the throes of an educational and humanitarian awakening and was feeling the initial thrust of the factory system.[3] In the later years of the nineteenth century, a number of new lines of development converged to produce a more active concern for child welfare. Humanitarian and reformist leaders organized settlement houses in the overcrowded, urban rabbit warrens. By the Nineties these "settlements" were actively engaged in fostering Mothers' Clubs. Just at this time, too, the influence of Froebel and others was being reflected in the United States by the rapid spread of the kindergarten movement. Paralleling this trend, and often intermingled with it, was the campaign

[2] *First National Congress of Mothers, February 17, 18, 19, 1897* (Washington, 1897), pp. 1-11.
[3] Elmer S. Holbeck, *An Analysis of the Activities and Potentialities for Achievement of Parent-Teacher Associations* (New York: Teachers College, Columbia University, 1934), pp. 7-9.

for the "scientific" study of child behavior launched by psychologist G. Stanley Hall and others. Across the country the new Mothers' Clubs worked in close harmony with kindergarten teachers and child study specialists.[4]

The final element in the picture was the emergence of the American middle- and upper-class female as club woman and militant crusader for "good" causes. Boldly heralding the advent of this new era of "organization woman" were such events as the founding of the American Association of University Women in 1882 and the establishment of the General Federation of Women's Clubs (along with the Daughters of the American Revolution) in 1889. No longer content merely with Shakespeare and Browning, or even gardening and Japanese prints, the indefatigable ladies' clubs of America were turning their attention to temperance, politics, child welfare, and public education.[5]

It should therefore come as no surprise that Mrs. Birney's first official call for a conference of mothers was read before a meeting of the General Federation of Women's Clubs in 1896. The previous summer the canny Mrs. Birney had encouraged her husband and his brothers to go on an extended fishing trip. She then headed for Chautauqua, New York, for her "vacation." At that renowned adult education center she sought support for a projected National Mothers' Congress. One afternoon a kindergarten teacher met Frances E. Newton of Kansas City, one of the most prominent advocates of the kindergarten crusade. "Come over with me to the Mothers' Building," she begged Miss Newton. "I want you to meet a little woman who has a beautiful dream she wants us to help her realize." And so at Chautauqua, Alice Birney had a chance to muster support for her plan, an essential prerequisite to getting the national women's club movement to back it.[6]

---

[4] Dorothy Sparks, *Strong Is the Current* (Chicago: Illinois Congress of Parents and Teachers, 1948), pp. 1-3; Mary L. Rogers, *A Contribution to the Theory and Practice of Parents Associations* (New York: United Parents Associations, 1931), p. 20; Margaret Lighty and Leroy Bowman, *Parenthood in a Democracy* (New York: The Parents Institute, 1939), pp. 20-23. Miss Elizabeth Harrison, president of the Chicago Kindergarten College, held a number of conferences in the mid-nineties to which mothers from all over the country were invited to hear expert advice from educators, psychologists, and physicians on how they should rear their children.

[5] Charles A. Beard and Mary R. Beard, *The Rise of American Civilization*, II (New York: The Macmillan Company, 1927), pp. 404-6, 752-53; Harvey Wish, *Society and Thought in Modern America* (New York: David McKay Co., Inc., 1952), pp. 124-25.

[6] Harry Overstreet and Bonaro Overstreet, *When Children Come First* (Chicago: National Congress of Parents and Teachers, 1949), pp. 40-43; Sparks, *Strong Is the Current*, pp. 1-3.

She still needed financial backing, however. Phoebe Appleton Hearst, widow of George Hearst, the multimillionaire mining king from California, had over the years become actively involved in a number of philanthropies, one of which was the kindergarten movement. Mrs. Hearst's financial aid was to play an indispensable role in making the 1897 Congress possible.[7]

And so the great crusade for better children (and better mothers) was launched. But how did the valiant crusaders propose to attain their primary objectives? At first they stumbled along with somewhat generalized and tenuous propositions, proclaiming a virtuous concern for child welfare in all its aspects. Thus the first charter of the Mothers' Congress, duly granted under the laws of the District of Columbia, published to the world the following sanguine hopes:

> The object of this organization shall be (1) to promote conference among parents upon questions vital to the welfare of their children; (2) to further develop the manifold interests of the home; (3) to cooperate with educators and legislators to secure the best methods in the physical, moral, and mental training of the young; (4) to enlighten motherhood on the problems of race development; (5) to uplift and improve the conditions of mothers in all walks of life; and (6) to this end to promote the formation of mothers' clubs and homemakers' clubs in all states and territories of the United States.[8]

In 1897 the fledgling organization was in effect just another women's club. According to its own professions, its purpose was solely to organize groups of mothers throughout the nation to study child psychology and improve the quality of child life. Although this concept was never completely abandoned, adventitious circumstances appreciably broadened the scheme as the years passed. As interest in the work of the Congress began to grow, it became evident that the project could not be confined to mothers alone. The child was also importantly influenced by fathers and by school teachers, and clearly both of these groups would have to be enlisted in the campaign.

The schools proved to be easier to assimilate to the campaign of the zealous and dedicated ladies than did the fathers. The Congress decided without much debate to sponsor a national drive for the organization

[7] Edgar E. Robinson, "Phoebe Appleton Hearst," *DAB*, 8, pp. 488-89; *First National Congress of Mothers*, p. 10.
[8] Martha S. Mason, ed., *Parents and Teachers, A Survey* (Boston: Ginn & Company, 1928), p. 282.

of parent-teacher associations. This effort went so well that very soon a special department had to be set up to coordinate it.[9] What the Congress had in mind was this: ". . . at least twice every month, from four to five in the afternoon, the teachers should open the school to the mothers, inviting them to be the guests of the school; and two or three times during the season an evening meeting, which would include the fathers and school directors, should be held, where frank, friendly discussion of some practical subject would be the feature of the evening." [10] While Father, as can be seen, was to be included in the evening meetings, the whole tone of the publication was such as to suggest that the prospective organization was to be the particular domain of *Materfamilias*.

And, in truth, men had little to do with the early stages of the parent-teacher movement in America. One reason is that American culture had certain definite, time-honored ideas about "woman's place" and "man's place." Man was the provider, the disciplinarian, the economic head of the family; woman was the moral head, the homemaker, the one who looked after the children. These hoary homilies received public approval from no less an authority than Theodore Roosevelt, President of the United States, when he addressed the Congress of Mothers in 1905. With all the pressures of tradition, custom, and self-esteem working upon them in this way, American men stayed away from the early parent-teacher meetings. Decades later many of them had not yet overcome a lingering disinterest or even distrust.[11]

Furthermore, certain members of the Mothers' Congress were somewhat less than eager to have their husbands join them in their lofty enterprise. Some of them undoubtedly accepted the traditional stereotypes at their face value and thought of their organization as predestined for a purely womanly sphere. Others, however, seem to have been burning with righteous feminist resentment against the established order and visualized the Mothers' Congress as yet another arm of the unending battle against male tyranny. While the Congress was circumspect enough not to commit itself on the then hot controversy over votes for women, there was more than a hint in early speeches of a bellicose women's rightist spirit. One such speech by a Mrs. Gardener openly

---

[9] Holbeck, *Parent-Teacher Associations*, pp. 10-14; Mason, ed., *Parents and Teachers*, pp. 284-85.

[10] *How to Organize Parents' Auxiliaries* (Washington, D.C.: National Congress of Mothers, 1901), pp. 3-5.

[11] William C. Kvaraceus, "PTA," *The Nation* (October 5 1963), pp. 200-201.

declared a deep resentment of "male domination." [12] Others may have silently shared her distaste for

> . . . the man who went around with the adult "boys." He could polish up his guns and go hunting, kill for the pleasure of it. He could swagger on the street corner, if he was that kind. He could pronounce the most flagrant political platitudes and prejudices and have them accepted as truth. He could get royally drunk, and if he came home and beat up his wife—well, he was a man, and a man had his rights.[13]

Though determined to see that the American mother did not continue to be, in Mrs. Gardener's vivid language, "a half-educated subordinate to masculine domination," the Congress could not very well overlook the fact that Father was still there. Whether through default or design, he could have an enormous influence for evil as well as good in the training of Junior. As time went on, sustained efforts were made by local units to recruit fathers as members. Often the only way this could be done, given the existing feminine context, was by founding separate Fathers' Clubs to cooperate with the schools.[14] As the number of interested male parents increased, it behooved the national leadership to change the name of their organization. This was finally done in 1908, when the group adopted the more inclusive title of National Congress of Mothers and Parent-Teacher Associations.[15] More and more fathers enrolled themselves in local PTA units, until by the 1930's separate fathers and mothers clubs were mostly ancient history.[16] As membership expanded and came to include both sexes, and as the concerns of the fellowship became more diverse, another change in name became inevitable. In 1924, what Mrs. Birney and her friends had started back in the Nineties as a mothers' crusade was henceforth to be known as the National Congress of Parents and Teachers.[17]

It takes more than a name, however, to completely overturn deep-rooted cultural and psychological realities. Although the PTA officially was no longer just another species of women's club, American males did not yet play a coequal role in it. This inequality may have been due to the necessity of earning a living as well as to the inhibiting in-

---

[12] *First National Congress of Mothers*, p. 26.
[13] Overstreet and Overstreet, *When Children Come First*, p. 89.
[14] Sparks, *Strong Is the Current*, pp. 171-72.
[15] Mason, ed., *Parents and Teachers*, p. 285.
[16] Sparks, *op. cit.*, p. 172.
[17] Mason, ed., *op. cit.*, pp. 286-93.

fluence of the mores.[18] As provider of the family, Father's time was more limited than that of his wife's, who could devote free hours to the volunteer work demanded of active PTA members. Often, furthermore, meetings were scheduled for the afternoon, when Father was occupied at work.[19] When the Parent-Teacher Congress in 1939 tallied up the findings of a questionnaire to discover the characteristics of the "typical" member, it announced significantly that, "*She* is a woman in her thirties; has two or three children; lives in a middle-class home . . . is not gainfully employed, but devotes her time and talents to her family." [20]

Meanwhile, the efforts of the parent-teacher movement attracted an increasing measure of public approval. The National Congress proudly announced in 1915 that over fifteen hundred ladies were helping its Home Education Division establish Parent-Teacher Associations in the schools. In that same year, Mr. Philander Claxton, United States Commissioner of Education, pledged his department's cooperation to the cause. Mr. W. P. Evans, State Superintendent of Instruction for Missouri, mailed a copy of the National Congress's pamphlet to every school superintendent in the state, with advice to encourage the movement "in every possible way." [21]

Membership grew, with a corresponding increase in the number of local units. The rate of expansion speeded up appreciably during the booming Twenties as enrollments in junior and senior high schools began to soar with all the sudden velocity of Jack's fabled beanstalk.[22] By 1956 the national organization could boast of 40,396 local Parent-Teacher Associations, 50 state branches, and 9,409,282 individual members.[23] Because of the racial problem, it had been necessary to form a distinct National Congress of Colored Parents and Teachers to work in those states that maintained separate schools for Negro children.[24] Yet another aspect of pluralistic American society was reflected in the

[18] Lighty and Bowman, *Parenthood in a Democracy*, p. 147; Sparks, *Strong Is the Current*, p. 172.

[19] Overstreet and Overstreet, *Where Children Come First*, p. 90.

[20] *The Parent-Teacher Organization* (Chicago: National Congress of Parents and Teachers, 1944), p. 70. The italics are mine.

[21] *Yearbook: 1915* (Washington, D.C.: National Congress of Mothers and Parent-Teacher Associations, 1915), pp. 16-17.

[22] Edna H. Edmondson, *The Indiana PTA: Its Organization and Its Program of Work* (Bloomington, Ind.: University of Indiana Press, 1928), p. 5.

[23] *Parent-Teacher Manual* (Chicago: National Congress of Parents and Teachers, 1956).

[24] Marguerite S. Taylor, *Evaluation of the Program of the Colored PTA in Missouri* (Jefferson City, Mo.: Lincoln University Press, 1957), pp. 18-19.

organization of 245 Parent-Teacher Associations in Roman Catholic parochial schools, with an estimated membership of 23,725. The movement apparently had been endorsed by many bishops, diocesan school superintendents, and pastors. Such associations were proving invaluable in raising money for the purchase of phonographs, school furniture, maps, and supplementary reading texts, and in helping to support other auxiliary services.[25]

As American influence on the world stage grew more potent, it was inevitable that the PTA movement would begin to have foreign imitators. From Paraguay to Patagonia, from Belgium to Bulgaria, parents and teachers councils modeled on the American prototype made their appearance. The movement was fostered, before 1918, by an International Congress on the Welfare of the Child, which met triennially, and, after that date, by the International Bureau of Education in Geneva. Ultimately in 1927 an International Federation of Home and School was formed, with the president of America's PTA Congress serving as its first president. Following World War II, the PTA gospel was spread even farther as units were set up at American military bases in the Azores, Formosa, Morocco, Japan, Okinawa, the Philippines, and South America.[26] And, seemingly not even the "Cold War" could keep the idea from spreading to Soviet Russia, where in 1962 regular evening conferences of parents and teachers were held in Moscow public schools.

Some transplants to foreign soil simply will not take. Such was the case in England, Norway, India, South Africa, and France where friction developed as attempts were made to introduce the movement in its American guise. Such difficulties may have been due to the fact that the whole PTA concept was peculiarly and characteristically American, reflecting the outlook of a culture with considerable diversity, with local control of schools, and without an established, independently powerful educational caste.

And, we may ask, what *were* the objectives of the now rapidly expanding and extensive National Congress of Parents and Teachers of the United States? A glance at its 1926 handbook leaves the impression of a scattering of energies over a great number of areas not always directly related to its stated basic goals. Therein, the activities of the National Congress's six departments are described as follows:

[25] *Parent-Teacher Associations in Catholic Schools* (Washington, D.C.: National Catholic Welfare Conference, 1929), pp. 3-5.
[26] *Parent-Teacher Manual* (Chicago, 1956).
[27] Holbeck, *Parent-Teacher Associations*, pp. 4-6.

1. Organization: Child Welfare Day, Congress Publications, Membership.
2. Extension: Parent-Teacher Associations in Colleges, in High Schools, in Grade Schools, in Churches, Study Circles, Pre-School Circles.
3. Public Welfare: Citizenship, Juvenile Protection, Legislation, Motion Pictures, Recreation, Safety.
4. Education: Art, Humane Education, Illiteracy, Kindergarten, Extension, Music, School Education, Student Loan Fund, Scholarships.
5. Home Service: Children's Reading, Home Economics, Home Education, Spiritual Training, Standards in Literature, Social Standards, Thrift.
6. Health: Child Hygiene, Mental Hygiene, Physical Education, Social Hygiene.[28]

Besides its prescribed duties, the Congress was finding time to pass resolutions calling for many other objectives it felt worthy: enforcement of the prohibition laws; more effective child labor legislation; "clean" motion pictures; world peace; uniform marriage and divorce laws; restrictions on the sale of narcotics; limitations on the use of cigarettes by children; and bans on the distribution of "objectionable" literature.[29] Like many another national pressure group whose *raison d'être* was "do-goodism," the Parent-Teacher Congress could not resist the temptation to put its moralistic fingers into a number of controversial pies.

If the national movement betrayed some aspects of confusion of motive, the local associations displayed even more confusion.[30] Some units spent more time in staging plays or in raising money for sports equipment than in pursuing other "educational" activities relating to schools.[31]

As the crusade spread, some of the ideas which the progressive edu-

---

[28] *Handbook: 1926* (Washington, D.C.: National Congress of Parents and Teachers, 1926).

[29] Margaretta W. Reeve and Ellen Lombard, *Parent-Teacher Associations, 1924-1926* (Washington, D.C.: Government Printing Office, 1927).

[30] *Why and How of a Parents' Association* (New York: United Parents Association, 1932), pp. 10-12; Holbeck, *Parent-Teacher Associations*; Rogers, *Theory and Practice of Parents Associations*, p. 58.

[31] Reeve and Lombard, *Parent-Teacher Associations; Parents League of New York City: By-Laws, April 1915* (New York: 1915).

cators were bringing to the fore began to penetrate local PTA chapters and even national headquarters. The United Parents Association of New York City announced in 1932 that the emphasis in modern education was shifting to the personality and behavior of the "whole child," and that it behooved parents to catch up with this trend. "As parents educate themselves in child psychology," the UPA's handbook hopefully prophesied, "as they learn what the new school is trying to do, they will gradually become so aware of the effects of the educational processes of both home and school that their discussions on these matters will be helpful to school authorities." [32]

As early as 1914, there was published under the imprimatur of the National Congress a piece on "The Adolescent" by Professor Katherine Stillwell of the University of Chicago. This article enthusiastically endorsed Dewey's position.[33] Then, too, the famous Seven Cardinal Principles of the Committee on Secondary Education of 1918, reflecting a strong progressive influence, were in 1927 incorporated into the Congress's permanent platform. The national office regretted that "many parents and teachers think of education and the work of the school in terms so narrow as to restrict child growth and development." It was firmly convinced that the Seven Cardinal Principles gave "a broader basis for interpreting child growth." Besides this theoretical reasoning, however, there was a rather important practical consideration, which the Congress was quick to point out: "Increased enrollment today demands curriculums adapted also to the needs of students who will not attend college. . . . During the years since 1918 it has become increasingly apparent that these are the objectives not only of the high school, but of all education." [34]

The multi-million strong parent-teacher movement patently was an inevitable by-product of American popular education. The process, however, was not a smooth outgrowth. Even in the early days of launching the movement, a gnawing suspicion existed on the part of some superintendents of schools, members of boards of education, and teachers that the new organization proposed to meddle in their work. This antagonism was largely due to a fear that the local associations might seek to wield political power, and, as a matter of fact, a few of them did attempt to do just that.[35]

[32] *Why and How*, pp. 7-10.
[33] Mary H. Weeks, ed., *Parents and Their Problems* (Washington, D.C.: National Congress of Mothers and PTA Associations, 1914), pp. 228-32.
[34] *Educating For Seven-Point Lives* (Washington, D.C.: National Congress of Parents and Teachers, 1931).
[35] Overstreet and Overstreet, *Where Children Come First*, p. 79.

It was this potentiality of transgression which undoubtedly motivated E. H. Edmondson of the Indiana State Department of Education to write in 1920: "The Parent-Teacher Association . . . has for its field of activity the study and promotion of child welfare. Only subjects pertaining to that field can properly be considered by a Parent-Teacher Association as such." [36] Actually, some administrative officials favored PTA's only insofar as such organizations could serve as convenient vehicles for informing parents of the accomplishments and decisions of professional educators. Or as Miss Edmondson rather loftily put it in another publication: "It must be kept in mind that the function of a Parent-Teacher Association in this connection is not one of suggesting changes, but of understanding a system carefully planned by those fitted by years of experience and specialized study." [37] But some local associations were not ready to settle for a mere rubber-stamp role. After all, it was a deep-rooted American tradition that each sturdy local resident and taxpayer might be an authority on education to rival Pestalozzi or Froebel *redivivus* and had therefore the God-given, inalienable right to "sound off" and tell the world how the schools should be run. Bitterly resentful of such immoderate manifestations of the rampant democratic spirit was Miss Edith E. Hoyt, an official in the Wisconsin State Department of Education, who complained in 1918 that: "There have been instances . . . where the Parent-Teacher Association has meddled inexcusably with the academic work of the school; where it has discussed the dismissal or retention of teachers; or where it has used political methods to determine the personnel of the school board." This, Miss Hoyt noted caustically, "is plainly an unwarranted and improper use to make of the organization." And there were yet other abuses noted by this embattled critic. In some instances, she charged, the Parent-Teacher Association had become "an exclusive club, dominated by the socially elect, and used to further the social ambitions of a few leaders." Her conclusion was that, "The Parent-Teacher Association is not in any sense an organization whose function it is to sit in judgment upon the academic work of the school, or to interfere in its methods of instruction or administration." [38]

Although the leadership of the National Congress countenanced no

---

[36] Edna H. Edmondson, *Parent-Teacher Associations* (Bloomington, Ind.: University of Indiana Press, 1928), p. 31.

[37] *Ibid.*

[38] Edith E. Hoyt, *Parent-Teacher Associations* (Madison, Wis.: University of Wisconsin Press, 1918), pp. 4-5.

such meddling in local school concerns or political situations by affiliates, it did come to feel, as we have seen, that support for legislation affecting child welfare, if done on a purely nonpartisan basis, was justified.[39] Therefore, in 1922 when a Kentucky PTA chapter went on record as favoring a bill then being debated in Congress to regulate child labor, and in 1946 when the PTA Congress in Oregon teamed up with the State Association of School Boards to support a bill for increased school support, it was with the entire approval of national headquarters.[40]

Some local associations, however, insisted on a more active part.[41] In Chicago, at the time of the highly publicized ouster in 1927 of Superintendent of Schools William McAndrew by Mayor "Big Bill" Thompson, the local parents organization signally failed in an overt attempt to make its influence felt.[42] On the other hand, in New York City in 1915, ingenious politicians from Tammany Hall managed to mobilize the entire force of parents to help undermine the John Purroy Mitchel administration on the ground that it had committed the heinous crime of importing the allegedly aristocratic "Gary Plan" into the city's schools.[43]

Unfortunately Parent-Teacher Associations were likely to be criticized for doing too much and just as likely to be castigated for doing too little. To Marxist-minded Rex David, Parent-Teacher Associations were still in 1934 "mainly social clubs." They were "not concerned with the pressing problems of the school." They did not "organize struggles against overcrowding, starvation, unsanitary conditions, fire hazards, and closing schools." [44] By contrast, Victor Bahou of Cortland (New York) State Teachers College in 1959 berated PTA's for being used by a "power elite" to interfere arrogantly "with decisions which should be the exclusive prerogative of those professionally prepared both to formulate

---

[39] *Parent-Teacher Manual*, pp. 66-68, 78-79.

[40] *Yearbook: 1923-1924* (Kentucky Branch of the National Congress of Parents and Teachers), p. 37; Overstreet and Overstreet, *Where Children Come First*, p. 117; Rogers, *Theory and Practice of Parents Associations*, p. 65.

[41] Reeve and Lombard, *Parent-Teacher Associations*; Lighty and Bowman, *Parenthood in a Democracy*, pp. 146-48.

[42] Rogers, *op. cit.*, p. 17.

[43] *17th Annual Report, 1937-1938* (New York: United Parents Association, 1938); Angelo Patri, *A Schoolmaster of the Great City* (New York: The Macmillan Company, 1917), pp. 84-115; Lighty and Bowman, *Parenthood in a Democracy*, pp. 30-33; Rogers, *op. cit.*, pp. 25-28.

[44] Rex David, *Schools and the Crisis* (New York: International Publishers Co., Inc., 1934), p. 41.

and execute school policies and procedures." [45] A similar point of view was expressed as recently as 1962 by Charles Cogen, President of the New York City local of the American Federation of Teachers, who warned Parent-Teacher Associations not to "meddle so much" in education. While such groups "certainly have the right to consult with us," he said, "they should remember we're the experts."

Viewing the PTA movement in perspective, we see it as a characteristic, perhaps unique, manifestation of the American democratic culture as it expressed itself in a highly diversified, popularly controlled school structure. Louis Kaplan reported in 1959 that parent committees had contributed to the endeavors of the schools by developing instructional guides in various subjects, devising reporting systems, helping to plan courses for superior students, and even by publishing pamphlets on modern school procedures.[46] Perhaps, however, in the last analysis, both educators and parents were responsible for keeping the PTA's from realizing their full potential. Again, quoting Kaplan on this point:

> In many instances, school officials skillfully confine the PTA to innocuous programs concerned primarily with money-raising activities. Or, these organizations become so busy with their own structure, or with state and national programs, that they have little opportunity to discuss the problems of their own schools.
>
> Educators may hesitate to take too dominant a role in the PTA, thinking this to be an organization of parents which should be run by parents. Lacking close cooperation with educators, parents, because of their friendliness toward teachers, may avoid the discussion of critical issues which might imply dissatisfaction with the school program. They confine themselves instead to nonsensitive activities which do not tap the great potential of their organization for service to schools.[47]

Sustained by universal acceptance as an established feature of the educational scene, should this potent mechanism of the parent-teacher idea have been used more forcefully to bring about elevation of the academic standards of schools? It seems to the present observer that more, much more, could have been done in this sphere. One thing is certain. Achievement of this sort would be forthcoming only when PTA members themselves urgently strove to bring it about.

[45] Victor Bahou, "PTA Reconsidered," *School and Society* (November 7, 1959), p. 447.

[46] Louis Kaplan, *Mental Health and Human Relations in Education* (New York: Harper & Row, Publishers, 1959), p. 424.

[47] *Ibid.*

Foundations and Their Influence

In 1960 a reporter for *Newsweek* magazine asked F. Emerson Andrews, editor of the *Directory of Philanthropic Foundations*, "Why are so many big foundations flourishing in the United States today?" The editor's prompt reply minced no words. "Great wealth and smart tax lawyers," he snapped.[48] A review of the history of American philanthropic foundations, from their earliest days to the beginning of the twentieth-century's seventh decade, clearly demonstrates the truth of the above pithy characterization. And it discloses something else, besides. It shows how deeply involved these foundations have been in educational enterprises of various kinds. Here, then, is a force with portentous possibilities to sway the nation's schools. What has been done with this enormous power?

In 1900 there were only two foundations in the United States with interests in educational work, and their available funds amounted to less than five million dollars. By 1960 the total assets of America's more than 5,000 foundations were in excess of eleven *billion* dollars, and these institutions were growing at the rate of 100 a month! Much of this expansion was recent, 87 per cent of the foundations having been established after 1940. The top five leaders in terms of assets in 1960 were (in order of rank), the Ford Foundation, the Rockefeller Foundation, the Duke Endowment, the John A. Hartford Foundation, and the Carnegie Corporation of New York. Education received a liberal share from these fabulous dispensers of largess. A survey of the 154 largest foundations in the United States showed that 54 per cent of their grants went to divers educational causes, which amounted to $212,000,000 for the year 1960 alone. Trailing far behind was "scientific research," with 20 per cent of all grants, and "health and welfare," with 17 per cent.

Foundations, however, had placed their principal emphasis upon educational benefactions long before 1960. Writing in 1952, Abraham Flexner, long associated with foundation work, noted that "education is by all odds the field to which foundations have up to the present time given most of their energy, thought, and money, and in which, whatever may have been their errors, they have been most effective." [49] The first philanthropic foundation of national significance in United

---

[48] "Who's in the Money," *Newsweek* (July 25, 1960), p. 106.
[49] Abraham Flexner, *Funds and Foundations* (New York: Harper & Row, Publishers, 1952), p. 125.

States history was specifically charged with the task of improving education in the southern states. This was the Peabody Education Fund, generously established in 1867 by a wealthy merchant and banker from Baltimore, who was then living in London. In 1882, another ample endowment, also devoted to education, was donated by John F. Slater, a wealthy New England textile manufacturer. By terms of the trust, the Fund was designed "for the uplifting of the lately emancipated people of the southern states and their posterity, by conferring on them the blessings of Christian education." [50]

Educational interests were similarly prominent in the foundations formed in the early twentieth century. American philanthropy received an important impetus from John D. Rockefeller, Sr., the most fabulous of all foundation patrons. Working closely with his trusted adviser on philanthropies, former Baptist preacher Frederick Taylor Gates, the "Augustus" of the oil industry began in 1902 a series of lavish donations to the General Education Board, which was thereby enabled to accomplish significant work in rural and secondary education in the South, as well as in a host of other fields.[51] Then, in March 1906, Congress approved an act incorporating the Carnegie Foundation for the Advancement of Teaching. Although the primary purpose of steelmaster Carnegie's ten-million dollar endowment was to provide retirement allowances for college professors, it soon became necessary, in order to carry out this program, to establish national norms for secondary education. Other Carnegie grants soon redounded to the benefit of American education. The Carnegie Corporation, created in 1911, made many awards to educational and scholarly institutions. Nor should we overlook the Russell Sage Foundation, founded in New York in 1907; the Anna T. Jeanes Foundation, established in 1908 by a Philadephia Quakeress interested in the welfare of rural Negroes; the Phelps-Stokes Fund, incorporated in 1911 under provisions stated in the will of Miss Caroline Phelps-Stokes of New York; the Julius Rosenwald Fund, set up in 1913 by a mail-order Midas; and the Commonwealth Fund, established in 1918 by Mrs. Stephen V. Harkness, of the Standard Oil Company Harknesses. All of these organizations were active in educational enterprises of one sort or another.[52]

[50] Leonard P. Ayres, *Seven Great Foundations* (New York: Leonard P. Ayres, 1911), p. 12; Arnaud C. Marts, *Philanthropy's Role in Civilization* (New York: Harper & Row, Publishers, 1953), p. 144.

[51] Ayres, *op. cit.*, pp. 41-49; Flexner, *op. cit.*, pp. 24-47.

[52] Ayres, *op. cit.*, pp. 53-77; Flexner, *op. cit.*, pp. 120-22; Frederick P. Keppel, *The Foundation, Its Place in American Life* (New York: The Macmillan Company, 1930), pp. 77-79.

In more recent times, the most gigantic establishment in the philanthropic field, and the one of greatest significance for the development of American education, has been the Ford Foundation. Possessing assets estimated to be from half a billion to a billion dollars, the Ford Foundation busied itself with a number of areas vital to modern civilization.[53] As a vehicle for bringing about improvements in the elementary and secondary schools of the nation, it sponsored in April, 1951, the establishment of a new organization, The Fund for the Advancement of Education. During the Fifties, this small, specialized Fund became involved in a number of highly publicized experiments designed to steer America's schools into new and more fruitful channels. Its announced concept was that grants should be confined to "short-term, pilot-plant efforts." Visualizing its resources mainly as "risk capital," it underwrote during the next ten years some 500 more or less experimental projects, with grants totaling some fifty million dollars.[54]

Most of the attention of the Fund was devoted to ways and means of improving standards of teaching. A number of grants were given to explore various "fifth-year programs" in which bright college graduates who had not majored in Education would have a chance to receive postgraduate teacher training. The most ambitious project of this type was introduced in Arkansas, which, coincidentally, aimed to strengthen the liberal-arts and general-education courses in four-year teachers colleges. Furthermore, in order to find better ways of teacher utilization, the Fund hopefully supported ventures employing teacher aides (as at Bay City, Michigan), team teaching (as at Lexington, Massachusetts), and television instruction (as at Hagerstown, Maryland). Another of its major concerns was to discover some workable plan which would make possible better identification of and more challenging instruction for the exceptionally capable student. It was also interested in bridging more intelligently the troublesome gap between school and college by sponsoring an Advanced Placement program and an Early Admission to College plan. Finally the Fund worked hard to overcome three stubborn barriers to equal educational opportunity: poverty, geography, and ethnic origin. One result of its constant search for improved techniques of recruiting potential college students was the drafting of a blueprint for what eventually became the National Merit Scholarship program.[55]

[53] Marts, *Philanthropy's Role in Civilization*, p. 145.
[54] *A Decade of Experiment* (New York: The Fund for the Advancement of Education, 1961), pp. 14-17.
[55] *Ibid.*

The Fund for the Advancement of Education, like the Carnegie Corporation and the Rockefeller Foundation, was a serious-minded, reputable philanthropic organization. Unforutnately, not all private foundations established during this era were. Sinclair Lewis' fictional foundation executive, Dr. Gideon Planish, was given surprisingly true-to-life "inside information" about the situation by an associate:

> Old Man Heskett was no philanthrobber, and neither were quite a few of the other moguls that set up Foundations. Here's their idea: With the increase in taxes, especially this damn income tax and surtax, a man can't afford to have too much income. And yet he wants to keep control of the big corporations in which he owns a majority of stock. So he places a big block of it in a Philanthropic Institution, in a trust fund—he doesn't get the interest, but he doesn't have to pay any pyramiding taxes, and he or his agents—that's me, for the Hesketts—hold the voting proxies on the donated stock, and control the corporation as much as before.[56]

That these were not merely vain imaginings was made clear by the Ways and Means Committee of the U.S. House of Representatives in a report in 1950 which indicated that foundations were being used in some instances purely as a screen for tax avoidance.[57]

A dramatic case in point may have been the intricate system of trusts organized by Royal S. Little for the benefit of his Textron, Inc., holdings. The primary purpose of these "philanthropic" operations, the committee alleged, was to build up tax-free funds as venture capital to aid in the expansion of Textron, Inc. Treasury agents, moreover, discovered that some individuals who had established personal foundations were paying themselves salaries as officers of these very same foundations. Others had arranged for their foundations to loan them money without interest charges from the capital funds with which these institutions had been entrusted. Still others had utilized foundations to avoid paying stiff estate taxes. The result of these revelations was furious public indignation, which, in turn, led Congress to pass a number of amendments to the Revenue Act of 1950 to plug existing loopholes. As late as 1962, however, a subcommittee of the House Small Business Committee found that the less reputable foundations were still up to their old tricks. A survey of 522 of the nation's tax-exempt foundations disclosed that of

[56] Sinclair Lewis, *Gideon Planish* (New York: Random House, Inc., 1943), pp. 223-24.
[57] Ernest Kurnow, *The Modern Foundation* (New York: New York University Press, 1953), pp. 6-7.

their total seven-billion dollar income over ten years, one and a half billion dollars came from stock sales. The subcommittee charged that these transactions included attempts to dodge capital-gains tax and involvement in proxy fights for control of profit-making corporations. Representative Wright Patman characterized the development of tax-exempt foundations as "far more dangerous than anything that has happened in the past in the way of concentration of economic power." [58]

Discussion of tax abuses in connection with philanthropic foundations deepened the suspicions already held by some sections of the public. Strangely enough, the foundations had found themselves under attack in earlier years for being too "conservative," while during the 1950's they were lambasted for being too "liberal"! In 1915 a dramatic investigation of foundations was made by a special committee of the United States Senate, headed by Senator Frank P. Walsh. This investigation came not long after the so-called "Ludlow massacre," which had occurred during a strike at the Colorado Fuel and Iron Company, a Rockefeller corporation. Militant Senatorial progressives charged that the Rockefeller Foundation was planning a study which would white-wash the "crimes" committed by the industrial corporation. It was further angrily asserted that the foundations were dominated by "big business," and that they were using their power and influence to defend inequities in the *status quo* and, incidentally, to mold education in a conservative direction. The majority of the committee agreeing with this point of view recommended rigid federal controls as a corrective. No congressional action was forthcoming, however.[59]

The foundations were not put on the witness stand by Congress again until 1952, but this time the attack came not from the Left, but from the Right. Harried by fears of Communist subversion in the hobgoblinish atmosphere of the Cold War, some Americans after 1945 began to suspect that their educational system was riddled with economic heresy, disloyalty, and faulty (i.e., Marxist) interpretations of the social sciences. Seeking an explanation for such a parlous state of

[58] *Ibid.*; Marts, *Philanthropy's Role in Civilization*, pp. 146-47; Rene A. Wormser, *Foundations, Their Power and Influence* (New York: The Devin-Adair Company, Publishers, 1958).

[59] Joseph Kiger, *Operating Principles of the Larger Foundations* (New York: Russell Sage Foundation, 1954), pp. 85-91; Horace Coon, *Money to Burn* (New York: David McKay Co., Inc., 1938), pp. 306-10; F. Emerson Andrews, *Philanthropic Foundations* (New York: Russell Sage Foundation, 1956); *Industrial Relations* (Final Report and Testimony Submitted to Congress by the Commission on Industrial Relations, 64th Congress, 1st Session, Senate Document No. 415 [Washington, D.C., 1916]).

affairs, they fixed their gaze upon the foundations, among other things. In his column in the New York *Daily News*, the Right-Wing journalist, John O'Donnell, sounded the alarm by proclaiming his discovery of "the incredible fact" that "the huge fortunes piled up by such industrial giants as John D. Rockefeller, Andrew Carnegie, and Henry Ford were today being used to destroy or discredit the free-enterprise system which gave them birth." [60] Reflecting this prevailing mood of anxiety, a Select Committee was created by the House of Representatives, on the motion of Eugene E. Cox of Georgia, on April 4, 1952. It was directed to investigate fully the activities of educational and philanthropic foundations to determine whether such organizations were "using their resources for un-American and subversive activities or for purposes not in the interest or tradition of the United States." [61] After 18 full days of public hearings and much effort spent in compiling the results of an exhaustive questionnaire, the committee voted unanimously to give the foundations a clean bill of health. "The committee believes," said its final report, "that on balance the record of the foundations is good." [62]

Not entirely satisfied with these findings, although he had signed the report (with reservations), Representative Brazilla Carroll Reece of Tennessee sponsored another House investigation in May and June, 1954. After 16 acridly controversial sessions, three of the five members of the committee issued a majority report sharply criticizing the foundations, and alleging what amounted to a diabolical socialist conspiracy on the part of these organizations to undermine the American system of government and society. Notwithstanding this strong language, the committee presented no firm and final specifications for legislation to remedy the situation. The other two members continued to dissent sharply from the majority conclusions. [63] Although no further action was taken, the majority of the Reece Committee, like the majority of the Senate Industrial Committee of 1915, remained convinced that foundations were dominating American education and influencing it in the wrong way: "It [the foundation] can exert immense influence on educa-

[60] Wormser, *Foundations*, p. vii.

[61] *Final Report of the Select Committee to Investigate Foundations and Other Organizations* (U.S. House of Representatives, 82nd Congress, 2nd Session, House Report 2514 [Washington, D.C., 1953]), p. 2.

[62] *Ibid.*, p. 8.

[63] *Report of the Special Committee to Investigate Tax-Exempt Foundations* (83rd Congress, 2nd Session, U.S. House of Representatives Report No. 2681 [Washington, D.C., 1954]).

tional institutions, upon the educational processes, and upon educators. It is capable of invisible coercion through the power of its purse." Thus the reasoning and the motivations—in 1915 and 1954—may have been different, but the conclusions came out the same.[64]

Controversial the foundations clearly were, but were they really as influential as their critics maintained? More particularly, was American education in essence mere putty in their hands, to be shaped at will? Rene Wormser, who had been employed by the Reece Committee as a research consultant, flatly asserted that "foundations have become the directors of education in the United States." He solemnly declared that the foundations had used Teachers College, Columbia, and the National Education Association to fasten John Dewey's "radical" philosophy on the schools and, that they were subsidizing the "crypto-Socialist" textbooks of dangerous pedagogues like Harold Rugg.[65] From a totally different ideological viewpoint, Horace Coon found that the foundations had secured control of the schools and were holding a club over educational and other social science researchers. "Nearly everybody who might criticise foundations or their policies," he said, "has received favors from them. The human nature that seeks foundation help, the reasons why that help is sought, the state of sycophancy, politics, wire-pulling, pan-handling which is indulged in to get foundation support might be worth consideration." [66]

Other observers have not been so sure in all respects of the decisive influence of the foundations. I. L. Kandel wondered whether the mere existence of philanthropic foundations did not actually inhibit efforts to solve pressing educational problems. American schoolmen seemed to feel that no issue could be dealt with without first asking a foundation for financial assistance. "One can only ask," Kandel pondered, "whether all thinking and investigating would stop if foundations ceased to exist." [67]

Abraham Flexner presented interesting evidence, based upon his own experiences in foundation work, suggesting that many foundations had frittered away potential influence for good by unwise administrative

---

[64] It would seem to be inevitable that the officers of foundations would strive to advance, through their allocations of funds, the particular educational philosophies which they happened to favor.

[65] Wormser, *Foundations*, pp. 139-60.

[66] Coon, *Money to Burn*, pp. 336-37.

[67] I. L. Kandel, "Educational Foundations and Progress," *School and Society*, 76 (July 26, 1952), p. 59.

practices and by scattered efforts. Too many small, ineffectual grants were being made to too many small projects. Flexner cited as one example a 1952 grant of ten thousand dollars by the General Education Board to the Progressive Education Association, which later became the American Education Fellowship. A letter of inquiry to the latter organization was returned by the Post Office as "unknown." Flexner asked: "Who actually got the money, what was done with it, and what happened when the two-year grants expired?" This kind of thing, he remarked tartly, was going on all over the country, resulting in the wasting of millions of dollars. "It is impossible," he maintained, "for any man or any group of men to administer intelligently funds so freely distributed to agencies, the competency of which no man or group of men could possibly judge." [68] Furthermore, he complained, most grants were slighting the humanities in favor of the social and physical sciences. Literature, history, languages, and the fine arts were fighting a losing battle in the United States. Why, Flexner inquired, had no foundation "interested itself in this—one might fairly say—most crying need of modern America"? [69]

Frederick Keppel, who for many years headed the Carnegie Foundation, recalled how perplexing was the task of finding individuals and projects worthy of being given support. The larger foundations, he observed, were faced with more than 1000 applications a year for diverse projects. With limited resources at hand, which of these were to be selected for foundation backing? [70] It was perfectly evident, Keppel concluded, that the bulk of foundation decisions "have been made from the heart rather than the head." [71]

Not only were foundations berated for not exerting intelligently the full influence of which they were capable; some critics charged further that the easy giving pattern set up by these organizations was simply reinforcing mediocrity rather than fostering creativity or the exploration of new frontiers. Kenneth J. Brown, Director of the Danforth Foundation, stated in 1958 that very often "it is we, not the institutions, who are without imagination, with eyes glued on education's yesterday, scarcely mindful of education's today, and totally indifferent to education's tomorrow." He expressed the hope that "sanctification of the

---

[68] Flexner, *Funds and Foundations*, pp. 86-89.
[69] *Ibid.*, p. 130.
[70] Frederick P. Keppel, *American Philanthropy and the Advancement of Learning* (Providence, R.I.: Brown University Press, 1934), pp. 9-10.
[71] Keppel, *The Foundation*, p. 39.

established may never become a major end of foundation benefits." [72] Somewhat blunting the force of this indictment, Frederick Keppel reminded us of the examples of "real courage" on the part of the foundations, such as the decision by the Rockefeller Foundation to work with the League of Nations (at a time when American public opinion was wary of League entanglements), and the revolutionary report by the Carnegie Foundation on the subject of medical education.[73] Earlier we noted that The Fund for the Advancement of Education had publicly announced its main purpose to be one of supporting new and untried programs. Theoretically, then, the foundations were on the right track. Furthermore, Robert M. Hutchins, one of the Associate Directors of the aforementioned Fund's parent organization, the Ford Foundation, went on record as stating that the proper function of private organizations of this type was to take calculated risks in controversial areas such as education, the social sciences, and human relations—areas where public agencies and other institutions dared not go.[74] In actual operations, however, how many foundations in twentieth-century America followed the venturesome path recommended by Dr. Hutchins?

Admittedly any effort to measure precisely the influence of a particular group of organizations or institutions in a given society is perilous. Nevertheless the evidence seems convincing that the foundations have played a significant role in modern American education. Even if we accept the rather critical estimates of Kandel, Flexner, and Brown as nearest to the truth, the impact of such institutions, if only in a negative and constrictive sense, has been considerable. On the other hand, the assertions of extremists like Wormser and Coon, with respect to the total dictatorship over the educational world enforced by these organizations, seem, in historical perspective, to be badly overdrawn. Severe critic that he was, Flexner had only praise for the fact that the Rockefeller and Carnegie Foundations alone had up to 1951 distributed grants totaling more than a billion dollars. This meant, he noted, that "Carnegie and Rockefeller appropriations have led to the increase of the educational resources of the country by two or three billions." [75] Furthermore, philanthropy of this type had brought about *some* obvious improvements.[76] Secondary education in the southern states had profited greatly

[72] Kenneth J. Brown, "The American Foundation: Conservor or Pacemaker?" *Saturday Review of Literature*, 41 (September 13, 1958), p. 24.

[73] Keppel, *The Foundation*, pp. 42-43.

[74] Kiger, *Operating Principles of the Larger Foundations*, pp. 52-53.

[75] Flexner, *Funds and Foundations*, p. 126.

[76] Keppel, *The Foundation*, pp. 112-13.

from the appropriations of the General Education Board. Techniques of basic research in various fields of educational theory and practice had been significantly advanced.[77]

We must not overlook at the same time the limitations which in mid-twentieth-century America barred the way to the unchallenged dominion of the foundations. Under the National Defense Education Act of 1958, a National Science Foundation (purely a governmental agency) had been set up with extensive involvement in science education. Under the Act, funds were provided for science, mathematics, and foreign language instruction in the elementary and secondary schools. The NSA's total budget for 1963 was $257,000,000. By contrast, the total of major foundation grants in 1960 for the same purposes was $79,000,000. Thus the federal government was increasingly displacing the private foundation as a source of financing for educational and research activities as the nation entered the Space Age. Then, too, by the very nature of the case—the complexity and diversity of the American educational system and the size of the country—there was just so much that a foundation, no matter how well endowed, could hope to accomplish. As The Fund for the Advancement of Education soon discovered, a private endowment could not "expect either to create or to halt large trends in education." It could, however, "study the power structure of the educational system, gauge the temper of the times, appraise the array of forces for and against any particular change, and then throw its weight at the right moment behind the most promising trends in the hope of converting them into dominant ones." [78] In other words, it could select, with shrewdness and foresight, "areas of contingency" and then make, through skillful timing, relatively small efforts count for large effects. And this is exactly what was done when the Carnegie Unit for college admissions was established, Advancement Placement was pioneered, liberal-arts–oriented fifth-year programs in teacher training were set up, and the National Merit Scholarship Corporation was formed.

Such accomplishments were of no mean significance. Against the rigidities of monolithic government and the vagaries and conformities of irrational or badly informed local groups, independent educational foundations would seem to have performed a valuable role in American society. Their purpose remained one of elevating taste, defending intellectual freedom without fear or favor, and prodding the schools to

[77] *Ibid.*, pp. 80-81; Keppel, *American Philanthropy*, pp. 18-20.
[78] *A Decade of Experiment*, p. 16.

seek quality at the expense of popularity. In that sense, at least, the statement of the Select House Committee of 1952 seems justifiable. The committee said then that "the present need for foundations is even greater than it has been in the past and that there is great likelihood that the need will prove an increasing one in the future." [79] If, however, through intimidation or willful choice, philanthropy's role shrank to that of justifying the obvious, of pandering to harmful pressures, or of courting popularity by avoiding attempts at educational improvement which ran counter to prejudice, then that need would unquestionably be at an end.

The Role of the Professional Administrator

American life in the twentieth century has been characterized by an ever-increasing complexity in administrative structure. This phenomenom has been as true in the realm of government and the professions as it has been in transportation, industry, and finance. In the years following World War I, the cult of "scientific" management spread rapidly across the land, largely as a consequence of the potent influence of industrial engineer Frederick Winslow Taylor and his "rationalizing" movement. In universities, schools of business administration, and public administration institutes, the new gospel was given powerful support. "Administration" as an applied science had arrived. In the field of education, the new era was distinguished by the emergence of a distinct class of professional intermediaries between school boards and the teaching force.[80]

Although the superintendency of schools was present in America as early as the second quarter of the nineteenth century, the office acquired real power only in later decades and, more particularly, in the years after 1900. Indeed, as late as 1906, a writer of a textbook on school administration noted that "American conditions do not seem to favor an easy, simple, and effective administration of schools." As one of the reasons for this unsatisfactory state of affairs, he mentioned the traditional localism of the American people and their aversion to centralization of any kind. Other difficulties, in his opinion, were the predominance of political considerations in the election of school officials, the

[79] *Select Committee to Investigate Foundations,* p. 4.

[80] Roald F. Campbell and Russell T. Gregg, eds., *Administrative Behavior in Education* (New York: Harper & Row, Publishers, 1957), pp. 84-98.

vast size of the country, and, in some sections, the sparse population.[81] Whatever the reasons, the early superintendents of schools appear to have been little more than clerks for their boards of education, while principals had even less power or prestige. Their time was consumed mainly by routine mechanical problems of school organization and management; they had little to say about program or policy.[82] At best, as one of their number recalled, they were regarded as business managers. Just as school teaching itself was then looked down upon by many as merely a temporary activity requiring no special preparation, so the school superintendent was thought of as a plodding man whose task it was "to attend to the details of the work, to keep the educational machine properly oiled, his selection seldom being dictated by any particular qualification of a professional character."[83] When young Ellwood P. Cubberley came to San Diego in 1896 to become Superintendent of Schools, he discovered that the local Board of Education minutely controlled almost every phase of school policy. The board members busied themselves with such questions as repairing broken windows, ordering plants out of classrooms, purchasing flags, demanding flag salutes, forbidding teachers to use a textbook in conducting recitations, and the like. The superintendent was looked upon as a glorified errand boy for the Board's committees.[84]

Changes in the public's attitude toward educational administrators came very slowly, even in the largest cities. Politicians were even slower to alter their outlook. In 1915 Charles H. Judd, Director of the School of Education at the University of Chicago, pointed out that in many cities the boards of education did not yet have regulations to which the superintendent could appeal or even a legal definition of his functions. Judd asserted that personal influence was "the strongest instrument which the superintendent has at his disposal." Furthermore, the Director continued, "when matters are conducted on the purely personal basis, there is likely to be an exercise of personal influence on the part of board members." There were "chairmen of committees on teachers

[81] John T. Prince, *School Administration* (Syracuse, N.Y.: Bardeen School Supplies, 1906), p. v.

[82] Lotus D. Coffman, "The Control of Educational Progress through School Supervision," *NEA Proceedings* (1917), pp. 187-88; B. J. Chandler and Paul V. Petty, *Personnel Management in School Administration* (New York: Harcourt, Brace & World, Inc., 1955), pp. 41-42.

[83] A. J. Ladd, *On the Firing Line in Education* (Boston: Richard G. Badger, 1919), p. 195.

[84] Jessie B. Sears and Adin D. Henderson, *Cubberley of Stanford* (Stanford: Calif.: Stanford University Press, 1957).

whose consent must be secured before it is possible to make in school programs changes that seem to school executives to be of obvious importance." Sometimes, he added, "an unprincipled seeker of influence has secured a place on the Board of Education because he wants to supervise the purchase of janitorial supplies." Such a man would be perfectly capable of preventing action on a new course of study "until an order for mops was properly placed." Judd seriously doubted, in view of these discouraging realities, that a high-minded professional control of the schools would develop automatically in the future simply through hoped for "growth of intelligence." [85]

Following World War I, claims were more frequently made that education was becoming a specialized profession, and that it was acquiring many of the attributes of a "science." It was then that the "chore boy" concept of the school administrator was drastically modified.[86] The cumulative effects of social and economic change began to tell. Accelerating urbanization and industrialization made the country one big market, and ways of life became increasingly standardized. Rapid means of transportation and communication broke down the local barriers against change. In this setting, the educational administrator came into his own.

As state governments became more active in determining minimal educational standards, their school commissioners began to exercise more policy-making power. Concomitantly many states began to require that the holder of this office possess some expert professional qualifications. By 1940 32 states had made some legal ruling to this effect. By this time, too, the chief school official was chairman of the Board of Education in 11 states, its secretary in 18 others, and an *ex officio* member of the Board in 25. Meanwhile the professional staffs within state Departments of Education were increasing. By 1950 there were 3,548 full-time professional staff members employed in such departments across the country. Nine states were recorded as having educational staffs of 100 or more (California, Georgia, Louisiana, Massachusetts, Michigan, New York, North Carolina, Tennessee, Virginia). Moreover, as state compulsory school attendance laws were extended and strengthened, additional personnel had to be appointed to deal with truancy problems, child labor, and related matters. It was also necessary to establish new

[85] Charles H. Judd, "The Protection of Professional Interests," *NEA Journal* (1915), p. 268.
[86] Chandler and Petty, *Personnel Management in School Administration*, pp. 3, 27, 40-41.

state agencies to deal with the education of the handicapped, the mentally retarded, and the incorrigible.

The complexities of school administration were also increasing on governmental levels other than that of the state. The United States Bureau (later Office) of Education, during the first half of the twentieth century, enlarged its professional staff, expanded the variety and scope of its activities, and extended its influence (which remained, however, mostly indirect) to state and local school systems. In rural areas, school officials known as county superintendents came to acquire heightened professional status. By 1930 a number of states were requiring educational qualifications for holders of this post and were giving these officials power over school budgets, apportionment of funds, and enforcement of school attendance legislation. It was, however, in the booming city school systems that professionalism attained its widest scope. By 1932, according to a study made for the National Education Association, most city superintendents of schools had won a dominant position for themselves as the initiators and executors of educational policy. More than 95 per cent of them were taking the initiative in the selection of teaching personnel. Urban boards of education, on the other hand, were now concentrating upon basic policy questions involving buildings and finances and other matters outside the realm of internal administration.[87] By this time, states one student of American public administration, the urban school administrator was achieving a "career pattern," which was "akin to that of the modern city manager." He was the recognized educational leader of the area, the spokesman for the schools, the expert trusted by the Board. His position was an important one in the structure of American public administration, one which had "mobility, influence, and potential permanence." [88]

Professionalism in educational administration was advanced, too, by the development of the field as a subject studied systematically in colleges and universities. Previously the only preparation for the job was the training received in the school through "Experience, the universal Mother of Sciences." By 1900, however, learning by doing in this vital area began to be supplemented by courses in educational administration at the larger American universities. By 1910 courses in school finance,

[87] The foregoing material is drawn from a memorandum prepared by the author for the National Citizens Committee for the Public Schools. See Willis Rudy, "Administration of Schools, 1890-1950" (typescript) (National Citizens Committee for the Public Schools, September 5, 1952).

[88] Thomas H. Eliot, *Governing America* (State and Local Supplement) (New York: Dodd, Mead & Co., 1961), p. 159.

school law, research in school administration, and school housing were being made available to the aspiring superintendent. By the 1920's, many other specialized courses had been added to the curriculum. Doctorates of Education were now awarded in the educational administration field.[89] Paralleling the differentiation and diversification of course offerings was an equally rapid growth of professional literature. In 1875 the first American publication on educational administration broke into print, a little 207 page treatise entitled *School Supervision*. By 1930 hundreds of works on various aspects of the subject were available.[90]

The appearance of enterprising professional groupings in a special field usually indicates that the undertaking is in the process of developing an *esprit de corps* and a set of qualitative standards. This was certainly true in the case of the educational administrators. By the turn of the century, the Department of Superintendence of the National Education Association was established on firm ground, as were separate departments for Secondary School Principals and Elementary School Principals. Then, in 1937, these subdivisions were reorganized to form the influential American Association of School Administrators. Other harbingers of higher status now began to appear. Requests were made by a number of large school systems for detailed "scientific" study of their administrative procedures by outside experts. Thus began an era of exhaustive school surveys, with noted specialists on administration like Hanus, Judd, and Strayer leading the way.[91]

While the professional administrators were busy entrenching themselves as a respected and formidable body of educational leaders, they began to receive criticism for authoritarianism and arbitrariness. Bristling with resentment, Miss Sallie Hill, President of the League of Teachers' Associations of Denver, Colorado, told the NEA convention of 1919, "There is no democracy in our school systems today. Democracy cannot exist with the present system, which gives so much power to those who supervise." She felt that there were too many supervisors lacking in training, personality, and teaching experience. They demanded too much of the teacher. "In fact," she lamented, "our system is tottering because of too many of everything. Too many supervisors with big salaries and undue rating power." Apparently Miss Hill was not alone in her plaint.

[89] Jesse H. Newlon, *Educational Administration As Social Policy* (New York: Charles Scribner's Sons, 1934), pp. 84-87.
[90] Ellwood P. Cubberley, "Public School Administration," in I. L. Kandel, ed., *Twenty-five Years of American Education* (New York: The Macmillan Company, 1924), pp. 180-87.
[91] Judd, "Protection of Professional Interests," pp. 270-72.

Other commentators questioned American educational administration. Professor George Counts charged it with being "undemocratic and tend[ing] to dwarf the personality of the teacher." [92]

In defense of the administrative guild, Lotus Coffman, then Dean of the School of Education at the University of Minnesota, pointed out tartly that "neither stupidity nor talent belongs to any particular class or group." What American schools needed was not less but more supervision. Pity the poor administrator. He has to work under conditions where "nearly everyone feels that he is competent to pass an expert opinion upon any phase of school work." He has to reckon with "the almost universal faith that the ordinary citizen has the ability to pass judgment upon the schools." [93]

The attitude of the modern school administrator was also condemned for being too slavishly modeled on that of efficiency-seeking business organizations. Indeed, one writer charged in a national magazine that pressures upon the school superintendent in the area of externals had grown so great that the latter was obliged to give the major share of his time and attention to business matters rather than to intellectual concerns.[94] Dr. Finis Engleman, Executive Secretary of the American Association of School Administrators, agreed with this indictment when he stated, "The superintendent must be given more time for study and contemplation if he is to fulfill his primary purpose, which is to be an educator and a cultural leader, not a jolly good fellow."

Every culture not unnaturally looks for a reflection of its own image in the leadership which represents it. Many twentieth-century Americans in their increasingly business-dominated and technological-minded civilization visualized educational administrators as practical-minded men in gray flannel suits with a sharp eye for the best procedures in cost accounting and budget making. This attitude was spelled out in 1916 by Thomas Churchill, then President of the New York City Board of Education. The school superintendent, he declared, "must purge himself of the fallacy that scholarship is the main desideratum in himself or in the school system." The public did not tax itself for scholarship. It wanted common sense, practical intelligence, know-how. Since scarcely

[92] Sallie Hill, "Defects of Supervision and Constructive Suggestions Thereon," *NEA Proceedings* (1919), pp. 506-9; George S. Counts, *The American Road to Culture* (New York: The John Day Company, Inc., 1930), pp. 152-53.

[93] Lotus D. Coffman, "Need for the Substitution of a Cooperative Type of Organization for the Present System," *NEA Proceedings* (1919), pp. 376-77; *idem,* "Control of Progress Thru Supervision," *NEA Proceedings* (1917), p. 191.

[94] George B. Leonard, Jr., "Educator or Businessman?" *Look,* 24 (June 21, 1960).

5 per cent of the population were destined to follow a path to which any form of scholarship led, it was "fatuous" and "dishonest" to stress academic values in the administration of public schools. The ideal superintendent of schools, Churchill concluded, was a red-blooded, "practical" man, a skillful organizer interested not in the training of scholars, "but in the output of human creatures who can think, reason, judge, and decide about the large concerns of personal and national life." [95]

To what extent did the men who served as superintendents of schools conform to the Philistine stereotype preferred by Board members like Thomas Churchill? A study in 1934 of some 850 holders of the office showed that the average superintendent was a native American "of long-established American ancestry and tradition." He was middle-aged, a married man with at least two children. He had been "reared in a large family on a farm by parents with a common school education who were church members and regular attendants." As for intellectual background, "his reading opportunities were narrow and his travel in boyhood limited, his work largely confined to the farm, and his avocations healthy but poor in the intellectual and aesthetic ranges." In his community situation, he was a "joiner" and an active participant in all "respectable" organizations. A member, active worker, and regular attendant at church, he also served as a member of the board of such groups as the Rotary Club, the Chamber of Commerce, the Masons, and the Young Men's Christian Association. "Probably much more than other professional men, he is drawn into all sorts of *ex-officio* relations, . . . the spread of his social and professional affiliations is from one to twenty [associations], and the average eight. . . ." [96] Substantially similar findings evolved from a study made about the same time of the status and activities of hundreds of junior high school principals.[97] Even more interesting, many of the same characteristics were found by the American Association of School Administrators to be true of the rank and file of school superintendents nearly 30 years later. They still came predominantly from small towns; they still came mostly from large families; and they still were primarily "joiners" rather than productive scholars or self-announced intellectuals.[98]

---

[95] Thomas W. Churchill, "The Superintendent As the Layman Sees Him," *NEA Proceedings* (1916), pp. 940-45.

[96] Frederick H. Bair, *Social Understandings of the Superintendent of Schools* (New York: Teachers College, Columbia University, 1934), pp. 80-81.

[97] Frank K. Foster, *Status of the Junior High School Principal* (Washington, D.C.: Government Printing Office, 1930).

[98] *Professional Administrators for America's Schools* (Washington, D.C.: American Association of School Administrators, 1960).

Specialized school administration, as it emerged, reflected rather accurately the dominant currents in the surrounding social matrix. The superintendents, school principals, and state education commissioners had to show themselves conventional and practical-minded enough to reassure the broad public, their constituency. The American public was well aware of the fact that the local superintendent of schools "is, or can be, the principal public school politician," and that in community "power structures," he figured prominently along with bankers and business men when important decisions were to be made with respect to the schools.[99]

By the early 1950's, a trend became apparent at the major universities training educational administrators, as illustrated by the work of Professor Roald Campbell of the University of Chicago. More systematic scholarly work in various of the social sciences and in administrative theory was being demanded of those proposing to secure an advanced degree in administration. By this time, too, more and more school systems were requiring their major administrators to earn a reputable doctorate. These trends seemed to reflect, on the one hand, a response to widespread public criticism of the inadequate scholarly credentials and poor professional preparation of an earlier generation of school administrators; on the other, it apparently represented the impact upon the educational field of the emergence of public administration and scientific business management, now recognized as new professions in twentieth-century American society.[100]

Perhaps, as George Counts suggested, past American attitudes in the selection of educational administrators reflected the predilections of a popular, activist culture, which was more interested in tangible symbols of achievement—figures of attendance, number of degrees granted, size of school buildings, amount of money spent—than in probing into the ultimate purposes of human institutions, including the school.[101] If ordinary Americans were during the first half of the twentieth century more wont to focus attention on the machinery and forms rather than on the spirit and intrinsic substance of education, the majority of their school administrators seemed to share this outlook. Whether a new trend was portended by the new approaches to the training of educational administrators remained for the century's later decades to disclose.

---

[99] Eliot, *Governing America*, p. 166.
[100] Campbell and Gregg, eds., *Administrative Behavior in Education*, pp. 445-52.
[101] Counts, *American Road to Culture*, pp. 148-54.

School Boards

In 1958 a journalist writing a feature article for a national magazine asked himself the question, "Who runs our schools?" His unequivocal answer was, "You do—you the people." Since the bulk of American school boards were elected by the voters, he believed that the people, in the last analysis, got the kind of public educational system they wanted.[102] His findings were indisputably correct. A factual review of the role of school boards in modern American government and in society manifestly bears out the truth of his assertion.

American public schools have traditionally been governed locally, on a township or county or school district basis, and the supreme authority on this grass-roots level has been the school board. Historic precedent for American localism in educational administration dates back to the Massachusetts Bay Colony of the 1640's. These practices were confirmed by frontier experience, the rise of democracy, and the acquiescence of the Federal Constitution.[103] During the nineteenth century, state legislatures began to assume increasing authority over the schools. But even though the local boards were now required by these legislative bodies to observe certain minimum standards in financing, hiring of teachers, and erection of buildings in order to qualify for state aid, they nevertheless retained considerable discretionary power.[104]

In early times the American school board performed both executive and legislative functions. Despite the rise of a university-trained profession of educational administration, many boards as late as 1917 were still slow to delegate their executive functions and power to professional administrators. The boards in the main had "not yet solved the problem of a judicious distribution of lay and professional control." [105] In the years that followed, organizations like the American Association of School Administrators fought for a "better type of organization" in

---

[102] George B. Leonard, Jr., "Who Runs Our Schools?" *Look*, 22 (June 10, 1958), pp. 79-88.

[103] Eliot, *Governing America*, pp. 157-58.

[104] Charles E. Reeves, *School Boards* (Englewood Cliffs, N.J.: Prentice-Hall, Inc., 1954), pp. 5-22; Thomas M. Gilland, *Origin and Development of the Power and Duties of the City School Superintendent* (Chicago: University of Chicago Press, 1936); P. Cubberley, *Public School Administration* (Boston: Houghton Mifflin Company, 1929).

[105] Walter W. Theisen, *The City Superintendent of Schools and the Board of Education* (New York: Teachers College, Columbia University, 1917), pp. 124-26.

which the people would have "a board of education represent them in formulating policies and a superintendent employed by the board to manage the educational effort in detail." [106] Certainly, by the 1930's, it had become a regular practice for the school boards to turn over to professional administrators important areas of educational responsibility. This they did in many cases readily, and in some instances almost eagerly and with a feeling of relief. But unfortunately, there were yet other boards that still insisted on keeping their superintendents tied securely to their apron strings.

The great majority of school board memberships were elective. A study by the Research Division of the National Education Association during the mid-1940's showed that nearly 85 per cent were elected by the people; the remaining 15 per cent were appointed.[107] This democratic, authentically Jacksonian approach was, beyond a doubt, characteristically American, but was it the best way to recruit a responsible educational leadership? An investigation in 1952 of the attitudes of more than 100 school superintendents in Massachusetts disclosed that one out of five considered his school board to be "a major obstacle" to satisfactory performance. Some school board members were found to be well motivated but badly informed. Others "felt their jobs were political-patronage posts and many of them sought election to the board to represent special segments of the community." This type of board member, especially in larger towns and cities, tended to regard his job primarily as a steppingstone to other, more influential political offices. Still others spent "a good deal of their time considering petty details rather than the fundamental problems of the schools." [108] In one small town, "Mineville" (scrutinized by a sociologist in 1932), the average school board member was "inhibited" from "fighting staunchly" for the good of the schools because he was afraid he might antagonize friends and business associates. In fact, some businessmen in "Mineville" frankly admitted that they did not want to serve on the school board because they believed they would make enemies by so doing and thereby lose trade at their stores.[109]

The interviewers in the previously cited Massachusetts study recorded

---

[106] *School Boards in Action* (Washington, D.C.: American Association of School Administrators, 1946).

[107] *Ibid.*

[108] Neal Gross, *Who Runs Our Schools?* (New York: John Wiley & Sons, Inc., 1958).

[109] Albert Blumenthal, *Small-Town Stuff* (Chicago: University of Chicago Press, 1932), p. 335.

some interesting comments by school superintendents on the school board members they considered to be "blockers," harmful to their community's educational program. One superintendent noted: "Our leading M.D. is a plain 'aginer.' He feels we spend too much money. He's active in community affairs and represents the older retired people that are worried over the tax rate. . . . He's got no faith in the common man and in the need for modern education." Another superintendent complained about ". . . the fellow who is the big blocker. He's a lawyer who has a narrow concept of education. He ridicules paying the teachers more money and anything we do to try to improve the schools. He's the spokesman for all the criticisms and minority complaints. He's cheap and no good. He's a thickhead." In order of frequency, the superintendents listed the following types of Massachusetts school board members or groups as doing the most to block public education in their communities: "Community officials, businessmen, taxpayer groups, older residents of the community, individuals with personal grudges against the schools, and Catholic groups." [110] A supplemental study of the same situation found that "regardless of the religion of the superintendent, the greater the proportion of Catholic school board members, the less the board conformed to professional expectations. . . ." [111]

There were also, to be sure, many dedicated, nonpartisan board members working hard to create better schools for their communities. For these truly nonpolitical boards, the early twentieth-century movement, usually denominated "progressivism," deserved much credit. In the era of Lincoln Steffens and Robert M. La Follette, Americans were fascinated by the watchwords "pragmatism" and "efficiency." They diligently sought to cleanse their political Augean stables of all dishonesty, waste, special interest, and partisan domination.[112] On state and municipal levels, progressive crusaders soon found themselves fighting for the short ballot, the initiative and the referendum, and a commission form of government. They also found it necessary to battle for more expert, nonpartisan management of schools by professional administrators responsible only to small public-spirited boards of education.[113] Teaching appointments were to be withdrawn from the realm of political patron-

---

[110] Gross, *Who Runs Our Schools?*

[111] Neal Gross, *et al.*, *Explorations in Role Analysis* (New York: John Wiley & Sons, Inc., 1958).

[112] Ralph H. Gabriel, *The Course of American Democratic Thought* (New York: The Ronald Press Co., 1940), pp. 336-38.

[113] Lawrence A. Cremin, "The Progressive Movement," *Harvard Educational Review*, 27 (Fall, 1957), pp. 259-60.

age and placed under the merit system, much like the classified civil
service.

It was more than a mere coincidence, therefore, that in New York
City it was the women's auxiliary of the Federation of Good Govern-
ment Clubs which in 1895 organized itself into the Public Education
Association, a society which actively worked for improvement of the
metropolis's schools.[114] The kind of political wire-pulling, noted by
Thomas Hunter, founder of Hunter College, to be endemic in the New
York public school system when he worked for it in the late nineteenth
century, was combatted by such "good government" organizations as
PEA.[115] Such leaders in the movement as Nicholas Murray Butler of
Columbia University fought hard for replacement of the highly political
"district system" of school administration by a city-wide Board of Education and for the appointment of a professional Superintendent of
Schools for all of greater New York. When William H. Maxwell was
appointed to the latter post, he worked sedulously with Butler and
other reform leaders to establish a merit system for teaching appointments based upon approval by a Board of Examiners. Other legislation
sponsored by PEA set up uniform salary schedules for teachers in all
boroughs, with provision for annual increments.[116]

On the state level, Butler and his associates campaigned to free New
York's State Education Department from the kind of political domination which had earlier resulted in the dismissal of the exceptionably
capable Andrew Sloan Draper as Commissioner of Education. The reformers maneuvered a bill through the legislature which placed this
office under the nonpolitical Board of Regents instead of, as previously,
under the thumb of the state legislators themselves. Draper was then
triumphantly brought back to Albany to resume his position.[117] In the
course of this controversy, which raged from 1894 to 1904, Butler came
to feel, as he later publicly stated, that "religion is probably the only
subject which excites controversy more bitter, more violent, and more
unreasoning than education." [118]

Despite all the efforts of the Progressive Era, there were conditions

[114] Lawrence A. Cremin, "The Origins of Progressive Education," *The Educational Forum* (January 1960), p. 138.
[115] Thomas Hunter, *Autobiography of Dr. Thomas Hunter* (New York, 1931).
[116] John L. Tildsley, "President Butler and Public Education," *Columbia University Quarterly* (June 1938), pp. 123-24.
[117] *Ibid.*; Nicholas Murray Butler, *Changes of a Quarter Century* (New York,
1929), pp. 2-4; James Sullivan, "Andrew Sloan Draper," *Dictionary of American
Biography*. Vol. 5.
[118] Butler, *Changes of a Quarter Century*, p. 4.

in some local school systems that continued to cry for reform. In 1934, for example, a visiting Australian educator noted that "political considerations" still "carried a good deal of weight in such matters in America." [119] About the same time, Professor George Counts of Teachers College, Columbia University, charged that control of the public school "has gradually come under the influence of the powerful commercial, financial, and industrial classes." According to Counts, "the successful businessman is the arbiter of educational enterprise in the United States today." [120]

To what extent were allegations such as these valid? Did school boards remain the private preserve of political manipulators and powerful propertied interests? First of all, it should be noted that considerable dissimilitude in school board personnel was bound to exist in a country as vast and diverse as the United States. Certainly not every American school board was recruited as was the one in "Jonesville," a little middle western town studied in the 1940's by sociologist W. L. Warner. There, "first, only men are eligible" and "second, Catholics, Jews, Irish, and Democrats are informally disqualified." To become a school board member, a man had to be "a Protestant, a Republican, a property owner, and a Rotarian or, at the very least, approved by the Rotarians." [121]

George Counts in 1927 and Claude Arnett in 1932 made studies designed to give a cross-sectional picture of school board members from coast to coast. After gathering information on 1,654 boards, Counts believed he had secured statistical validation for his belief that school board members "for the most part" came from "the dominant classes in our society"—merchants, bankers, manufacturers, lawyers, and physicians.[122] After polling the opinions of 1,076 school board members in 45 states, Arnett found that the majority gave a "conservative" response to questions involving freedom of speech, government ownership, religion, flag education, and patriotism.[123] To be sure, by the 1950's a tendency had developed in a few cities to select labor union officials

---

[119] Kenneth S. Cunningham, *Educational Observations and Reflections* (Melbourne: Melbourne University Press, 1934), pp. 20-21; see also J. B. Shouse, "Teaching Appointments and Political Patronage," *American School Board Journal* (February 1936), pp. 22-23.

[120] Counts, *American Road to Culture*, p. 156.

[121] W. Lloyd Warner, ed., *Democracy in Jonesville* (New York: Harper & Row, Publishers, 1949), p. 194.

[122] George Counts, *Social Composition of Boards of Education* (Chicago: University of Chicago Press, 1927), pp. 78-81.

[123] Claude E. Arnett, *Social Beliefs and Attitudes of American School Board Members* (Emporia, Kansas: Emporia Gazette Press, 1932), pp. 215-18.

for school board positions, but this continued to be the exception rather than the rule. The same was true with respect to the election of women to school boards.

That Americans, when voting in school board elections, tended to favor practical "men of affairs" was suggested by *Look* magazine in 1958, when it made a detailed study of one such contest in Cedar Rapids, Iowa. At the very least, it might be argued that Cedar Rapids was not atypical as an example of a small mid-continent city. In the election in question, 14 candidates campaigned strenuously for four school board vacancies. There was a record voter turnout. One of the candidates, a housewife with a degree in mathematics and Greek from Carleton College, called upon the local schools to elevate their intellectual standards and provide "mental discipline and real knowledge." She placed fifth from the bottom. Another candidate, a young professor of mathematics from Coe College, ran for the school board on the single-minded platform that: "The primary job of the schools is intellectual training. Everything else is secondary." He also went down in defeat. The four winners included a "jovial" hog buyer who had worked as a member of a citizens advisory committee on school construction; an engineering executive who favored attention to the needs of all kinds of students ("Let's not be stampeded into a program we may later regret. Let's not neglect all those who will be housewives, tradesmen, and mechanics"); a housewife and club-woman whose reaction to Sputnik was: "America's school philosophy is good compared to Russia's. We don't want automatons"; and a highly popular business manager of the local professional baseball team whose presence on the school board was expected to give Cedar Rapids what she had not had for many years, namely, a winning high school football or basketball team.

Back in the 1880's, Marshall Field, the department store tycoon of Chicago, was reported to have instructed one of his clerks with respect to the somewhat troublesome demands of a particularly difficult customer: "Give the lady what she wants!" The *Look* survey of Cedar Rapids indicated that the same slogan might well be applied to the American public school systems of the twentieth century. It is only simple realism to note, as *Look* reporter George Leonard, Jr., did, that "the residents get the kind of school program they want, including winning teams—if they want them badly enough." [124]

More than one foreign observer has noticed the relatively low esteem in which pure scholarship or disinterested intellectual achievement has

[124] Leonard, "*Who Runs Our Schools?*" pp. 79-86.

been held in the American culture. Scholarly discoveries have been admired by the American *demos* only if they gave promise of immediate utility in fields such as health, profit-making, national defense, or material standards of living.[125] Such being the case, how could one expect that professors, scholars, literary men, or educational philosophers would be given the direction of school boards? The "practical" man who could "meet a payroll" was the one who was trusted. In such a context, too, the major emphasis would customarily be placed on outward physical or material symbols of education, which the ordinary voter could see and understand, such as buildings, football stadia, salary schedules, and school budgets. A sociological study of Westwood, Massachusetts, a prosperous Boston suburb, illustrates this trend. There, after much wrangling, the town meeting authorized construction of a magnificent new high school building, "a palace of progress and modernity." Thereafter, according to this survey, the parents manifested little concern with the content of the actual curriculum taught within the building. "Their attitude seems to be that since the high school building has received numerous architectural awards, and the youths generally get into college, what more could one ask?" [126]

In the United States, as we have seen, public schools have been managed for 300 years in an authentic framework of popular control. *Vox populi, vox Dei.* Responsibility for basic policy has historically resided in the hands of democratically elected school board' members. Thus, the calibre, training, and outlook of school board membership has in the last analysis reflected the basic wishes of the American people. Or, to put an obvious truth another way, America's public schools have been what America's parents and voters have chosen to make them.

"Veto Groups"

The American sociologist David Riesman, in a perceptive little book published in 1956, uses the phrase "veto group" to describe those organized segments of the community that seek to exercise power over the public schools, usually to advance a special program or to protect

---

[125] Hugo Munsterberg, *The Americans* (New York: McClure, Phillips & Co., 1904); Gustave Lanson, *Trois mois d'enseignement aux États-Unis* (Paris: Librairie Hachette et Cie, 1912); André Potier, *Un Français à l'école Américaine* (Paris: Amiot, Dumont, 1951).
[126] David Fisher, "Changing Community," in Roger Hagan, ed., *Character and Social Structure* (Cambridge: Harvard University Press, 1960), p. 40.

a particular economic or ideological interest. Because of the very nature of modern American life, particularly its deep-rooted democratic and conformist tendencies, public school boards, superintendents, and teachers, in Riesman's view, are terribly vulnerable to onslaughts launched by such pressure groups.[127]

Much can be said for Riesman's interesting thesis. Not that all pressures of this kind on the schools are inherently evil; some may very well serve a useful purpose. What stands out here is the fact that the special-interest approach to which "veto groups" were dedicated could easily make impossible a balanced, objective, open-minded search for knowledge in the schools.

Recognizing the significance of pressure groups, Jesse Newlon pointed out: "Each of these lobbies represents one of the organized groups in society, and frequently a vital economic or social interest. Under our democratic form of government lobbies are not only inevitable; they perform a necessary function in the process of government if groups representing vital interests are to present their views to lawmaking bodies and to the public." [128]

A study of American suburban life in the 1950's reported that much of the organized political effort by local groups to influence the public schools represented "ideological politics." [129] Such pressures might sometimes be as petty and picayune as those exerted by a group of parents in 1961 in Levittown, New York. A loud and indignant protest was made there against the use of a textbook in United States history at the General Douglas MacArthur High School on the ground that the volume made mention of the quaint, if antiquated, colonial wooing custom known as "bundling." The harassed chairman of the social studies department thereupon tore the four pages containing the dangerous material from all copies of the book which had been innocently and unknowingly purchased by the Levittown school board, meanwhile doing a similar job of excision on books other students had purchased *for themselves*, thus arousing the wrath of *their* parents! Even more fascinating was the incident in Miami, Florida, in 1960, when a few parents complained about the placing of Aldous Huxley's *Brave New World* on the required reading list and George Orwell's *1984* on the supplementary list for high school seniors taking an English course.

[127] David Riesman, *Constraint and Variety in American Education* (Garden City, N.Y.: Doubleday & Company, Inc., 1958), pp. 122-39.
[128] Newlon, *Educational Administration As Social Policy.*
[129] Robert C. Wood, *Suburbia* (Boston: Houghton Mifflin Company, 1958).

After due investigation by the school authorities, the books were dropped from the reading list. The Superintendent of Schools explained: "It's our feeling here that no child should be required to read a book to which any appreciable number of parents object. There certainly must be enough books in the world." [130]

From time to time segments of the American business community made strenuous efforts to influence the schools. Prominent among these was the National Association of Manufacturers, which, during the early years of the century, campaigned for the establishment of separate trade or technical schools and, after 1913, continuation schools. [131] In the 1920's the NAM opposed a proposed amendment to the Constitution that would ban child labor and thus strengthen the compulsory education laws of the various states. At the same time it sought to induce public school systems to use more extensively the many free NAM teaching aids and materials made available to them, and to accept NAM guest lecturers. [132]

In the latter part of 1940, the NAM commissioned Professor Ralph Robey of Columbia University to survey public school textbooks in order to determine whether they contained "materials inimical to the American way of life." Dr. Robey's study, which drew much adverse comment, found that many school books did in fact contain such materials. The NAM also sponsored Business-Education days throughout the country, during which school children were taken on tours of local factories. [133]

Other organizations representing American business also sought to make their point of view known in the public schools. The American Institute of Banking was one of these. At its annual meeting in June 1940, S. N. Pickard declared: "Selling banking to the public is a definite objective of the American Bankers Association and it is a selling job. Banking has a reputation to sell; each bank has specific merchandise, valuable to the public and worthy of purchase. Both must be sold." [134] At the same session, Elton H. Thompson enthusiastically explained how this "selling" program could be carried on in the public schools:

[130] Murray Kempton, "Lost Horizon," *New York Post* (March 31, 1960).

[131] *Proceedings of the Annual Convention* (National Association of Manufacturers 1903), pp. 81-82 (1905), pp. 142-47 (1906), p. 51 (1913), pp. 195-97, 233 (1917), p. 95.

[132] *Ibid.* (1925), p. 195 (1926), p. 81 (1927), pp. 271-73.

[133] R. J. Havighurst, "Economic Propaganda in the Schools?" *School Review* (February 1943), pp. 72-73.

[134] *Proceedings* (American Institute of Banking, Public Education Conference, 1940).

How are we going to put these speakers to work? First, go to your county school superintendent and obtain a list of all high schools and their principals. . . .

After you have collected this information, go back to your desk and write your very best sales letter. Explain to these school superintendents that your organization has had the privilege of appearing before some of their classes and that you are desirous of repeating that appearance this year. After you have the permission of the superintendent, write to the heads of the commercial departments of the various high schools and tell them the same story. The teachers themselves and the heads of the departments should be approached for they are the ones who engage the speakers and it is before their classes that you appear. When you are initiating this activity concentrate on individual classes rather than on the whole student body. While the number of people you are talking to will not be large your reception will be much better.[135]

Underlying the pedagogical wisdom of the project was the tried-and-true adage, "The student of today is the voter and businessman of tomorrow."

Even more active in seeking a favorable hearing in the public schools was the utility industry. The power companies sought from time to time to secure the dropping of textbooks which they considered inimical to their interests. State and national committees and bureaus were set up to investigate such matters. Utility executives who served on such committees apparently found much to displease them. Thus, Frank W. Smith, Vice-President of the United States Electric Light and Power Company, complained at one time:

I must say that it was a great shock to me to be brought to a realization of what the situation is with respect to this subject.

For a long time we have all understood that much of the misunderstanding of the utility business and its problems was created in the minds of the young student by misinformed and radical educators, but I doubt if any considerable number of executives and utility operators appreciate the character of the stuff contained in these textbooks, . . . It has been talked of for a long time and there have been committees on the subject, but until some action is taken about these books that dish up such trash and absolutely criminal food for the digestion of school children, college students, etc., we can expect a new radical born or created every so often.

J. B. Sheridan, Director of the Missouri Committee on Public Utility Information, agreed with Mr. Smith one hundred per cent. After mak-

[135] *Ibid.*

ing a survey of a number of standard textbooks in the fields of economics and civics used in the public schools of the country, he found himself "irresistibly driven to the conclusion that the chief effort of the public schools appeared to be manufacture and production of socialists and communists." More sanguine, however, was the head of the Iowa Public Utility Information Bureau. "We believe," he happily stated, "we have this matter pretty well in hand here; after three years' work most of the really objectionable textbooks have been eliminated." [136]

The reader would be very wrong were he at this point to assume that all pressures upon the schools issued from management's side of the fence. Almost from the time of its beginnings in the 1880's, the American Federation of Labor campaigned to have the trade union point of view presented sympathetically in the schools and to secure public education programs that would advance organized labor's objectives. As a weapon against the highly unwelcome competition of child labor, A.F. of L. leaders on both national and state levels year after year called not only for more effective child labor laws but also for compulsory school attendance legislation. Moreover, the Federation went on record in its national conventions as favoring part-time continuation schooling, but not the kind of public school manual training desired by the NAM.[137]

As early as 1903, an A.F. of L. convention turned its attention to the curriculum of the schools and the contents of textbooks. In that year schoolmen were criticized because "they failed to inculcate the dignity of manual labor [and] failed to give due importance to the service of labor to society." Finally in 1919 the Federation established a committee to investigate the adequacy of textbooks currently in use. A full report, presented to the A.F. of L. convention of 1923, maintained that of 123 texts examined, many ignored subjects of concern to the wage-earning population and did not deal fairly with labor's point of view. The committee concluded that there were sinister forces operating upon the public schools, and that these forces could only be counteracted by unionization of the teaching force. In subsequent years the Federation worked continually to secure the revision or elimination of text-

---

[136] See Stephen Rauschenbush, *The Power Fight* (New York, 1923); Bruce Raup, *Education and Organized Interests in America* (New York: G. P. Putnam's Sons, 1936).
[137] Philip Curoe, *Educational Attitudes and Policies of Organized Labor* (New York: Teachers College, Columbia University, 1926); Jesse H. Newlon, *Educational Administration As Social Policy* (New York: Charles Scribner's Sons, 1934), pp. 41-42.

books it considered objectionable and threw its influence behind all efforts to expand work in the social studies, contemporary history, and physical training.[138]

Furthermore, much pressure was exerted by patriotic groups seeking to shape the course of American education. The American Legion and the Daughters of the American Revolution were active in sponsoring flag ceremonies, patriotic essay contests, and civic education courses in the schools.[139] "Scientific" temperance crusaders such as Mary Hunt and her embattled colleagues in the WCTU were successful in securing the revision of textbooks and the inclusion of teaching materials in public school programs which graphically illustrated the evils of "demon rum." Other special-interest groups, while not as strong as the foregoing, were still influential enough to oblige a large and populous commonwealth like California to require by statute that all its public schools faithfully observe such events as Bird Day, Arbor Day, Luther Burbank Day, and Susan B. Anthony Day! Indeed, such groups promoting one-idea platforms persuaded the California legislature to require the state's elementary schools to teach no less than *19* nonacademic subjects, including safety, fire prevention, morals, conservation of natural resources, manners, and something entitled "training for healthful living." [140]

On the local level, some school systems succeeded in resisting these incessant and importunate pressures; others gave in and ran up the white flag. Not every former superintendent of schools could state as did Jesse Newlon that he had "experienced all these pressures and resisted them for reasons that seemed to him valid from the standpoint of our social and political institutions and ideals." [141] Nor were they all as ingenious or as lucky as one Texas superintendent who was approached by a physician representing the local medical association. The visitor wished the schools to sponsor an essay contest devoted to the evils of socialized medicine and offered a $250 prize. The superintendent said: "Well, we have a policy here of barring *all* essay contests. Now, if

[138] Curoe, *Educational Attitudes of Organized Labor*, pp. 106-64.

[139] Bessie L. Pierce, *Citizen's Organizations and the Civic Training of Youth* (New York: Charles Scribner's Sons, 1933); Howard K. Beale, *Are American Teachers Free?* (New York: Charles Scribner's Sons, 1936); *Proceedings of the National Conventions, 1926-1935* (American Legion); J. Ray Murphy, "Americanism is the Soul of America," *American Legion Monthly* (February 1935); Earl L. Hunter, *A Sociological Analysis of Certain Types of Patriotism* (New York: Columbia University Press, 1932).

[140] Philip Reaves, "They're Stealing Time from Our Schools," *Coronet* (October 1959), pp. 102-3.

[141] Newlon, *Educational Administration As Social Policy*, p. 48.

you'd like us to re-evaluate that policy, we have here a similar request, with an offer of a $1,000 prize. It's from the local chiropractors." The physician made a hasty exit.

It is possible that some educational administrators did not fight strenuously against the demands of interest-group spokesmen because they really felt no undue pressure. Many of these public schoolmen shared the basic viewpoints and values of the "veto groups" in their communities and thus suffered no strain in helping to implement them in the schools.[142] At all events, the realm of group pressures in the American educational context is a most complex and tricky one. Riesman cautiously advanced the idea that a moderate "counter-cyclical" policy might be generated by bold and imaginative administrators and school systems to preserve some of the values of individuality and non-conformity in the increasingly "other-directed" mid-twentieth–century American society. With astute management, the "veto groups" might be checked somewhat, or even induced to cancel out each other.[143] Perhaps so, for the very heterogeneity and diversity of the American social matrix has to a certain extent produced the same results. As we have seen, a medley of proposals and designs bombarded the public schools, issuing from a host of minority groups, religious groups, business groups, labor groups, patriotic societies, reformist groups, and the like. From the pressures and counter-pressures thus brought to bear, something like a rough "checks and balances" has emerged in the American educational world. While, on the one hand, this situation has made the school superintendency what some would call the most "interesting" profession in the world (and which others would term the worst), it may also have left room for maneuvering, for the preservation of freedom in the face of the grinding impact of modern standardization. What would the alternative be for America? Judging by the experience of other cultures and times, it most likely would be a more centralized, authoritative, regimented, and hence even more conformable, educational order. A golden opportunity for educational freedom and intellectual independence remained inherent in the American public school framework and had by no means been blotted out by the growing power of pressure groups and "veto groups." But such an opportunity, unless consciously grasped by courageous and resourceful educators, could be lost forever, like the precious jewel locked in a box

---

[142] J. Flint Waller, *Outside Demands and Pressures on the Public Schools* (New York: Teachers College, Columbia University, 1932).

[143] Riesman, *Constraint and Variety in American Education*, pp. 162-74.

whose owners had long since forgotten when or where they mislaid the key.

The School Teacher in the American Social Order

In "Jonesville," U.S.A.—a middle western community of the 1940's—sociologists found two distinct policies in effect in the recruitment of teaching personnel. Administrators and high school teachers were secured from the outside, whenever possible. In the elementary schools, however, local girls were hired in the great majority of cases. Indeed, approximately three-fourths of the town's elementary school teachers had been born, reared, and educated in the community. After high school, these girls had gone away to gain professional training, whereupon they returned to town to take jobs in the local schools. They mostly came from lower-middle–class families and lived at home while teaching. These local girls usually followed one of two life patterns: they either taught a few years and then married and raised a family, or they remained year after year in the schools, eventually attaining the status of "maiden ladies." There was much less turnover among these teachers than among those from "outside," for the latter often left the system to accept better offers elsewhere.[144]

The situation in "Jonesville" was scarcely atypical, as a number of nationwide surveys of the social composition of the teaching population demonstrated. As early as 1911, a careful study by Lotus Coffman indicated that "feminization" of the teaching corps was proceeding rapidly in the United States, particularly on the elementary school level. Men were tending to concentrate in the upper grades or to leave the teaching field entirely. This was due, declared Coffman, "to the narrowing of the intellectual range or versatility required of teachers, and to the willingness of women to work for less than men." [145] A compendious survey of conditions in 1930 by the United States Office of Education produced similar conclusions. American public schools continued to be taught "predominantly by young, unmarried women with little teaching experience." In rural areas (where transiency was a severe problem), seven-eighths of all the teachers were women. Nineteen-twentieths of all other elementary school teachers were female, as were three-fourths

---

[144]Warner, ed., *Democracy in Jonesville*, p. 199.
[145] Lotus D. Coffman, *Social Composition of the Teaching Population* (New York: Teachers College (Columbia) Press, 1911), pp. 78-86.

of all the junior high school teachers, and nearly two-thirds of the senior high school teachers. Because of low salaries and other unfavorable circumstances, the investigators found that teaching was not considered a permanent career. That this state of affairs was slow to improve, at least salary-wise, was made clear by a report of the Office of Education in 1950, indicating that the average annual salary in public elementary and secondary schools was $4,156 during the school year 1955-56. This figure was $444, or ten per cent less than the personal income per member of the national labor force (which was then $4,600).[146]

Educational "inbreeding" constituted a vexing problem for the teaching staffs of many school systems. An intensive study of nine urban school systems in New York State during the 1940's revealed that policies favoring local candidates for teaching positions were in effect in more than two-thirds of the communities surveyed. The tendency toward inbreeding was greatest among women teachers (it applied to only 15 per cent of the men), and it was greatest at the elementary school level. About twice as many female outsiders as local women teachers were found to be married. The nonlocal teacher, furthermore, was more likely than her local colleague to have had college training, more years of teaching experience, and a record of activity in professional organizations and publications in her special field. What was the researcher's conclusion? Educational inbreeding contributed to the relatively low social standing of the teacher because it was associated with "the difficulty the local person often encounters in achieving adult status in the eyes of his friends and neighbors." It was also responsible for the predominance of women in the profession, brevity of tenure, low salaries, insecurity, and "a feeling of inferiority on the part of teachers themselves."[147]

What were further factors that contributed to the low status of the teacher in the community? One of these was what might be termed the "hired hand" concept, the contemptuous outlook which refused to accept the public school teacher, no matter how extensive his training, as a skilled professional similar to the lawyer, physician, or engineer. He might rank a notch or two above the school janitor and the principal's secretary, and then again he might not. The last-named worthies

[146] Edward S. Evenden, Guy Gamble, and Harold Blue, *Teacher Personnel in the United States* (Washington, D.C.: Government Printing Office, 1933), pp. 38-39; *Statistical Summary of Education: 1955-56* (Washington, D.C.: U. S. Office of Education, 1959), Chap. 1.

[147] Harold E. Snyder, *Educational Inbreeding* (New York: Teachers College (Columbia) Press, 1943), pp. 130-38.

were often difficult to replace and ordinarily would not be "pushed around," while teachers, in the eyes of some taxpapers, were members of a "third sex" and came a "dime a dozen" (especially if salary schedules were pushed up sufficiently in times of shortages).

Lest these remarks be deemed extreme, a survey of some of the obligations and duties imposed on Mr. or Miss "Organization Teacher" in certain actual schools of mid-century will prove that the "professional" teacher was little more than an automaton. Item, *re* the teacher's freedom to give pupils the grades he or she honestly believes they have earned, a letter from principal to teacher in one of the better suburban school systems of the Northeast:

February 1, 1960

_____:

Will you please review your marking of first and second terms and be sure that your policies are in keeping with our rules and regulations here at _____. It is my opinion that perhaps you are more severe in the grading than our policy of marking calls for, and I say this because in my opinion there would be no pupil in your period 1 or 3 who should have a grade much below B unless there had been very serious lack of effort during the term.

I would also say that your period 4 class should have high grades. I note that you marked your period 3 as a very good section and yet the distribution is not much above average.

Possibly you are thinking of some higher level of grading than we have here at the school and if so please revise that procedure in keeping with the general policy of marking recently issued. This is by no means a criticism but merely a desire to have our marking systems on the same basis regardless of which teacher happens to be having a section.[148]

Or, again, item, *re* the right of a teacher as a professional employee to eat or rest on the job in between a host of compulsory nonteaching obligations (lunchroom duty, corridor duty, playground duty, homeroom duty, detention duty, and study-hall duty):

November 6, 1959

Special Notice to Teachers:

We seem to have a situation that has arisen because some teachers, apparently, feel that they are entitled to thirty minutes in the dining room, which, of course, is not true. As of Monday, and for every day, teachers must be back in their rooms 25 minutes after they leave, which is 5 minutes before the class is to start. There have been some rooms

[148] Original copy in my files.

which I, personally, noted yesterday where pupils are ready to start and the teacher has not arrived.

Teachers are needed throughout this building at all times, and the 25 minutes allowed for lunch is ample time and more than most teachers get in most systems. In our school it is not a question of what has happened, but the possibility that exists of having bad troubles if we do not have proper supervision at all times.

Please assist in this respect and be sure that your group is taken care of, and that you help by not allowing pupils to loiter in corridors as they return from lunch. I am sure that we can improve this situation if we all work together.

_____ _____, Principal.[149]

Infringement of this kind on the teacher's time and energies by making him perform clerking or even janitorial duties was a nationwide scandal, J. Lloyd Trump, Associate Secretary of the National Education Association, declared in 1960. Trump charged that such impositions were demeaning the teacher as a professional, robbing him of status in the community, and discouraging the ablest young Americans from entering the teaching field. "Let teachers do the teaching, let clerks do the clerking, and let machines help out as learning aids," he told an educational conference in San Francisco. There is simply "too much togetherness in schools," Trump added, citing the fact that American teachers spent "at least *one-third* of their time performing clerical tasks or supervising student activities." [150]

Even attempts to "democratize" school administration and introduce a more cooperative "participatory process" in faculty relationships with colleagues or superiors tended to end in still more demands on the teacher. Using this objective as a *rationalê*, some school systems took away additional segments of the teacher's time, further constricted his individuality, and even more tightly regimented him. In the name of "democracy," he must now conform to the group and be one of the "cooperative" bananas on the bunch (although usually not the top one). New hours of "committee work" loomed ahead of him, whereby in a duly "participatory" fashion he could "democratically" arrive at decisions in agreement with his fellows, decisions which the administration and school board may have already determined upon. In some school systems, such activities were stated to be purely "voluntary," but even in outside-the-school matters, such as attending testimonial dinners for retiring administrators, the individual decision of Mr. "Organi-

---

[149] Copy in my files.
[150] *Champaign-Urbana Courier* (Illinois), July 14, 1960.

zation Teacher" might be "prodded" along by mimeographed notices from the office:

> . . . . Obviously, it seems to me, there should be a large representation of teachers from this school present on Saturday evening. Certainly the citizens, parents, former graduates, and invited guests will think it strange if the teachers are not present. . . .
> Some of us will attend *both* testimonials. Why not all of us? Our absence at either will be conspicuous. . . . Let us all be together on Saturday evening and again, by ourselves, on Tuesday evening.

All of this "participatory" draining off of the teacher's small remaining stores of creativity and strength was given the *imprimatur* of approval in 1943 in a treatise on "Democracy in School Administration" by Koopman, Miel, and Misner. Reflecting the ingenious concept that an American public school teacher is at no time more useful than when sitting on a committee, the authors querulously complained that "an analysis of any faculty will readily reveal that teachers, in general, lack a personal socialization and that they lack also a knowledge of how to help learners to become socialized." To remedy this "deplorable" situation and to properly "socialize" all recalcitrant individualists among the teaching personnel, the authors happily proposed the holding of many "functional, socializing" types of faculty meetings. They also advocated obliging all teachers to participate more actively in "cooperative activities which take place out in the community." Finally, to bring this Orwellian setting into being still faster, all teachers were to be required to take part in at least four school-wide committees: a "Socialization" Committee; a "Community-Relations" Committee; a "Teacher Affairs" Committee; and a "Curriculum Activities" Committee.[152]

Even more highly visible than the problem of the teacher's status within the school was that of his standing in the *outside* community. Here a number of studies by sociologists and others have documented at length the delicate and troublesome problems twentieth-century teachers faced in their relations with society, not only in small rural hamlets, but in larger centers of population as well. In 1941 Florence Greenhoe analyzed the community relationships of 9,122 public school teachers

---

[151] Copy in my files.
[152] G. Robert Koopman, Alice Miel, and Paul J. Misner, *Democracy in School Administration* (New York: Appleton-Century-Crofts, Inc., 1943), pp. 10-14, 170-81.

selected as a national sample. She found that in terms of away-from-the-job behavior, only ministers were more beholden to community "good will" than teachers.[153] A study made a couple of years earlier of 622 teachers in Ohio, West Virginia, and Pennsylvania (70 per cent of them in grade schools) found that "the mores governing the teacher's nonschool life are even more rigorous than at first suspected." Community disapproval of teachers dating students, drinking alcoholic liquors, smoking in public, or dancing was marked in both small towns and larger ones. On the other hand, teachers were "expected" to be active in such community organizations as Parent-Teacher Associations, churches, Sunday schools, lodges, and service clubs, whether willingly or otherwise. The explanation for these pressures, according to the authors, was that "area dwellers cannot take the teacher's assimilation for granted because too much is at stake. For one thing, the educator touches local life at its most sensitive point, its children. If traditional forms and norms of conduct are to survive at all, they must do so via the children." [154]

In pharisaical towns like "Mineville," however, community taboos were relaxed somewhat for influential local people. As late as the closing years of the 1920's, a teacher there was advised by friends not to apply for reappointment. The children had "spread to their homes a steady flow of information in regard to her poor class discipline and her disposition to become intoxicated." Then, at a Christmas party the teacher was seen dancing with "prominent citizens of the town" while in a state of intoxication. She was an outsider, and was not rehired. Interestingly enough, at the same time a "home-girl" teacher was known to be involved in very similar relationships with men, but she "was protected by the weight of family influence. Literally, people were afraid to talk about her excepting in a most muffled manner." In "Mineville," too (atypically, let us hope), teachers found that they might jeopardize their popularity with the community if they were stern with offenders in their classes. Past history had shown that they might "easily lose their jobs by arousing the wrath of influential families. Even though the children of such families be positive nuisances, the teacher is obliged to proceed as if they are no different from the rank and file of the students." [155]

[153] Florence Greenhoe, *Community Contacts and Participation of Teachers* (Washington, D.C.: American Council on Public Affairs, 1941), pp. 77-81.
[154] Lloyd A. Cook, Ronald Almack, and Florence Greenhoe, "The Teacher and Community Relations," *American Sociological Review* (April 1938).
[155] Blumenthal, *Small-Town Stuff*, pp. 329-41.

In some small communities (such as one in Texas), conforming to community desires required dextrous footwork. With saloon-keepers and gamblers prominent in town politics, and with the Methodist and Baptist churches highly influential in local affairs, one member of the teaching staff, Lawrence Washington, soon found himself looking for another job. As he tells the story:

> I had allied myself with one church and thus affronted the other. I neither drank nor gambled, so I was unpopular with the saloon faction. My politics did not suit some, and the women as a group condemned my wife for being stuck up and unsocial. Too, we bought most of our groceries and supplies in Houston. I might be a good schoolmaster but I was not a good citizen.

Luckily for him, Washington managed to exchange jobs with a young man who was teaching in a nearby town. Profiting from Washington's example, the new teacher "taught in the Baptist Sunday School, sang in the Methodist choir, and gambled and drank with the frequenters of the saloons." [156]

The amazing thing, says Howard K. Beale, is that many teachers were not *themselves* even *aware* that their freedom was being curbed in any way.[157] Many of them shared the community's outlook and accepted its standards of conduct without inner conflict. This thesis is confirmed by the findings of the Cook, Almack, and Greenhoe study and is also validated by Snyder's investigation of educational inbreeding.[158] The latter makes a further observation about the sort of personality types likely to accept without question local community restrictions on teachers:

> Obviously, submission to peculiarly rigid mores or enforced adherence to a prescribed code of behavior is distasteful to many of the ablest teachers. . . . It is particularly difficult under such circumstances to secure and retain good nonlocal teachers. Teachers who submit to such restrictions will tend to be docile individuals from whom one can scarcely

---

[156] Lawrence D. Washington, *Confessions of a Schoolmaster* (San Antonio, Texas: The Naylor Company, 1939), pp. 382-83.

[157] Howard K. Beale, *History of Freedom of Teaching in American Schools* (New York: Charles Scribner's Sons, 1941).

[158] Cook, Almack, and Greenhoe, "The Teacher and Community Relations," p. 173; Snyder, *Educational Inbreeding*, pp. 143-44.

expect dynamic creative leadership. . . . This may lead to a pyramiding of cultural and educational isolation and smugness.[159]

As urbanization advanced in the mid-twentieth-century, certain communities came to be more diverse in population makeup and, consequently, in mores and social outlook. Teachers in such communities became somewhat freer to lead their own private lives. But growing freedom in one sphere tended to be paralleled by growing intolerance in another, the area of "academic freedom." While no longer required to be a teetotaling Puritan, the teacher was still expected "to be a 'good guy,' warm and friendly, not too eccentrically dedicated to interests in which the community cannot share." [160] In substance, this meant, beginning with the World War I era, that the teacher had better not express opinions on political or economic subjects which influential people in the community might be likely to deem "radical." In the small midwestern city called "Middletown," the local DAR and other patriotic organizations in the mid-1930's felt that the high school had "some pretty pink teachers." Important citizens had their children check up on what was going on in the classrooms of suspected teachers. When a social studies teacher spoke favorably about the United States joining the World Court, an editorial in the local paper warned teachers to remember that the schools were supported by the taxpayers. "Middletown" teachers, under these circumstances, very often feared to discuss candidly any searching questions that their students might throw at them in class and even apprehensively ended conversations with remarks such as: "I don't know whether I should discuss these things *even with you.*" [161]

By 1937, 21 states had enacted legislation imposing loyalty oaths on teachers. It is worthy of note that *all but one* of these oaths were adopted in the years following World War I and the Russian Revolution. The Daughters of the American Revolution and the Hearst chain of newspapers were most active in mobilizing public sentiment to support such measures. Discussing what it termed the "gag on teaching," the American Civil Liberties Union reported in 1937 that "it is hazardous in most communities for teachers to discuss in the classroom,

---

[159] Snyder, *op. cit.*, p. 143.
[160] Riesman, *Constraint and Variety in American Education.* p. 125.
[161] Robert S. Lynd and Helen M. Lynd, *Middletown in Transition* (New York: Harcourt, Brace & World, Inc., 1937).

and often outside, one or another of the subjects of Communism, Soviet Russia, Socialism, pacifism, trade unions, public ownership of industry, free trade, government regulation of industry, dishonest banking, civil liberties for radicals, racial equality, birth control, and sex hygiene." [162]

In addition to those forces both within and without the school which have operated to affect the teacher's feelings of status, independence, and professional *esprit de corps*, there may possibly be another factor. This factor Riesman has labeled "inner vulnerability." It reflected the influence of a culture profoundly influenced by a nonauthoritarian, "child-centered," Be-a-Pal-with-Your-Son-or-Daughter philosophy of child-rearing. In this setting, some teachers might allow their dedication to rigorous standards of work to be weakened by a compulsive desire to gain the approval of the pupils. Teachers with this kind of Achilles heel (at least, in part, culturally conditioned) "need to be liked by the children, . . . to have evident and immediate response." And, in turn, the children, "good operators that they are," are quick to take advantage of their teacher's vulnerability. They "include among *their* social skills the ability to exploit the adult need for affection and approval—skills the young people have been taught in the child-centered middle-class home." [163]

At first slowly, haltingly, and then with increasing speed after 1920, the public school teachers of America labored to win recognition by forming professional associations on the local, state, and national levels. Best known of these, of course, was the National Education Association, founded in 1857 but not really successful in attracting a mass membership until the years following World War I. The NEA was viewed by radicals as "a kind of company union . . . controlled by superintendents and administrators who depend on the favor of employers for their jobs." [164] It was condemned by the rival American Federation of Teachers, which during these same years was trying, not too successfully, to sell teachers the idea of trade union organization, as an ineffective "fraud" which at best was little more than a "chowder marching society." Nevertheless, the NEA worked steadily, and with increasing boldness, to do whatever it could as a national pressure group to improve teacher welfare and status, particularly with respect to vital mat-

[162] *The Gag on Teaching* (New York: American Civil Liberties Union, 1937), pp. 22-28.
[163] Riesman, *Constraint and Variety in American Education*, pp. 140-41.
[164] David, *Schools and the Crisis*, p. 32.

ters such as salaries, tenure, sick leave, and pensions.[165] In the realm of academic freedom, it went on record during the 1950's as upholding the teacher's "freedom to present all points of view without danger of reprisal, intimidation, loss of position, reduction of salary, loss of opportunities for advancement, or deprivation of their usual assignments and authorities." [166] To implement this sweeping resolution, NEA committees on Tenure and Academic Freedom and on the Defense of Democracy through Education earnestly sought to defend teachers who had been unfairly and unprofessionally deprived of their civil liberties and academic freedom.[167]

The NEA seemed to move more definitively in the direction of greater militancy when its membership increased to include greater numbers of classroom teachers. Up to this point, it had been described as "a holding company, the parent organization of a number of branches and subprofessional groups." [168] One such influential subgroup was the American Association of School Administrators. Local and state associations, much closer to the grass roots, have in many instances been even more successful than the national organization in securing legislation and administrative rulings which have enhanced teacher welfare. They have also come to have an influential voice in the affairs of some state education departments. Nevertheless one would have to look through the rosiest of rose-colored glasses to conclude that these efforts attained the degree of professional recognition already accorded to the legal, medicine, and engineering corps. Unlike the American Bar Association or American Medical Association, the NEA could not hope to tightly control professional training or standards of practice, nor through cooperating state agencies, could it determine, like AMA, who should or should not be admitted to the craft. Then, too, the vast majority of NEA members were employed by public agencies. As government employees in a country where it was presumed that the people rule, could teachers ever hope to attain a truly independent status? "If the opinions of the nonprofessional public clash with those of the profession, who is to run the schools?" [169] Furthermore, the preponderance of women in the field caused a much higher turnover than in law and medicine. Public

---

[165] Wesley, *NEA: The First Hundred Years* (New York: Harper & Row, Publishers, 1957), pp. 334-52.

[166] *Platform and Resolutions* (Portland, Oregon: National Education Association, July 1-6, 1956), p. 96.

[167] Wesley, *NEA: The First Hundred Years.*

[168] Eliot, *Governing America,* p. 176.

[169] *Ibid.,* p. 176.

opinion, moreover, remained considerably more suspicious of the body of professional knowledge on which educational science was said to rest (especially that which was dispensed in teachers colleges and schools of education) than of time-hallowed judicial, technological, and medical wisdom. This being the case, taxpayers were likely to consider themselves at least as "expert" as educators. Finally, many persons seemed to be more deeply impressed with the value of a profession such as medicine, which dealt with physical survival, or law, which protected the people, than with school teaching. Whatever its importance (and many citizens were ready to concede that it was immense), teaching did not seem to be wholly as much a matter of life-or-death.

Professor Beale questioned whether the modern American social matrix made it possible to attract and retain the very ablest persons in the land to teach the nation's young. "The world today," he observes, "desperately needs men and women of courage and integrity. Can teachers who are cringing, obedient 'hired men,' cowards, and hypocrites create citizens of courage and integrity?" [170] But, we may ask, do people really care? How many citizens unthinkingly still believe that teaching is an overpaid "snap" job with short hours, long summer vacations, and nothing much to do while at work? It would probably come as a surprise to many taxpayers to hear one contemporary teacher's story: "I find that after working with a roomful of lively children for six hours, I face four to six more hours of school work each day, and almost every weekend is taken up with school work. This situation has recently been getting worse instead of better. I have given up hobbies and recreational, church, and community activities." Nor would they be more likely to place credence in the words of another overburdened teacher: "We have in-service teacher meetings, such as art workshops, general curriculum workshops, grade level meetings, building meetings, district meetings, county institutes, PTA meetings, child-study meetings, and book review meetings. I counted the hours I spent in these meetings and the extra time devoted to clerical work, and found that during the school year it amounted to six weeks to two months of overtime counted on the basis of eight-hour days." A recent student of mental health and human relations in American education adds that when a teacher's time is still further taxed by being required, as remains true in many communities, to participate in "scout activities, youth centers, Sunday schools, and similar functions, he has little time to lead a normal life." [171]

[170] Beale, *Are American Teachers Free?*, p. 775.
[171] Kaplan, *Mental Health and Human Relations in Education*, pp. 408-12.

Every one of life's callings has its difficulties as well as its rewards, and school teaching is certainly no different in this respect from any other occupation. The problems facing the teacher in contemporary America have been, as we have seen, numerous and formidable. But for those persons whose intrinsic remuneration came, no matter what the stumbling blocks, from the opportunity to make young minds sparkle and from the hope of seeing callow youth glow as it senses for the first time its potential, there could be no other vocation.

CHAPTER FOUR

The "Adjusted" Child

Concepts of Proper Adjustment

In 1958 a professor of Child Development at the University of Rhode Island wrote in *Parents' Magazine* about the usual weekly schedule of Dorothy, "an attractive seventh grader blessed liberally with intelligence and good looks." In addition to school attendance and a half hour a day for cello practice, she had to spend at least one or two hours on homework daily. Because the girl was in the school band and chorus, she had no time to do her homework at school. Then, too, the band stayed after school for meetings and extra practice every Monday, and Dorothy had to rush off to dancing school on Monday nights. Tuesday was Girl Scout day, and, being an officer in her troop, she was always active in their campaigns. The neighborhood orchestra of which she was a member practiced on Wednesday, often till late at night. "It was such an honor to be asked that her mother hated to have her turn it down."

On Thursdays, after a trip to the orthodontist, Dorothy hurried to the church for junior choir practice. While nothing was formally scheduled for Friday evening, the neighborhood youngsters considered that time to be "movie night" and "date night." On Saturdays Dorothy might clean up her room, but she might also go to Girl Scout affairs or bird-watching parties. Saturday night might bring more social activity or an occasional baby sitting job. On Sunday the choir had to be at the church school half an hour before the other children. Sometimes Dorothy went to church as well as Sunday school. About the only time the parents and all the children had an opportunity to do something together was on Sunday afternoon, and then they usually watched favorite television programs. Often Dorothy had to miss some of these to catch up on her homework.

Dorothy's parents were proud of their daughter and her broad-range "adjustment to life." They were happy that her interests both in and out of school were so diverse and that she was developing a full, "well-rounded" personality. Says the Child Development expert: "Sometimes, it's true, parents want to give their children certain opportunities simply because they missed out themselves. . . . Limiting activities may look like depriving, and depriving is the last thing we want to do. Dorothy's mother is practically a taxi driver, running cheerfully from orthodontist to choir practice, from Scouts to music lesson. Her father willingly makes out the checks." [1]

More and more, the public school in twentieth-century America came to be the institutional focus of "life adjustment," or, as Luther Halsey Gulick put it as early as 1911,

> . . . the foundation of democracy. Communities must have, therefore, material and social machinery by which various classes shall come to know each other; some instrument that shall cross-section racial, financial, and social strata; something that shall go beneath these and touch fundamental human interests. Of these the central one is the love of children, and the machinery, most natural, as well as most available, is the public school system.[2]

Concepts of democracy in education and education for a democratic social order, most prominently associated with John Dewey and his disciples, were increasingly used as intellectual underpinnings for the "life adjustment" approach. Thus, in 1914, Charles Hughes Johnston, Professor of Secondary Education at the University of Illinois, stated that it was now universally accepted that "public education in America, and especially high school education, should be primarily a socializing process." He added that beyond the "more conventional" academic

---

[1] Mollie Smart, "Is Your Child Over-Organized?" *Parents' Magazine*, 33 (December 1958), pp. 52-53, 80-81.

[2] As quoted in Clarence A. Perry, *The Community-Used School* (New York: Russell Sage Foundation, 1911), p. 9.

subjects were "informal yet highly effective modes of schooling which come, through play, imitation, rivalry, social intercourse, and initiation under supervised school control and direction, into the various sorts of industrial and moral give-and-take which actual life later provides." This type of extracurricular as well as curricular training would produce a well-adjusted, socialized individual. There would be little interest in the "capricious or freakish, unsocial or purely individualistic genius," since he was "powerless and useless because he lacks contact with actual social forces." The high school must be "socializing and collectivistic in its operation, must pointedly seek to reduce eccentricity, as such, and [must] definitely and systematically plan to train the students' powers as the best social usages and common life demand." [3] Much the same terminology was employed at a round-table meeting of school superintendents held in conjunction with the NEA convention of 1917 which considered what the earmarks of an efficient school system might be. [4]

The "Life Adjustment" idea was given considerable publicity during and after World War II as a result of conferences organized by the United States Office of Education. A National Commission on Life Adjustment Education for Youth was established. In 1953 a series of regional meetings on the subject was held at the suggestion of a White House Conference on Education. The sessions for the New England area arrived at the following statement of basic philosophy:

> Life Adjustment Education does not mean a complete reorganization of current subject offerings nor the introduction of a complete new set of subjects. However, it does imply an emphasis . . . on the fact that the adjustment of youth to personal problems of a vocational, educational, social, and emotional nature are of significant importance. Also the adjustment of youth to current environment in the school, home, and community and preparation for the life experiences ahead, in the home, community, and vocation selected, are real responsibilities of all, including the school, who come in contact with youth during the period of adolescence, and previous to that time. [5]

As the drums beat ever more loudly for adjustment-oriented education, an inevitable reaction set in. This was most noticeable during the

[3] Charles Hughes Johnston, *et al*, *The Modern High School* (New York: Charles Scribner's Sons, 1914), pp. 3-5.
[4] Fred M. Hunter, "Earmarks of an Efficient School System," *NEA Proceedings* (1917), pp. 821-26.
[5] *Report of Conference on Life Adjustment Education* (Storrs, Conn.: University of Connecticut, May 14 and 15, 1953). (Mimeographed copy in possession of the author.)

national soul-searching which followed the launching of the first Soviet Sputnik. Dr. Francis Horn, President of the University of Rhode Island, reflected this uneasy mood of self-criticism and reappraisal when he told an educational conference in New York City: "We have had enough of this togetherness. . . . Children should be taught not to want to belong, not to lean on others, even on members of one's family. What we should educate for is independence, independence of thought, action, and character." Expressing a similar point of view was April Oursler Armstrong who commented in the November, 1961, issue of *Saturday Evening Post,* "I do not want my children to be well adjusted." Machines, she pointed out, could be adjusted, but not people. Adjustment too frequently meant conformity "to the current and often phony pattern of the world, . . . making yourself fit an assembly-line mold, paring off the rough edges of your curiosity and faith, your eccentricity and idealism in order to be well liked and safe. Frankly, I would rather be all the way dead." [6]

But how does this involve our busy, well-adjusted "organization child"? Does this seventh grader, and others like her, have *too much* to do, too much pressure to "belong," to "participate"? The observer of Dorothy's particular case admits that "the more a youngster crams into his schedule, the more he misses of freedom—freedom to be truly himself, to do what he wants, to do nothing, to make decisions, to grow." The result might very well be fatigue, harassment, worry. Yet these conforming, joining, "adjusting" school children of the Fifties and Sixties were probably only reproducing in their own juvenile sphere an activist way of life which adults were busy setting before them daily as the preferred model. Mother was in many instances so busy with "PTA meetings, church suppers, den mothers' duties, hospital volunteer work, and hobby clubs" that she hardly had time to notice whether her children were overburdened by their own "group dynamics" rounds. Father when not on the job might very well be involved in a similar series of activities. Children could only conclude that this was the authentic way to be adult, to really live.

The Role of the Extracurriculum

Within the school environment itself, officially sponsored extracurricular activity was the most conspicuous instance of efforts to pro-

[6] April Oursler Armstrong, "I Don't Want 'Well-adjusted' Children," *Saturday Evening Post* (November 11, 1961), p. 10.

vide "life adjustment." This development was in the main a post-World War I phenomenon, as a detailed survey of 275 public high schools indicated. In the majority of these schools, football had been accepted as a recognized activity before 1900; in less than 25 per cent of these institutions had any other activities been organized. Following 1920, however, many schools introduced student councils, student publications, music, tennis, golf, swimming, wrestling, and hockey, all under official sponsorship.[7]

Advocates of the expansion of extracurricular programs took much inspiration from the "Cardinal Principles of Secondary Education" report issued in 1918 by the Committee on the Reorganization of Secondary Instruction. High school teachers in Little Rock, Arkansas, even enrolled in a course in 1924 to find out to what extent various forms of extracurricular activitie met the seven basic aims set forth by this NEA Committee. "The results of the study convinced all members of the class that to best provide for adolescent needs in meeting the aims of education, there must be a definitely planned program broader than is now generally provided in the curricular programs of secondary schools." [8]

A few years later, a specialist on extracurricular matters defined the objectives of such activities as basic to the attainment of life adjustment. According to E. K. Fretwell, the purpose of these activities was to prepare the student for life in a democracy, to make him increasingly self-directive, to teach cooperation, to increase the interest of the student in the school, to "foster sentiments of law and order," and to develop special abilities.[9] Elaborating on the fourth and fifth of the above points, an educational sociologist, Willard Waller, shrewdly noted that *sponsored* extracurricular activities, in contrast to informal or spontaneous ones, had the advantage of facilitating faculty control. This was particularly important, he remarked, in a period when mass enrollments and compulsory education were bringing to America's classrooms thousands of youngsters who did not want to be in them, and who, indeed, could not possibly hope to understand what was going on in them.[10] To this,

[7] Galen Jones, *Extracurricular Activities in Relation to the Curriculum* (New York: Teachers College, Columbia University, 1935), pp. 28-29.

[8] Charles F. Allen, *Outlines in Extracurricular Activities* (Little Rock, Ark.: Little Rock High School Print Shop, 1924), p. 3.

[9] Elbert K. Fretwell, *Extracurricular Activities* (Boston: Houghton Mifflin Company, 1931), pp. 4-7.

[10] Willard Waller, *The Sociology of Teaching* (New York: John Wiley & Sons, Inc., 1924), pp. 118-19.

Dr. Fretwell added that a formally sponsored extracurriculum should help motivate the regular work of the school; that it definitely should be given school time; that the entire school must be made to participate; that management of such activities should be considered as part of the regular program of teachers; and that these same teachers were to "accept, wholeheartedly, the responsibility of developing the school's extracurricular activities." All of this was now necessary because "in both curricular and extracurricular activities there has been too much of a *laissez-faire* policy." Everything had to be more thoroughly coordinated, organized, and planned.[11]

And how did the children themselves react? One observer detected a trend among them in recent times toward "social sophistication," toward a favoring of nonintellectual values over academic ones. To these teenagers the really important things in school were athletic teams, school newspapers, drama clubs, and social affairs.[12]

A study of student opinion in a New York high school in 1960 revealed that, in order of "acceptability," eight types of students were ranked as follows:

1. Brilliant Nonstudious Athlete
2. Average Nonstudious Athlete
3. Average Studious Athlete
4. Brilliant Studious Athlete
5. Brilliant Nonstudious Nonathlete
6. Average Nonstudious Nonathlete
7. Average Studious Nonathlete
8. Brilliant Studious Nonathlete

It was notable that the four top-ranked characters were athletes, while studious, nonathletic types occupied the lowest rungs. "Brilliance" hurt a boy's status only if he was "studious" as well.[13]

Somewhat similar findings resulted from a study in 1957 of the social patterns in vogue among the 576 students of a suburban high school in a midwestern metropolitan community. In this instance, the dominant

[11] Fretwell, *op. cit.*, pp. 6-15. One treatise even proposed to give school credit toward graduation for participation in such activities. See Harold Meyer and Clara Cole, *The High School Society* (Chapel Hill, N.C.: University of North Carolina Press, 1924), p. 17.

[12] James S. Coleman, *Adolescent Society* (New York: Free Press of Glencoe, Inc., 1961), pp. 315-16.

[13] Abraham J. Tannenbaum, "Adolescents' Attitudes Toward Academic Brilliance" (Ph.D. dissertation, New York University, 1960), as quoted in *ibid.*, p. 310.

motivation was found to be the achievement and maintenance, not of a scholarly status or reputation, but of a general "social status" within the human-relations framework and organization of the school. The student accepted "roles in the various groups which enhance his position in the informal network of personal relationships within the school." In doing so, he strove mightily to gain prestige by conforming to the expectations of the members of both informal and formally organized adolescent groups. Analysis of the social structure of this particular high school produced "documentary evidence of a highly conformity-oriented system of action around highly valued patterns of dress, dating, moral behavior, and prestige-differentiated clique structures." The criterion for such prestige was definitely not intellectual attainment. "Social position of the student in school seems least significantly related to grade achievement," concluded the author of the study. The system of extracurricular student organizations, on the other hand, played an important part, along with informal personal and clique relationships outside of school, in "differentiating the students into a prestige hierarchy." [14]

As extracurricular activities became increasingly important during the 1920's, attempts were made to evaluate their impact upon the educational process. Many of these early studies were made by proponents of these activities and, not surprisingly, arrived at conclusions which were either wholly favorable, or, at the very least, distinctly not unfavorable.[15] A study by Wayland J. Hayes in 1930, centering attention on extracurricular activities at Cliffside Park High School, Grantwood, New Jersey, asserted that "there is positive correlation between voluntary school group activities and intelligence." The high participating group was found to be getting much higher grades than the nonparticipating group, in spite of the fact that the former spent less time on study (and *needed* less time to get high grades). He concluded that voluntary school group activities were selective in character. "The values they offer are sought after in the greater number of cases by the most intelligent, socially select. . . . Others seek values through community leisure time activities or work for wages or are occupied with home duties or studies." [16]

[14] C. Wayne Gordon, *The Social System of the High School* (New York: Free Press of Glencoe, Inc., 1957), pp. 1-5, 130-34.

[15] The findings of these studies are summarized in L. V. Koos, "Evaluating Extracurricular Activities," *National Society for the Study of Education*, 25th Yearbook, Part II (1926).

[16] Wayland J. Hayes, *Factors Influencing Participation in Voluntary School Group Activities* (New York: Teachers College, Columbia University, 1930), pp. 71-76.

Even in the early 1920's, however, some observers were not happy about the effect of extracurricular activities. Willard Waller pointed out that such activities were in many cases flourishing only at the expense of other important components of the school's schedule, most notably its effort to impart academic knowledge.[17] Some years later, another sociologist, studying the high school extracurricular program in a small midwestern town, described it as "the circus side of school," a kind of theatrical performance which entertained both students and town adults in their leisure time. The Board of Education, the superintendent of schools, the principal, indeed most of the teachers and students of that particular community, emphasized such activities primarily for their entertainment and public relations value. This is why they were eager for their athletic teams to win interscholastic games and their musical organizations to perform creditably at public concerts. Although one-third of the student body (particularly those of lower-class origin) did not participate in extracurricular activities of any kind, other "Jonesville" High School boys and girls were so actively "adjusted" to the "socializing" life that they belonged simultaneously to 11 or 12 different student organizations. It was particularly noteworthy that those activities that did not have broad or spectacular public relations value received little attention from students or townspeople. Thus, "girls' athletics, student government, school clubs, and dances" were found to be "tolerated, but not encouraged." [18]

Many new "voluntary" activities were introduced in public school systems by World War II as a result of pressures brought by special-interest groups. In Portland, Oregon, a high school principal in 1959 calculated that 2,155 class periods were annually devoted to that city's Rose Festival. About the same time in New Britain, Connecticut, 14 charity organizations were given permission to hold fund drives during class periods. The local superintendent of schools reported: "Our teachers seemed to be spending too much of their time doing clerical work for nonschool groups." Some students were said to have skipped classes and even examinations to work on these fund drives. Finally, the situation became so drastic that these drives in New Britain's schools were severely curtailed. But the pressures were kept up in many other parts of the country. Philip Reaves observed in 1959, "In suburban communities like Long Beach, New York, and Clayton, Missouri, parents

[17] Waller, *The Sociology of Teaching*, p. 119.
[18] W. L. Warner, ed., *Democracy in Jonesville* (New York: Harper & Row, Publishers, 1949), pp. 210-11.

want their children to be 'well-rounded' college material. In small Iowa towns, local merchants want winning basketball teams. In industrial towns in Ohio, employers want students trained in 'practical' subjects." Sometimes pressure groups "laid down the line" with brutal frankness to school officials. "You approve our program," the superintendent of schools in one Ohio town was told, "or we'll see to it that your next building bond issue is beaten." And later he ruefully recalled, "They beat it, too." [19]

The highly organized aspect of the extracurricular movement implemented within the school's environment the conviction widely held in the surrounding society that the individual must seek to "adjust" himself to life, not through narrow, specialized, or nonconforming interests, but through a broadly based involvement in the diverse organizational activities of his fellows. This approach was termed "education for life," and it was expected to produce a wholesome, well-rounded, "participatory" personality. There were those who continued to wonder, however, whether the game was worth the candle. Dr. Cuthbert Hurd, electronics director for IBM, told sociologist David Riesman at a conference held in the mid-fifties that he had his doubts "whether today's high schools could turn out the youngsters capable of the abstract and mathematical thinking that would increasingly be requisite when every pressure would be on the boys to become 'normal' in the sense of not caring to be prodigies, not caring to be immersed in some impersonal intellectual hobby (and when their teachers, too, would be under pressure not to be one-sided themselves or to encourage one-sidedness in their students)." [20] One could only hope, in the "Age of Adjustment," that the liberal and liberating arts, whatever their dollar-and-cents or national defense value, ultimately would be viewed as having an indispensable role to play in helping young persons "adjust" to a life meaningful in the deepest sense of the word.

School Athletics

The program of well-rounded youth "adjustment" that proved to be most popular with twentieth-century Americans was interscholastic

[19] Philip Reaves, "They're Stealing Time From Our Schools," *Coronet* (October 1959), pp. 103-4.
[20] David Riesman, *The Oral Tradition, The Written Word, and the Screen Image* (Yellow Springs, Ohio: Antioch Press, 1956), p. 25.

and intercollegiate athletics. "Big-time" sports took some time to win complete public acceptance, however. Before 1900, little was done to promote systematically interscholastic team sports. In those days, secondary school teams were almost exclusively informal and played few outside games. Players bought their own uniforms or improvised them at home. Professional coaching was unknown, and there was little attempt at supervision by school authorities. Interscholastic games were thought of primarily as amusements that were outside the proper province of a school. At a widely publicized national Physical Training Conference held in 1889, only two of the 33 participants mentioned team sports for schools, and then only in terms of out-of-school pastimes. Systematic gymnastics was considered to be the form of exercise best suited to promote the proper physical development of school children.[21]

Although some public schoolmen in the 1890's sought to ban all student participation in interscholastic games, these prohibitions usually proved to be unenforceable. By the turn of the century, the typical attitude on the part of public school authorities was one of uneasy toleration, or at the very least, disinterest. Competitive high school sports were gaining considerable impetus from publicized athletic contests between colleges,[22] especially from those contests waged in football. Only a year after Harvard and McGill, in 1875, played one of the pioneering American football games, Andover Academy initiated secondary school football by fielding a team which battled Exeter. In 1887, Boston Latin Shcool played Boston English High School, thereby inaugurating a traditional rivalry.[23] As football fanned out across the land to other high schools, the sport became the leading extracurricular activity.

The really impressive developments did not come, however, until the 1920's. The first high school to hold a game at night was that of Westville, Illinois; the date was 1928. Since many more spectators could be attracted to high school games in this way, the night game rapidly attained popularity, particularly in Texas and California. Investment of time and money in high school football snowballed, until in 1959 the National High School Federation was able to report that 14,034 organ-

[21] William Geer, "Athletic Situation in High Schools," *Harvard Alumni Bulletin* (May 1, 1924), pp. 1-10; Frederick W. Cozens and Florence Stumpf, *Sports in American Life* (Chicago: University of Chicago Press, 1953), p. 63.
[22] Harry A. Scott, *Competitive Sports in Schools and Colleges* (New York: Harper & Row, Publishers, 1951), pp. 42-43.
[23] Harold Claasen, ed., *Ronald Encyclopedia of Football* (New York: The Ronald Press Company, 1960), p. 825.

ized interscholastic teams were cavorting on the gridirons and were using the talents of 614,471 players during the current season. Even intersectional trips, like those of "big-time" colleges, were being made by high school teams in order to compete for championships in "bowls" and tournaments drummed up by local promoters.[24]

Although still undeniably the kingpin sport, football soon had a rival for the affections of high school students and sports fans in the community. The potential usurper was basketball, a game invented in the United States in 1892 by two Springfield (Massachusetts) YMCA college instructors, Luther Gulick and James Naismith. They sought to devise a competitive sport that would be less rough than football and that could be played indoors, thus avoiding the loss of interest in physical activity which occurred among many students during the winter months. Their fast-moving game proved to be enormously popular, especially among smaller high schools. By 1945 it was being played by 98 per cent of all American high schools, and perhaps as many as eighty million spectators a season were witnessing these contests. From coast to coast new high school gymnasiums were constructed to accommodate the thousands of people who wished to see basketball games.[25]

Other team sports which gained an interscholastic following were ice hockey, track and field, tennis, fencing, and baseball. With the exception of the last named, however, they did not begin to attract the enthusiastic attention and support given to football and basketball.[26]

Resistance among educational leaders to competitive and team athletics in schools generally weakened considerably by World War I. New conceptions of the curriculum and of methodology, in part stemming from the kindergarten movement and in part from the Neo-Herbartians and John Dewey, led to a readier acceptance of the idea of play, team sports, and physical recreation in secondary schools. Sports and games, according to this viewpoint, would help "adjust" the youth to life. They would influence young people in the direction of better citizenship, teamwork, and good sportsmanship. They would help assimilate and "Americanize" children from diverse ethnic and racial backgrounds and effectively "democratize" the coming generation.

[24] *Ibid.*, pp. 825-26; John A. Krout, *Annals of American Sport* (New Haven, Conn.: Yale University Press, 1929), pp. 258-59.

[25] Ethel J. Dorgan, *Luther Halsey Gulick* (New York Teachers College, Columbia University Press, 1934), pp. 34-35; William A. Healey, *Coaching and Managing High School Basketball* (Danville, Ill.: The Interstate Printers & Publishers, Inc., 1945), pp. 20-22.

[26] Elmer D. Mitchell, *et al.*, *World History of Physical Education* (Englewood Cliffs, N.J.: Prentice-Hall, Inc., 1953).

In 1903 Luther Gulick, director of physical training of the New York City public schools, succeeded in organizing a Public School Athletic League. Backed by many well-known individuals and private organizations, the League staged track and field meets, as well as many other athletic competitions. In 1907 there were 106 baseball teams competing under its program. The basic purpose of the organization was to "provide healthful, joyous, and constructive play, folk dancing, and athletics for every boy and girl." [27] Seventeen other American cities formed similar school athletic associations patterned on the one in New York.[28] The school sports movement received further encouragement from the Playground and Recreation Association of America, founded in 1906, which was sponsoring the establishment of urban playgrounds and stressing the value of out-of-door play. The organized camp movement and the Boys and Girls Club movement similarly made rapid progress at this time, strengthening the public's interest in providing opportunities for organized recreation for school children. There were also increasing community demands now for "wider use of the school plant," a concept notably appealing to taxpayers. This new attitude was gradually opening up school gymnasiums and playgrounds to all types of physical recreation and competitive sport.[29]

The increased interest in high school sports necessitated standardization of policies, resulting in the founding of a number of athletic associations. Once again the high schools followed a pattern established by the colleges. (In 1905, after a particularly bad series of football injuries, the Intercollegiate Athletic Association of the United States had been created.) The first tentative step was usually the setting up of an organization within a single institution to establish rules for player eligibility and for other athletic practices. Then associations were formed between two or more schools, and finally a state-wide organization was formed. The first state associations appeared in the Middle West. By 1925, however, such organizations could be found in every state.[30]

In May, 1920, the secretary of the Illinois High School Athletic Association, L. W. Smith, invited representatives from neighboring states

[27] Lee F. Hammer, *Athletics in the Public Schools* (New York: Russell Sage Foundation, 1910), pp. 3-4.

[28] *Ibid.*, pp. 72-73; Scott, *Competitive Sports in Schools and Colleges*, pp. 42-43.

[29] Mitchell, *et al.*, *World History of Physical Training*; Cozens and Stumpf, *Sports in American Life*, pp. 70-71; Elmer D. Mitchell and Bernard Mason, *The Theory of Play* (New York: A. S. Barnes & Co., 1941), p. 42.

[30] George E. Shepard and Richard E. Jamerson, *Interscholastic Athletics* (New York: McGraw-Hill, Inc., 1953), pp. 20-21; Cozens and Stumpf, *op. cit.*, p. 74; Scott, *Competitive Sports in Schools and Colleges*, p. 35.

to Chicago to discuss establishing an organization with wider scope. The result was the formation of the Midwest Federation of State High School Athletic Associations. This organization proved to be so successful that it was quickly converted into a national one. In 1922 representatives from 11 states combined to establish the National Federation of State High School Athletic Associations. Eventually most of the state associations affiliated themselves with this central body. Among other things, it formulated national policies with respect to sports equipment, eligibility regulations, and interstate competition. It worked in close collaboration with the National Collegiate Athletic Association, the Amateur Athletic Union, the YMCA, and the Canadian Physical Education Association to standardize or revise the rules for the major competitive sports.[31]

At first, competitive sports were entirely extracurricular, with only small groups of students participating. As Elmer Mitchell related, "both of the more prominent departments of physical exercise, to wit, Physical Education and Varsity Athletics, were so concerned with their own needs that the athletic needs of the great mass of students were almost entirely neglected." [32] By the mid-1920's, however, some schoolmen attempted to bridge the gap between athletic sports and formal physical education in an effort to make some of the presumed values of the former available to the students who were required to take work in the latter.

This was the intention of the state of California when it introduced school sports programs for the mass of the students. A number of other states followed suit, and the emphasis in physical education began to change gradually from formal gymnastics to sports. In general, the impact of World War I heightened public interest in health questions and physical fitness training. By 1929, 27 state legislatures had enacted legislation making physical education and health care compulsory in the public schools.[33] The profession of physical education and sports coaching grew by leaps and bounds. From 1918 to 1950, the number of men and women employed in the profession increased approximately from 10,000 to 75,000.[34]

[31] Charles E. Forsythe, *The Administration of High School Athletics* (Englewood Cliffs, N.J.: Prentice-Hall, Inc., 1948), pp. 10-19; Mitchell, *et al., op. cit.*; Scott, *op. cit.*, pp. 35-36; Shepard and Jamerson, *op. cit.*, p. 21.
    [32] Elmer D. Mitchell, *Intra-Mural Sports* (New York: A. S. Barnes & Co., 1939), p. 4.
    [33] Cozens and Stumpf, *Sports in American Life*, pp. 80-82.
    [34] Scott, *op. cit.*, p. 48; Bruce L. Bennett, "Contributions of Dr. Sargent to Physical Education," *Research Quarterly* (May 1948), pp. 78-86.

Experience in World War I with sports competition between members of the armed forces helped foster spectator interest; the decade which followed was characterized by a veritable "boom" in sports. Public demand now led to the building of stadiums and gymnasiums on the grounds of schools and colleges. Professional training programs in colleges and universities designed for prospective physical educators and coaches became more elaborate and diversified.[35]

An even more ambitious attempt to bridge the gap between physical education and interscholastic athletics was represented by the intramurals movement. This program of organized team competition between groups drawn from the general student body within a school began to gain a significant foothold in the colleges about 1915. Under the banner of "athletics for all," intramurals began to penetrate the junior and senior high schools approximately ten years later. In some schools, groupings made in physical education were carried over into intramural activities. Much more common, however, were formation of teams by grades, classes, and home rooms. Despite the fact that much greater numbers of children directly participated in these programs than in interscholastic competition, few schools awarded credit for such activity, and intramural contests were usually held in after-school hours. The student interested in participating, wrote one specialist, "either for competition or recreation, . . . should be permitted his chance just as much so as the student who tries out for the varsity, or the student who prefers to follow music, debating, dramatics, reading, or some other specialty or hobby." [36]

What, then, are we to conclude with respect to the relationship between interscholastic athletics and the physical education programs of the public schools? P. R. Brammell, after making a survey of hundreds of junior and senior high schools in the early 1930's, found that interscholastic athletics were largely independent of, and often dominated,, other phases of the physical education program. At some schools when new playing fields, gymnasiums, or stadiums were constructed, no thought was given to the possibility of making these facilities serve both athletics and physical education. Sometimes such installations were located too far from the school building to be of any use to physical

[35] Cozens and Stumpf, op. cit., pp. 81-82; H. Harrison Clarke, "The Extent of Graduate Study in Physical Education in the United States," Journal of Health and Physical Education, V (April 1934), pp. 31-33.
[36] Mitchell, Intra-Mural Sports, p. 14; see also Mitchell and Mason, Theory of Play, p. 43; P. Roy Brammell, Intramural and Interscholastic Athletics (Washington, D.C.: Government Printing Office, 1933), pp. 44-47.

education classes during the day. Very often these structures were equipped only for interscholastic sports and had dressing rooms, showers, and lockers that accommodated small groups only. Furthermore, Brammell's survey revealed that interscholastic competition was confined mainly to a few sports, "most of which have no recognized carry-over value." The sports in which the largest number of pupils participated were not necessarily the sports having the longest playing seasons. In listing problems in connection with school sports programs, the one pointed out to Brammell as the most serious was that too few students derived benefit of any kind from these activities. Next in order, educators were concerned that many communities tended to rank the success of their schools in terms of the records of athletic teams. Also frequently mentioned were the physical hazards which menaced interscholastic contestants, and the problems presented by the offering of financial inducements to high school athletes by private individuals— alumni, businessmen, and persons interested in recruiting for college teams.[37]

The last point brings up the moot question of economic motivation. In 1933, Brammell reported, the amount of money spent in American schools for interscholastic athletics was greater than for any other extra-curricular activity. In 16 high schools visited by him the average amount of money taken in during the football season was $2,230. In one year the total athletic activities fund in Upper Darby Senior High School in Pennsylvania reached $43,231.[38] Practically all of these school systems required their interscholastic athletic programs to be self-supporting, with the exception of coaching salaries which were usually paid by the local Board of Education. Where then did the money come from? Some of it was raised by an activity fee levied on, or available to, all students. Some of it was derived from the receipts of school carnivals, magazine sales, suppers, plays, card parties, Parent-Teacher Association events, individual gifts, school store profits, and civic club contributions. Another source of revenue was income from concessions for the sale of pennants, souvenirs, stickers, foods, drinks, and game programs. The bulk of the support for interscholastic athletics however, came from gate receipts. This hard fact, in turn, created a situation where schools almost inevitably wished to have winning teams in order to attract bigger crowds which would mean larger gate receipts. Commented Shepard

[37] Brammell, *Intramural and Interscholastic Athletics*, pp. 104-9, 140-43.
[38] *Ibid.*, pp. 81-93.

and Jamerson: "Many of the current malpractices, unfavorable attitudes, and poorly administered athletic programs stem from the necessity of financing the total program from gate receipts." [39]

Frederick Rogers was of the opinion that there were other factors at work besides the financial need for winning teams that kept public interest in interscholastic sports at a fever pitch. The press constituted one such force. The *New York Times* during one week in November, 1888, carried only 151 inches of news of interscholastic and intercollegiate athletics; for a comparable week in November, 1928, the total had grown to an incredible 2,433 inches! "Sports writers," declared Rogers, "are determined to maintain this journalistic emphasis in order to preserve their prestige and pecuniary safety." Newspaper publishers were acting on the belief that sports news sold perhaps a fourth of their papers. A 1928 study of five New York metropolitan dailies made by Henry Fairfield Osborne and Charles N. Nager at the Columbia School of Journalism showed that 9 per cent of all newspaper space was devoted to sports. This percentage was more than that devoted to any other single news topic, and was surpassed only by fashion advertising, which claimed 16½ per cent. Nevertheless, sports ranked far ahead of domestic news, foreign news, and the like.[40]

Another group with a vested interest in maintaining and heightening the public's enthusiasm for interscholastic and intercollegiate athletics was the sporting goods manufacturers, retailers, and salesmen. In 1899, according to statistics compiled by the United States Department of Commerce, there were only 217 manufacturing establishments in this field, with a total of 2,934 employees and a value of goods shipped amounting to $5,277,000. By 1958 the number of factories had grown to 1,169, the total number of employees to 37,164, and the value of goods shipped to an impressive $577,815,000, or approximately one hundred times greater than the figure of 60 years before. In 1958, too sporting goods retail sales throughout the nation totaled $573,474,000.[41]

[39] Shepard and Jamerson, *Interscholastic Athletics*, pp. 164-67.
[40] Frederick R. Rogers, *Future of Interscholastic Athletics* (New York: Teachers College, Columbia University, 1929), pp. 10-14; see also James E. Sullivan, *Schoolyard Athletics* (New York: American Sports Publishing Co., 1909), for an example of the promotional work of a leading sports publisher.
[41] *Census of Business*, II (U.S. Department of Commerce [Washington, D.C., 1958]), 1-6; *Census of Manufacturing* (U.S. Department of Commerce [Washington, D.C., 1958]); *Industry Statistics* (U.S. Department of Commerce [Washington, D.C., 1958]), pp. 39-B-4, 5; A. B. Gunn, E. H. Clark, and F. C. White, *All-Around Athletics* (New York: American Sports Publishing Co., 1903).

By this time American manufacturers were happily turning out one and one-half million football, baseball, and basketball suits per year.[42] Over $6,000,000 annually were being spent just for helmets and pads, and over $21,000,000 for athletic shoes.[43]

Thus, the thriving world of school and college sports had given rise to a vast industry and an important element in the nation's prosperity. In the high schools the purchase of athletic equipment and supplies represented the largest item in the entire interscholastic sports budget.[44] By 1962 a Massachusetts coach estimated that it now cost nearly $5,000 simply to equip a high school ice hockey team for interscholastic competition.[45] Any move to "de-emphasize" school sports would have struck directly at not only the livelihood of thousands of salesmen, workers, and other employees, but also the investments, totaling many millions of dollars, of numerous stockholders. Therefore such people having a financial interest were quick to repel any and all attacks on interscholastic athletics. Furthermore, they would profit directly from any increase in the public's interest in such competition.[46]

The steadily growing army of coaches also had a vital pecuniary interest in the survival and growth of school sports. By 1928 it was estimated that there were at least 15,000 coaches of interscholastic teams in the United States. In many cases their success was evaluated by the local community in terms of their ability to turn out winning teams. Very often their salary averaged higher than that of other faculty members. In hiring such important personages, more attention was given to the candidate's own record as a player or builder of winning teams than to his training in physical education or any other field of education.[47] Any development which threatened to reduce or destroy public interest in interscholastic or intercollegiate competition would willy-nilly be stubbornly resisted by the numerous, well-organized coaching fraternity.

There were other persons, too, who had a personal stake in the continuing flourishing of school sports. Among such faithful lobbyists for sports we should not be surprised to find athletic managers, state athletic association secretaries, national sports officials, stadium maintenance workers, and, finally, the vastly influential persons who ran so-called

[42] "Sporting Goods," *Life*, 36 (March 22, 1954), pp. 115-23.
[43] Ernst and Ernst, *Athletic and Sporting Goods Sales for the 1960 Year* (Athletic Goods Manufacturers Association, 1961).
[44] Shepard and Jamerson, *Interscholastic Athletics*, p. 123.
[45] *The Sudbury Valley Advertiser* (Mass.), March 8, 1962, p. 8.
[46] Rogers, *Future of Interscholastic Athletics*, p. 15.
[47] Brammel, *Intramural and Interscholastic Athletics*, pp. 99-103.

"coaching schools" or clinics.[48] In some of these latter sessions, nationally famous football and basketball coaches conducted classes showing their high school *confreres* how to produce winning teams. At least one such clinic in New York State in 1958 was financed, interestingly enough, by A. G. Spalding Company, manufacturers of sports equipment.[49] Rogers, looking at the over-all picture, concluded accusingly, ". . . . Money plays a major role in interscholastic athletics, representing the ulterior motives and selfish aims of tens of thousands of highly trained, strategically placed, well-paid, and unusually alert and competitive adults." [50]

Many further studies have been made of the impact of organized sports upon the life of schools and colleges. The literature in the twentieth century has been particularly extensive, with many differing viewpoints expressed. More and more, however, the final assessment has been critical, not necessarily of athletics *per se*, but of commercialization and the all-too prevalent overemphasis on winning.[51]

It is not altogether surprising that many coaches and former players were ready to testify publicly to the virtues of interscholastic and intercollegiate competition, but they were by no means the only spokesmen for the cause. Some school administrators, whether because of background or personal preference, joined the sports professionals in putting a favorable estimate of athletics on the record. Ethel Percy Andrus, Principal of Lincoln High School in Los Angeles, told the NEA in 1917 that "the splendid school spirit" at her institution was "largely" due to its thorough and passionate involvement in interscholastic competition. The students and the team members had "learned the greatest lesson of good sportsmanship—to be good losers." [52] Expressing much the same point of view in 1923, T. C. Hart, chairman of the school board in Palatine Township, Illinois, argued that properly conducted school athletics would boost the morale of the students and townspeople. Team members would have an added incentive for attaining good grades in order to remain on the eligibility list. Athletic competition, furthermore, would act as "a sort of general drawing card for the school."

[48] Cozens and Stumpf, *Sports in American Life*, p. 81; Scott, *Competitive Sports in Schools and Colleges*, pp. 46-47; Harold C. Evans, "College Football in Kansas," *Kansas Historical Quarterly*, 9 (August 1940), pp. 310-11.

[49] *New York Times*, June 29, 1958.

[50] Rogers, *Future of Interscholastic Athletics*, pp. 18-19.

[51] W. Carson Ryan, Jr., *A Study of the Literature of American School and College Athletics* (New York: Carnegie Foundation for the Advancement of Teaching, 1929).

[52] Ethel Percy Andrus, "School Spirit," *NEA Proceedings* (1917), pp. 528-30.

Through interest in the local athletic teams, "the public is gradually drawn into acquaintance with the school itself and becomes familiar with the institution, its position in the community, and its hopes, its aims, and its needs." [53]

From the standpoint of educational sociology, Willard Waller conceded that there might be a basis for some of the preceding claims. Interscholastic athletics did as a matter of fact have the effect of unifying an entire student body in support of a common objective. Moreover, a skillful use of the athletic craze among students might "simplify the problem of police work in the school." The highly influential team members could be used as a kind of extension of faculty control. "It is a powerful machine which is organized to whip all students into line for the support of athletic teams," Waller observed, "and adroit school administrators learn to use it for the dissemination of other attitudes favorable to the faculty and the faculty policy." [54]

One of the most frequent arguments advanced by coaches, physical educators, and others on behalf of competitive athletics was that it possessed superb character-building potentialities. Such was the argument used by Walter Camp, perhaps the most renowned coach and rule-maker in the early history of American football.[55] "We wish," he wrote, "to have every man . . . take his athletics in the highest spirit. He should in the best sense 'play the game' fairly, honestly, and earnestly. . . . In fact, he is better prepared by his athletic experience in school and college to take up the drudgery at the bottom than a man who has not acquired exactly that experience in sports. . . ." [56] Writing in a similar vein, Abel J. Gregg, an active worker in the YMCA athletic program, argued that basketball leagues could play an important part in inculcating ideals of sportsmanship and Christian character. Such games, however, should not be used merely as an incentive to increase Sunday school attendance. It should be recognized, he insisted, that they were intrinsically valuable *in themselves* in leading to character development.[57]

Other commentators on school sports were less sure that such activities

---

[53] T. C. Hart, "Athletics as an Aid to School Morale," *Education* (March 1923) pp. 434-39.

[54] Waller, *Sociology of Teaching*, pp. 116-20.

[55] See the biographical sketch by Norris G. Osborne in *Dictionary of American Biography*, III, pp. 444-45.

[56] Walter Camp, *Athletes All* (New York: Charles Scribner's Sons, 1919), p. 275

[57] Abel J. Gregg, ed., *Basketball and Character* (New York: Association Press 1934), pp. 5-11.

were leading to beneficial results. Attacks on abuses in intercollegiate sports date back at least as far as the 1870's. Indeed, for a period of time in the late Eighties, the Harvard authorities prohibited all participation in intercollegiate football. Indictments by responsible educators, plus a revulsion of public feeling following a number of appalling football injuries, led in 1905 to the historic intercollegiate conference which modified the rules of the game and set up a more effective general supervisory organization.[58]

As early as 1924, William Geer, Director of Physical Education at Harvard, listed a number of weak points in secondary school athletics, including pre-season coaching, playing of post-season games in response to pressure from alumni and other "boosters," a mania for state and national championships, unnecessary showering of honors and gifts on winning athletes, and commercialism in athletic administration due to the drive for larger gate receipts. Such unsavory phenomena, Geer caustically remarked, made a mockery of sportsmanship and school loyalty. The root cause, in his opinion, was the failure to maintain firm institutional control of, and responsibility for, interscholastic competition.[59]

Five years later, as high school athletics assumed more and more the proportions of a "big-time" operation, Frederick Rogers excoriated what he called the "painfully ludicrous" copying of intercollegiate competition by secondary schools. Just as leading college towns take Roman holidays on football days, he said, "so does Gopher Prairie bedeck itself for its own high school games. Local newspapers announce the victors and scores in front-page headlines of the same size as those used to announce a new president of the United States. The teams have their pictures on the sporting page; and private trains are chartered to transport townspeople to state championship contests."

Rogers was convinced that most of the harmful aspects of schoolboy sports resulted from pernicious adult interference (usually by outsiders) which overorganized and excessively commercialized what otherwise might be healthy and spontaneous leisure-time activity. The elaborate system of sports leagues, associations, and championships had been developed and was being controlled, in his opinion, by nonplayers who had "wholly selfish adult motives almost irrespective of the interests of players." School administrators and coaches, he charged, cared more "for the advertisement of their own cleverness or for the advertisement of

[58] Ryan, *Literature of School and College Athletics*, pp. xxi-xxiii.
[59] William Geer, "Athletic Situation in High Schools."

their departments or schools than for the physical, mental, or social development of their pupils." Gain, usually pecuniary gain, was often the sole motive.[60]

A similar argument was presented by Reed Harris, a young Left-Wing editor of the Columbia University *Spectator*. Expelled in 1932 from the university by President Butler for, among other things, protesting conditions in the school's dining halls, Harris promptly penned a bitter diatribe against intercollegiate athletics which he entitled *King Football*. "The god of materialism," he asserted, "has an able high priest in King Football." Students were being taught, not how to think or how to acquire knowledge, but rather to appreciate football, fraternities, and bridge. This state of affairs had come to pass, Harris surmised, because in large part education in America was thought to be "for everyone." The average student had to be carefully coddled and distracted with inanities like football. American centers of learning were turning out hundreds of thousands of unthinking, rigid conformists each year, he bitterly declared. "Instead of weeding out from the student body those who are not concerned with the intellectual opportunities offered, our universities adjust their courses to conform to the aptitudes and abilities of the students. The emphasis . . . is, therefore, upon making the system suitable for the exalted 'average man.' " [61]

By way of a partial rebuttal, ex-player Barry Wood published a cautious analysis of organized athletics. Wood conceded that football might be run as "a commercial racket" in some institutions, but he insisted that this did not need to be the case. The key to the situation was the school's athletic director. A competent man in this post could check ballyhoo, overemphasis, and commercialism and could preserve football as a healthy competitive sport for young people. Overemphasis, he maintained, was due ultimately not to players, coaches, or even athletic directors, but to "His Majesty, the spectator." In the last analysis, then, it was the public which was responsible for the abuses that had crept into school sports. Too many "old grads" were hot for victory at any price. When the public's attitude changed for the better, conditions would improve.[62]

Many years later, Francis Wallace, one-time athletic director at a

[60] Rogers, *Future of the Interscholastic Athletics*, pp. 8-14, 128-30.

[61] Reed Harris, *King Football* (New York: Vanguard Press, 1932), pp. 16-17, 163, 241-52.

[62] Barry Wood, *What Price Football?* (Boston: Houghton Mifflin Company, 1932), pp. 154-58.

large university, thoroughly reviewed the situation. Amateur athletics in schools and colleges, he declared in 1951, shaped up "like a Rube Goldberg invention." Why so? Because, he pointed out, "everybody knows there hasn't been an honest amateur in big-time football for quite some time now. The faculty men certainly know because, in one form or another, they are the people who permit or condone the pay." The schools realized that they could not make money without a winning team; "that they cannot have a winning team without superior players; that to get superior players, most of whom are poor boys, somebody must provide some financial assistance. . . ." The result, according to Wallace, was "a four-year course in deception, a bootlegging system that closely parallels prohibition days, with the only crime being careless or indiscreet enough to be caught." [63]

Agreeing regretfully with these conclusions was Richard Miller, a former physical education teacher and high school football player. Football as it was being conducted, he wrote, "serves neither amateurism nor the sports ideal." Instead, it was a form of big business, "deleterious in its effects upon both the athlete and the nonathlete and the sponsoring institution itself." Small schools were losing money on the game, due to soaring costs. Teams at big colleges required expenditures as high as $200,000 to $400,000 per season. For example, each University of North Carolina player needed a new $18 pair of shoes per season. The squad wardrobe consisted of 146 complete uniforms at $132 each. The latest type of plastic headgear cost nearly as much as a whole uniform did in the 1920's.[64]

Additional problems were specified in a report issued in the same year as Miller's book by the Educational Policies Commission of the NEA. Overemphasis on high school varsity teams, according to this publication, was bringing pressure upon teachers to excuse athletes from regular assignments or to lower academic standards in order to keep such players on the eligibility list. The Educational Policies Commission report called particular attention to the pressure on high school coaches to produce winning teams. Their tenure and status in the community often depended on such results, and they were driven in too many instances to questionable means in order to succeed. They might

[63] Francis Wallace, *Dementia Pigskin* (New York: Holt, Rinehart & Winston, Inc., 1951), pp. 21-22.

[64] Richard I. Miller, *Truth About Football* (New York: William Sloane Associates, Inc., 1953), pp. 2-31.

even "pursue a program that may result in athletes injuring health or sacrificing character." [65] Richard Miller mentioned a number of such ugly incidents on the college level of deliberate injuries inflicted on stars of rival teams in order to win games. He added: "Today, with the 'get-away-with-what-you-can' viewpoint altogether too common in daily living, it is not surprising that some of this attitude has rubbed off on football players. The unfortunate thing is the lack of positive correction on the part of many coaches." [66]

Peter Dawkins, a West Point football star who went to England for postgraduate study, called attention in the *New York Times* in 1960 to the win-at-all-costs psychosis that characterized the whole American attitude toward competitive sport. At English schools and universities, Dawkins found, young people played games such as rugby for the sheer love of the game. The fun of playing was more important for them than winning or losing. In American schools and colleges practically anything that a player could "get away with" was considered appropriate as long as it contributed to victory. [67] According to Dr. James B. Conant, as he toured the country making his study of public junior and senior high schools, again and again at the end of one of his visits, after discussing curriculum and teaching problems, a superintendent would tell him: "We haven't yet talked about my chief problem which, to be quite frank, is the record of the high school teams. Let's face it—what this city demands is that I get coaches whose teams will win, or out I go." [68]

The dependence on gate receipts to support a school's athletic program contributed, in the opinion of the Educational Policies Commission, to more than just an overemphasis on winning. Additional abuses resulting from this situation included scheduling of games at night or cramming the schedule with too many games. In both cases, the objective was obviously to make as much money as possible. In addition, schools very often would play games in bad weather, endangering the health of the players, in order, among other reasons, not to forego anticipated income. Then, too, games would very often be scheduled with unequal opponents in order to build up a winning record. To ac-

[65] *School Athletics* (Washington, D.C.: National Education Association, Educational Policies Commission, 1954).

[66] Miller, *Truth About Football*, pp. 54-55.

[67] Peter Dawkins, "We Play to Win, They Play for Fun," *New York Times Magazine*, April 24, 1960, pp. 34-35.

[68] James B. Conant, "Athletics, The Poison Ivy in Our Schools," *Look*, 25 (January 17, 1961), p. 58.

commodate larger and larger paying crowds, some schools even winked at violations of fire and safety codes. Financial aid, moreover, was frequently forthcoming to school athletic programs from "downtown merchants" and "interested citizens" who made direct contributions or bought advertising space in the programs sold at the games. These patrons subsequently felt that they had by such benefactions acquired a vested right to determine the local school system's athletic policy.[69]

The Commission further noted that the kind of sports craze generated in some towns by excessive emphasis on winning led to "problems of crowd conduct that are harmful to students and troublesome for the school staff." Members of opposing teams in such places were regarded as enemies and reviled and jeered. Game officials became "targets for primitive, hysterical outbursts of derision, sometimes resulting in physical violence. . . . Appreciation of the game is lost in the wildly partisan, unsportsmanlike manifestations of the crowd." [70] In 1959 post-game violence of this kind was all too obvious in various communities in Massachusetts. Following the Foxboro–Mansfield high school game, the "customary" football victory riot that ended in ripping up the goal posts led to the killing of a teenage girl who was struck by one of the metal posts. Foxboro police were too busy breaking up fist fights to stop the crowd of more than 100 students that assaulted the posts. Meanwhile, in Everett five men under the grandstand after a game tried to beat up a police sergeant with whiskey bottles. In Lynn girl cheerleaders were assaulted. In Watertown a mob staged a battle outside the football field. Three years later, following a Nashua (New Hampshire)– Lowell (Massachusetts) high school football game, a Nashua girl was admitted to the hospital with head and other injuries after being attacked by three Lowell girls, and a Nashua boy had a bone broken in his neck by a rock thrown through the rear window of a car in which he was riding. Another Nashua youth was charged with assault and battery on a police officer and drunkenness.

A further disparaging aspect of interscholastic–intercollegiate football competition reported on by the Educational Policies Commission was the bad athletic practice resulting from the interest of colleges in recruiting star high school players for their teams. This pernicious system demoralized not only the colleges involved but also the high schools. Teenage boys were taken to a college campus, entertained lavishly, and given "tryouts." Attractive financial inducements were dangled before

---

[69] *School Athletics* (Educational Policies Commission).
[70] *Ibid*.

their eyes. Admission requirements were blandly waived or evaded for them.

A high school principal wrote to Dr. Conant in the late 1950's: "Until Bill _____ came along, our quiet little school was virtually unknown to the overwhelming majority of collegiate institutions. However, thanks to the tremendous physical ability of this lad, our school became a virtual meeting place of admission officers and college coaches. . . . Bill finally went to _____, where he received a full scholarship, private tutoring to make certain he passed his courses (in physical education and business education), a job for his father on the campus, a low-rent apartment for the family, and spending money, exact sum unknown." [71]

What concepts of life would be fostered among young people who discovered that opportunities for a "college education" were more readily available to star athletes than to those who ranked high in scholarship? Miller asked whether such scandals as the college basketball prosecution of 1951 were due, not only to the machinations of professional gamblers and "fixers," but to the fact that coaches and schools had permitted recruiting of athletes to proceed "in such a manner that the boys concerned found little difference between original inducements and the bribes later offered to them by gamblers." [72]

One of the most widely criticized aspects of American football was the serious incidence of physical injury to players. In 1931 the University of Michigan coach Fielding Yost compiled a list of fatalities directly chargeable to football and found that there had been 21 such deaths in one year. Seven of the fatalities occurred among college players, seven among high school players, and seven among "sandlot" players.[73] Other studies of the injury problem resulted in equally grim findings.[74] Even more depressing was the circumstance that some football fatalities among high school players tended to occur during so-called "pre-season" practice, before the regular season's games had even begun. Such early practice was usually banned by state interscholastic athletic associations, but the striving for victory on the part of some high schools was so great that they brazenly violated the ban. It was just such an illegal session which resulted in the death in August, 1962, of a fourteen-year-old football player for St. Cecilia High School of Englewood, New

[71] Conant, "Athletics, The Poison Ivy in Our Schools," pp. 59-60.

[72] Miller, *Truth About Football*, p. 68; on this topic see also Cozens and Stumpf, *Sports in American Life*, pp. 90-92.

[73] Fielding Yost, *Football Fatalities of 1931* (n.p., 1932?).

[74] Ryan, *Literature of School and College Athletics*, pp. XXXIV-XXXIX.

Jersey. Death was due to a cardiac malfunction. Since the New Jersey State Interscholastic Athletic Association prohibited football teams from starting practice before September 1st, St. Cecilia secretly sent its entire team out of the state to "work out" at the Carmelite Seminary in Hamilton, Massachusetts. The St. Cecilia coach Ralph Cavalucci explained to the press: "I felt that a three-week period was insufficient to get our team in shape for the opening game." St. Cecilia, by the way, had won the Tri-County championship the previous year. Other schoolboy deaths occurred during the same month in the course of early practice sessions. A fourteen-year-old student of Xenia, Ohio, died of a brain hemorrhage suffered during pre-season practice with the John Carroll High School football squad. A fifteen-year-old member of the Gillespie, Illinois, High School team died shortly after another pre-season workout.[75]

Most stultifying of all was the fact that after several decades of emphasis, indeed overemphasis, on big-time sports in their schools and colleges, Americans were less physically fit than ever. In December, 1961, President John F. Kennedy noted that five out of every seven young men called up for army service were being rejected. Three of these rejections were because of physical defects and two for mental disabilities. The President observed that the rejection rate was increasing year by year; this discouraging trend indicated that the American people were underexercised and had become a nation of spectators.

One of the most perplexing problems posed by the craze for interscholastic sports, which the Educational Policies Commission was quick to spotlight, was "the effort to introduce highly organized varsity-type competition in elementary schools and junior high schools." [76] This movement reached giant proportions in the years following World War II, much in the same way that the vogue for high school competition had developed following World War I. The public allegedly demanded it. This public demand, however, may very well have been stimulated purposefully and skillfully (despite warnings from medical and recreational authorities) by interested parties with special axes to grind.[77] Child-sports promotion appealed to high school coaches as a means of establishing "feeder lines" whereby they could recruit talent in the junior high schools for their varsity football and basketball teams.

[75] New York Times, August 30, 1962, p. 21.
[76] Mortimer H. Morris, "Does Sports Equal Fitness?" New Republic (April 29, 1957).
[77] School Athletics (Educational Policies Commission), pp. 32-35.

Manufacturers and salesmen of athletic equipment quickly recognized in the competition of teams made up of young children a vast new market for their products and moved in every way they dared to encourage the novel trend. Shrewd local promotors found that they could create profitable jobs for themselves setting up "little league" baseball, "Pop Warner" football, "Biddy" basketball, and even "Iddy Biddy" basketball. Some imaginative entrepreneurs made efforts to spread the burgeoning midget fad to tennis, golf, auto racing, boxing, and ice hockey! Local sponsors and merchants were quick to back these programs, no doubt recognizing the advertising possibilities of using the participating children as "baby billboards." [78]

These ingenious athletic promotions very soon reached intersectional proportions. Thus, on Thanksgiving Day, 1961, a "Turkey Bowl" football game was played at Elizabeth City, North Carolina, between the "champs" of the Long Island Midget Football League, representing the Grenville Baker Boys Club of Locust Valley, Long Island, and the midget all-star team from the Elizabeth City Boys Club. Both groups were affiliated with the Boys Clubs of America. The players ranged in age from ten to twelve and averaged 100 pounds to 108 pounds in weight. The star of the Long Island team was its 85-pound halfback, Carmine Abate. Despite his 4′ 9″ size, this twelve-year-old had scored ten touchdowns and seven extra points during the season. Hank Banach, 106-pound quarterback of the team, and also twelve, was quoted as saying: "I think it's about the best thing that ever happened to me. I didn't think I'd ever get to play in a bowl game—except in college." More than 150 proud-as-punch parents and other relatives drove to North Carolina with the excited children. The boys were entertained by generous North Carolina hosts at a Thanksgiving dinner and even attended a dance after the game.

Public school systems by the hundreds joined the bandwagon in the 1950's and introduced competitive team sports for younger boys. Pleading sheer self-defense, public schoolmen argued that unless the schools did something about the matter, it would be impossible to head off community-run sports programs organized by commercial promoters outside the schools and aimed at children as young as eight or nine! Such unsupervised and uncontrolled sports leagues would be more dangerous to the health of the children than would regular interscholastic compe-

[78] Morris, *op. cit.*, p. 14; George Weinstein, "Can Junior Football Hurt Your Boy?" *Good Housekeeping*, 151 (October 1960), pp. 167-68.

tition.[79] In any event, it soon became clear what form this "regularized" sports competition among children of pre-high school age would assume. Soon football games were being played in stadiums at night (with admission being charged) between junior high school teams made up of twelve- and thirteen-year-old boys. Marching bands of children pranced up and down the field, majorettes cavorted, and cheerleaders howled, all aping the hallowed tradition of big-time college games.[80]

The interest of high school coaches in such goings-on was enthusiastic. A director of school health services in a Texas city was quoted in 1960 as saying: "In some of our junior high schools, there is as much or more time spent on pep rallies and encouraging the boys to go out there and win for the glory of the school as there is in senior high schools. We have several towns even in Texas that have organized football from the fourth grade up. Coaches for the various elementary schools are selected, as I understand it, on the recommendation and approval of the head coach, in order that they be taught the style of football the coaches want the boys to play when they reach senior high school." In Steubenville, Ohio, a more-than-ordinarily football-mad town, the entire physical training program in the elementary and secondary schools was geared to one objective—the grinding out of material for the high school team, which was a perennial contender for the state championship. Six coaches were assigned to leagues starting at the fifth-grade level. These men had the assigned mission of putting interested youngsters through a spartan system of high-powered drills and grueling competition to get them ready for the high school varsity. "By the time they come to the varsity," the local high school coach was smugly quoted as saying, "we don't have to waste much time."

A succession of reputable medical and physical education experts testified, to no avail, that children under fourteen were not mature enough for hard contact sports such as football, and that the risk of permanent bone and joint injuries was great. Strenuous and fatiguing competition of this kind, they warned, could put a damaging overload on immature lungs, hearts, kidneys, and brains. To make matters worse, in many communities medical supervision of the junior footballers was totally inadequate. In one town in the late 1950's, a junior high school squad started its football practice without even a pretense at a medical

[79] Conant, "Athletics, The Poison Ivy in Our Schools," p. 57; Weinstein, *op. cit.*, pp. 166-68.
[80] Morris, *op. cit.*, pp. 14-15; Conant, *op. cit.*, pp. 57-58.

examination, and on the very first day of the workouts a child-player dropped dead of a heart ailment. In many institutions it was left to the discretion of the coach, not an attending physician, whether an injured youngster continued in a game. Furthermore, few elementary or junior high schools could afford the expensive equipment which was necessary to help safeguard the players. Their teams might therefore go into action without helmets and safety pads, or with old helmets with the padding worn "so thin that when a boy was hit, the hard shell passed it on to the skull, instead of absorbing the blow." Also dangerous was the condition of many of the playing fields. Several deaths among the junior high school age group in 1959 were due to the hard, poorly grassed, or even stony fields on which the youngsters were gamely trying to perform.

What, we may ask then, was the great appeal of interscholastic athletics to the youngsters participating in them? It was clearly not just physical exercise or recreation, not just boyish fun—there was too much commercialized hoopla, too much high-powered publicity and organization, too much fanatical community identification with the fortunes of the picked varsity gladiators for the above to be the explanation. It appears, rather, that the motivating force, much like that of the American adults who sponsored these circus-style competitions, may well have been a drive for prestige. A thoughtful eleventh-grade boy in a midwestern high school put it this way in an interview with a sociologist:

> The athletic field is definitely an important basis of prestige. In order to be a success on the athletic field, you usually have a good physical make-up and a good personality. These traits are much sought after and important. The amount of prestige you gain from athletics depends on the sport you participate in. Basketball rates highest, football next, baseball, track, wrestling and tennis is the lowest, I think.
>
> If you are a good basketball player, you get a lot of prestige. In dating this is most important. If a girl is asked out to a dance by the star center of the basketball team or the star halfback of the football team, she will probably be more thrilled than if some nobody asks her. This is for the first few dates, but after the get-acquainted period, the personality is what determines how long the two will go together.
>
> The reason sports are so important in school, I would think, is first, because they make money, that is, some of them do. They are a social event. Then there is the school spirit point of view. Which team is better as referred to which school is better. Then, if you were on the team it is an accepted way of showing off or bragging of what you can do.
>
> Another thing, the school has a better chance to witness your work

more than they do, say, the work of the president of the class. These factors are what make sports an important prestige builder-upper.[81]

Why did not the American school and its supporting community make as great a hero of the star scholar as it did of the star varsity athlete? Big-time sports were inherently nonintellectual and nonscholarly, but had a marked entertainment value. Therefore the vast majority in the community could enthusiastically support and appreciate sports without feeling resentful or inferior. The achievements of star athletes were more highly "visible" and more readily comprehensible to the masses than those of star scholars, and the school and town population could therefore identify more readily with the former than with the latter.

The emotional drives aroused by fighting in harness with other team members for a common cause and "winning for the school" were deep-seated in the human personality. Commenting on the worth of school sports, Luther Gulick saw that "their final justification is in the spirit of the athletes, the loyalty to school, the social consciousness which includes in its grasp all the students, not merely those who compete." [82] So basic to youth was the honor and appeal of competing on teams for the glory of the greater social organism, the school, that sociologist James Coleman dreamt of harnessing the drive for intellectual purposes. This could be done, he wrote, by substituting as much as possible interscholastic and intramural competition in *scholarly* matters (through contests, science fairs, debate teams, current events tournaments, and the like) for interpersonal competition for grades, which had always existed.[83]

There is one other factor which may help to explain the vogue for interscholastic athletics in the United States. A perceptive British observer, Denis W. Brogan of Cambridge University, may have put his finger on it when he noted that in a nation of immigrants, "the political function of the schools is to teach Americanism, meaning not merely political and patriotic dogma, but the habits necessary to American life." And interscholastic sport, as he saw it, was a uniquely American vehicle for speeding up this "Americanization," this acceptance. It united parents, children, and community—*E Pluribus Unum.* New-

[81] Gordon, *The Social System of the High School*, p. 104.
[82] Ryan, *Literature of Athletics*, pp. xx-xxi.
[83] Coleman, *Adolescent Society*.

comers gifted with the ability to excel in competitive athletic contests were able to win quickly personal, community, and institutional glory. Professor Brogan continued:

> The main political achievement of the high schools and grammar schools is to bring together the young of all classes and origins, to provide, artificially, the common background that in an old, rural society is provided by tradition, by the necessary collaboration of village life. The elementary schools—the "grade" schools—do this, too, but as far as an American town is broken up into racial blocs, the Ethan Allen Public School may have mainly Polish pupils, the Zachary Chandler mainly Welsh. Only in the Warren G. Harding High School is [there] a big enough common pool formed in which Americans can be made. . . .
>
> . . . . a Greek would know where he was at a basketball game uniting boys and girls, parents and civic leaders, in a common passion for competitive achievement. . . . And sport is rigorously democratic. The sons of Czechs and Poles can score there, can break through the barriers that stand in the way of the children of "Bohunks" and "Polacks." . . . The Ohio high school that produced the great Negro runner, Jesse Owens, was prouder of him than if he had made Phi Beta Kappa at Ohio State. . . . The great athlete performing for the glory of the school, college, state, or nation is a less egotistic figure than the great scholar pursuing his own studies with an undemocratic concentration. . . .
>
> The cheer leaders, the new "jongleurs de Notre Dame," the "majorettes," shapely young women more or less involved with musical instruments, the massed cheering sections of the students, the massed yelling sections of the alumni—these are the equivalent of the crowds at the great Hellenic festivals in which barbarians were not allowed to compete. The Rose Bowl, the Cotton Bowl, the other intersectional games—these are instruments of national unity. . . .[84]

Granted that the school sports mania was produced by the peculiar circumstances of a polyglot society and its basically democratic and equalitarian bias, we may well ask whether America, or any other nation, could afford such overemphasis on competitive athletics in an era of Sputniks and thermonuclear bombs. James B. Conant, former president of Harvard University, answered this question with an emphatic No! Writing for a national magazine in January, 1961, Conant described big-time varsity athletics as the "poison ivy" which had crept into American schools. Conant pointed out that overemphasis on athletics was one big reason why American school systems were hard put to keep up with the intellectual quality of European schools. He reminded his

[84] Denis W. Brogan, *The American Character* (New York: Alfred A. Knopf, Inc., 1944), pp. 136-37, 141-43.

readers that "there is no equivalent in Europe for interscholastic athletic competitions with marching bands." He recalled American schools he had visited "in which the life of the school revolves around the athletic field, not the classroom." In such schools children were being "conditioned to become future members of a cheering section. A child sees such a school not as a place to develop his own intellectual and physical talents, but as a place to applaud the skillful performance of athletic heroes." There was a time, he remembered, "when cheerleaders were still amateurs and not yet trained in choreography, when there were no marching bands, no majorettes, no flag twirlers, no drill squads, no color guard." Should the function of a school, he asked, be the entertainment of the public? "Can we afford in these days of peril . . . the luxury of so much misdirected effort?" [85] American educators, community leaders, and parents would do well to give careful thought to Dr. Conant's question.

Nonathletic "Activities"

August B. Hollingshead, in the course of a study of social patterns in a small midwestern community, noted in 1949 that the "circus" features of the extracurricular program were by no means limited to athletic competitions. In Elmtown, he observed, "an elaborate extracurricular program brings the schools' activities before the public on a broader front than its teaching functions. This side of school life entertained "students, parents, and Elmtowners in their leisure time." They wanted their athletic teams to win games, their musical organizations to perform publicly at all possible times in a creditable manner, and their dramatics group to produce plays that would not be criticized but enjoyed. Furthermore those extracurricular activities that patently lacked spectator appeal and "broad public relations value," such as student government or subject-matter clubs, received little support from either the Board of Education or the community.[86]

The situation in Elmtown's schools during the 1940's was not necessarily atypical. There were a number of school systems where similar conditions existed. Paralleling the rise of interscholastic athletics, the first large-scale development of nonsports interests in pub-

---

[85] Conant, "Athletics, The Poison Ivy in Our Schools," pp. 57-60.
[86] August B. Hollingshead, *Elmtown's Youth: The Impact of Social Class on Adolescents* (New York: John Wiley & Sons, Inc., 1948), pp. 192-94.

lic high schools came in the years following World War I.[87] At this
time community after community was supporting the concept that the
adolescents who were thronging into the schools must be "prepared for
life." This meant in most cases that they must participate in extracurricular activities. Homerooms came to be utilized in many institutions
as a staging point from which students could be funneled into such
"socialized" goings-on.[88] Some schools (about *one-fifth* of those covered
in one extensive national survey in 1932) *required* that all students
participate in some activity of this sort.[89] In other schools pressures
from teachers and fellow students to participate were so great as to be
almost the equivalent of a requirement. Apparently the bookish lads or
lasses who went to school primarily to study were no longer to be permitted to go their own way without challenge.

The most popular side of the extracurriculum in a great number of
schools was that which had the greatest "show" value. Under these
circumstances school dramatics began to attain much popularity in the
Twenties. Once again, as in interscholastic athletics, the colleges and
universities appear to have blazed the trail for the high schools. School
dramatic productions and courses in dramatic arts began to flourish during the "golden" Twenties.[90] But here, as in spectator sports, all too
often the main emphasis was on public relations and entertainment
rather than on inherent educational value for the youngsters themselves.
Instead of spontaneous play-acting or informal dramatizations in connection with literature studies, high school dramatics in such instances
emerged as a highly organized and frantically coached extracurricular activity. All that counted was the quality of the final performance and
the impression this would make upon the community.[91]

Advocates of serious dramatic work in the schools were disappointed
with the way in which drama was being utilized in American public
school systems. Instead of being approached as an aesthetic and recreational field which could help develop the creative impulse of young
people and improve their standards of literary appreciation and under-

[87] William C. Reavis and George Van Dyke, *Nonathletic Extracurriculum Activities* (Washington, D.C.: Government Printing Office, 1933), pp. 13-14.

[88] Harry C. McKown, *Extracurricular Activities* (New York: The Macmillan Company, 1929), pp. 20-25.

[89] Reavis and Van Dyke, *op. cit.*, pp. 73-74.

[90] Kenneth MacGowan, *Drama in the High School* (New York: Samuel French,
Inc., 1929), pp. 3-5; Samuel J. Hume and Lois M. Foster, *Theater and School*
(New York: Samuel French, Inc., 1933), pp. 4-11.

[91] John Merrill and Martha Fleming, *Playmaking and Plays* (New York: The
Macmillan Company, 1930), pp. xviii-xix.

standing, high school dramatics was looked upon by some as a frill possessing no lasting worth other than public entertainment.[92] Writing in the *Quarterly Journal of Speech* in 1946, Ernest Bavely bitterly complained that "the dramatics program often consists of little more than the production of one or two class plays, staged for the sole purpose of securing funds for any one of a dozen possible projects—yearbooks, class outings, equipment for the football team, spare parts for the boiler room, and the like." The superintendent of schools and the principal, he maintained, often had, at best, only the vaguest idea of the problems inherent in play selection and production, or of the educational values to be found in a well-established dramatics program. "The appointment of the dramatics 'coach' is often made on the basis of availability during certain school hours, with complete disregard for the qualifications and interests of the candidate. . . ."[93]

Another characteristic "display item" in the American high school's jam-packed extracurricular showcase was the music program. In some school systems the main emphasis in music education was on preparation for public performance, again reflecting a community obsession with publicity value. In "Elmtown," for example, local organizations relied heavily on the high school for free musical entertainment on special occasions, ranging from the American Legion's Armistice Day Dinner to the Rotary Club's Annual Ladies' Night. In 1941-42 the school furnished 131 programs out of 140 requests which it had received. "Fifteen different musical groups were supported and used in these programs: marching band, concert band, girls' chorus, mixed chorus, swing band, violin ensemble, brass quartet, cornet trio, girls' glee club, and three girls' and three boys' quartets. The larger groups such as the marching band and the mixed chorus included practically all students able to play an instrument or sing well enough to do chorus work. Seventy-nine students (20 per cent of the student body) carried the load of this extensive activity."[94]

Musical groups also represented schools at interscholastic concerts and tournaments. The two types of musical organizations most frequently involved in melodic competition of this sort were the band and

[92] *Teaching Dramatic Arts in the Secondary Schools* (High School Committee of the American Educational Theatre Association, 1945); Corinne Brown, *Creative Drama in the Lower School* (New York: Appleton-Century-Crofts, Inc., 1929), pp. 209-19.

[93] Ernest Bavely, "Dramatic Arts in Secondary Education," *Quarterly Journal of Speech* (February 1946), pp. 39-40.

[94] Hollingshead, *Elmtown's Youth*, pp. 198-200.

the glee club. Again, because of the public relations possibilities, boards of education quite often contributed money to finance their entries, while additional funds were raised from the sale of tickets and dues collected from students. Many schools provided special coaching for participants, somewhat in the same way as they prepared athletic teams to represent them on the field of interscholastic combat, although by no means in as frenzied and compulsive a manner.[95]

Another extracurricular activity which received an important stimulus from interscholastic competition was debating. Here was a student activity which went all the way back to mid-nineteenth century high schools and their literary societies. In turn, those early schools modeled their oratorical program on the pioneering efforts of college debaters in the colonial period. Forensic contests and debates between teams representing competing high schools continued to attract a good deal of interest throughout the late nineteenth century and on into the twentieth century.[96] Debating leagues in many regions were organized on a state-wide basis and sponsored interscholastic contests in both extemporaneous speaking and formal debates.[97] As late as 1955, one such league which had existed in Iowa for 50 years loftily announced its aims as being "to achieve with its students the goals of self-realization, economic efficiency, human relationships, and civic responsibility. . . . Likewise, it [debating] provides for a direct approach to developing in students the ability to think effectively, to communicate thought, to make relevant judgments, and to discriminate among values."[98] Undoubtedly, community and student identification with a school's forensic champions in terms of prestige and institutional superiority were an important feature of these elocutionary contests.

Even school publications became involved, with the rise of journalism schools and the emergence of a journalistic profession, in interscholastic competition, There was much attendant publicity and the giving of awards for the student newspapers and magazines adjudged the best. School journalism, like debating, was one of the earliest extracurricular activities to appear in American secondary schools. Senior annuals,

<hr />

[95] Reavis and Van Dyke, *Nonathletic Extracurriculum Activities*, pp. 129-30, 147-49.

[96] Henry C. Davis and Reed Smith, *Debating for High Schools* (Columbia, S.C.: University of South Carolina Extension Division, Bulletin No. 83, February 1920).

[97] *Second Annual Report of the Interscholastic Public Speaking League, 1915-1916* (Berkeley, Calif.: University of California Extension Division).

[98] *Extension Bulletin, 1954* (Iowa City: State University of Iowa, Iowa High School Forensic Events, 1954-1955), pp. 8-9.

school newspapers, and student literary magazines had a history dating
from the nineteenth century.

In surveying the broad spectrum of extracurricular activities, we
should not overlook the many subject-matter and special interest clubs,
offshoots, more or less, of existing subdivisions in the course of study. In
this category may be placed the ubiquitous Cercles Francaises, the
Latin clubs, the English clubs, the history clubs, the home economics
clubs, and even the typing and stenographers' clubs. Here, too, we must
list such organizations as student government clubs.[99]

What final estimate can be made of the significance of extracurricular
activities in the twentieth-century history of the American school? A
professor of sociology at the University of North Carolina noted in the
mid-twenties that the development of such activities among adolescents
was perfectly natural. "The gregarious tendency is strongest at this
time," he said. "The gang spirit shows itself in many ways." The school,
he argued, should organize, direct, and supervise such activities to make
sure that they serve as a "constructive instrument of educational advancement." These activities could be made to further the social education of
youngsters, to teach them important lessons in loyalty, cooperation, and
idealism, and to "socialize" them and adjust them to life.[100]

But were school administrators always aware of these lofty objectives?
The survey made by Reavis and Van Dyke in 1932 revealed that many
of them were not. It was found that "the aims and purposes of extracurriculum activities, even in outstanding schools, very often are not
clearly defined." There was no clear idea of the purposes either of individual clubs or of the entire school's extracurricular program.[101] Given
this confusion as to basic purpose, philosopher Horace Kallen saw such
activities, both in schools and colleges, as contributing to little more
than "the social prolongation of infancy." Far from contributing to
maturation, far from preparing for or adjusting to adult life, the *extracurriculum*, as it was enthusiastically elaborated and meticulously
overorganized in American educational institutions simply prolonged
"the pre-pubertal dependence, its juvenility and social nonresponsibility
to the twenty-second or twenty-third year of life." [102] Frederick Rogers
raised an additional point of criticism when he acridly asked why school

---

[99] Maris M. Proffitt, *High School Clubs* (Washington, D.C.: Government Printing
Office, 1934).

[100] Meyer and Cole, *The High School Society*, pp. 11-12.

[101] Reavis and Van Dyke, *Nonathletic Extracurriculum Activities*, p. 90.

[102] Horace M. Kallen, *The Education of Free Men* (New York: Farrar, Straus &
Company, 1949), pp. 67-79.

children's extra-class interests in sports, dramatics, journalism, debating, or music were made to "serve the selfish interests of ambitious coaches." Why, he wondered, did school administrators strive to extend the school day so that it included every moment of the pupil's time on school property? Why the careful pacing and "currying for the public stage" of champion spellers, champion bands, champion public speakers, and champion debaters? Could it be that school boards and school administrators, principals, coaches, and supervisors "care more for the advertisement of their departments or schools than for the physical, mental, or social development of their pupils?" [103]

A strong case could be made for the proposition that the extracurricular program represented the imposition of the competitive and status-seeking standards of the adult world upon the life of the young. Anthropologists, however, tell us that such initiation patterns have been demanded in countless other human societies, ranging from the primitive to the most complex. The community-identification that came with successful extracurricular performance and the advertising and prestige values that resulted from such proceedings have their counterparts in other culture patterns. What seemed to be uniquely modern and typically American was the concentration of these various societal functions within the formal school structure. This trend, in turn, was apparently accelerated by the mass-enrollment in public junior and senior high schools in the years following World War I. Now it was necessary for schoolmen not only to mobilize and retain community support; they also had to find ways of making school life interesting for great numbers of youngsters who were not interested in intellectual or academic values as such. However, not all children could be easily adjusted, nor were they all adjusted in the same way. And in the end, as Willard Waller reminds us, in spite of all the adult organizing and theorizing, the matters which affected the life of the students most deeply were those which spontaneously appealed "by presenting to them behavior patterns of considerable intrinsic interest." [104]

[103] Frederick Rogers, *Future of Interscholastic Athletics*, p. 129.
[104] Waller, *The Sociology of Teaching*, p. 112.

CHAPTER FIVE

Education for All

Writing in the *Columbia University Forum* in 1961 sociologist Seymour Martin Lipset noted that American society had evolved in such a way as to bring into prominence two basic values "which are not entirely compatible and never have been." These were Equality and Achievement.[1] Emphasis on these two keynotes has pervaded much of American culture, including important aspects of the country's educational outlook and practice. Legislation in the educational field, as in other spheres of human life, Charles H. Judd once shrewdly observed, most often follows fundamental social change rather than causes it.[2] Therefore, to explain adequately the reasons for the uniquely American system of mass education by legislative fiat, we must first comprehend the total social context which gave it birth. And to understand why a dogged search for excellence came increasingly to concern many American public schools in the middle of the twentieth century, we must first take into account the circumstances which led to this eager quest. It is to these two trends, then, viewed in the framework of the developing American social order, that we now address ourselves.

[1] Seymour Martin Lipset, "Equal or Better in America," *Columbia University Forum* (Spring, 1961), p. 17.
[2] Charles H. Judd, *Problems of Education in the United States* (New York: McGraw-Hill Book Company, 1933), p. 20.

Democracy in the School

Beginning with Massachusetts in 1852, a procession of American states enacted legislation requiring school attendance for a specified period of time each year for all children within certain specified age groups. Limited in applicability at first, the required time period was steadily lengthened until it included eight to ten months of schooling, and the mandatory age limits were continuously extended down toward the kindergarten level and up toward the threshold of maturity. State governments began to set up for the first time during the 1920's effective enforcement divisions which required local officials to see that the compulsory school laws were obeyed.[3] To be sure, even then sporadic resistance continued, especially in small towns and rural areas. In the small midwestern community of "Jonesville," as late as the 1940's members of the local school board held fast to the opinion that high school education should not be universal. Many boys and girls would be better off if they stayed "on the farm" or "down at the mill." [4] Public opinion, however, generally favored the new trend of compulsory schooling. Changing family and societal expectations, independently of legislative requirements, were inducing youth to remain longer in school. In representative "Middletown" during the 1930's, the watchword came to be: "The more education any child can get the better." [5]

What produced this remarkable phenomenon? Undoubtedly one factor was the increasing awareness, in an age of mass immigration, of the need for a common background and citizenship. Ever since the mid-nineteenth century "Educational Awakening," this goal had been prominently in the minds of the nation's leaders, and in the early twentieth century the "Americanization" movement brought it forward more urgently than ever.[6] Henry Steele Commager traced the development of education for all to the "melting pot" composition of American so-

---

[3] Nelda Umbeck, *State Legislation on School Attendance and Related Matters* (U.S. Office of Education Circular No. 573 [Washington, D.C.]). Forest C. Ensign. *Compulsory School Attendance and Child Labor* (Iowa City: State University of Iowa Press, 1921), pp. 7-35, 128-80, 235-36.

[4] W. Lloyd Warner, ed., *Democracy in Jonesville* (New York: Harper & Row, Publishers, 1949), p. 196.

[5] Robert S. Lynd and Helen M. Lynd, *Middletown in Transition* (New York: Harcourt, Brace & World, Inc., 1937), p. 200.

[6] Lawrence A. Cremin, *The American Common School: An Historic Conception* (New York: Teachers College, Columbia University, 1951); Merle E. Curti, *Social Ideas of American Educators* (New York: Charles Scribner's Sons, 1935), pp. 232-35.

ciety, when, in contrasting the American school system with that of Europe's, he noted that we require our schools "to train citizens competent to govern themselves (a requirement not urgent in the Old World), to absorb and Americanize millions of newcomers from the Old World and elsewhere, to encourage and strengthen national unity, and to teach the habits and practices of democracy and equality and religious tolerance." [7]

Important, too, were the new attitudes toward child welfare which flourished during the early years of the twentieth century. A drive for social justice sponsored by humanitarian reformers, women's club members, progressive political leaders, and spokesmen for organized labor, led, among other things, to an attempt to limit or abolish child labor and, as a correlative movement, to enforce school attendance upon children of potential working age. As late as 1910, 18 per cent of all American children between the ages of ten and fifteen were to some extent gainfully employed. As the campaign for something like a "welfare state" grew stronger and stronger, the concept of compulsory prolongation of schooling gained wider acceptance. [8]

During World War II, it was increasingly impressed upon the American nation that its very survival depended upon intelligent utilization of manpower resources and that the key to such effective use was systematic education at all levels. Americans were shocked by the reports of Selective Service officials which revealed the existence of substantial numbers of citizens who could neither read nor write or who were functional illiterates. In all, 676,000 men were rejected for military service during the war years because of educational deficiencies, meaning that they had less than four years of schooling. Of this number, 350,000 signed their names with a mark. [9]

Even more alarming were indications following the war that the nation's schools were not turning out a sufficient number of skilled persons to meet the demands of a rapidly changing technological society. Complaints were constantly heard about shortages of scientists, engineers, technicians, medical men, school teachers. A survey in 1960 re-

[7] Henry Steele Commager, "A Historian Looks at the High School," in Francis S. Chase and Harold Anderson, *The High School in a New Era* (Chicago: University of Chicago Press, 1958).

[8] Judd, *Problems of Education*, pp. 20-22; Margaret Mead, *The School in American Culture* (Cambridge, Mass.: Harvard University Press, 1951).

[9] I. L. Kandel, ed., *The Impact of the War upon American Education* (Chapel Hill, N.C.: University of North Carolina Press, 1946), pp. 41-42; Eli Ginzberg and D. W. Bray, *The Uneducated* (New York: Columbia University Press, 1953).

vealed that 46 per cent of the youth of the country with an I.Q. of
110 or over completed high school but did not go on to college, while
another 10 per cent did not even finish high school.[10] Many Americans
interpreted such findings as indicative of the fact that national security
as well as national prosperity urgently required an expansion of mass
education at both the elementary and the higher grade levels. In accordance with the mounting concern, President Truman's Advisory
Commission on Higher Education recommended in 1948 that the
American system of free public education be extended upward to include two years of study beyond high school. These opportunities
should, according to the Commission, be extended to the masses by
means of a nationwide network of community colleges.[11] Although not
agreeing in every detail with the President's Commission, the influential
Educational Policies Commission of the NEA published a report in
1957 which similarly recognized that growth in various types of post-
secondary school training "should be substantial." While priority should
be given to ability, opportunities for such training should be made
available to ever "larger proportions of the population." [12]

Another factor making for the triumph of mass education was the
emergence of what John Galbraith has called "the New Class." With
the development of a complex and highly interrelated technological
society, thousands of new job opportunities for skilled technicians and
professionals appeared. The ranks of this new upper-echelon class,
"whose primary identification is with their job, rather than the income
it returns," began to be numbered in the millions. The chief qualification for entering the New Class, with its relatively more pleasant and
satisfying way of life, was formal education.[13] As a result, more and
more parents insistently demanded that their children be given the
training which was indispensable if they were to move up the social
ladder into the expanding ranks of the New Class (or the "Diploma
Elite," to use Vance Packard's term).[14]

[10] Henry David, ed., *Education and Manpower* (New York: Columbia University
Press, 1960), pp. 18-23.

[11] "U.S. President's Commission," *Higher Education for American Democracy:
A Report* (New York: Harper & Row, Publishers, 1948), I, pp. 27-28, 41-42, 100-
102; V, pp. 56-68.

[12] *Higher Education in a Decade of Decision* (Washington, D.C.: National Education Association, Educational Policies Commission, 1957), p. 147.

[13] John K. Galbraith, *The Affluent Society* (Boston: Houghton Mifflin Company,
1958), pp. 342-46.

[14] David Riesman, "The College Professor," in Brand Blanshard, ed., *Education
in the Age of Science* (New York: Basic Books, 1959); Vance Packard, *The Status
Seekers* (New York: David McKay Co., Inc., 1959).

Mutatis Mutandis, an ever-increasing proportion of America's youth found itself in attendance at some type of educational institution, and for longer periods of time than ever before in the nation's history. The most dramatic consequence of this campaign was a mass influx into the high schools. By the mid-point of the twentieth century American education had crossed "two historic benchmarks." In 1949-50, a clear majority of all high school students (59 per cent, to be exact) actually graduated from high school. Second, a majority of these high school graduates were then going on to some form of post-secondary training. Other mid-century statistics testify to the signal triumph of mass education. In 1890, for example, 202,963 children were enrolled in four-year public high schools; in 1952, 5,695,514 were so enrolled. In 1890, 3.8 per cent of the fourteen- to seventeen-year age group were enrolled in ninth- through twelfth-grade programs; in 1952, the figure had jumped to an impressive 65.3 per cent. In addition, in the latter year an additional 1,526,998 students were enrolled in junior high schools. Enrollments at all grade levels continued to soar during the Fifties and early Sixties.[15]

What were the vital consequences of this clear-cut triumph of education for all? Lawrence Cremin properly observed that "had there never been a progressive movement, had there been no social settlements, municipal reform associations, country life commissions, or immigrant aid societies, no William James, Stanley Hall, Edward Thorndike, or John Dewey, the mere fact of compulsory attendance would have changed the American school." [16] Junior and senior high schools were now flooded with youngsters who would not have been in any school in earlier times. Many of these children had no motivation to learn and did not really wish to remain in school. Others lacked ability to learn even the rudiments. In 1951 a careful study of the "I.Q." scores of entering New York City high school students revealed that more than 60 *per cent* of those going to vocational high schools had I.Q.'s below 90, and 20 per cent of the academic high school students had similarly low scores.[17] In overcrowded Chicago slum areas in the late 1950's, public school classrooms often had a turnover of 100 per cent in one year! Eighth-grade reading levels in such areas lagged four years behind those in nonproblem areas. Schools in these rundown districts had 11 times as

---

[15] David, ed., *Education and Manpower,* pp. 6-15.
[16] Lawrence A. Cremin, *Transformation of the School* (New York: Alfred A. Knopf, Inc., 1961), p. 128.
[17] Frances Wilson and Morris Krugman, *Studies of Student Personnel* (Albany, N.Y.: New York State Department of Education, 1951).

many pupils who were overage for their grades as was normal. At a meeting of superintendents representing the nation's 14 largest cities, statistics were presented showing that while in 1950 only 10 per cent of urban students were "culturally deprived," ten years later this percentage had risen to 33. In 1970, they feared, it might well reach 50 per cent.

It was manifest that compulsory education had transformed the American public high school, which now had to perform a variety of functions not required a half century before. To meet the needs of the new, more highly diversified student body, high schools were obliged to introduce many new course offerings, particularly vocational ones. Courses in typewriting, shorthand, bookkeeping, printing, the manual arts, mechanical skills, electrical work, and commercial art were springing up on every side. Many cities founded new trade schools, technical high schools, and commercial high schools, or expanded previously existing ones.[18]

The sweeping implementation of the fast-evolving conception of compulsory formal education up to age sixteen (or even eighteen in certain cases) posed grave challenges for the nation's public school system. In underprivileged slum areas schoolmen would have to deal with youth (and parents) who could see no value in formal schooling. Slum dwellers with this outlook saw life as rigged against them, bitterly felt in their bones that, given their racial, ethnic, or economic origins, the American dream promised little or nothing to them. Cynically dismissing the possibilities of achievement by means of legitimate effort, such children might end by running in gangs, fighting back at society via juvenile delinquency; in so doing they converted the atmosphere of the classroom into a "Blackboard Jungle." [19]

In many communities public school systems sought to adapt themselves to these disturbing realities by establishing special disciplinary classes, industrial schools of a reformatory type, non-English speaking classes, and special classes for the mentally retarded. State education departments launched similar programs. But in the opinion of some observers, the situation was too serious to be handled by mere palliatives. Americans were vainly trying to ride an "education-for-all" tiger which their oversimplified educational philosophy in no way prepared them to control. In May, 1960, Dr. James Bryant Conant made this very point where he said that juvenile delinquency arose because of the ex-

[18] Noel P. Gist and L. A. Halbert, *Urban Society* (New York: The Thomas Y. Crowell Company, 1941), pp. 522-23.
[19] David, ed., *Education and Manpower*, pp 21-23.

istence of a body of "academically frustrated youth who are unemployed." He added that he was not one to judge a high school harshly solely because its drop-out rate was high.[20] As early as 1907, Edward L. Thorndike had discovered that the main cause of elimination from school was "incapacity for and lack of interest in the sort of intellectual work demanded by present courses of study." [21] Some educators in Thorndike's time had been ready to call all drop-outs an "American tragedy." [22] Yet Conant asked parents and citizens to consider "the danger of trying to force down the throats of all children of high school age a diet suitable only for those with academic talent."

Although the consultants concurred on the nature of the disease, few agreed on its cure. Some believed that a positive program to rehabilitate drop-outs could help them come back to school or find jobs. During the late Fifties, Livingston E. Beane of Riverside, California, reported, a representative group of such potential or actual juvenile delinquents were sought out at their homes, at pool halls, and on the street. These "J.D.'s" were followed in and out of jail. Personal counseling was given as well as training for certain kinds of jobs. Twenty youths out of 52 returned to school. A group of Chicago guidance workers, social workers, and psychologists in 1962 recommended that more extensive counseling be made available to such maladjusted children in school as well as out, and that special schools be established which they could attend. Such institutions would have a "combined educational-therapeutic milieu created by a staff of educators, psychiatrists, psychologists, and social workers." [23]

Dr. Conant preferred to approach the problem from a different and possibly more realistic angle. "It is worse for a boy," he emphasized, "to remain in school and become continually frustrated by his academic difficulties than to leave school and get a satisfying job." Not every child in school was preparing to be a future scientist, medical man, lawyer, or research scholar. Why, then, should they all be expected to profit from the same public school curriculum? If their future vocations required a shorter period of formal training, and if they were aca-

[20] James Bryant Conant, "Public Concern for *All* American Youth," *Ladies' Home Journal* (May 1960), p. 30.
[21] Edward L. Thorndike, *Elimination of Pupils from School* (U.S. Bureau of Education Bulletin No. 4, 1907 [Washington, D.C., 1908]).
[22] A. J. Ladd, *On the Firing Line in Education* (Boston: Bruce Humphries, Pubs., 1919), pp. 192-93; see also Solomon O. Lichter, *et al.*, "Prevention of School Drop-Outs," *School and Society* (April 7, 1962), pp. 159-68.
[23] Lichter, *et al.*, *op. cit.*, p. 166.

demically handicapped by being slow readers, why not allow them, by the eleventh and twelfth grades, to take a satisfying job and continue their education on a part-time or continuation-school basis? Then came an important suggestion. For a few with problems of genuine mental retardation, it might even be desirable, Conant argued, to terminate *all* formal education after the completion of grade ten. And for the great mass of children who were not college-bound but who had good general ability and could profit from remaining in school through grades eleven and twelve, why not develop more frankly and fully than at present such "practical" courses as home economics, typing, stenography, auto mechanics, and shop work? In this way, Conant concluded, American society would avoid engendering, through its public schools, a rebellious spirit among youth toward both schoolwork and the community. It would cease "producing, through neglect, even a small number of thwarted and resentful youth." [24]

Many Americans found it difficult, if not impossible, to face up realistically to the explosive problems spotlighted by Dr. Conant. Their deep and long-established commitment to a philosophy of unqualified equalitarianism stood in the way. Would not any attempt to differentiate, to establish special classes or programs, openly introduce invidious, "undemocratic" distinctions? In the schools of the mid-century, it was considered more expedient to demonstrate to the taxpayers—*all* the taxpayers—that equality reigned. This feat was accomplished in many cases by means of such mechanisms as "social promotion," which employed a questionable educational psychology to justify keeping school children moving along from grade to grade with their own age group, no matter how low their level of scholastic achievement. It was also considered desirable in many classrooms to avoid annoying practices which might single out for public attention the brighter or more hardworking students. Such recognition was castigated as "undemocratic" and nonegalitarian because it might hurt the feelings of the less bright and slower members of the class. An example of this attitude was seen in the opposition of the embattled mayor of "Mineville" toward a local grade school principal, as reported in Blumenthal's 1932 sociological survey *Small-Town Stuff*:

> Burger is another one I would put out if I had my way. He does some things that are pretty crazy. . . .
> Burger isn't fair by giving the leadership to a few who happen to lead

[24] Conant, "Public Concern for *All* American Youth," pp. 30, 184.

in scholarship. He favors a few. It isn't fair to kids who work hard but aren't bright enough to lead. Just because a kid is born bright, he shouldn't have privileges over those who weren't born bright. The favors should be passed around.

All I've got to say is that I'd have done something to get him if my kid were in that school again this year. But she is in high school now, and so I don't know how things are going over there now.[25]

It was in just this kind of watered-down educational atmosphere that one suburban high school principal in 1958 issued the following directive on marking standards to all members of his teaching staff:

2) We are teaching the AVERAGE PUPIL in our classes, giving special opportunities for the SUPERIOR pupils to do more extensive and intensive work, and special attention to the "slow learner." Marks, therefore, are to be established with the AVERAGE pupil as the basis . . . rather than by picking out one or two leaders and comparing all others to them. The presence, or lack of presence, of such superior pupils in any class should not materially affect the grades of the average pupils.
3) The total grades issued by any teacher . . . should conform IN GENERAL to a normal curve of distribution. . . .

. . . .

5) All teachers are to mark the same, as nearly as possible. . . . The day of "hard markers" and "easy markers" has passed. . . .

. . . .

7) High per cents of failure NEVER indicate high standards in a school, and may indicate low standards of teaching skill. . . .

. . . .

9) . . . . A high grade of accomplishment should be demanded, but accomplishment of combined groups should be the basis for determining whether too much or too little is expected. What CONSCIENTIOUS pupils (of average ability) show by ACCOMPLISHMENT that they CAN do, and what may be EXPECTED of them at times, may be entirely different quantities. The FORMER and NOT the LAATER should be the basis for marking. True marks can never be safely established by numerical averages of grades, unless extreme caution was used in establishing the individual marks entering into the averages.[26]

Carrying the above philosophy one step further, Dr. Jack Abramowitz, Supervisor of Social Studies in the Farmingdale, N.Y., public schools, proposed that "simplified" schoolbooks be used to keep the slow

[25] Albert Blumenthal, *Small-Town Stuff* (Chicago: University of Chicago Press, 1932), p. 336.
[26] "School Policy in Regard to Accomplishment Marks" (1958). Mimeographed announcement. Copy in author's files.

learner happy in school. Twenty per cent of the public school population fell into this "slow" category, Abramowitz averred, and this group
was the major source of school drop-outs. He was especially alarmed
by the fact that 500,000 drop-outs aged sixteen to twenty-four were
listed by the U.S. Department of Labor in 1961 as being unemployed.
Thus the "slow learner" became the "low earner," often ending up on
relief rolls altogether. Happily Dr. Abramowitz had a panacea ready to
handle this threatening situation. Slow learners would be given simplified
booklets instead of standard textbooks and thereby would "learn" in a
form understandable to them. Words in these booklets would not be
difficult, sentences would not be long, and content would be simplified.
In this way slow children would not develop a "defeatist" attitude.
They would come to *feel better* as they got the impression that they
were "accomplishing something" during the years the compulsory education law forced them to remain in school. Closely related to Abramowitz's pat solution was the growing interest in educational television and
"programmed" learning, which about this time was mushrooming not
only because of a wish to help solve the perplexing post-World War II
teacher shortage, but also because it was thought these gadgets would
better serve pupils of below-average ability and motivation. The so-called
"teaching machine" phase of this movement was set into motion by
a series of experiments begun at Harvard by psychology professor B. F.
Skinner.[27] One skeptic asked whether by such experiments "we are
quietly accepting that state of electronic imbecility which is already
familiar in the popular equation of intellectual accomplishment and
the winning of quiz shows." Just as weather reports were compiled by
meteorologists but recited by models, this tongue-in-cheek critic saw no
reason why Hollywood starlets should not in the future be used to gain
the attention of classes in solid geometry, or why "our curriculum of
core and social studies and controlled reading should not be designed
once and for all by the NEA and filmed in Hollywood for use and re-
use, until the happy day when the Single-Shot Education Injection is
invented." [28]

Some educators did not share the irreverent attitude of the above
commentator. Lustily lambasting the old, narrow, academic-minded,

[27] Richard Franko Goldman, "The Little-Read Schoolhouse: The Videogogue and
His Pedavision," *Columbia University Forum* (Winter, 1961), pp. 16-22; Donald A.
Cook, "Programmed Learning: A Revolution in Instruction," *Columbia University
Graduate Faculties Newsletter* (November 1960).
[28] Goldman, "The Little-Read Schoolhouse," pp. 20-22.

college-preparatory type of curriculum, Harl Douglass of the University of Colorado warned in 1952 that "parents and other laymen are seriously questioning whether *students and taxpayers are getting their money's worth* in secondary education today." [29] Douglass went on to point out:

> Pupils have a diminishing degree of faith in the sales talks which teachers give them about subjects in secondary education. With the development of movies, television, and the automobile, the pupils lead a much richer social life than formerly. A great part of their learning activities as devised by secondary school teachers seems drab and out of proportion. There is, therefore, a distinct need for a much more appealing and much more challenging curriculum, involving, no doubt, much more participation of the youngsters in setting up the goals and the materials of their own learning activities. [30]

Attempts to maintain meaningful intellectual standards in mid-century schools were undermined not only by an unwillingness to offend the lowest common denominator, but also, curiously enough, by a remarkable tenderness for the feelings of children with real mental ability. In the age of the "Organization Man," the emphasis in many urban and suburban communities—particularly those dominated by middle-class outlook—was more and more on "getting along" with the group rather than on individual improvement or independent personality development. Hence for school children, as for their parents, the main stress was now on social not intellectual or scholastic values.

Perhaps the very "interplay" of the ideals of Equality and Achievement helped contribute to an American oversensitivity to the judgment of others, or what David Riesman has labeled "other-directedness." European travelers in America noted this phenomenon as early as the late eighteenth century, and many later visitors professed to see a close relationship between such behavior and the fundamentally equalitarian American values. Thus Alexis De Tocqueville observed in the 1830's that "the more equal social conditions become, the more men display this reciprocal disposition to oblige each other." And John Graham Brooks, summarizing in the early twentieth century comments made by various British observers of the American scene, wrote:

> One deeper reason why the English are blunt and abrupt about their rights . . . is because class lines are more sharply drawn there. Within

---

[29] Italics are mine.

[30] Harl Douglass, *Secondary Education for Life Adjustment of American Youth* (New York: The Ronald Press Company, 1952), p. 4.

these limits one is likely to develop the habit of demanding his due. He insists on his prerogatives all the more because they are narrowly defined. . . . In a democracy everyone at least hopes to get on and up. This ascent depends not upon the favor of a class, but upon the good-will of the whole. . . . To make one's self conspicuous and disagreeable is to arouse enmities that block one's way.[31]

American educators and social scientists following World War I agreed with foreign observers in regard to the increasing importance of conformable, "other-directed" tendencies in the United States. Said President Nicholas Murray Butler of Columbia University in 1922: "There has grown up among us a passion for conformity with its necessarily resultant mediocrity, that is in sharp contrast to the old American spirit which built the nation and steadily pushed its western frontier to the Golden Gate." And he gloomily added:

We are told that an explanation of all this is to be sought in the fact that about one-half of our total population consists of morons, persons of stunted, twelve-year-old intelligence, who cannot think adult-fashion and who cannot be taught so to think. If this be a real and adequate explanation of the odd phenomena that surround us, then the cause of popular government . . . has burdens to bear that have not hitherto been suspected.[32]

Writing in 1930, Professor George Counts of Teachers College, Columbia University, argued that American group solidarity had in the early republic a different purpose from that which was motivating it in the twentieth century. In early times it was associated with a radical political ideal and ambitious programs of social reconstruction, but in modern times it had become conservative, demanding conformity to things as they are. Counts strenuously denied that even the individual-success ideal that animated so many Americans contradicted his basic thesis. The very emphasis on outward success constituted an emphatic denial of genuine individualism. Counts maintained that "the urge to success may prove to be the most austere and merciless of masters." [33] And, in point of fact, Arthur Miller's tragic "Salesman," Willy Loman, had not yet appeared before the footlights when these prescient observations were committed to paper!

[31] As quoted in Lipset, "Equal or Better in America," p. 20.
[32] Nicholas Murray Butler, *Toward Higher Ground* (An address delivered October 17, 1922).
[33] George S. Counts, *The American Road to Culture* (New York: John Day Co., 1930), pp. 118-21.

If anything, the whole impact of World War II and its aftermath was to accelerate conformable, group-oriented trends. Historian Eric Goldman wrote that the total socio-economic situation made genuine attitudes of individualism "not so much wrong as irrelevant." The very manner of living in the late Forties and early Fifties furthered a sheep-like outlook. The trend was toward suburban homes, "mushrooming miles" of mass-produced, standardized middle-class homes. In such communities "the prime virtue was adjustment to what the neighbors thought and did." The average worker now belonged to a union and worked for a large, impersonal corporation. The average farmer was deeply involved in his own special interest group or occupational organization. The typical executive was not an owner but an employed manager of a complex, impersonal business organization. In the era of the "welfare state" an intricate "web of relationships bound most Americans in with state and federal governments." Under these circumstances, the dominant urge was "for getting oneself into the most profitable and comfortable relationship with some larger group or organization." [34] George Orwell's "Big-Brother" land of 1984 had not yet arrived, but was it coming, after all, ahead of schedule?

Some of the most searching comments on the developing American situation were those made in 1950 by sociologist David Riesman in his widely discussed book *The Lonely Crowd*. Riesman argued that with the slowing down of social mobility and the spread of mass education, competition for openings was heightening. This phenomenon, taken in conjunction with the growing organizational and impersonal nature of American business and professional life, was producing a change in personality type from what Riesman called the "inner-directed" man to a new "outer-directed" one. The "inner-directed" type, which predominated during the nineteenth century, was brought up under a more or less authoritarian code in home and school to accept certain absolute values. He then proceeded with "zeal and ruthlessness" to carve out whatever kind of career he could for himself in an expanding frontier and a dynamically growing industrial order. The "outer-directed" man of the mid-twentieth century also sought to achieve, but his success "depends less on what one is and what one does than on what others think of one—and how competent one is in manipulating others and being oneself manipulated." Putting it another way, Riesman advanced the theory that when the basic physical plant of a society is built, "or

[34] Eric Goldman, *The Crucial Decade* (New York: Alfred A. Knopf, Inc., 1956), pp. 262-64.

rather when the building can be routinized by management-planning, there begins to be room at the top for the other-directed person who can see the subtle opportunities given in the human setting." Therefore, at this stage of social development *"the product now in demand is neither a staple nor a machine; it is personality."* William Whyte, Jr., made much the same point in his perspicacious study of *The Organization Man.* The new middle class of the mid-twentieth century (and the people of the lower classes influenced by their behavior patterns) manifested distinctly "other-directed" tendencies at home, at work, in community relationships, and in child-rearing. To "get ahead" one now had to "differentiate" one's personality, but not move too far out of line from the conventional mass mode. To such people, "work meant . . . primarily getting along with people. They saw advancement—and, beyond that, happiness—in terms of improving their social skills." [35] Although Riesman's sharp distinction between twentieth-century "outer direction" and nineteenth-century "inner direction" eventually came under the sharp criticism of fellow sociologists such as Seymour Lipset, the history of American education would seem to furnish considerable data indicating that Riesman was essentially on the right track.

Social psychologist Erich Fromm saw this change in social attitude as flowing from a change in Western man's relationship to authority. Traditional Western civilization, as he interpreted history, had evolved a definite authority—rational or irrational, but, in any case, tangible, overt. By the middle of the twentieth century, however, authority had essentially changed its character. It was now anonymous, invisible, alienated. Instead of authority being somebody or something, it was now an impersonal "it." No longer in business, government, or social relationships were orders generally given as such; rather one suggested, one coaxed, one manipulated. The mechanism through which this anonymous authority operated was a heightened conformity. "I ought to do what everybody does, hence, I must conform, not be different, not 'stick out.' I must be ready and willing to change according to the changes in the pattern; I must not ask whether I am right or wrong, but whether I am adjusted, whether I am not 'peculiar,' not different." Such a society produced, according to Fromm, "alienated personalities, incapable of true interpersonal relationships, lacking stable, meaningful

[35] David Riesman, *The Lonely Crowd* (New Haven, Conn.: Yale University Press, 1950), pp. 46-48; William H. Whyte, Jr., *The Organization Man* (New York: Simon and Schuster, Inc., 1956), pp. 63-100.

goals or standards of value, and *incapable even of understanding them-selves.*" Virtue and vice could be adjusted like all the rest.[36]

Documenting these conclusions was an intensive study of one of the new "mass-produced" suburbs which showed that privacy itself was clandestine there and the desire for it practically a crime. To be "intro-verted" was to be mentally aberrant. Lack of conformity to mass mores was taken to indicate a high degree of neuroticism and personal insta-bility. "Friendships" were formed not on the basis of individual liking and attraction but in terms of the location of one's house or apartment in relation to others. In many instances children dictated these relation-ships; their social contacts, "filiarchy"-style, set the basic design for Mother's and Father's "socializing." With the surrounding society so perplexingly kaleidoscopic and complex, with so many "status-seekers" and transients in the community, the individual found that his existence could have meaning only in so far as it contributed to the social harmony of the group and was adapted to the group's concepts of "togetherness" and "outgoingness." [37]

The "other-directed" tendencies in modern American society rein-forced the basic equalitarianism which had long been deeply imbedded in our culture. This brings us back to our original question: Was the atmosphere in classrooms of mid-century American public schools, in-fluenced by the "other-directed" norms of the community, one which would exact from those capable of doing so their maximum intellectual effort? In communities where "other-directedness" held sway uncritically in school as well as ranch house, "scientific" norms of child-rearing taught parents not to give commands, not to interpose overt authority. Rather they were to suggest that the child would "want to do this." Thus the behavior manipulation that had been developed by "human relations" experts and personnel managers in industry and the profes-sions had become a guide for "democratic" relationships within family and school groupings as well. As Fromm pointed out, some "outer-directed" parents, lacking fixed principles or convictions themselves, would almost inevitably end up by seeking to guide their children to do whatever the current law of conformity expected.[38] Often being themselves out of touch with such "latest" revelations, they found them-

[36] Eric Fromm, *The Sane Society* (New York: Holt, Rinehart & Winston, Inc., 1955), pp. 152-67.

[37] William H. Whyte, Jr., "The Transients," *Fortune Magazine*, 47 (May, August, 1953).

[38] Fromm, *The Sane Society*, p. 153.

selves being instructed by their children as to what parental attitudes should be on dating practices, schoolwork, and the like. For such modern parents, increasingly in doubt as to how to rear their children, "expert" child psychologists, columnists in national magazines, neighbors on the block, and fellow-members of the PTA became the authority. And above all else, "approval itself, irrespective of content [became] almost the only unequivocal good." [39] This *desideratum* frequently came to subsume within its meaning approval by the very children who supposedly were to be "guided" by the adults.

This paradoxical situation was complicated by the fact that ever since the "Cardinal Principles" report of 1918 a number of influential educators had been informing the public that the primary function of America's schools was not so much the passing along of an intellectual heritage as it was the socialization and acculturation of American youth. It was this sort of argument that Edgar B. Wesley presented in 1935 when he wrote that the modern age was a "socialized" one, and that the schools must get in step with the times by developing a "socialized education." Where formerly the family, the neighborhood, and the church performed many of the vital functions of socializing the young and preparing them for an adult role, now larger, more highly integrated units had to accomplish this task. The public school must therefore take on educative roles, previously assumed by parents and friends, in preparing youth to adjust to "the transition from the age of individualism to that of the integrated economy into which we are moving." [40] James H. Bossard in 1949 discerned that twentieth-century urban America was moving out of a situation where "primary groups" such as the family were all-important in educating and acculturating the young and into one in which impersonal and specialized "secondary groups" were having to do what parents and friends once did. "In secondary group life, such as one finds in the superficial and anonymous life of a large city, the group controls of behavior come from many specialized sources. . . . The simplicity of the code is lost, the unity and consistency of behavior requirements are gone." Under these circumstances, Bossard concluded, the school, *as a character-building agency*, had an even greater importance than it had ever had in the past.[41]

Approving of the *gesellschaft* trend in 1952 Harl Douglass proposed

[39] Riesman, *The Lonely Crowd*, pp. 48-49.

[40] Edgar B. Wesley, "Education for Social Control," *Annals of the American Academy of Political and Social Science*, 182 (November 1935).

[41] James H. Bossard, "Social Change in the United States," *ibid.*, 265 (September 1949). Italics are mine.

that the public school boldly assume many of these new social functions and even be assisted financially to do so. "The school," he wrote, "must upon occasion face the question of whether it should not provide some type of education which was formerly provided by some other social agency or phase of our life. If the home or industry no longer functions in giving certain types of educational experiences that it formerly did, the school should consider whether or not it should fill the gap." Pursuing this interesting thought further, Professor Douglass asked whether, in view of the fact that "the family no longer functions as it should in the realm of child-rearing," it would be expedient for the school to "take a larger part in nursery schools for lower ages and . . . enter other phases of education more gradually and fully than formerly." On the other hand, he mused, it might be preferable for school systems to try to make their major socialization contribution on the secondary level by "(a) educating young people . . . better for parenthood and (b) providing adult education for the training of parents, thereby preparing the family to resume the responsibility for its function. . . ." [42]

Undoubtedly in the years following World War I public school administrators took more seriously than ever before socialization duties such as those specified above. Expressing this ideal as completely as any of its advocates could desire was a statement issued in 1931 by the Granite Consolidated School District in Utah. This document began by emphasizing that: "The education of all the children of all the people is an ideal that has received nationwide acceptance in the United States." Noting that Utah had attempted to translate that ideal into practice, the authors went on to assert that "education is more than school attendance:" it "is the work of adapting a child to his environment. Education, in the large sense, includes the duty of following up every child to the age of eighteen for 365 days of the year, in and out of the classroom, with the aim of helping him develop his capacities to their greatest usefulness." In order to realize these comprehensive socializing goals, the Granite School District authorities ambitiously planned for:

1) Child accounting, since the plan obviously called for a complete and constant check up. . . .
2) Collection of data which would enable school authorities to guide each child to healthy living, to the full development of his abilities, and to the best use of leisure time. . . .
3) Placement of each child in school, work, and leisure all year around.

[42] Douglass, *Secondary Education for Life Adjustment*, Chap. 3.

Ever since the Americanization movement of the early years of the century, a primary "acculturative" task of the public schools had been that of assimilating the large numbers of immigrants pouring into the country. One of the main objectives of the Granite District schools, it was stated, was "to Americanize thoroughly and systematically the foreign born who have come here to live with us." Another sweeping purpose enunciated in this document was "to train the youth through the twelve months of the year in the discharge of those industrial, civil, social, and moral duties that make a people happy and a state prosperous and secure." To attain such all-embracing goals, many kinds of specialized workers were needed. The Utah report listed, in addition to the regular staff, the following personnel: a "work-and-school coordinator"; special teachers of industrial and agricultural subjects; a teacher to supervise the 4-H Clubs during the summer months; a secretary to supervise the child accounting system; a school dentist; three school nurses; teachers for the "special-opportunity summer school"; and "three home-economics teachers for summer months for vocational project work in home economics, recreation, health, and citizenship." [43]

Sharp-eyed observers like Whyte, Fromm, and Riesman, in attempting to evaluate such programs for educating the "whole child," pointed out an interesting phenomenon. In addition to training for democracy and for citizenship, such schools were also predisposing youngsters to consider it important to "get along" at all costs with the group. In Riesman's opinion, it was no longer sufficient in many lines of work to be merely "good" on the job; one also had to be "cooperative," one of the gang. "Business and professional success now depend much more than ever before on one's ability to work in a team in far-flung personnel networks; the man who works too hard or in too solitary a way is, by and large, almost as unwelcome in the executive offices, the universities, or the hospitals of urban America as he would be in a union shop." [44] Applied to the schoolroom situation, these circumstances meant that many parents who wished their child to be successful and happy would be more worried about the youngster's "adjustment" to his peer group than his grades in academic subjects. If their child was rejected by his classmates, such parents would be sincerely alarmed. Perhaps the child's differences and "introverted" tendencies were a danger to his "personality

[43] Francis W. Kirkham, *Educating All the Children of All the People: A Year-Round Preparation for Life Program for Youth up to 18 Years of Age in Granite Consolidated School District of Utah* (Washington, D.C., 1931).

[44] David Riesman, *Individualism Reconsidered* (New York: Free Press of Glencoe, Inc., 1954), pp. 266-67.

development." Very often, such fears might be fed by warnings from guidance counselors and other school officials that such lack of "team spirit" was indeed woefully detrimental to the youngster.

In the nineteenth-century era of inner direction, classroom procedures were often authoritarian, but the emphasis was on the attainment of a specific academic goal. This made it possible for the regnant intellectual standards to be "internalized" both by those who succeeded and those who failed. "They are felt as real and given, not as somebody's whim. Thus the school reinforces the home in setting for the child goals that are clear to all and that give direction and meaning to life thereafter." [45]

However, in the later setting of mass education and ascendant outer direction, much of the foregoing was changed. A pattern of teaching developed in which the instructors were specifically trained "to be more concerned with the child's social and psychological adjustment than with his academic progress—indeed, to scan the intellectual performance for signs of social maladjustment." Even the physical arrangements in grade school classrooms were now designed to symbolize the new keynote—informality rather than alphabetical seating plan, movable tables instead of stationary desks, teacher sitting with the "family circle" rather than behind a formidable raised dais, and walls covered with paintings by the children or clippings from *Life* assembled by the social studies class. Although this kind of grade school religiously de-emphasized grades and report cards, the bulletin board displays seemed, in Riesman's opinion, to be always asking the happily "adjusted" children: "Mirror, mirror on the wall, who is fairest of us all?"

The new-model outer-directed teacher strove not so much to be a mentor as an "opinion leader." Since the major emphasis was on voluntary "cooperation," her frequently contentless lessons were conveyed, as in the case of the outer-directed parent, by means of reasoning and manipulation. Learning was supposed to be "fun." Children were supposed inherently to want to "cooperate." And what was the basic message such a progressive, new-style teacher imparted? "She conveys to the children," wrote Riesman, "that what matters is not their industry and learning as such but their adjustment in the group, their cooperation, their (carefully stylized and limited) initiative and leadership." Perhaps such a role was indeed something like that of the industrial relations department in a modern factory which was also "increasingly concerned with cooperation between men and men and between men

[45] Riesman, *The Lonely Crowd*, pp. 57-59.

and management, as technical skill becomes less and less of a major concern." In the factory, just as in the other-directed schoolroom, there might even be established "a pattern of democratic decision on moot matters—occasionally important because it affects piecework rates and seniority rules, but usually as trivial as the similar decisions of grammar school government." [46]

In the modern-minded suburb of Park Forest, Illinois, the schools very early sought to implant the concept explained by one parent as follows: "The adjustment to the group does not seem to involve so many problems for them [the children]. I have noticed that they seem to get the feeling that nobody is the boss—there is a feeling of complete cooperation. Partly this comes from early exposure to court play." One Park Forest mother told an interviewer: "Johnny has not been doing so well at school. The teacher told me he was doing fine in some respects but that his *social adjustment was not as good as it might be*. He would pick *one or two friends to play with—and sometimes he was happy to remain by himself*." [47] What, after all, in the schools of an other-directed, mass culture, could be a worse crime than that?

In many modern-minded schools, such as those of Park Forest, grading systems became happily "flexible." "To use fixed standards of performance," the Park Forest authorities felt, "would strait-jacket the child. As a consequence, the primaries, as in many other schools, are ungraded, and in later classes formal reports of the A-B-C-D-F percentage type have been discarded." Mrs. Lucille Thimblin, a curriculum consultant for Park Forest, explained that this action had been taken because it was impossible for a teacher to "reduce *the many-sided* aspects of a *pupil's development* to an accurate numerical value." [48] While this system, Mrs. Thimblin admitted, did decrease the competition for scholastic leadership, it had the compensating feature that it made for better adjustment (and presumably would not hurt the feelings of the academically slower children and their taxpaying parents). Instead of rating a child's academic progress on the basis of individual achievement and in terms of some arbitrary norm, the pupil could be conveniently rated in terms of his social or peer group, and all he would have to do would be to meet the general standards which had been established as *attainable* for *every member* of the group! [49]

[46] *Ibid.*, pp. 63-64.
[47] Fromm, *The Sane Society*, pp. 154-56.
[48] Italics are mine.
[49] Whyte, Jr., *The Organization Man*, pp. 382-86.

An even more dramatic expression of a mass culture's educational values was evident in Park Forest's high school. The basis of the high school's curriculum was openly stated to be "life adjustment." To this end, the community's new $1,600,000 high school building was described by Dr. Baber, then head of the institution, as a "learning laboratory." Baber was of the opinion that American high schools of mid-century were still far too much concerned with purely intellectual education. Except for a small coterie, he asked, what was the value to most people of traditional academic disciplines? "The so-called 'bright' student is often one of the dumbest or least apt when he gets away from his textbooks and memory work." To Baber, this profound proposition was convincingly proved "by the fact that many $20,000-to-$100,000-a-year jobs in business, sales, sports, radio, and TV are held by persons with I.Q.'s of less than ninety."

Thus it came to pass that in Park Forest, where (as in other middle- or upper-middle class suburbs) a majority of the public high school children were *going on to college anyway*, nearly *half* the secondary school curriculum was devoted to noncollege preparatory courses (life adjustment and vocational offerings primarily). One of the key offerings of the latter curriculum was listed by the school as "Family Living" and included units of study such as money management, everyday social relationships, care of the sick, nutrition, food management, clothing, housing the family, and preparation for marriage. The intended emphasis in this course was on "shared responsibility" in building a happy, successful home. "Unified Studies" classes meanwhile discussed such problems of a personal, group, or community nature as town government or juvenile delinquency. Other "preparation-for-life" courses in high favor included journalism, speech, radio, and TV work in the school's well equipped communications laboratory. Dr. Baber was proud of the fact that his school was performing a definite socialization function and was by no means purely an institution of academic learning. "Ours is an age of group action," he solemnly declared, adding that the public high school must acculturate the rising generation to this portentous reality. "We emphasize," he continued, "*general education* and the development of understandings, skills, and critical thinking directly related to current problems of social living. If I were to attempt to define the bases of our educational program, I believe it would be in terms of three fundamental concepts: (1) the philosophy of experimentalism, compromised somewhat by the pressures of tradition, (2) an organismic (or Gestalt) psychology, and (3) democratic educational leadership." [50]

The Search for Excellence

In October, 1957, the Soviet government announced to a startled world that Russia had launched into space its Sputnik I, history's first man-made earth satellite. A stunned American public began to ask itself searching questions. Why had not the American system of popular education, with its vast endowments and well-nigh universal public support, produced a sufficient number of capable scientists and technicians to maintain national technological leadership both on earth and in orbit? A United States Senate document prepared by the Library of Congress in 1958 revealed that Soviet Russian education, like that of other European countries, was "tougher" than that of the United States and bore down much more heavily on pure and applied science than did the more easy-going American schools. [51] People came to feel at this juncture of world history that America must have more and better schools, not just because democratic citizenship and intellectual growth required them, but because the nation's very security depended on them. The keynote of the times was to be a search for excellence.

Actually, the crusade for quality in the schools began even before Sputnik and represented not so much a complete change in direction as an eleventh-hour return to former affirmations. As we have observed, American culture from early days had been deeply involved not only in a drive for Equality, but also in an equally fervent dedication to the ideal of Achievement. The very concept of equality, Alexis De Tocqueville noted, helped to entrench the concept that "success" should be a goal of all, no matter what the origin of the person. When a rigidly stratified aristocratic caste was in complete control, as in Great Britain, members of the "establishment" could afford to follow a customary code appropriate to their station and to "play the game" well for its own sake. [52] But with the "bitch-goddess, success" gnawing at the vitals of a relatively open society, as in America, the emphasis came to be on

[50] Quoted in *Ibid.*, pp. 384-90.
[51] *A Collection of Excerpts and a Bibliography Relative to American Education and Certain Other Educational Systems* (U.S. Senate Document No. 109, 85th Congress, 2d Session [Washington, D.C., 1958]).
[52] Anthony Bailey, "The Establishment: The Institution That Runs Great Britain," *Esquire* (February 1960), pp. 71-76.

"winning the game," no matter what means were used to win it. Indeed, many Americans, as we have seen in our discussion of interscholastic and intercollegiate sports, knowingly tolerated sharp practices if it became apparent that such unsavory measures were efficacious in attaining the one supreme goal—success. As Lipset astutely pointed out, American society pressed its students, ethnic groups, businessmen, union leaders, politicians, and even research scholars to "achieve, to 'get ahead,'" and then, incongruously, it wondered "why there is cheating on exams, rackets among low-status ethnic groups, embezzlement in white-collar jobs, dictatorships in unions, and graft among politicians." [53]

There was a further consequence of the frantic campaign for fame and fortune in a relatively fluid society. Deep human drives in those who had achieved "success" led them to seek by roundabout methods to retain and pass on their privileged position to their children. This ironical development within the framework of a culture officially devoted to equalitarianism was nowhere seen more clearly than in the nation's school system. Despite the public obeisance paid to the slogan, "Education for All," many of the nation's "success *elite*" privately sought to provide *their* children with instruction superior to that available to others. Other things being equal, such educational opportunities were expected to ensure that those whose fathers were already high up on the socio-economic ladder would themselves be able to cling to a similar position. All of which brings to mind that wonderful situation depicted in George Orwell's *Animal Farm* where all pigs started out by being equal, only some pigs came to be "more equal" than others.

A number of studies of mid-century public schools by sociologists have documented at length the theory that, despite official protestations to the contrary, class distinctions did in reality affect many aspects of school life. One observer Bevode McCall stated flatly: "It is a fallacy to say that we have mass education in this country." Vance Packard charged that the teaching staffs in many schools, the parents, and the members of the school boards, far from deemphasizing differentiation among the students on the basis of socio-economic background, actually fostered it. By the time most youngsters reached the fifth or sixth grade, said Packard, they had been made amply aware by all the forces in their environment of the social-class origins of their playmates and with

[53] Lipset, "Equal or Better in America," p. 20. That cheating on examinations has not, however, been limited historically to modern American schools is emphasized by William W. Brickman in "Ethics, Examinations, and Education," *School and Society* (December 2, 1961), pp. 412-14.

whom they should and should not associate. Packard concluded, writing in 1959, that despite all the talk about education for all, America was moving for a number of reasons more and more toward a rigid, stratified society.[54]

The impact of social class upon American public education was even more tangibly felt on the secondary school level. By the time of high school graduation, many children from the lowest rungs of the socio-economic ladder had left school to go to work, while the handful of local youngsters from the real "upper class" (especially in the East) had in many cases been shipped off to private schools. As William L. Warner put it: "Captains of industry educate their sons to take their places or to occupy similar places in other industries." Whereas 80 per cent of the upper- and upper-middle-class children (in terms of family income) in the 1950's actually went to college, only 20 per cent of the lower-middle- and less than 5 per cent of the lower-class children were able to continue their higher education. This trend did not necessarily correspond to I.Q. and general intellectual potential, but was determined in most cases by family expectations and economic capabilities.[55]

In a wealthy suburb like Wellesley, Massachusetts, the clique spirit among students came out into the open. There a sociologist found the local high school to be sharply divided between the sons of upper-class and upper-middle-class "organization men" and those of local servants and blue-collar workers, i.e., the "hot-rod group" comprised mainly of "villagers." Only a very "maverick" member of the lower-class group in a community such as Wellesley was "able to ignore the rejection by the upper clique, resist the temptation of hot-rods and 'broads,' and embark on a college preparatory career." [56] When Hollingshead in 1949 made his study of "Elmtown," he discovered that the children, teachers, and parents in that middle western community had a fairly good understanding of the impact of class status upon the schools. One senior citizen told him, "The high school kids know what is what, and who is who; we don't fool them any." In "Elmtown," the great majority of the children in the two lowest social classes dropped out of school by the end of the eighth grade or shortly thereafter. Only a small number in these working class circles were actively discontented. The majority be-

[54] Packard, *The Status Seekers*, pp. 227-30, 290-96.

[55] W. L. Warner, *et al.*, *Social Class in America* (Gloucester, Mass.: Peter Smith, Publisher, 1957), pp. 24-28.

[56] David Fisher, "Changing Community," in Roger Hagan, ed., *Character and Social Structure* (Cambridge, Mass.: Harvard Printing Office, 1960), p. 42.

lieved that nothing could be done to challenge the position of the "inner ring." Summing up, Hollingshead reported:

> Class V parents were indifferent to the future; they did not look forward to anything better for themselves or their children than they had known. Their school experience had been limited almost exclusively to the elementary grades. Dropping out of school by the end of the eighth grade was the rule, and to go beyond this point was not approved generally by the class culture.[57]

As already suggested, many ambitious parents anxious to provide superior educational opportunities for their children sent their youngsters to private or "independent" schools. About 2 per cent of America's school-age children at mid-century attended such institutions. Sociologist E. Digby Baltzell, himself a graduate of St. Paul's, asserted that the private schools (along with the "Ivy League" universities) served "the sociological function of differentiating the upper class in America from the rest of the population." Influential parents felt they must patronize reputedly "fashionable" independent schools in order to prove and fortify family status. Such persons were firmly of the opinion that famous schools like Andover, Exeter, Groton, Choate, and St. Paul's gave an education for excellence that was academically superior to anything available in the public schools, besides serving as a tool to maintain social status.[58] At schools of the "St. Grottlesex" [59] type the boys were "taught how to dance and dress and talk and comport themselves." And as for the private-school girls, writes Vance Packard, "typically, party lists planned by proper parents for their youngsters are drawn from, and checked against, school-enrollment lists. And most of the schools, aware of their role in screening future socialites, demand students whose fathers have commanding business positions, have membership in proper clubs, and have proper addresses." [60]

Although many of the "exclusive" boy's boarding schools were visibly

[57] August B. Hollingshead, *Elmtown's Youth* (New York: John Wiley & Sons, Inc., 1949), pp. 148-50; Gordon claims that the impact of class has perhaps been overemphasized in terms of its impact upon social relationships within the American high school, and that individual personality factors had a modifying effect, but he also concedes that parental occupation "with its derived cultural manifestations is a significant basis of differentiation." C. Wayne Gordon, *The Social System of the High School* (Glencoe, Ill.: The Free Press, 1957), pp. 100-102.
[58] Robert Gutwillig, "The Select Seventeen: A Guide to Upper-Class Education," *Esquire* (November 1960), pp. 166-85.
[59] Six fashionable eastern boarding schools, most of them Episcopal.
[60] Packard, *The Status Seekers*, pp. 236-37.

modeled after the great English "public" schools such as Eton, Harrow, and Winchester, Robert Gutwillig raises the question whether they effectively imitated their English prototypes in anything but superficial social polish. The English schools, after all, were "products of an old, small, limited, highly structured society and country that continually requires well-educated, well-trained, and well-bred men to lead and guide it at home and abroad." The American private schools, on the other hand, were purposefully created as a kind of artificial hothouse "in a small almost-old corner of a large new nation whose society is certainly stratified, but whose entrance into and exit from the higher levels can be accomplished in one or two generations, and whose basic requirement has always been and continues to be money, despite all protestations to the contrary." [61] Furthermore, the English schools produced not only well-bred gentlemen, but the great statesmen of modern British history. Many of their graduates seemed to feel that special privilege brought with it a solemn responsibility for service and leadership, not only in government, but in art, religion, science, and education. And the English people have in the past readily accepted leadership by this "public school"- and Oxford and Cambridge-trained *elite*. *Per contra*, very few American private school products, given the special circumstances of United States political life, went on to become great statesmen. Indeed before 1960 only a small percentage of them entered public service at all. The vast majority took positions in brokerage or banking firms or became corporation lawyers and executives, usually on Wall Street.[62]

The increasing difficulty in the Fifties and early Sixties of gaining admission to a good college accentuated a kind of hysteria among parents, as did also the post-"Sputnik" concern for early intellectual development. Some parents in New York City were firmly convinced that the path to "success" ran from Brick Church Nursery School to Buckley Elementary to Exeter to Yale. Another educational ladder, this time for girls, which was considered by the *cognoscenti* to be highly efficacious Achievement-wise, was Hunter Elementary to Hunter High to Radcliffe. With such feverish pressures building up, it should not surprise us to discover that Hunter Elementary School (which, being public and tuition-free, was in this instance the exception that proves the

[61] Gutwillig, *op. cit.*, p. 170.
[62] *Ibid.*, pp. 170-72. Franklin D. Roosevelt was a notable exception, but he was denounced by many of his fellow Groton graduates as a "traitor to his class." John F. Kennedy (Choate) was another, but only time will disclose whether his elevation to the Presidency signalized the beginning of a new trend.

rule) had in 1962 over 2000 applications for only 70 vacancies in its nursery school, kindergarten, and first grade. And even so, many anxious parents were probably aware of the fact that less than 60 per cent of the high I.Q. graduates of Hunter Elementary were able to pass the stiff entrance examination for Hunter High.

The above data pertaining to Hunter Elementary and Hunter High suggests that if such high-quality schools had been available in greater numbers under public, tax-supported auspices, many parents enrolling children in private schools might have instead sent their youngsters to these public institutions. Where academic excellence was not available under public auspices, some parents would inevitably seek it out under private ones. Moreover, the "select" private schools were themselves changing somewhat in character following World War II and were putting more stress on intellectual achievement and less on socio-economic status. Claude M. Fuess, former headmaster of Phillips Andover Academy, pointed out in 1962 that an independent school "in which more than one-third of the pupils are receiving financial aid towards their education and in which no student is actually paying the full budgeted tuition cost can hardly be regarded as 'exclusive!' " [63] As the "name" colleges of the Northeast more and more sought out the student with exceptional intellectual talent and/or preparation, it behooved the independent schools to look to their own academic laurels. The better of them moved swiftly to meet the challenge.

Even before the pressure of mounting enrollments hit America's schools and colleges and even before Sputnik I soared into orbit, eloquent voices were heard in the land arguing that dedication to a democratic ideal need not eliminate an equally fervent commitment to high-quality schooling for those able to profit from it. Education for all need not produce conformity to mediocrity nor need it displace a continuing search for excellence. Such was the concept which may be found in the ambitious educational blueprint which Thomas Jefferson in the 1770's presented for consideration to his native Virginia.[64] Obscured somewhat by the equalitarian currents of the Jacksonian era and the rising West, Jefferson's hope never died out in America. In the early twentieth century instructive critiques of American mass education from a qualitative point of view continued to appear; and as enrollments mounted in

---

[63] Claude M. Fuess, "Golden Days for Independent Schools," *Saturday Review of Literature* (August 18, 1962), p. 48.

[64] Roy Honeywell, *The Educational Work of Thomas Jefferson* (Cambridge, Mass.: Harvard University Press, 1931).

the years between the great world wars, upholders of this position became more vocal than ever before.[65]

Comparing the U.S. system in 1913 with that of the secondary schools of England, France, and Germany, Henry A. Perkins asserted that two years were lost in the American educational program. These years of adolescent intellectual training were never recovered at any later stage of mental development. The author believed that the United States could not afford to allow such a loss to go on if she wished to hold her own as a leading power. What were the reasons for this deplorable state of affairs? "In Europe," wrote Perkins, "a child of ten is supposed to be able to work and work hard, and there is little pity shown either to the dull or the lazy." As a result, European school children were gaining two whole years on ours. American parents were too soft, the writer concluded. Reacting against the stern parental discipline which they themselves had known back in the Seventies and Eighties, they were permitting their children to become too flabby, too lazy.[66]

Professor Arthur G. Webster of Clark University, who had spent the summer of 1919 at the Sorbonne in France, published somewhat similar observations in November, 1920. In the United States, he said, the only criterion of success was the amount of money that a person had made. But in Europe an educated man was looked upon as superior solely on the basis of his intellect. Europeans "consider the chief aim of man not to be the accumulation of a certain number of millions of francs, but the accomplishment of some creative task." This is why, Webster explained, French boys and girls of fifteen and sixteen could pass the examinations for entrance to the Sorbonne but American children most certainly could not. The French children were not inherently brighter than American boys and girls, but the former looked upon education as a serious business. "The trouble with education in the United States is with the community, with the fathers and mothers, who do not insist that their children shall do anything that requires exactitude, [shall] stick to it and not let up until they get it done." What suggestions did the professor have to offer to remedy the situation? First of all he called for the end of American self-satisfaction. "We are not the best educated nation in the world. We do not produce the most original

[65] I. L. Kandel, *Impact of the War* (Chapel Hill, N.C.: University of North Carolina Press, 1948).

[66] Henry A. Perkins, "The Schoolboy's Two Lost Years," *The Yale Review* (October 1913), pp. 138-40.

ideas in learning or in invention." Second, he argued that Americans must dispense with the illusion that "the chief thing in life is to have a good time. . . . Youth is the time for work; youth is the time for beginning to learn." [67]

More than a decade later William S. Learned, a member of the staff of the Carnegie Foundation for the Advancement of Teaching, published an analysis of American education which criticized it for being overorganized and overstandardized in its effort to cater to the lowest common denominator. The pupil was imprisoned in a "strait-jacket" curriculum. Attendance, recitations, quizzes all had to be uniform regardless of individual ability. Each standardized stage must be satisfied down to the very last item in order to establish the theoretical equality of the "credit" which was then finally allowed. If the student thereupon went on to college, the same routine was repeated there. Learned conceded that the "neat and convincing bookkeeping" in the American system of mass education helped schoolmen solve otherwise thorny problems of admission, placement, transfer, and the like. But, he asked, was this really education? [68]

Dr. Charles Judd, agreeing with many of the previous comments, declared that "American society must share with the schools responsibility for the existing situation." The high regard for intellectual training in Europe, according to Judd, was to some extent due to the stratification of Old World society and the existence there of a recognized *elite*. European aristocrats understood that their superior social position depended in large measure on superior education. "They respect education more than do many of the members of a democratic nation, which often bestows rewards on people who exhibit energy but lack the refinements belonging to aristocracy." A case in point, claimed Judd, was the fact that the "average intelligence" of the members of the British Parliament was far higher than the "average intelligence" of the members of the United States Congress. Because of the absence in America of the long tradition of culture and breeding, taken for granted in Europe, the purposes of many American young people in seeking a secondary education were exceedingly nebulous. The result was a regrettable flippancy on the part of many American high school pupils.

[67] Arthur G. Webster, "Education and Learning in America," *Science Monthly* (November 1920), pp. 422-46.

[68] William S. Learned, "Credits Versus Education," *Proceedings: Associated Academic Principals of the State of New York* (New York, 1933).

Was there a remedy? Judd stated flatly that in his opinion the palliative "cannot be provided by teachers unless they are supported by a changed attitude in society." [69]

In the years following World War II, American critics of routinized, watered-down public education redoubled their efforts. Alan Valentine, criticising many aspects of contemporary mass culture, saw most Americans as too easily impressed by outward signs of educational progress, by desks and dollars. American democracy had become so static, so smug that it was actually impairing meaningful education. There was a vast difference, Valentine pointed out, between Thomas Jefferson's dream of a national system of public education and the current reality, "yet the average American assumes that Jefferson's plan has been magnificently realized." American schoolmen had concentrated so heavily on one essential aspect of democracy, namely, equal opportunity for all, that they had neglected the second prime ingredient, which was "opportunity and recognition for the exceptional." As a result, "more time and money is spent in bolstering the academically feeble than in developing the strong." Such an approach was dangerous. Democracy could not "afford to be static in its levels of human excellence; it must always be moving consciously toward self-improvement, infused with a spirit of lifting the average to the superior. It cannot safely preach complacency, conformity, or equalitarianism." [70]

Agreeing with Valentine's basic conclusions was David Riesman, who observed that contemporary American parents were being told that children should not read too much, "that it is better for them to learn through experience and to spend their time with other children—as if life were long and varied enough to find out very much about people without the aid of the social storehouse of books and other artistic works." The paradoxical result, as Riesman saw it, was that a veritable fear of books and bookishness had been instilled in the very social groups that once upheld intellectual standards, on the ground that books might interfere with a child's personality development. The child might, God forbid, grow up to be a bookworm and thus lack a well-rounded psyche! [71]

Similarly critical of mid-century schools was William H. Whyte, Jr., who observed that "Organization Men" deprecated the value of purely

---

[69] Charles H. Judd, *Education and Social Progress* (New York: Harcourt, Brace & World, Inc., 1934), pp. 16-19.

[70] Alan Valentine, *Age of Conformity* (Chicago: Henry Regnery Co., 1954), pp. 136-42.

[71] Riesman, *Individualism Reconsidered*, p. 258.

asocial, highly intellectual disciplines for their children. Accordingly, "We find many teachers treating a course less as a worthy discipline in its own right than as a vehicle for stimulating interaction. In many institutions, as a consequence, the yardstick of a teacher's performance is the amount of interaction he develops in the group, and those who keep the students' focus on the discipline are apt to find themselves under censure." [72]

Strongly counterattacking and in so doing reasserting in uncompromising terms the virtues claimed for education for all was the influential Education Policies Commission of the NEA. In 1944, in 1948, and again in 1952, this august body raised its voice in the name of the entire American teaching profession to affirm "that every youth in these United States—regardless of sex, economic status, geographic location, or race—should experience a broad and balanced education." From a close reading of its reports, one gathers that the Commission was more interested in stressing the common qualities of American youth than possible differences. Not surprisingly, it found these common qualities to be seven in number, closely paralleling the classic Seven Cardinal Principles of secondary education which the NEA's special committee had promulgated more than three decades before. All American youth, gravely proclaimed the Commission in 1952, were citizens and would become qualified voters in the future. This meant that "all require education for civic responsibility and competence." Furthermore, all American youth were members of family groups and consequently required "an understanding of family relationships." Next, it was carefully noted that all American youth were products of American culture; all therefore required "an understanding of the main elements in that culture." All American youth, moreover, needed to maintain physical and mental health, and to this end should be given "instruction to develop habits of healthful living, understanding of conditions which foster health, and knowledge of ways of preventing disease, avoiding injuries, and using medical services." All American youth had in addition to learn to earn a living and therefore required occupational guidance and training. Finally, all American youth, it was confidently stated, were capable of rational thought and would be able to make choices involving values, good and bad. Therefore they had to be given an appreciation of the rational process and an insight into the "preferred values" of American democracy.[73]

[72] Whyte, Jr., *The Organization Man*, pp. 50, 392-93.
[73] *Education For All American Youth, A Further Look* (Washington, D.C.: National Education Association, Educational Policies Commission, 1952), pp. 28-30.

In order to implement the ambitious "life adjustment" program outlined above, the Commission proposed that the United States make its public school system truly comprehensive for all youth from age three through twenty, beginning with public nursery schools and including six-year elementary schools, junior high schools, senior high schools, and community colleges. These schools were to provide a training for each American youngster which would

> (1) equip him to enter an occupation suited to his abilities and offering reasonable opportunity for personal growth and social usefulness; (2) prepare him to assume the full responsibilities of American citizenship; (3) give him a fair chance to exercise his right to the pursuit of happiness; (4) stimulate intellectual curiosity, engender satisfaction in intellectual achievement, and cultivate an ability to think rationally; and (5) help him to develop an appreciation of the ethical values which should undergird all life in a democratic society.[74]

Lawrence Cremin has pointed out how influential were these Educational Policies Commission reports during the Fifties.[75] State departments of education from coast to coast followed with few dissents the Commission's suggestions for a broader based pre-primary and elementary school program, with much group work and community projects as well as traditional rudiments. They similarly followed with little change the Commission's proposals for secondary education involving a common program for grades seven through nine and a "partially differentiated program" for grades ten through fourteen. This plan was to be closely linked with a continuous program of vocational, educational, and personal guidance, and with new "general" course offerings which would be functional rather than academic in orientation. All this made a deep impression on many school systems, and was further supported by the recommendations made by President Truman's Commission on Higher Education in 1948. These two studies were similar, most notably with respect to extending the principle of education for all at the public expense through grade fourteen. A few years later, another presidential committee, this time set up by the Eisenhower administration, again focused attention on the need in an expanding economy for enlarging

[74] *Education For All American Youth* (Washington, D.C.: National Education Association, Educational Policies Commission, 1944).
[75] Cremin, *Transformation of the School*, pp. 330-32.

the training of young men and women beyond the high school level.[76]
Then in October, 1957, came Sputnik. The almost instantaneous
national mood of panic and alarm was typified, in its educational aspect,
by a "public service" advertisement which, some months later, appeared
in *Newsweek* magazine and was reprinted in *Reader's Digest* and other
mass-circulation periodicals. "Johnny had *better* learn to read," the statement began. "It no longer matters whether he wants to or would like
to or may learn when the spirit moves him. Johnny now has no choice.
He had better learn to read—and read well—or we may wind up in a
world where no English is written any more. . . . We Americans don't
want to move the world. But we don't want anyone else to, either. So
Johnny had *better* learn to read. Because you can bet Ivan is spending
a lot of time on *his* books." [77] Against the backdrop of an aroused and
piqued public opinion, critics of the existing situation in the schools
had a field day. They made the welkin ring with charges that "inanities,"
"frills," and "life adjustment" in the classroom were actually endangering
American national security.

Fifteen months before Sputnik, Caspar Green had asked in the *Atlantic Monthly*, "What shall we do with the Dullards?" [78] The answer
now more and more seemed to be: Do not allow them to interfere with
the education of the gifted, the training of future leaders! Educational
journalist Fred M. Hechinger summed up the disenchanted mood of
the hour when he wrote: "Through the years 'excellence' became the
forgotten word, while the 'open door' was made the permanent symbol.
In time, despite the 'open door,' many children were no longer offered
true equality of opportunity, because behind the 'open door' the shelves
were often bare." [79] In a similar vein, three authors of a volume on
secondary school teaching pondered the far-reaching implications of the
change in national outlook for the future of the high school:

> Can the richest nation in the world afford to have schools serving as
> custodial agents for all the children of all the people through the eighteenth
> or twentieth year? Is it possible to meet the social, cultural, intellectual,

[76] This body, set up in March, 1956, was known as The Committee on Education
Beyond the High School. See Albert R. Munse and Edna D. Booher, *Federal Funds
for Education* (U.S. Office of Education Bulletin No. 2, 1959. [Washington, D.C.,
1959]).

[77] *Newsweek* (October 20, 1958).

[78] Caspar D. Green, "What Shall We Do with the Dullards," *Atlantic Monthly*
(May 1956), pp. 72-74.

[79] As quoted in *AAUW Journal* (March 1962), p. 162.

and athletic needs of all adolescents under one roof? . . . Are the extreme ranges of ability accommodated by mass education? . . . And with the prevailing stress upon the gifted child, what proportion of the tax dollar and the teacher's time should be devoted to his care, nurture, and guidance? The American system of values presumably will govern the future of the secondary school; if and when the philosophy changes, so will the school change its organization, purposes, and procedures.[80]

That such a fundamental reorganization was in process became more and more manifest as brickbats aimed at existing mass education practices flew thick and fast. Professor Harold C. McCurdy, a psychologist at the University of North Carolina, published a study in 1960 of 20 creative geniuses of history, noting that these exceptional people in childhood had received much attention and love from their parents and were in constant association with adults, but were relatively isolated from other children. As children, furthermore, many of these geniuses had experienced rich fantasies. Professor McCurdy maintained that existing mass education reduced such factors to a minimal value and thus, in essence, had the effect of suppressing genius and creativity. Agreeing with the fundamental outlines of his indictment, the newly installed Dean of Teachers College, Columbia University, Dr. John H. Fischer, declared in June, 1960, that American schools must give priority to "the intellectual competence" of students instead of acting as centers of "entertainment, civic development, and charitable enterprises." The Dean of the institution once considered the most influential bulwark of "life adjustment" in education further told his audience: "A school free to concentrate on those services that only schools can give is in a position to do more effective teaching than one that must be all things to all children and their parents, too."

Equally significant in showing which way the pedagogical winds were blowing was the new concern for academic education exhibited by members of the United States Congress. The solons were mightily interested in finding out why the nation had fallen so badly behind the Russians in the race for space. Among others, Secretary of Health, Education, and Welfare Marian B. Folsom was summoned before the Senate's Committee on Education in 1958 and asked to explain what was wrong with American education. Folsom testified that Russian schools were indeed requiring, and obtaining, work of higher quality,

[80] H. Orville Nordberg, James M. Bradfield, and William C. Odell, "Teachers and the Pursuit of Excellence," in *Secondary School Teaching* (New York: The Macmillan Company, 1962). First published in *School and Society* (February 24, 1962), p. 86.

particularly in the natural sciences and languages, than were American schools. "Great care is taken," he said, "to see that able Soviet youth are prepared to serve the state in the most effective possible way." Nevertheless, because of their authoritarian aspects, Folsom declared that Soviet educational methods would not work at all for the American system or national purposes. Soviet education was opposed to the whole idea of individual liberty and freedom. Yet Americans, continued the Secretary, might have carried freedom too far. "We offer to youth still too young to know the importance of their decision the choice between taking more difficult courses which will open greater opportunities to them and easier courses which may not produce the same long-range benefits." The result was that only one in three American high school graduates had taken as much as one year of chemistry, only one in four had pursued any course in physics, and only 15 per cent of all high school students were studying a foreign language. This situation, Folsom told the senators, represented an appalling waste of human talent. While the nation's striving for universal education was commendable, what was needed most now, he said, was "a new emphasis on the pursuit of learning, a new esteem for academic teaching and academic accomplishment. In many of our schools and homes we need more hard work in fundamental academic subjects and higher academic standards." [81]

Even before the challenge posed by Soviet space technology, significant plans and programs for attaining just such "a new emphasis on the pursuit of learning" as Secretary Folsom had called for had begun to appear. While it is true that the progressive movement of the pre-World War II period brought forth some promising programs for breaking the academic lockstep and permitting gifted students to proceed at their own pace (notably the Eight-Year Study),[82] the most influential experiments along these lines were launched in the early 1950's. Why this swing of the pendulum away from education for all

[81] *Senate Document No. 109, 85th Congress, 2nd Session* (Washington, D.C.: Senate Committee on Education, 1958), pp. 5-10.

[82] Thayer, *The Role of the School,* pp. 166-167; *Twenty-third Yearbook,* II National Society for the Study of Education (1924), 256-58; Wilford M. Aikman, *The Story of the Eight-Year Study* (New York: Harper & Row, Publishers, 1942), pp. 4-21. The Eight-Year Study was an experiment sponsored by the Progressive Education Association's Commission on the Relation of School and College in which some 300 colleges from 1932 to 1940 agreed to waive their formal admissions requirements for recommended graduates of 30 cooperating secondary schools. A flexible program was followed in these schools which permitted more attention to the needs of the individual student than was customarily given.

and toward education for excellence should have come in the early 1950's is not entirely clear. Perhaps it was simply a long overdue reaction to the main trends of the Twenties and Thirties, which had, particularly on the high school level, gone too far. Perhaps, as Thomas Eliot suggests, the reaction set in because in the years following World War II it was becoming more and more difficult for high school graduates to gain admission to the college of their choice and there consequently arose a demand for "beefing up" the academic side of the secondary school curriculum.[83] Or perhaps it was because the Ford Foundation was set up about this time, and through its educational subsidiary, the Fund for the Advancement of Education, had decided to pump some of the vast funds at its disposal into the subsidy of education for excellence in the nation's schools. The Fund, reviewing its first ten years of operation, endorsed the general proposition that everyone should have an equal opportunity to as full an education as possible, but also enunciated a number of other fundamental convictions:

> One such is the Fund's conviction that a liberal education is the first essential in the education of every American, and particularly of every teacher. Another is that it is in no way undemocratic to seek out and nurture superior talent and that, in fact, the democratic way of life is bound to suffer if this is not done. A third is that American schools, if they are to produce any significant number of intellectually superior human beings, must re-establish the priority of the intellect.[84]

One of the first moves by the Fund to achieve these objectives was sponsorship of an Advanced Placement program in America's schools and colleges. In 1953 this program was launched as an experimental project with 18 secondary schools and 12 colleges participating. In 1955 the program was established as a continuing project of the College Entrance Examination Board. A signal success from the start in helping to provide education for excellence, the Advanced Placement movement grew by leaps and bounds. By 1959, 355 secondary schools and 279 colleges and universities were taking part in the program. Some 3,700 high school seniors and an additional 10,000 ninth, tenth, and eleventh graders were benefiting from it.[85]

[83] Thomas Eliot, *Governing America* (New York: Dodd, Mead & Co., 1961), p. 177.

[84] Fund for the Advancement of Education, *Decade of Experiment* (New York: Fund for the Advancement of Education, 1961), p. 19.

[85] Harold Howe, II, "The Advanced Placement Program," *NEA Journal* (January 1959), pp. 28-29; Fuess, "Golden Days for Independent Schools," p. 48; *A Guide to the Advanced Placement Program and the Advanced Placement Examinations: 1958-1959* (College Entrance Examination Board, 1958).

The first step in the program involved the establishment of college-level courses in secondary schools for especially able and ambitious students. Conferences between college and secondary school teachers prepared course outlines at a college-freshman level in 11 subjects: mathematics, French, German, Spanish, Latin, physics, chemistry, biology, American history, European history, and English. Then, each May, the College Entrance Examination Board offered students the chance to take stiff Advanced Placement Examinations in these subject areas based on the specific courses as described in the Advanced Placement Syllabus. Each of these examinations was prepared by a committee of teachers from colleges and secondary schools, assisted by a specialist from the Educational Testing Service. Once a student in the program was admitted to college, his scores were reported to that institution. The colleges were thereupon requested to follow one of three procedures in dealing with such students: grant actual semester hours of college credit; give advanced placement in college standing; or release the student from required course work which had already been satisfactorily completed in high school. Practices varied, of course, from college to college. It is certainly worthy of note, in this connection, that in 1958 some 30 boys went straight from secondary school into the sophomore class at Harvard.[86]

Charles R. Keller, Director of Advanced Placement from 1955 to 1957, saw the program as one containing "more by way of intangibles, by-products, derivatives, and hopes than of tangibles and realized gains." He further declared, "I have developed an 'iceberg theory' of the Program. So much more lies below the surface than appears at or above the surface." And it seems beyond doubt that Advanced Placement, once it gained momentum, sent a shock-wave through the entire American secondary school system, raising intellectual standards and generating a genuine search for academic excellence. The College Entrance Board itself defined the significant by-products of the movement five years after its launching as the following:

1) The Program provides challenging experiences for able secondary school teachers as well as for able students.
2) Schools and colleges are encouraged to think of students as individuals.
3) Attention is directed to subject matter and to the teaching of this subject matter.
4) College teachers who know what the schools are doing become 'duplication conscious' and re-think all their courses.

[86] *The Key Reporter* (April 1958), p. 7; *Advanced Placement Program Newsletter*, No. 7 (May 1959); *A Guide to the Advanced Placement Program*.

5) Constructive and creative curricular thinking has been encouraged in the schools, curricular flexibility in the colleges.
6) Schools and colleges are working together in an effective way, with the colleges showing an increasing interest in what the schools are doing.
7) The head start enjoyed by Advanced Placement students enables them when in college either to broaden their education or to intensify or accelerate study in their chosen fields.[87]

One of the most important by-products of Advancement Placement was the formulation of new "honors" (college level) courses for high schools, often under the sponsorship of a national learned society. While this trend went back at least as far as 1953, it was greatly accelerated by the impact of Sputnik. Organizations such as the American Historical Association, the Modern Language Association, the Association of American Geographers, the American Political Science Association, and the American Economic Association now became more actively interested in problems of instruction at the pre-college level than they had been at any previous time in their history.[88] A revolution in the teaching of English was held by some to be in the making.[89] The American Institute of Physics undertook to advise high schools on ways to make science instruction more palatable and comprehensive, specifically proposing, in the bargain, two new types of secondary-level physics courses. Similarly new and penetrating courses in chemistry, biology, mathematics, modern foreign languages, Latin, and even grade school reading (through the aid of phonics) were worked out by committees set up by the Advanced Placement Program, the learned societies themselves, or other groups of educational experts. Soon the whole American educational order was humming with the excitement of a busy and sedulous search for quality.

The parent organization of the Fund for the Advancement of Education made a notable contribution to the quest for academic excellence two years before Sputnik crossed the night sky. At that time it invested $20,000,000 in grants payable over a ten-year period to found and finance a National Merit Scholarship Corporation. The stated purpose of this new body was "to discover, recognize and encourage exceptionally able young people, as a means of helping them receive the kind of education that will assure to themselves and the nation the full benefits

[87] *A Guide to the Advanced Placement Program.*
[88] *American Council of Learned Societies Newsletter,* Vol. XIII, No. 5 (May 1962).
[89] *School and Society* (September 22, 1962), p. 282.

of their unusual abilities." To this end the Corporation was to grant Merit Scholarships so that highly capable young people in the nation's secondary schools might go on to college. By 1960 it had in fact granted more than 3000 such scholarships, in collaboration with more than 100 business corporations and other sponsors such as the Carnegie Corporation of New York, setting in motion the largest independently supported scholarship program ever undertaken.

In order to make its selection, the Corporation was obliged to hold special examinations in public, parochial, and independent secondary schools. By 1960 more than 1,500,000 youngsters had been so tested. Stipends varied from $100 as token awards to students not actually in financial need to as much as $2,200 a year for four years. Of the Merit Scholars finally selected, 86 per cent during the first five years of the program came from public schools, 8 per cent from parochial schools, and 6 per cent from private schools. Certificates of Merit and Letters of Commendation were given during that period to another 55,000 outstanding secondary school students who did not for one reason or another actually qualify for one of the scholarships. Of this number, at least half were assisted thereby in obtaining scholarship aid and admission to colleges of their choice. In 1962, 80 special scholarships in addition to the nearly 900 regular ones were established by the Corporation for "Exceptional Merit Scholars." These were to be awarded to students "whose records indicate exceptional creative promise; who, while showing superior attainment and promise in one field, are not as distinguished in many fields as the typical National Merit Scholar; who have shown an ability to depart from the traditional academic time pattern by entering college, . . . with less than four years of secondary school education; and to students of marked academic ability who also have demonstrated an exceptionally determined effort to overcome severe financial and related disadvantages." [90]

The Fourth Annual Report of the National Merit Scholarship Corporation called attention to the larger significance of the experiment. Merit Scholars, it declared, had already become the very embodiment of that national *elite* of academic talent which the founders of the program had envisioned. The first 21 Merit Scholars to graduate all had distinguished careers in college. Several had contributed to original

[90] The question of the validity of the selection procedures of the National Merit Scholar program for children who came from homes where there was little experience with the use of verbal and mathematical symbols was raised by Horace Mann Bond. See his "The Productivity of National Merit Scholars by Occupational Class," *School and Society* (September 28, 1957), pp. 267-68.

research. Most of them were elected to Phi Beta Kappa or other campus honorary societies. Twenty-one of the 26 had gone on to graduate or professional school. Although most of the more than 3000 scholarship holders had chosen to attend colleges with rigorous academic standards, 82 per cent were able to secure a place in the top quarter of their respective college classes.

Another area in which foundation funds played an important role in elevating academic standards was that of in-service teacher training. The John Hay Fellows Program, which was begun in the late 1950's by the Greenwood Fund, provided stipends to enable approximately 85 senior high school teachers annually "to pursue studies in the humanities, to enrich their teaching, and to stimulate creative, imaginative contributions to American education." For this purpose the teachers selected for the program were subsidized during a Fellowship year in advanced studies in their own fields and related ones at a number of leading universities. There was also a four-week John Hay Fellows Summer Institutes Program at four regional college centers which had similar objectives, but which was open also to public school administrators.[91]

During this same period of time the federal government began to move impressively to elevate standards in the schools. An important first step came in 1950 when Congress established the National Science Foundation as an independent agency of the United States government. The stated purpose of the new federal organization was "to promote scientific progress primarily by supporting basic research and education in the sciences." By the fiscal year 1961, $176,000,000 was being appropriated annually for the Foundation's program, which included the improving of course content in the natural sciences and assistance to science teachers, students, and advanced scholars. A subsequent act directed the National Science Foundation to administer a teacher-institute in-service program to improve the competence and deepen the knowledge of teachers of science and mathematics.[92]

Even more far-reaching was a direct consequence of the national debate over the educational implications of Sputnik, namely, the National Defense Education Act of 1958. This omnibus bill provided for a number of things that had a direct relationship to the search for excellence. By Title III elementary and secondary schools procured fed-

[91] Robert Quick, ed., *Fellowships in the Arts and Sciences, 1963-1964* (Washington, D.C.: American Council on Education, 1962), pp. 26-27, 71.

[92] F. Emerson Andrews and Ann D. Walton, eds., *The Foundation Directory* (New York: Russell Sage Foundation, 1960), p. 80.

eral funds to be used for new or remodeled equipment for education in science, mathematics, and modern foreign languages. Money was also appropriated by this Title to state educational agencies to expand or improve their supervisory or related services in the above-mentioned subject-matter fields. Title VI provided for federal subsidies to encourage the teaching in the United States of important but rarely studied languages, to finance through special language institutes the advanced training of elementary and secondary school teachers, and to introduce new language teaching methods and instructional materials in the schools. Other vital educational provisions of the Act dealt with guidance and counseling and specialized training on the college and university level.[93]

The National Defense Education Act was enacted during the second administration of President Dwight D. Eisenhower, who opposed more sweeping proposals for federal aid to education as advanced by the NEA and other organizations. When John F. Kennedy succeeded Eisenhower as President in 1961, he announced support for an ambitious program of federal aid to the schools, which, however, failed in Congress again and again, largely because of the church-state issue (see Chap. 6). An important part of the Kennedy Administration's unrealized educational blueprint for 1962 called for large federal appropriations to improve the quality of American public education. New support for the search for excellence, under this plan, was to be provided by means of federal scholarship grants to teachers in *all* academic fields, not just those in science, mathematics, and modern languages. This program, reminiscent of the John Hay Fellows Program, intended to support short-term institutes for teachers staged at selected colleges and universities. Furthermore, federal grants would have been made available to the states for the education of gifted children, the encouragement of new and better methods of instruction, and the acquisition by local school systems of improved equipment and better libraries. Administration officials supporting these proposals described them as a "seed money" approach—that is, "planting the seeds for a quality education program that in years to come would blossom at local, state, and federal levels." [94]

What was the balance sheet of the search for excellence by the early

[93] Theodora E. Carlson, *Guide to the National Defense Education Act of 1958* (Washington, D.C., 1959), pp. 7-10, 16-18; *Progress of Public Education in the United States of America, 1958-1959* (Washington, D.C.: U.S. Department of Health, Education, and Welfare, 1959), p. 2.

[94] *New York Times*, July 31, 1962, p. 26; *ibid.*, November 24, 1962, p. 18.

1960's? Manifestly, the drive for intellectual quality had scored significant gains. Particularly in fields such as the natural sciences, mathematics, and vital foreign languages like Russian, measurable progress was being made from coast to coast with new types of course organization and instructional materials. Specialized courses in these fields were being introduced for the first time into public high schools.[95] An intensive study of developments along this line in New York State revealed that by 1961, aided by grants from the legislature, a notable increase had occurred in the number of school systems offering specific programs for the gifted. More and more, these systems were requiring higher I.Q.'s for admission to such programs, were forming special small-size classes to give better attention to pupil needs, were providing more accelerated and advanced placement programs than ever before, and were taking specific measures to improve the teaching of the gifted.[96] At Miami University in Ohio a special variant of acceleration was launched in 1958 (again, as in earlier experiments, with money provided by the Fund for the Advancement of Education) whereby selected high school students were admitted, generally during the summertime, to college-level courses taught by university instructors either on or off campus. This University Study Program for Superior High School Students proved, after a trial of three years, to be most useful for the 179 high school sophomores and juniors who enrolled in it and received college credits for work completed.[97]

It would be correct to say, as the U.S. Office of Education's report on the *Progress of Public Education* for 1958-1959 pointed out, that the American people had rejected "the recommendations of some who had maintained that a more selective type of institution was necessary to insure quality in education." But it also was a fact that "many school systems were experimenting along a line of compromise by establishing special classes for gifted pupils in the comprehensive high schools." While this was the usual pattern established, a few communities preferred to seek academic excellence by maintaining specialized high schools catering to especially talented students. Certain public high schools of this type, such as Boston Latin School and Girls Latin School in Roxbury, Massachusetts, had distinguished reputations going back

[95] *Progress of Public Education in the United States, 1958-1959*, pp. 16-17.

[96] Cyril W. Woolcock, "The Gifted in the Public Schools of New York State, 1961," *School and Society* (February 10, 1962), pp. 62-64.

[97] Joseph R. Baxter and Reginald L. Jones, "Acceleration of Superior High School Students," *School and Society* (February 10, 1962), pp. 64-66.

to colonial times. Although more recent developments made it increasingly difficult for these schools to maintain their traditional standards of excellence, they continued in the main to deserve their fame.[98] Other special institutions such as previously mentioned Hunter Elementary and Hunter High were twentieth-century establishments which admitted only the highly gifted, and which put them through a rigorous academic program. A similar institution in the New York City area, which came to be particularly well known during the 1950's, was the Bronx High School of Science. In isolated cases, moreover, the formation of new regional or consolidated schools, a phenomenon which became increasingly common by the middle of the century, gave an opportunity for the building up of institutions specifically pointed toward the education of the gifted. Thus at the new Bridgewater-Raynham Regional High School in Massachusetts, which began operation in 1961, the entire emphasis was on a drive for academic excellence. Periods were 60 minutes long ("to give the teacher a better leverage on the subject"), homerooms and study halls were abolished as time wasters (students reported directly to their first class), teachers had no lunchroom duty and their clerical duties were held to a bare minimum, and no fund-raising or other disruptive "extra" activities were allowed to take place during school time. In addition, all students were grouped in classes according to intellectual ability (with Honors classes in a number of subject-matter fields), and all students were expected to carry five major subjects a year in place of the traditional four. Examples such as these gave dramatic proof of what could be accomplished by the American public high school system to further the search for excellence, should the people decide to sponsor Honors institutions specifically dedicated to the education of an intellectual *elite*.

The pendulum had swung far, then, as Americans entered the challenging 1960's, in the direction pointed out by the fervent advocates of the crusade for educational excellence. The big question, however, remained: How far? One team of observers, looking at the over-all picture in 1962, argued that no really profound change had occurred: "While man-made satellites, automation, astronauts, intercontinental missiles, and revelations of what the competitor is producing and achieving all make an initial shock and impression on some people, yet there appears to be no universal awakening in the schools to match the events

[98] See "Boston Latin: Its Decline and Fall?" *Boston Globe*, September 3, 1961, pp. 1, 33.

. . . the same old things generally tend to be taught in the same old ways."[99] Certain it was that many educational administrators were loath to change their policies; their thinking in many cases was still running in the same old grooves. A sampling of opinion among professional educators made by Phi Delta Kappa (an honorary educational society) in 1960 revealed that 48 per cent of the schoolmen polled were opposed to reduction of nonacademic schooling to permit greater emphasis on the basic disciplines. Another 41 per cent recorded themselves as favoring the idea, but only with reservations. Only 11 per cent of America's professional educators, according to this sample, unreservedly approved of a renewed academic emphasis in the schools.[100]

Noting possible distortions in the current mania for intellectual upgrading, Paul Woodring warned that it was "not a sign of excellence that school pressures are creating neurotic anxieties in parents and students about grades, test scores, and getting into the 'right' colleges." He further declared, commenting on the vogue for "beefing up" science education programs (sometimes at the expense of the humanities), that "excellence is not achieved merely by piling on more work or by shifting the emphasis from poetry and history to science and mathematics."[101] Even greater difficulties were involved in the process of selecting the "top cream" of the nation's youth in terms of its potential for special academic programs, as evidenced by the problems which bedeviled the work of the National Merit Scholarship Corporation. In this connection, a Dean of Admissions at Harvard College, Wilbur J. Bender, declared in his final report for the 1960 academic year that he did not believe it would be wise for Harvard to limit admission to the top 1 per cent of high school students as recorded on nationwide tests. Such a policy, he believed, far from producing first-rate intellectual power, might instead produce "simply a high level of dull, competent, safe academic mediocrity," an army of future Doctors of Philosophy who would do plodding, useful work but would possess no originality. In reaching these conclusions, Dean Bender had the following considerations in mind:

The student who ranks first in his class may be genuinely brilliant. Or he may be a compulsive worker or the instrument of domineering parents' ambitions or a conformist or self-centered careerist who has shrewdly

[99] Nordberg, Bradfield, and Odell, *School and Society* (February 24, 1962), p. 75.
[100] Richard E. Gross, "Education's Centennial Dilemma," *School and Society* (February 13, 1960), p. 66.
[101] Paul Woodring, "The Meaning of Excellence," *Saturday Review of Literature* (April 15, 1961), p. 51.

calculated his teachers' prejudices and expectations and discovered how to regurgitate efficiently what they want.[102]

Nothing Bender had to say, however, lessened the basic importance of the new programs of education for excellence. If anything, he simply emphasized the necessity of a more sophisticated and knowledgeable approach to the problem. Whatever the criteria involved, it was generally agreed that American schools must locate and identify individuals with unusual potentialities for excellence. And as Cyril Woolcock pointed out, it was most important that such gifted children be identified at the earliest possible age. Furthermore, something had to be done to modify the rigidities of American school laws, which prevented entrance into school until age five or six and then required a slow grade-by-grade mass-production type of progress through a standardized course of study. Many bright children, Woolcock noted, were "mentally at least two or three years advanced and correspondingly a year or two advanced socially and physically over five- and six-year olds found in the beginning grades of school." [103]

In any event, it was obvious that American education, for a complex of reasons, had turned a significant corner as it entered the seventh decade of the twentieth century. Without abandoning the characteristically American commitment to education for all (in the comprehensive form it had assumed by that time), a renewed emphasis was being placed upon the equally traditional, if not always compatible, goal of Achievement. This latest drive in no way denigrated the immense value of what had already been achieved by the nation's school system. To appreciate this accomplishment we have only to compare the developed educational resources of the United States in the year 1960 with those of some of the smaller, poorer, "under-developed" countries of the world such as Burma, the Congo, Nigeria, or Pakistan.[104] In such a comparison, the American material lead immediately becomes apparent: indeed, many of these struggling new countries were actively seeking educational assistance from the United States. The twentieth-century American problem, essentially, was how best to make use of the extensive educational machinery which had already been constructed. And here it may well be argued that it was precisely because so many Americans in the Space Age held ambitious expectations with respect

[102] *New York Times*, October 19, 1961, p. 31.

[103] Cyril W. Woolcock, "Needs of Gifted and Talented Students," *School and Society* (November 5, 1960), p. 413.

[104] On this point, see David, ed., *Education and Manpower*, pp. 6-15, 35-37.

to popular education that the crusade for excellence got under way
with such a dramatic impact. In any event, the consequences of the
new course were soon apparent. Not only did the American secondary
school enter upon a period of readjustment "unparalleled in the past
half-century." The total effort Americans were making to shape their
educational structure to meet the modern world's demands for *both*
well-trained citizens *and* gifted leaders also promised, said *Business
Week* in 1958, to "reshape our ways of living, patterns of spending, and
scales of social values for the next 50 years."

CHAPTER SIX

Church, State, and School

"For, whatever you may say in the future, your record of anti-Catholicism stands for all to see—a record which you yourself wrote on the pages of history which cannot be recalled—documents of discrimination unworthy of an American mother!" [1] These angry words were addressed to a former First Lady of the United States by one of the highest ranking ecclesiastical dignitaries of the Roman Catholic church in America. The date was July 21, 1949, and the personalities involved were, respectively, Mrs. Eleanor Roosevelt and Francis Cardinal Spellman, Archbishop of New York. The outburst came in the midst of a bitter controversy over proposals in Congress for federal aid to education and the relationship of such a program to church-supported private schools. The Roosevelt-Spellman controversy brought to a head important issues involving the relations of church, state, and school which, in their origins, went back to the very beginnings of the American Republic. In the twentieth century these thorny questions were placed by the march of events in an ever sharper focus and increasingly attracted the attention of legislators, courts of law, and ordinary citizens of the land.

[1] Anson Phelps Stokes, *Church and State in the United States,* II (New York: Harper & Row, Publisher, 1950), p. 749.

The Nineteenth-Century Background

Before the American Revolution truly secular schools did not exist in America. Sectarian religious groups had a strong control over curriculum, course content, school procedures, and teaching personnel. Reflecting Old World precedents, religious indoctrination was considered a perfectly appropriate undertaking at every level of the educational process. With the separation from Great Britain and the adoption of a national constitution, a powerful movement got under way on both the state and federal level to separate church and state and establish full rights of conscience. This development was bound to have an impact upon the public school systems which were beginning to be established by some of the now independent states. Although teaching of the characteristic religious doctrines of the most numerous and influential Protestant denominations continued to be the practice, there was less of this than before. Sectarian jealousies and jockeying for position strengthened the stand of those who advocated rigid exclusion of all doctrinal teachings from the public schools. In 1827 Massachusetts, the first state to take legal action, enacted an influential statute forbidding sectarian textbooks or teachings in her common schools. When Horace Mann became secretary of the Massachusetts Board of Education in 1837, he enforced this law vigorously, over the strenuous objection of a number of clerical leaders. Mann kept religion in the public schools by means of generalized ethical teaching and the reading of the Bible to the pupils, but he excluded all teaching of the doctrines of a particular sect.[2]

This solution of the problem of church-public school relations seems to have appealed widely to majority sentiment in America during the early and middle period of the nineteenth century. By 1861 most states had put into effect a program similar to that of Massachusetts, banning sectarian teaching and schoolbooks but encouraging the inculcation of a nondenominational, basic Protestant Christianity. Despairing of being able individually to dominate the fast-growing common school systems in the multidenominational American setting, the most powerful Protestant churches settled for this system as the best possible solution under the circumstances.[3]

While this arrangement satisfied the Protestant group, based as it

[2] R. Freeman Butts, *The American Tradition in Religion and Education* (Boston: Beacon Press, 1950), pp. 43-101, 130-34; William K. Dunn, *What Happened to Religious Education?* (Baltimore: Johns Hopkins Press, 1958), pp. 304 7.

[3] Dunn, *What Happened to Religious Education?*

was upon mutually acceptable readings from the King James Version of the Bible, it definitely was not satisfactory to a growing religious minority—the Roman Catholics. The vast immigration from Europe in the 1840's and 1850's had swelled the numbers of Catholics in the United States to an important degree, especially in the large East Coast cities. These new arrivals felt that their children were being discriminated against in existing public schools, and that justice required that the tax moneys they were being asked to contribute be allotted to the support of Catholic-controlled schools or schools staffed by Catholics.[4] The Catholic attitude of this period was one of protest against favoritism:

> But while the public schools of those days professed to be nonsectarian, they were really Protestant institutions, used to pervert Catholics. The Protestant version of the Bible was King James's, which Catholics hold to be incomplete and false. It was read every morning in the presence of the Catholic children; and the teachers, who were all Protestants, made comments on the text unfriendly and insulting to Catholic convictions. Protestant hymns were sung, and Protestant prayers, expressing Protestant doctrines, were recited. The whole tendency of this system of education was to make Catholic children indifferent to their religion or apostates to it.[5]

In Lowell, Massachusetts, beginning in 1835, separate schools for Irish Catholics were absorbed into the local public school system and given public support.[6] Horace Mann, replying to an inquiry about this system, characterized it as "very intelligent" as long as such schools and their instructors were "subject to examination and . . . to visitation by the Committee in the same manner as other teachers and schools." [7] However, efforts by Catholic leaders to spread this arrangement to other American communities or, failing in that, to eliminate the required attendance at readings from the King James Bible met with signal failure. In some cities such proposals provoked mob violence, fostered mainly by the "Know-Nothings" and other militant nativists.[8]

[4] Leo Pfeffer, *Creeds in Competition* (New York: Harper & Row, Publishers, 1958), p. 75.

[5] Rev. Henry A. Brann, *Most Rev. John Hughes* (New York: Dodd, Mead & Co., 1892), pp. 69-70.

[6] J. A. Burns and Bernard Kohlbrenner, *History of Catholic Education in the United States* (New York: Benziger Bros., Inc., 1937), pp. 156-58; *School Committee of Lowell, Massachusetts, Annual Report* (March 1836), p. 3.

[7] Mary Mann, ed., *Life and Works of Horace Mann,* III (Boston, 1865), p. 262.

[8] Townsend Scudder, *Concord—American Town* (Boston: Little, Brown & Co., 1947), pp. 194-218, 289-91; John Higham, *Strangers in the Land* (New Brunswick, N.J.: Rutgers University Press, 1955).

The most dramatic of these pre-Civil War controversies arose in New York City. In 1840 Bishop John Hughes denounced the Public School Society of that community for fostering an anti-Catholic atmosphere in its schools and demanded that the share of taxes Catholic citizens were paying to support education be turned over to schools under Catholic control. A battle royal followed in the City Council and in the New York State Legislature, ultimately having an important effect upon the election campaign of 1841. The final result was not completely satisfactory either to the Bishop or to his Protestant opponents. The Public School Society, which had been dominated by a "nonsectarian Protestant outlook" was abolished by the Legislature and in its place a purely secular New York City Board of Education was set up to manage all the local public schools. Henceforth public moneys were not to be paid to any schools under denominational auspices. Thus the consequence in this particular instance was an acceleration of the trend toward a separation of church and public school.[9] Bishop Hughes clearly appreciated this aspect, for he noted in a confidential memoir some years later,

> Immediately after the breaking up of the Public School Society, a new system was introduced, very different indeed from what I would have recommended; but yet an immense improvement on the one which it replaced. I was obliged to tolerate the attendance of our poor children at these schools until we should, with time and the blessing of Almighty God, be enabled to erect schools of our own for their *exclusively* Catholic training.[10]

Catholics tried repeatedly, during ensuing decades, to secure public moneys for their schools, but they continually found this line of attack unprofitable and increasingly turned to the building up of a parochial school system which would be supported by the American Catholic community. It is true that at Poughkeepsie, New York, an arrangement much like the earlier Lowell system went into operation during the 1870's, but this was the exception rather than the rule.[11] Church coun-

---

[9] Brann, *Most Rev. John Hughes*, pp. 83-86; Butts, *The American Tradition in Religion and Education*, pp. 134-35; W. O. Bourne, *History of the Public School Society of the City of New York* (New York, 1873), pp. 192-93; John R. Hassard, *Life of Archbishop Hughes* (New York: Appleton-Century-Crofts, Inc., 1866), pp. 226-51; Lawrence Kehoe, ed., *Complete Works of the Most Rev. John Hughes*, I, (New York: Lawrence Kehoe, 1865), pp. 292-95.

[10] Rev. Henry J. Browne, ed., "Memoir of Archbishop Hughes," *U.S. Catholic Historical Society: Historical Records and Studies*, Vols. 39-40 (1952), pp. 152-53.

[11] Burns and Kohlbrenner, *History of Catholic Education in the United States*, pp. 160-62. The attempt was finally terminated in 1898.

cils, particularly in the Middle West, where German-Americans were strongly attached to the parochial school idea, came to demand stricter ecclesiastical legislation that would require all parishes to establish such institutions.[12] The decisions of a number of plenary councils held between 1852 and 1884 included important moves in this direction.[13]

Speeding this trend were pressures from Rome. Following the momentous Vatican Council of 1870, with the victory for the ultramontane point of view as evidenced by the promulgation of the doctrine of papal infallibility, the Papacy displayed a new activism in many areas of the Church's affairs. Thus when certain American bishops appealed to the Propaganda for stricter enactments on parochial schools, the Roman Congregation (Papal department), which had jurisdiction in American church matters, responded in 1875 with a rigorous "Instruction . . . concerning the Public Schools." Forbidding the attendance of Catholic children at such schools as dangerous to their souls, the Congregation declared that the only possible exceptions to this rule would be in cases where no Catholic schools existed.[14]

This authoritative utterance from Rome served as the basis for much of the legislation on schools adopted by the celebrated Third Plenary Council of Baltimore, which met in the fall of 1884. Eleven archbishops were in attendance, together with 60 bishops, and a number of other officials of the American hierarchy. Following in every important respect the Instruction of 1875, the Council decreed the parochial school to be the norm for the elementary education of all Catholics and ordered ecclesiastical authorities to establish such schools within two years time in every parish. Catholic parents were strictly enjoined to send their children to parochial schools, unless they were given permission by the bishop, "on account of a sufficient cause," to send them elsewhere. This legislation of the Third Plenary Council was to remain in full force during the years that followed as the final and authoritative statement of the Catholic hierarchy of the United States on questions of education.[15] Subsequent pastoral letters on the subject simply represented efforts to implement the sweeping decrees of 1884. While such attempts

---

[12] *Ibid.*, pp. 137-38.

[13] *Ibid.*, pp. 138-39; Orville H. Zabel, *God and Caesar in Nebraska* (Lincoln, Neb.: University of Nebraska Press, 1955), p. 130.

[14] Burns and Kohlbrenner, *History of Catholic Education in the United States*, pp. 140-42; Reuben Maury, *The Wars of the Godly* (New York: Robert M. McBride & Company, 1928), pp. 199-200.

[15] Thomas T. McAvoy, *The Great Crisis in American Catholic History* (Chicago: Henry Regnery Co., Publishers, 1957), pp. 30-34; Burns and Kohlbrenner, *op. cit.*, pp. 142-46, 156.

were constant and unremitting, it proved difficult for a number of reasons for American Catholics to fully realize the Third Plenary Council's ambitious goal of "every Catholic child in a Catholic school." [16]

The new activism of Catholic leadership provoked a strong reaction from the Protestant community. Speaking at a veteran's reunion at Des Moines, Iowa, in the fall of 1875, President U.S. Grant declared: "Let us . . . leave the matter of religious teaching to the family altar, the church, and the private school, supported entirely by private contributions." The President followed this statement by proposing, in his annual message of December 7, 1875, that a constitutional amendment be passed forbidding the appropriation of public funds for denominational schools.[17] The relation of these proposals to Rome's Instruction of 1875 seems rather clear. It has been further suggested that Grant's actions were motivated by the approaching election campaign of 1876. Administration politicos were anxious to divert the public's attention from Reconstruction problems in the South and national political scandals. In any event, the Democratic-controlled House of Representatives proved to be cool to the project, and, when James G. Blaine introduced the proposed amendment, it failed to secure the necessary approval.[18]

The church-state issue with respect to the public schools was hotly debated during the next few years. Renewed demands by Catholic spokesmen for financial support of parochial schools were met with charges that Rome was "plotting to take the nation's life by corrupting the minds of the young." [19] Then in 1887, the American Protective Association made its debut. This new nativist organization, which was particularly influential in the Middle West in the early 1890's, opposed "all attempts to use the public funds for any sectarian purpose whatever" and fervently upheld what it termed "the principles of one general unsectarian free school organization." [20] The APA brought pressure

[16] Burns and Kohlbrenner, *op. cit.*, pp. 144-46.

[17] Alvin W. Johnson and Frank Yost, *Separation of Church and State in the United States* (Minneapolis: University of Minnesota Press, 1948), p. 30.

[18] Higham, *Strangers in the Land*, pp. 28-29; Butts, *The American Tradition in Religion and Education*, pp. 142-44.

[19] Bishop Bernard McQuaid, *The Public School Question As Understood by a Catholic American Citizen* (Boston: The Free Religious Association, 1876); L. K. Washburn, *The Catholic Menace to Our Government* (Boston: J. P. Mendum, 1888); Justin D. Fulton, *Washington in the Lap of Rome* (Boston: W. Kellaway, 1888), pp. 214-30; Joseph Henry Crooker, *Religious Freedom in American Education* (Boston: American Unitarian Association, 1903), pp. 23-37.

[20] Higham, *op. cit.*, pp. 62-63; George Potier, *The American League (U.O.D.)* (Chicago? 1890?), pp. 19-20, 24-25, 81-82, 91-93.

wherever possible to prevent Catholic teachers from being appointed to the public schools and to secure the dismissal of those already employed in them. In some small middle western communities, there is evidence that this campaign was at least temporarily successful.[21] Not only did the APA oppose Catholic pressures on the public schools, according to one angry Catholic observer, but its program in essence contemplated "the absolute suppression of all parochial and church schools." [22] While this charge may have exaggerated somewhat the dimensions of the APA challenge to Catholic education, the movement clearly represented the most virulent manifestation of Protestant nativism since "Know-Nothing" days.

In this setting of acrimonious denominational wrangling, proposals for federal aid to education such as the Blair bills of the 1880's fell by the wayside. Sponsors of this legislation agreed with contemporary observers that one major obstacle to its passage was the Catholic objection to it unless it included aid to parochial schools and the equally vehement Protestant insistence that no aid whatsoever be given to such schools.[23] Meanwhile, on the state level, prohibitions against the use of public funds for sectarian purposes of any kind and against religious instruction in public schools were becoming general. Such provisions were incorporated in most state constitutions by 1900. For its part, Congress in its appropriation acts for the District of Columbia in 1896 and 1897 specified that it was national policy to make no contribution to any institution under sectarian control.[24]

Any assumption that the Catholic position during these years was monolithic is negated by the famous "school controversy" which produced bitter polemics and sharp divisions in American Catholic ranks. By the 1890's an important faction known as the "Americanists," led by eminent churchmen such as Cardinal Gibbons, Archbishop John Ireland of St. Paul, Minnesota, and Bishop John Keane, Rector of the Catholic University of America, had emerged within the American hierarchy. These ecclesiastics were eager to adjust their church as completely as possible to the democratic American environment without surrendering any of its basic principles. Opposing them in the ranks of

[21] H. J. Desmond, *The APA Movement* (Washington, D.C.: The New Century Press, 1912), pp. 38-43; Rev. J. J. Burke, *The Rural Rector* (New York: The Longfellow Press, 1942), p. 47.
[22] Rev. J. J. Tighe, *The APA* (New York: D. P. Murphy, Jr., 1894), pp. 8-17.
[23] Gordon Canfield Lee, *The Struggle for Federal Aid* (New York: Teachers College, Columbia University, 1949), pp. 46-47, 121-23, 159-68.
[24] Butts, *The American Tradition in Religion and Education*, pp. 137-45.

American Catholic clergymen was a conservative faction, led by Archbishop Corrigan of New York, which rejected all compromise with the American Protestant and secular culture as representing an unjustifiable surrender of essential Catholic truth. Strong in support of the conservative faction were German-American Catholics of the Midwest and many members of the Jesuit order.[25]

The liberal or "Americanist" churchmen were eager above all to establish their good will toward the American public school system. "I am a friend and an advocate of the state school," Archbishop Ireland told the NEA convention of 1890. "In the circumstances of the present time I uphold the parish school. I sincerely wish that the need for it did not exist. I would have all schools for the children of the people to be state schools." [26] Cardinal Gibbons even went so far in 1893 as to use his influence to stop a movement which had begun among some Maryland priests and Catholic laymen to petition for state aid for parochial schools.[27] Faced with frontier conditions in late nineteenth-century Minnesota, which made it difficult to raise funds for an independent parochial school system, Archbishop Ireland made arrangements similar to those which had been instituted earlier at Lowell and Poughkeepsie for the sharing of school facilities between local Catholic parishes and public school systems. This arrangement was widely publicized as the "Faribault Plan." [28]

Conservative Catholics bitterly denounced the "Americanists'" friendliness to public schools as a betrayal of the parochial schools and an open defiance of the decrees on education of the Third Plenary Council. Nor were they any happier with Ireland's Faribault Plan, which they regarded as a dangerous compromise risking submergence of the Catholic parochial school in a sea of Protestant "nondenominational" influence. Most bitter in their denunciations of such concessions were German-American churchmen, who regarded parochial schools not only as their first line of defense in preserving orthodox Catholicism, but also as indispensable vehicles in maintaining their

[25] John T. Ellis, *American Catholicism* (Chicago: University of Chicago Press, 1956), pp. 118-20; Robert Cross, *Emergence of Liberal Catholicism* (Cambridge, Mass.: Harvard University Press, 1958), pp. 139-41.

[26] John Ireland, *The Church and Modern Society*, I (New York: D. H. McBride & Co., 1903), p. 217.

[27] Allen S. Will, *Life of Cardinal Gibbons*, I (New York: E. P. Dutton & Co., Inc., 1922), pp. 478-79.

[28] Burns and Kohlbrenner, *History of Catholic Education in the United States*, pp. 162-63; James P. Shannon, *Catholic Colonization on the Frontier* (New Haven, Conn.: Yale University Press, 1957), pp. 192-94.

ethnic and linguistic identity.[29] Archbishop Katzer bluntly put this attitude into words when, in a pastoral, he denounced Ireland's attitude on schools:

> Liberalizing opinions, always injurious to the true Catholic interests, sentimental phrases of closer communion with our separated brethren, appeals to a false and unreal American patriotism, lying charges of foreign and disloyal nationalism, high-flown and indiscriminate praise of the public school system together with a scornful and unfair criticism of our parochial schools, a hypocritical sympathy with the poor "double-tax" ridden Catholics, even the silly spectre of a conflict with the political powers—all this was brought into play to make the Catholics of this country understand that parochial schools, Catholic schools, were no longer opportune.[30]

When the conservatives finally appealed to Rome to outlaw such arrangements as the Faribault Plan, Ireland presented a memorial to the Pope defending his position and the liberals' convictions. In April, 1892, Rome announced in the letter *Tolerari potest* that under prevailing circumstances in America, Archbishop Ireland's plan could be tolerated. All bishops were exhorted to labor "with harmony and unanimity." [31]

Meanwhile the school controversy had been considerably deepened and embittered in November, 1891, when Father Thomas Bouquillon, a professor of Moral Theology at the Catholic University of America, published a pamphlet entitled *Education: To Whom Does It Belong?* Bouquillon, a distinguished Belgian scholar in the fields of ecclesiastical history, bibliography, and moral philosophy, argued on purely abstract and universal grounds that "the doctrine of the Church is not opposed to a reasonable liberty or to the just prerogatives of the state in matters of education." [32] The publication of his views provoked new outbursts of rage from the conservative faction, the sharpest rejoinders coming from members of the Jesuit order who contended that Bouquillon's argument had undercut the whole theoretical basis for maintaining in-

---

[29] Cross, *Emergence of Liberal Catholicism*, pp. 132-44; Most Rev. Edwin V. O'Hara and Richard Purcell, *Archbishop Ireland, Two Appreciations* (St. Paul, Minn.: College of St. Thomas Press, 1948), p. 24; Ellis, *American Catholicism*, pp. 108-9; McAvoy, *The Great Crisis in American Catholic History*, pp. 64-67.

[30] As quoted in James H. Moynihan, *The Life of Archbishop John Ireland* (New York: Harper & Row, Publishers, 1953), p. 103.

[31] *Ibid.*, p. 94; Burns and Kohlbrenner, *op. cit.*, p. 165.

[32] William J. Kerby, "Thomas Joseph Bouquillon," in *Dictionary of American Biography*, II, 48182; "Thomas Bouquillon," *Catholic University Bulletin*, 9 (January 1903), pp. 154-56; Cross, *op. cit.*, p. 143; Moynihan, *op. cit.*, p. 86.

dependent Catholic parochial schools. The indignant conservatives were well aware that the rector of Catholic University, who had invited Bouquillon to join its faculty, was Bishop John Keane, a charter member of the "Americanist" group.[33]

Again angry appeals were made to Rome. This time Pope Leo XIII directed Monsignor Francis Satolli, sent over to America in the fall of 1892 as representative of the Holy See to the Columbian Exposition, to settle the whole troublesome controversy. To a distinguished assemblage of American archbishops in New York on November 16, Satolli presented 14 propositions on the school question. Although reaffirming in general the decrees of the Third Plenary Council, these postulates "sanctioned virtually everything Ireland and Bouquillon had contended for." [34] Priests were forbidden to deny the sacraments to parents whose children attended public schools when no adequate parochial school existed. There was no reason "absolutely and universally speaking" why children should not be instructed in public schools, if they were purged of features objectionable to the church.[35]

These findings produced a "near mutiny" among the conservative prelates. Leo XIII remained firm through all the clamor, backing up his official representative with a letter to Cardinal Gibbons on May 31, 1893, which pointed out that the Satolli propositions in no way invalidated the decrees of the Third Plenary Council.[36] Observers were quick to note, however, that in succeeding years the Pope attempted to right the balance within the American church by favoring conservatives for high ecclesiastical appointments and by issuing his celebrated letter *Testem benevolentiae* of January 22, 1899, condemning any tendencies toward a false "Americanism" which would construct a theology far removed from that of orthodox Catholicism. For his part, Cardinal Gibbons quickly put upon the record his view that the "Americanism" condemned by the pontiff had "nothing in common with the views, aspirations, doctrine, and conduct of Americans." [37]

Both liberals and conservatives maintained that they had been vindicated by the Pope's statement. What, then, was the final result of the school controversy? Certainly the "Americanists" had by no means been removed as an important influence within the American Catholic

---

[33] Burns and Kohlbrenner, *op. cit.*, pp. 163-65.

[34] *Ibid.*, pp. 165-67; Cross, *op. cit.*, p. 144.

[35] Cross, *op. cit.*, p. 35.

[36] Theodore Roemer, *The Catholic Church in the United States.* (St. Louis: B. Herder Book Company, 1950), p. 295; Moynihan, *op. cit.*, pp. 100-101.

[37] Ellis, *American Catholicism*, pp. 118-20; Cross, *op. cit.*, pp. 196-204, 223-24.

Church. As a matter of fact, their influence was to grow by leaps and bounds in the twentieth century. The decrees of the Third Plenary Council on schools still stood, but the concessions which the liberals had been able to induce the Holy See to approve during the 1890's made possible a more flexible approach to the public school structure. As one perspicacious observer put it: "American Catholics no longer needed to jeopardize their good relations with neighbors in proving their orthodoxy by violent attacks upon the public schools. Instead of being forced to choose between an American culture bent on giving youth the finest possible secular education and a Church which insisted that an inadequate parochial school, or no school at all, was better than a nonsectarian one, *Catholics were freed to accept profitable compromises with the state schools,* even while they worked to develop, under either state or Church auspices, a perfect Catholic educational system." [38]

Catholic leaders of both liberal and conservative persuasion made it unmistakably clear in the early twentieth century that they remained united in their desire for state aid for parochial schools and a greater consideration of their religious viewpoint in the existing program of the public schools. Perhaps the most eloquent and articulate spokesman for these views was the scholarly bishop of Peoria, Illinois, John Lancaster Spalding.[39] The nonsectarian school was a failure, he contended, because it failed to educate the whole man. The state should have concentrated upon aid to private educational enterprises and encouragement to the various religious denominations to found and maintain their own schools.[40] If this had been done, "it would have acted in harmony with our theory of government, and we should be today a worthier, more religious and not less enlightened people; while, from an economic point of view, education would have been made vastly cheaper." [41]

It was during these turn-of-the-century years that the first evidences of strong organization by Catholic educators along national lines became apparent. In 1902 a group met in Chicago to form the Parish School Conference and in the same year the *Catholic School Journal*

[38] Cross, *op. cit.,* p. 145. Italics are mine.
[39] Rev. John Lancaster Spalding, *Progress in Education* (Notre Dame, Ind.: Ave Maria Press, 1901), pp. 44-56.
[40] Rev. John Lancaster Spalding, *Means and Ends of Education* (Chicago: A. C. McClurg & Co., 1901), pp. 141-42.
[41] Sister Agnes C. Schroll, *Social Thought of John Lancaster Spalding* (Washington, D.C.: Catholic University of America Press, 1944), pp. 74-75.

was founded. In 1904 the Catholic Educational Association began its operation and incorporated the pre-existing 1902 organization within its framework. To improve the quality of teachers in parochial schools, normal school training was developed by various Catholic religious orders. Concern over the "influence of naturalistic literature on religious teachers" led to the founding of the Catholic Sisters College in Washington, D.C., in 1911.[42] There soon developed, as a response to state certification requirements, a characteristically American "credit-chasing" on the part of teaching nuns and brothers, necessitating summer session study, weekend classes, extension and correspondence courses, with in-service training rather than pre-service preparation being the dominant Catholic teacher-training pattern. Prominent, too, was a trend in the direction of standardization and centralized supervision in school administration. Supervisory tasks were now delegated by the bishop in most cases to a diocesan school superintendent or secretary for education. Between 1889 and 1910 more than a dozen dioceses including large cities such as New York, Boston, Cincinnati, and Philadelphia appointed school superintendents. Closely related to this development and destined to have important influence was the opening in 1905 of the Department of Education of the Catholic University of America, which announced as its express purpose the training of diocesan superintendents.[43]

An even more potent mechanism was forged during World War I. To aid the nation's war effort a National Catholic War Council was established in 1917. This brainchild of the Paulist father Rev. John J. Burke was designed to serve not only as a welfare organization to meet a temporary emergency but also as a means of establishing an effective and expeditious unity of American Catholics. The liberal "Americanizing" prelates were active in the immediate postwar period in moving for the continuance of the new organization as a permanent institution.[44] For this very reason conservative leaders of the American hierarchy felt impelled to protest to Rome against the Council as a potentially dangerous precedent for a "Gallican"-type church in America and as an infringement on the canonical authority of the bishops within their dioceses. The Holy See responded to these protests in 1922 by

[42] Rev. Henry J. Browne, "The American Parish School in the Last Half Century," *Proceedings of the National Catholic Educational Association*, L (August 1953), p. 325.

[43] *Ibid.*, pp. 323-25, 327-31; L. D. Putz, ed., *The Catholic Church, U.S.A.* (Notre Dame, Ind.: Fides Publishers, 1956), pp. 114-15.

[44] Cross, *Emergence of Liberal Catholicism*, pp. 214-15.

withdrawing the tentative approval it had given to the organization. However, after a series of consultations in Rome the Curia issued a new decree (July 2, 1922) accepting the original plan with the one important exception that the new body was to be known as the National Catholic Welfare *Conference*, rather than Council, and that therefore it was understood to be a purely voluntary organization. As time passed, the fears of conservative bishops were shown to have been groundless and the entire Catholic hierarchy in America came to participate in the annual meetings of the Welfare Conference. On its Administrative Board sat ten of the leading prelates of the land whose pronouncements, after being approved by the annual conference, were accepted as being the most authoritative statements of the American Church. Most important, from the point of view of church-state relations in education, was the organization within the National Catholic Welfare Conference of a permanent Department of Education with offices in Washington, D.C. This subdivision was specifically commissioned to look after Catholic interests with respect to any school legislation which might come before Congress, and also to survey the expanding field of international educational relations. Furthermore, the Department was to carry on many important special activities such as collecting statistics, registering teachers, and preparing curricular blueprints for Catholic schools.[45]

These new Catholic efforts to attain power and influence through unity produced, as in the 1840's and the 1890's, a nativist Protestant reaction which was nationwide and fervent. The strongholds of this latest anti-Popery crusade were the rural areas of the nation, although some anti-clericals in urban centers joined in the attack on the Church, seeing it as a citadel of reaction.[46] Typical of the new anti-Catholic crusaders was Tom Watson of Georgia, a frustrated Southern ex-Populist. The most active national organization in the drive was the revived Ku Klux Klan, which made its debut in 1915. These forces were particularly powerful in the years immediately following World War I, and it was not long before their agitation began to bear fruit. In at least five states—Nebraska, Ohio, Iowa, Michigan, and Oregon— a serious challenge developed to the legal right of the parochial school to exist.

In Nebraska special legislation was enacted prohibiting the teaching

---

[45] Ellis, *American Catholicism*, pp. 139-41; Leo R. Ward, ed., *The American Apostolate* (Westminster, Mo.: The Newman Press, 1952), pp. 243-44, 272-73.
[46] Arthur M. Lewis, *Ten Blind Leaders of the Blind* (Chicago: Charles H. Kerr & Co., 1910), pp. 187-88; Higham, *Strangers in the Land*, pp. 179-81.

of foreign languages in primary schools. Similar laws were adopted in Ohio and Iowa. Actually at stake here was the existence of Catholic and Lutheran parochial schools where German was taught. In the case of *Meyer v. State of Nebraska* (1923) the Supreme Court of the United States voided this legislation as violating the Fourteenth Amendment.[47] In upholding a private school's right to teach foreign languages, the Court laid down a ruling which had much broader implications. It supported the right of the parent, as against the state, to regulate the education of the child, thus setting limits to the power of the state to control education. By so doing, the Court, in effect, recognized the right of private and parochial schools to exist.[48]

In Michigan an amendment to the state's constitution was proposed in 1920, requiring all children between the ages of five and sixteen to attend public schools. After a heated campaign, this measure, which would have effectively closed all parochial schools in the state, was defeated in a popular referendum on November 2, 1920. Ku Klux Klan and other anti-Catholic elements made another attempt in 1924 to secure approval of the amendment. Again the proposal was defeated, the vote being 421,472 in favor and 760,571 against. The extent of the interest aroused by the controversy is indicated by the total of 1,182,043 votes cast as compared to a presidential vote in Michigan in the same year of only 1,160,918.[49]

An even more significant struggle occurred in Oregon. After prolonged agitation by the local Ku Klux Klan, the voters of that state on November 7, 1922, approved by a vote of 115,000 to 101,000 an initiative proposal to compel every parent or guardian to send all children between ages eight and sixteen to public schools. The law was to become effective on September 1, 1926. Violations of the act were defined as misdemeanors, punishable by fines ranging from $5 to $100 and imprisonment for not more than two nor less than thirty days.[50]

This act would clearly have had the practical effect of abolishing private and parochial schools in Oregon. Its supporters argued that it would foster "Americanism" and promote assimilation of the foreign born. By mingling all elements of the population in the great "melting

[47] 262 U.S. 390 (1923).

[48] Zabel, *God and Caesar in Nebraska*, pp. 132-49; Pfeffer, *Creeds in Competition,* p. 83.

[49] *Ibid.*, p. 132; Burns and Kohlbrenner, *History of Catholic Education in the United States*, p. 169; Higham, *op. cit.*, p. 292.

[50] *The Outlook*, 140 (June 10, 1925), p. 205; Burns and Kohlbrenner, *op. cit.*, p. 167.

pot" of the public school, divisive influences would be overcome and good citizenship stimulated. Fighting the law was a Catholic Civil Rights Association organized by Archbishop Christie. This group was joined by representatives of the various private schools of the state. The Society of the Sisters of the Holy Names of Jesus and Mary, which conducted a number of parochial grade and high schools, filed suit against the act on the ground that it was unconstitutional under the Fourteenth Amendment. Their petition was granted by the federal circuit court in March, 1924, whereupon Oregon appealed to the United States Supreme Court.[51]

On June 1, 1925, a unanimous Court rendered its decision. The opinion, written by Mr. Justice McReynolds, found the Oregon act unconstitutional as violating the "due process of law" clause of the Fourteenth Amendment. The Court found that the educational enterprise upon which the Society of Sisters was engaged amounted to a "remunerative" business and "the successful conduct of this business" required long-time contracts with teachers and parents. The Compulsory Education Act of 1922 had already "caused the withdrawal from its schools of children who would otherwise continue, and their income has steadily declined." Furthermore, the act infringed upon the right of the schools and teachers involved "to engage in a useful business or profession." It was also found to interfere with "the liberty of parents and guardians to direct the upbringing and education of children under their control." [52] In a powerful plea for the individual's freedom from coercion by the state, the Court stated:

> As often heretofore pointed out, rights guaranteed by the Constitution may not be abridged by legislation which has no reasonable relation to some purpose within the competency of the state. The fundamental theory of liberty upon which all governments in this Union repose excludes any general power of the state to standardize its children by forcing them to accept instruction from public teachers only. The child is not the mere creature of the state; those who nurture him and direct his destiny have the right coupled with the high duty to recognize and prepare him for additional obligations.[53]

The Court's decision in the Oregon case was one of the most significant it had ever rendered on an issue affecting the schools. Counsel for Oregon had argued that the state was merely exercising its legitimate

[51] Pfeffer, *op. cit.*, p. 83; Burns and Kohlbrenner, *op. cit.*, pp. 167-68.
[52] The doctrine of *Meyer* v. *Nebraska* was cited as a precedent.
[53] *Pierce* v. *Society of Sisters*, 268 U.S. 510 (1925).

reserved powers in the educational field, and that if various state acts respecting compulsory school attendance were constitutional then this one must also be so. But the Court had rejected this contention and for the first time had clarified the question of state power under the Constitution to compel school attendance or to regulate, supervise, or inspect all schools within its jurisdiction. "No question is raised," the Court emphasized, "concerning the power of the State reasonably to regulate all schools, to inspect, supervise and examine them, their teachers and pupils; to require that all children of proper age attend some school, that teachers shall be of good moral character and patriotic disposition, that certain studies plainly essential to good citizenship must be taught, and that nothing be taught which is manifestly inimical to the public welfare." But compulsory attendance legislation could not be used as a device to force children to go only to a *public* school. Equivalent training at a properly certified private school would satisfy the requirement; the state could not use compulsory attendance legislation to stamp out private and parochial schools.[54]

The decision was widely praised. *The Outlook* was happy to see the Oregon law invalidated and noted that "tyranny is none the less tyranny when it is imposed by a temporary majority." [55] *The Nation* found the decision to be "undoubtedly in line with the spirit of our Constitution and our institutions. . . ." The Oregon law was held to be "a bigoted measure inspired by the Ku Klux Klan" which was "well out of the way." [56] The *New Republic* saw the Oregon decision, "like its Nebraska forerunner," as giving "just cause for rejoicing." In its opinion, the Supreme Court "did immediate service on behalf of the essential spirit of liberalism. It put the quietus on two striking manifestations of post-war obscurantism." [57] The passage of the years has not tended to reverse these contemporary judgments nor dimmed the significance of the decision. The case was a victory not for Catholic parochial schools alone but for the principle of cultural pluralism in America. The American system of constitutional liberty was held, as one observer in the 1950's put it, to preclude the conferring upon the public schools "a monopoly in the shaping and transmission of cultural patterns and values." [58] The Oregon decision thus stands not just as the Magna Carta of American private schools, but also of a pluralistic America.

[54] *Ibid.*
[55] *The Outlook*, 140 (June 10, 1925), p. 205.
[56] *The Nation* (June 10, 1925), p. 641.
[57] *New Republic* (June 17, 1925), p. 86.
[58] Pfeffer, *Creeds in Competition*, p. 83.

Was there, however, more here than meets the eye? Even while noting the portentous implications of the Oregon decision, the *New Republic* carefully noted important questions which had been left unsolved. Still not determined was the expediency within the American educational system as a kind of *imperio in imperium* of an important group of religiously dominated schools such as the Roman Catholic parochial schools. The original Oregon law of 1922 did not call for measures regulating the type of instruction to be given within all schools, a power which under the Constitution the state unquestionably possessed. The Oregon statute made no effort to define what it considered to be "good" or "bad" school practices. It had nothing to say about the merits of religious instruction in the schools nor did it comment on the quality of the educational training given in parochial schools. This lack of specification, the *New Republic* suggested, was due to the fact that the very advocates of the Oregon law, while wishing to exclude all teaching of a special creed or theology from the schools, subscribed to the traditional Protestant concept which was equally eager to keep out anything that could be alleged even remotely to be impiety or irreligion. "A spirit of reverence must pervade the schoolroom, but it must be reverence of 'Christianity-in-general'. . . ." [59] Molded as they were by their own conception that the people's schools should be "godly," if nonsectarian, the Protestant sponsors of the Oregon act were hardly in a position to spell out state-wide school regulations that would have made it impossible for the Roman Catholic Church to continue to put into effect their particular version of what a "godly" school should be like.

Drawing the Line

With its legal right to exist now firmly established, the Catholic parochial school system turned with a new confidence and vigor during the 1930's and 1940's to a crusade for public aid and support. In some ways this latest campaign was more formidable than the earlier Catholic drives of the 1840's and 1870's, mainly because American Catholics were better organized on a national scale now than they had been before. Their parochial schools by this time certainly represented a much more considerable investment in money and effort than any that had existed in the nineteenth century. By 1930, 2,222,598 pupils

[59] *New Republic* (June 24, 1925), pp. 115-16.

were enrolled in Catholic elementary schools alone, of which there were 7,923 then in existence, according to the National Catholic Welfare Conference.[60] From the Catholic point of view, such figures lent color to the oft-repeated complaint that American Catholics were subject to double taxation since they paid money to the state to support the public schools, which their children did not attend, while at the same time, for conscience's sake, they contributed hundreds of millions of dollars to help maintain the parochial school structure.[61]

The opening trumpet blast of this renewed drive for "distributive justice" was sounded in Rome by Pope Pius XI who on December 31, 1929, published an Encyclical Letter *On Christian Education of Youth.* The Pontiff here upheld in plain language the legitimacy of Catholic requests for public support of the parochial schools, arguing that such schools were saving money for the state, and that Catholic citizens were already contributing their full share to the maintenance of public schools. Catholics, in his view, could never accept a so-called "neutral" or "lay" school from which religion was excluded. They must have truly Catholic schools, permeated throughout by a religious spirit. "That this can be done to the full satisfaction of families," Pius declared, "and to the advantage of education and of public peace and tranquillity is clear from the actual experience of some countries comprising different religious denominations. There the school legislation respects the rights of the family, and Catholics are free to follow their own system of teaching in schools that are entirely Catholic. Nor is distributive justice lost sight of, as is evidenced by the financial aid granted by the state to the several schools demanded by the families." [62]

The Pope's encyclical provoked a storm of criticism from defenders of American secular schools while, contrariwise, it seemed to stiffen American Catholics in their determination to secure public assistance for their parish schools without loss of their existing independent status.[63] The *New York Times* protested in an editorial on January 13, 1930, that the papal pronouncement "sounds a note that will

[60] Burns and Kohlbrenner, *History of Catholic Education in the United States,* p. 145.

[61] Bernard Kohlbrenner, "Indomitable Schools," in Leo R. Ward, ed., *The American Apostolate,* p. 184; see also Rev. K. J. Alter, "Does State Aid to Education Mean Union of Church and State?" *Catholic Educational Review* (February 1935), p. 69.

[62] Pius XI, *On Christian Education of Youth* (Encyclical Letter), (Washington, D.C.: National Catholic Welfare Conference, 1930), p. 31.

[63] Henry J. Browne, *Proceedings of the National Catholic Education Association,* L, p. 332.

startle Americans, for it assails an institution dearest to them—the public school—without which it is hardly conceivable that democracy could long exist." The *Times* went on to note: "If the declaration of the encyclical were scrupulously obeyed by those to whom it was addressed, the public school would be emptied of all its Catholic pupils except as the bishop in his discretion in special circumstances may permit them to remain." The *New York Telegram*, for its part, observed that: "It is the Pope's conception that the church should predominate in educational matters." To this viewpoint, the paper wished to reply that "religious freedom is guaranteed by the Constitution of the United States, and there can be no religious freedom where any church or group of churches dominates the entire educational system." [64]

Catholic proponents of public financial assistance to parochial schools were confronted with the sobering fact that, at least in part due to the "nativist" campaigns of the mid and later nineteenth century, practically every state in the Union now had either a constitutional or a legislative ban on any and all grants to denominational schools or any other sectarian establishments.[65] Nevertheless, the great depression of the 1930's hurt certain parochial school systems so grievously that a desperate drive for direct public aid was launched in Ohio in 1933 and in Connecticut in 1937. These efforts were defeated, however, after much bitter debate.[66] Much more characteristic of the point of view of the American Catholic leadership, after World War I, was a growing demand for public funds for "auxiliary services"—i.e., public welfare benefits for all children who attended nonpublic as well as public schools. Such "fringe benefits" would include medical and dental services, school bus transportation, vocational training, and school lunches. This new strategy envisioned Catholic opposition to any proposed plan for federal or state grants for such services that would exclude private school pupils. The argument upholding such grants rested heavily on the "child-welfare" theory: it would be primarily the *child* that would gain by such public assistance, not the *school*. Any incidental benefits that might accrue to the schools themselves would in any case be of

[64] Joseph M. Dawson, *Separate Church and State Now* (New York: Richard R. Smith, 1948), pp. 62-63.

[65] Rev. Edward M. Connors, *Church-State Relationships in Education in New York* (Washington, D.C.: Catholic University of America Press, 1951), pp. 130-38.

[66] Burns and Kohlbrenner, *History of Catholic Education in the United States*, p. 169; Mason, *Church-State Relationships in Connecticut* (Washington, D.C.: Catholic University of America Press, 1953), pp. 260-63.

social and educational value to the community if such private schools were legally established and acceptable educationally to the state's regulatory authority. There was no violation of the constitutional separation of church and state here, it was asserted, because the benefits were given to all children without regard to the kind of public, private, or religious school they might attend. Moreover, since children were legally permitted to attend religious schools in fulfillment of state compulsory attendance laws (as validated by the United States Supreme Court in the Oregon case), it was only fair that such children be granted the same benefits and services as public school children. Unless this were done, the former would be discriminated against just because they sought to exercise their constitutional rights of religious freedom.[67]

All-out opponents of government subsidies to denominational schools opposed the Catholic program for "child welfare" grants just as they had earlier opposed proposals for direct government aid. As R. Freeman Butts put it, "Aid to all religious groups is as clear a violation of separation as is aid to one religious group in preference to others. The line between direct aid and indirect aid is so difficult to draw that the American people would be well advised to stop short of indirect aid if they wish to avoid the entanglements that plagued the nation for well over a hundred years." [68] According to this school of thought, if the child's needs for education were to be the only consideration and could by the "fringe benefit" theory be divorced from the question of denominational controls, what was to stop some future public authority from making financial grants to parochial schools for school buildings, operation and maintenance costs, libraries, scientific and athletic equipment, perhaps even teachers' salaries? These items could all be shown to have an important effect on "child welfare"! The end result would be stimulation of divisive forces in community life and increasing state entanglement with religion.[69]

The question of state aid for the aforesaid "auxiliary services" was admittedly a most difficult one. For one thing, it was new, peculiar to the twentieth century and, as such, necessitated the working out of a

[67] Rev. William E. McManus, "Should Public Funds be Used to Support Parochial Schools," *PM* (New York, August 24, 1947); Kohlbrenner, "Indomitable Schools," in *The American Apostolate*, pp. 184-85; Sister Mary Mason, *op. cit.*, pp. 288-93.

[68] Butts, *The American Tradition in Religion and Education*, p. 150.

[69] *Ibid.*, for this viewpoint, see also Edward J. B. Barrett, *Rome Stoops to Conquer* (New York: Julian Messner, Inc., Publishers, 1935).

whole new series of definitions of the boundary line between church and state. The nineteenth-century school had not customarily provided these child-welfare benefits—bus transportation, lunches, health services. Its twentieth-century counterpart did, dedicated as it was increasingly to the concept of care for the *total* welfare of the child within the context of a welfare-minded state.

Even more troublesome was the question of just what constituted "indirect" aid to a religious institution. Could tax exemption for parochial schools be so defined? If so, it had been furnished to them in many states for years. One observer suggested that the very permission accorded to religious groups to substitute their schools for the public schools might be considered a form of "indirect" aid and certainly led to the furnishing of such aids.[70] Thus once this permission was granted, public funds were appropriated to pay the salaries and expenses of state inspectors who were obliged to visit the private and parochial schools. In addition, the state compulsory school attendance laws which appeared everywhere in the twentieth century aided the parochial schools by ensuring regular attendance in them also. In most states publicly paid truant officers were provided by law to see that this was so, possibly another important type of "indirect" aid! Then, too, the affording of certain incidental services such as fire and police protection to parochial school buildings and the furnishing to parochial school teachers of books on fire dangers, civics, and health matters at the public expense might, in the technical sense of the term, be similarly classified as public aid.

In the final analysis, under the American constitutional system it was left to the federal courts to work out solutions to this intricate and controversial question and, in so doing, to lay down new and authoritative boundary lines between the respective spheres of church and state. As we have seen, the United States Supreme Court in the *Meyer* v. *Nebraska* and the *Oregon* cases upheld the right of parochial schools to exist and to be free of excessive regulation by the state. But just what constituted permissible regulation of such schools by the state was not clearly defined, beyond the ruling that it did *not* include a flat ban on the teaching of foreign languages. The vital question of the extent to which a state may "indirectly" aid parochial schools was a related problem, and the high court turned its attention to this important issue for the first time in 1930.

When the state of Louisiana put into operation legislation furnish-

[70] Zabel, *God and Caesar in Nebraska*, p. 154.

ing free textbooks to parochial school pupils as well as to those in the
public schools, a taxpayer's suit was brought to enjoin the authorities
from expending public funds for that purpose. It was claimed that the
law violated the state and federal constitutions. The case, *Cochran* v.
Louisiana State Board of Education, was appealed to the United States
Supreme Court, and on April 30, 1930, that high tribunal rendered its
decision. Chief Justice Hughes, speaking for the Court, upheld the constitutionality of the Louisiana act on the ground that the textbooks in
question were given to the individual children, not to the schools, and
these books were the same as those used in the public schools and
consequently not "adapted to religious instruction." [71] In holding that
constitutional separation of church and state was not violated by this
particular instance of auxiliary aid, the Court formulated for the first
time the "child-welfare" theory as a justification:

> One may scan the acts in vain to ascertain where any money is appro-
> priated for the purchase of the school books for the use of any church,
> private, sectarian, or even public school. The appropriations were made
> for the specific purpose of purchasing school books for the use of the
> school children of the state, free of cost to them. It was for their benefit
> and the resulting benefit to the state that the appropriations were made.
> . . . . The schools . . . are not the beneficiaries of these appropria-
> tions. They obtain nothing from them, nor are they relieved of a single
> obligation because of them. The school children and the state alone are
> the beneficiaries.[72]

While only a handful of states, in subsequent years, actually chose
to furnish free schoolbooks to parochial school pupils, the Supreme
Court had established an important precedent which could be cited by
state and federal judges to uphold the constitutionality of other measures providing "auxiliary" benefits to such children. In essence the Supreme Court was saying that there might be instances where the state's
constitutional right to enact general welfare legislation for the benefit
of the child superseded the implications for education of the prohibition
against "an establishment of religion" in the First Amendment.

The next important test of the Court's new principle involved one
of the most important and controversial of auxiliary aids—free bus
transportation for parochial school pupils at public expense. This issue

---

[71] Johnson and Yost, *Separation of Church and State*, pp. 146-49; Butts, *The
American Tradition in Religion and Education*, pp. 170-72; Stokes, *Church and
State in the United States*, II, pp. 716-17.

[72] *Cochran* v. *Louisiana State Board of Education*, 281 U.S. 370 (1930).

had become particularly acute since World War I as a result of the new importance of the automobile and the consolidated school. The states were by no means of one mind on how to solve it. In some, bus transportation for parochial school children was outlawed by legislative enactment or judicial ruling as violative of the constitutional separation of church and state. In 14 states, some provision had been made by 1947 authorizing such services.[73]

This was the setting when Arch R. Everson, a resident of Ewing Township in New Jersey and secretary of a taxpayers' league, decided to challenge the constitutionality of a law passed by the New Jersey Legislature in 1941 providing reimbursement from public funds to parents of parochial school pupils for their children's bus fares. The case was appealed to the Supreme Court and on February 10, 1947, that tribunal rendered its decision. By a paper-thin five-to-four majority, the court voted to uphold the New Jersey statute, using the "child-welfare" concept as the principal basis for its finding. Speaking for the majority, Justice Hugo Black asserted:

> . . . The fact that a state law, passed to satisfy a public need, coincides with the personal desires of the individuals most directly affected is certainly an inadequate reason for us to say that a legislature has erroneously appraised the public need.
> . . . It appears that these parochial schools meet New Jersey's requirements. The state contributes no money to the schools. It does not support them. Its legislation, as applied, does no more than provide a general program to help parents get their children, regardless of their religion, safely and expeditiously to and from accredited schools.
> The First Amendment has erected a wall between church and state. That wall must be kept high and impregnable. We could not approve the slightest breach. New Jersey has not breached it here.[74]

An important aspect of the majority decision was the powerful plea that it made for separation of church and state, a statement which was, in the view of Anson Phelps Stokes, "among the most important ever drafted by the Supreme Court in its efforts to define and protect religious liberty":[75]

> The "establishment of religion" clause of the First Amendment means at least this: Neither a state nor the federal government can set up a church. Neither can pass laws which aid one religion, aid all religions, or

---

[73] Johnson and Yost, *op. cit.*, pp. 152-57; Stokes, op. cit., pp. 696-97.
[74] *Everson v. Board of Education of Township of Ewing*, 67 U.S. 504 (1947).
[75] Stokes, *op. cit.*, p. 704.

prefer one religion over another. Neither can force nor influence a person to go to or to remain away from church against his will or force him to profess a belief or disbelief in any religion. No person can be punished for entertaining or professing religious beliefs or disbeliefs, for church attendance or nonattendance. No tax in any amount, large or small, can be levied to support any religious activities or institutions, whatever they may be called, or whatever form they may adopt to teach or practice religion. Neither a state nor the federal government can, openly or secretly, participate in the affairs of any religious organizations or groups and *vice versa*. In the words of Jefferson, the clause against establishment of religion by law was intended to erect "a wall of separation between Church and State." [76]

It is especially worthy of note here that by this eloquent and forceful declaration the Supreme Court had finally and specifically made the "establishment of religion" clause of the First Amendment binding on the states through the power of the Fourteenth Amendment. And this obligation was defined in terms of a sweeping concept of a "wall of separation" between church and state, a wall which absolutely forbade the appropriation of public tax funds for the support of any branch or agency of a church that taught or practiced religion. Both the court majority and the minority in the *Everson* case were in firm agreement on this vital point. But the majority went on from there to reason that New Jersey could not under the First Amendment exclude individuals of any faith *"because of their faith or lack of it"* from receiving the benefits of public welfare legislation." [77] School bus transportation was seen as belonging in the latter category. The *Oregon* decision of 1925 had established that parents might "send their children to a religious rather than a public school if the school meets the secular educational requirements." Hence the exclusion of one group of children from general welfare benefits such as bus transportation simply because they attended denominational schools would constitute religious discrimination.

The minority saw a clear contradiction between the majority's reasoning and their conclusions. One of the dissenters Justice Robert H. Jackson asserted: "Catholic education is the rock on which the whole structure rests, and to render tax aid to its Church school is indistinguishable to me from rendering the same aid to the Church itself." Jackson did not accept the theory that there was a vital difference, from a constitutional point of view, between rendering financial aid directly

---

[76] 67 U.S. 504 (1947).
[77] *Ibid*. Italics are mine.

to a parochial school and aiding pupils to be transported to such a school. Justice Wiley Rutledge, another of the dissenters, concurred in this view:

> Here parents pay money to send their children to parochial schools, and funds raised by taxation are used to reimburse them. This not only helps the children to get to school and the parents to send them. It aids them in a substantial way to get the very thing which they are sent to the particular school to secure, namely, religious training and teaching.
> . . . it cannot be said that the cost of transportation is no part of the cost of education or of the religious instruction given. That it is a substantial and a necessary element is shown most plainly by the continuing and increasing demand for the state to assume it. . . .

In a long review of the history of the struggle to establish separation of church and state as an essential part of the American constitutional system, Justice Rutledge reminded his colleagues of the key role Thomas Jefferson had played in this achievement. Citing the third President's views, Rutledge concluded: "I cannot believe that the great author of those words . . . could have joined in the [majority] decision." [78]

The *Everson* decision by no means represented a final settlement of the school bus issue or the larger one of "auxiliary services." A number of states continued to withhold such services from parochial school children. And some state courts continued to regard as invalid under their own state constitutions laws similar to that of New Jersey. Catholic spokesmen and publications generally approved the high court's decision while objecting to the reasoning that led to it. Conversely, many Protestant, Jewish, and secularist observers approved the reasoning of the court majority but deplored its decision! [79] One student of the problem saw the *Everson* case as representing the most momentous judicial spelling-out in a century and a half of the meaning of the "no-establishment" clause in the Constitution. And he maintained that it was no coincidence that the clarification should have occurred in response to a Roman Catholic challenge to a pre-existing situation. This is shown by the Court's final decision explicitly to interpret the First Amendment "as conferring the force of constitutional law on the principles of the Protestant dissenter secular humanist alliance," principles which dated from the period of the framing of the Constitution.[80] But confusion was implicit in the unexpected twists and turns of the majority's

[78] *Ibid.*
[79] Stokes, *op. cit.*, 708-11.
[80] Pfeffer, *Creeds in Competition*, pp. 46-47.

opinion. Noting this, one Protestant leader commented: "I personally cannot see how the reasoning of the Court that the Constitution prevents giving aid to one religion can then be made to justify a program that does substantially that." [81]

Whatever its impact on the state level, the *Everson* decision had the effect of encouraging an energetic Catholic campaign to secure federal financial grants for auxiliary services. The new concern for the public welfare which had resulted in the social legislation of the "New Deal" and "Fair Deal" periods brightened prospects for securing such aid. Programs such as those of the NYA and CCC seemed to point the way. With World War II came a new concern for the welfare of veterans, resulting in the G.I. Bill of Rights. This latter piece of legislation served as a particularly significant precedent to the advocates of federal grants for auxiliary services because under it educational benefits were awarded to individual students, without regard to whether they attended a public, private, or denominational school.

Supporters of aid to church-affiliated schools under the "child-welfare" philosophy won a new triumph in 1946 when Congress passed the National School Lunch Act. This measure provided for federal subsidies to the states to pay for the school lunches of children in both public and parochial educational institutions. Even more important from the Catholic point of view, it specified that federal funds might be allocated *directly* to nonpublic schools in any state (and these included 27 at the time) where "the state educational agency is not permitted by law to disburse the funds paid to it under this chapter to nonprofit private schools. . . ." [82] Catholic Archbishop John McNicholas, in a letter to the 1947 convention of the National Education Association, expressed the hope that the school lunch program would be only the first step in a comprehensive governmental program to provide essential school services for nonpublic school children. "It is inconceivable," said the Archbishop, "that this large body of distinguished educators would recommend that parochial school children be rejected from public school buses, or that health services be denied to those children. We hope that the Association in no uncertain terms will recommend that essential school services be furnished to all children regardless of the school they attend." [83]

[81] Merrimon Cuninggim, *Freedom's Holy Light* (New York: Harper & Row, Publishers, 1955), p. 112.
[82] Zabel, *God and Caesar in Nebraska*, p. 158; Butts, *The American Tradition in Religion and Education*, p. 176.
[83] Stokes, *op. cit.*, p. 667.

This was by no means the last word from Catholic spokesmen, however. Events were soon to disclose that, while calling for a due share of federal child-welfare benefits for their schools, they had not abandoned their conviction that they were entitled also to more direct aid. In April, 1948, the United States Senate passed a bill sponsored by Senator Robert Taft and others which provided $300,000,000 in general federal aid to schools to help "equalize" educational opportunities in all the states. Those states spending the least per capita on public education would receive the most funds. The money was, however, not necessarily barred from going to private and parochial schools. This controversial question together with the equally explosive one of racial segregation in the schools was by-passed by a provision allowing the states themselves to decide how to use the federal aid. The bill, first of its kind to pass either House of Congress since the late nineteenth century, died in the House of Representatives.[84] The following year the Senate, again with Taft as perhaps the most active proponent, pushed through a federal aid to education bill with practically identical terms.[85] Once more the measure ran into trouble in the House. Leadership in that body had in the interval switched from the Republicans to the Democrats, not making the path of the federal aid bill any smoother.

The principal difficulty was that now the issue of federal aid to parochial schools had come out into the open. On May 11, 1949, Congressman Graham A. Barden of North Carolina introduced a federal aid to education bill which would have made assistance available to the states "in bearing certain costs of public elementary and secondary education." Unlike the Senate version, however, this bill did not leave distribution of the moneys to the discretion of the states, but specified that they could go only "for current expenditures for public elementary and secondary schools within such states." The measure further provided that in case any taxpayer felt that the above provisions were being violated or about to be violated, he might make application to the proper United States court for an order "enjoining such acts or practices, or for an order enforcing compliance with the first sentence of this section." Accompanying the act were a series of "Definitions" which stated specifically:

> The term "current expenditures" does not include expenditures for transportation or for interest, debt service, or capital outlay, and does not

[84] *Time Magazine* (April 12, 1948), p. 82.
[85] *Ibid* (May 16, 1949), p. 24.

include expenditures for health services for the prevention, diagnosis, or treatment of physical or mental defects or conditions.[86]

The Barden bill thus flung down the gage of battle to those who supported giving federal aid to parochial schools. Supporters quickly lined up on both sides of the fence. The influential National Education Association, in a series of public statements, made it clear that it supported federal aid only for *public* elementary and secondary schools. The Association pointed out that any direct aid for parochial schools had just been finally and conclusively held to be unconstitutional by the United States Supreme Court in the *Everson* and (as we shall soon see) the *McCollum* cases. Equally firm in support of Congressman Barden's position were a number of nationally prominent Protestant, Jewish, and secular leaders, and the new organization of Protestants and Others United for Separation of Church and State, organized in January, 1948, for the specific purpose of preventing the use of public funds for parochial schools.[87] Even though Roman Catholic demands in recent years had centered on requests to share in appropriations for auxiliary services, it now became clear that the fundamental Catholic position in favor of a share in direct aid as a form of "distributive justice," which had led to Catholic opposition to the federal aid bills of the 1880's, had not yet been abandoned. The fact that the Supreme Court had ruled such aid to be unconstitutional apparently had no effect on their position, nor did the fact that the Barden bill inferred that such matters could be provided for in *separate* bills lessen their opposition.[88] Leading Catholic spokesmen centered their fire upon the mandatory provision of the Barden bill that the federal aid *must* go to public schools only, demanding a measure more like the Senate version which would allow the individual states to decide the question. In this position they came to have the support of Representative John Lesinski, Chairman of the House Committee on Education and Labor, and an important number of other House members. House supporters of the Barden bill were just as adamant in their position as were the opponents. The result was that after much bitter wrangling (at one point the House Education and Labor Committee debated the issue heatedly for 19 days behind closed doors), the federal aid bill finally was killed.[89]

[86] Stokes, *op. cit.*, p. 746.

[87] *School and Society*, 70 (September 10, 1949), pp. 171-72.

[88] In this respect, the Barden bill seems to have taken into account the fact that the Supreme Court in the *Everson* case had ruled aid to such services to be constitutional.

[89] *School and Society*, 70, p. 171; Stokes, *op. cit.*, pp. 745-46.

The First Lady and the Cardinal

So matters stood on the eve of the Roosevelt-Spellman controversy. On June 23, 1949, Mrs. Roosevelt, in her "My Day" column in the *New York World Telegram,* noted that Francis Cardinal Spellman, Archbishop of New York, had declared that Catholic schools should share in any federal funds which might be voted for aid to education. Mrs. Roosevelt did not agree with the Cardinal: "Those of us who believe in the right of any human being to belong to whatever church he sees fit, and to worship God in his own way, cannot be accused of prejudice when we do not want to see public education connected with religious control of the schools, which are paid for by taxpayers' money." And the former First Lady added, by way of emphasis, that private schools, whether denominational or nonsectarian, "should not receive federal funds; in fact, no tax funds of any kind." She concluded: "The separation of church and state is extremely important to any of us who hold to the original traditions of our nation. To change these traditions by changing our traditional attitude toward public education would be harmful, I think, to our whole attitude of tolerance in the religious area."

When in subsequent weeks Mrs. Roosevelt received some letters accusing her of being anti-Catholic, she commented on the issue once again in her columns of July 8 and July 15. On these occasions she reiterated her stand in favor of the constitutional separation of church and state and denied that this position was motivated by religious prejudice. Although her position agreed with that of the Barden bill, she noted: "I have not read the bill carefully, and I have been rather careful not to say if I am for or against any particular bill or bills." Finally, she stated her approval of aid for individual student-veterans such as the benefits of the G.I. Bill of Rights which could be utilized at institutions of the student's own choosing, including Roman Catholic schools and colleges. Thus, implicitly, she endorsed the principle of aid for auxiliary services in denominational schools under the student-welfare concept.[90]

Cardinal Spellman responded to these statements with a wrathful letter to Mrs. Roosevelt dated July 21 which he directed should immediately be made public. He charged her with aligning herself with the proponents of the Barden bill—"the now famous, infamous bill that would unjustly discriminate against minority groups of America's

---

[90] Stokes, *op. cit.,* pp. 747-49.

children"—and with condemning him "for defending Catholic children against those who would deny them their constitutional rights of equality with other American children." [91] Alleging that Mrs. Roosevelt had made a personal attack upon him and had consistently carried on an anti-Catholic campaign in her newspaper columns, the Cardinal declared that she "could have acted only from misinformation, ignorance, or prejudice, not from knowledge and understanding." Closing his case, he told Mrs. Roosevelt that "even though you may again use your columns to attack me and again accuse me of starting a controversy, I shall not again publicly acknowledge you." [92]

A flood of comments came from the press and the country as the full import of the Cardinal's blast sank in. In general, Catholic spokesmen upheld the Cardinal and non-Catholics defended Mrs. Roosevelt. Dr. John W. Behnken, President of the Lutheran Church-Missouri Synod, a group supporting the largest system of parochial schools in American Protestantism, flatly stated that his denomination did not seek federal aid for its schools and upheld the separation of church and state as a matter of fundamental principle.[93] Herbert H. Lehman, former Governor of New York, issued a public statement expressing shock at the attack on Mrs. Roosevelt. "The issue," Lehman declared, "is not whether one agrees or disagrees with Mrs. Roosevelt on this or any other public question. The issue is whether Americans are entitled freely to express their views on public questions without being vilified or accused of religious bias." He added that in Mrs. Roosevelt's record as a public figure for 25 years, he did not know of "a single act or word that would in the slightest degree indicate bias or prejudice against any

[91] Apparently the Cardinal remained convinced many years after the conclusion of the controversy that Mrs. Roosevelt had specifically endorsed the Barden bill. In a letter to the author in October, 1959, he stated: ". . . I have no further comment to make about the Barden bill and its endorsement by Mrs. Roosevelt" (Francis Cardinal Spellman to Willis Rudy, October 30, 1959). In any event, the Cardinal apparently continued to believe, 11 years after his controversy with Mrs. Roosevelt, that it would be unjust to enact federal aid to education legislation that did not include parochial schools. This he indicated in a strong public statement on January 17, 1961.

[92] Stokes, *op. cit.*, p. 749. According to Stokes, the bitter tone of the Cardinal's letter was due to the fact that "there had been several matters over the years in Mrs. Roosevelt's comments on public events which had irritated the hierarchy." This included her lack of sympathy for Franco Spain and her failure to condemn Communist nations during and after the war as unequivocally as the Catholic Church would have liked.

[93] *Time Magazine* (August 8, 1949), p. 54.

religion or any race." The *New York Times* came to a similar conclusion two days later when it published an editorial entitled "It Is the Child That Matters." Noting that the government could not constitutionally subsidize religious education as such, the *Times* stressed the "child-welfare" doctrine.

> The emphasis should be, as we are sure Cardinal Spellman would agree, on the child, not on the school. This paper feels that Cardinal Spellman will come to realize that Mrs. Roosevelt can not be justly charged with prejudice or bigotry. We do not believe she ever discriminated against Catholic soldiers, or those of any other faith, when she went the rounds of the war hospitals, or that she would be less compassionate toward a needy or hungry Catholic child than she is toward other children.[94]

With public sympathy clearly swinging to her side, Mrs. Roosevelt broke the silence which she had temporarily self-imposed. In her newspaper column she pointed out that she had supported Alfred E. Smith, a Roman Catholic, in every political campaign that he had made. "I have no ill feeling," she added, "toward any people of high or low estate because they belong to any religious group." She was sure that the Cardinal had stated his views "in what to him seems a Christian and kindly manner," and she expressed her wish to do the same.[95] In a letter to the Cardinal dated July 23 she restated her conviction that no direct public aid could, under the American system, go to church-controlled schools. The question of auxiliary services, she conceded, was something else and remained a debatable one. But in all such matters the nation should proceed with caution since "anyone who knows history, particularly the history of Europe, will, I think, recognize that the domination of education or of government by any one particular religious faith is never a happy arrangement for the people." Mrs. Roosevelt concluded by denying any intention of attacking the Cardinal personally, or of attacking the Roman Catholic church. She would, of course, "continue to stand for the things in our government which I think are right. They may lead me to be in opposition to you and to other groups within our country, but I shall always act, as far as I am able, from real conviction and from honest belief." Her record, she suggested, was not anti-Catholic or anti- any religious group. And she had no sense of being an unworthy American mother. "The final judg-

[94] Stokes, *op. cit.*, pp. 750-52.
[95] *Time Magazine* (August 1, 1949), p. 11.

ment, my dear Cardinal Spellman, of the worthiness of all human beings is in the hands of God." [96]

In his original statement Cardinal Spellman had flatly stated that he would not again publicly acknowledge Mrs. Roosevelt. However, Mrs. Roosevelt one day early in August picked up the telephone at Hyde Park, and on the line was the Cardinal, who sounded in a much more genial mood that he had earlier. Gone was the indignant resentment. In its place, the prelate now spoke with the voice of sweet reason. He had written a new statement on the school question which was designed to make the Roman Catholic position crystal clear. He would like Mrs. Roosevelt to read it before it was released. Would she be willing to do so? The former First Lady readily assented. She found the Cardinal's statement both "clarifying and fair," and it was released to the press on August 6. To it Eleanor Roosevelt appended a short statement of her own, which the Cardinal's office in Manhattan also released, in which she emphasized: "I am firm in my belief that there shall be no pressure brought to bear by any church against the proper operations of the government and that there shall be recognition of the fact that all citizens may express their views freely on questions of public interest." Later that same month, Francis Cardinal Spellman on his way to dedicate a chapel in Peekskill dropped in at Hyde Park to see the world-renowned lady of the house. They chatted in a friendly manner for nearly three-quarters of an hour and Mrs. Roosevelt served her guest a glass of iced tea.[97]

The Spellman-Roosevelt controversy was over, but in the process it had produced perhaps the most detailed and authoritative statement of the position of the Catholic Church in America on relations of parochial schools to public education to be issued in the twentieth century by a high-ranking prelate. By refusing to compromise on the basic issue of direct public aid for Catholic schools, Mrs. Roosevelt had succeeded in securing a significant clarification of the position of the American Catholic hierarchy and one, incidentally, which represented a considerable retreat from that which the Cardinal himself had originally maintained. In his carefully worded public statement of August 6th, Cardinal Spellman had the following to say:

> It is important that everyone should understand clearly what we are asking for under constitutional law, and, for what we are not asking. We

[96] Stokes, *op. cit.*, pp. 753-54.
[97] *Ibid.*, pp. 757-58.

are not asking for general public support of religious schools. In the state of New York, as in practically every other state, the state constitution prohibits the use of public funds for the support of sectarian schools. The Supreme Court of the United States has interpreted the federal Constitution in the same sense.

Under the Constitution we do not ask for nor can we expect public funds to pay for the construction or repair of parochial school buildings or for the support of teachers, or for other maintenance costs.

There are, however, other incidental expenses involved in education, expenses for such purposes as the transportation of children to and from school, the purchase of nonreligious textbooks, and the provision of health aids. These are called "auxiliary services". . . .

Our New York State constitution expressly allows the use of public funds for the transportation of children to any school, public or parochial. . . . In all states many communities supply public health services to pupils in all schools. The Supreme Court of the United States has upheld these practices as constitutional.

What precisely are we asking for? We believe in federal aid for needy states and needy children. We further believe that Congress should guarantee, as it did in the School Lunch Act, that all children of whatever race, creed, or color and no matter what schools they attend will share alike in the "auxiliary services" for which these federal funds are spent in the states.

We do not think it should be left to each state to decide for itself whether or not to distribute federal funds in a discriminatory way. . . .

We are asking Congress to do no more than to continue, in its first general aid-to-education measure, the nondiscriminatory policy it has followed in the School Lunch Act. . . .[98]

Cardinal Spellman's pronouncement was momentous in that it marked the first time that a leading spokesman of the American hierarchy had conceded publicly that under the American constitutional system direct public aid for parochial school teachers' salaries and for the building programs of Catholic schools was both invalid and impossible. But the statement also served notice that, faced by the soaring costs of running an ever expanding parochial school system and by the increasing difficulties of finding the teaching personnel to staff it, the hierarchy would fight all the harder for all the "indirect" aid it could get. Specifically, the Church would now demand, as the *quid pro quo* for its support of a general federal aid to education bill, that a program be included in that bill providing for federal assistance to the states for "auxiliary services" along the mandatory lines of the School Lunch Act. The reason the latter format appealed to the hierarchy so highly

[98] *Ibid.*, pp. 754-55.

was that it took away from state educational authorities the right to decide whether to distribute federal child-welfare funds only to pupils in publicly supported and controlled schools. Where states, either through constitutional prohibition or through specific legislation, so limited the distribution of funds, the federal government stepped in and paid the lunch money directly to the private and parochial schools involved. Thus were this formula to be adopted, it would ensure that money from the federal government would flow in a steady stream to parochial schools *in every state of the Union.*

Later Developments

The touchy question of the relationship of public education to church-controlled schools calmed down somewhat during the 1950's, but the dispute reached new heights of polemical fury in the early weeks of 1961 when President-Elect Kennedy's "task force" on education proposed a vast program of federal spending in aid to education. Because this proposal omitted any provision for governmental aid to Catholic elementary and secondary schools, Francis Cardinal Spellman in a strong public statement blasted it as discriminatory and unacceptable.[99] Soon thereafter the American Catholic hierarchy upheld the Cardinal's point of view, while a number of Protestant and other leaders of American opinion just as firmly condemned his position.[100] Despite the furor, President Kennedy refused to include in his proposal for federal aid to education any provision for public money for parochial elementary or secondary schools when the bill was finally sent to Congress.[101] This, he said, would be unconstitutional, though he did feel free to recommend federal aid to colleges (on an individual scholarship and loan basis) which would without doubt go eventually to church-controlled schools, as well as to nonsectarian institutions. On this last point, it is rather significant that the American Civil Liberties Union, always a zealous defender of the principle of separation of church and state, declared in August, 1961, that it saw no constitutional barrier to the granting of such aid to church-related *higher* education. This principle would apply, however, the ACLU was careful to empha-

[99] *New York Times,* January 18, 1961, pp. 1-2, 15-16.
[100] *Ibid.,* May 9, 1961, p. 18; June 6, 1961, p. 34M; June 7, 1961, p. 26.
[101] *Ibid.,* February 21, 1961, p. 22; June 2, 1961, p. 22; *Christian Science Monitor* (June 7, 1961), p. 1 (June 15, 1961), p. 1; Edward T. Folliard, "Kennedy's Dilemma," *Saturday Review of Literature,* 44 (April 15, 1961), pp. 56-57.

size, only to institutions which actually concentrated on higher learning rather than on the inculcation of religious doctrine.[102]

The result of all this flaring up once again of the fires of religious controversy was that no federal aid to public schools was authorized by Congress. In addition, the aid to colleges bill also went down the drain for the nonce. (It was finally to pass in 1963.) The *New York Times*, in a series of bitter editorials, roundly condemned the "obstructionism" by Congressmen and pressure-group leaders which had killed the chance for urgently needed federal aid to schools.[103] The demise of the legislation, in the opinion of the *Times*, constituted a tragic "chapter of legislative irresponsibility and inept executive leadership." Much of the burden of the defeat, the newspaper declared, rested with those in the Kennedy administration who "mismanaged the measure. Inept behind-the-scenes talk of compromise, particularly the offer to use the National Defense Education Act as a vehicle for backdoor aid to non-public schools, consolidated the opposition and disheartened supporters." [104]

Efforts by the Kennedy administration to gain Congressional approval of the aid to education project were also blocked in 1962.[105] The *Boston Globe* commented: "Actually, 1962 turned out to be just a bitter echo of 1961 when the religious issue and the separation of church and state argument brought President Kennedy's federal aid to education bill to disaster." [106] Thus the drive for federal aid in the early Sixties was impaled on the horns of the aid-to-parochial-schools dilemma. In an effort to find a way out of this impasse, a bipartisan Citizens Committee for Federal Aid for Public Elementary and Secondary Education came forward in December, 1962, with a plan under which all federal funds would be "intermingled" with state aid to the schools immediately after receipt of the money at the state level. All accounting to the federal government would be made by the state education authorities, and matching funds would be required of the states. The proposal was designed to bypass the controversy over funds for private and parochial schools by shifting the responsibility to the states for fund allocation. If a state's use of "intermingled funds" were to be declared unconstitutional on any count, the eventual court test

[102] *Civil Liberties* (American Civil Liberties Union, September 1961).
[103] *New York Times*, June 17, 1961, p. 20; June 22, 1961, p. 30; June 24, 1961, p. 1; August 25, 1961, p. 13.
[104] *Ibid.*, "School Aid Debacle," September 1, 1961, p. 20.
[105] *Ibid.*, September 24, 1962, pp. 1, 18.
[106] *Boston Globe*, October 7, 1962, p. A-7.

would have to come at the state level, and thus federal aid on a nationwide scale would no longer be held up.[107] While this compromise
seemed reasonable to some, others remained dubious of its implications.
One possible application on the state level of this compromise approach was now spelled out, namely, the "shared" use of federally
aided public school facilities by children enrolled in parochial schools
in such nonreligious areas as physical education, home economics, industrial arts, and cafeteria service. A poll of 275 school administrators
by *The Nation's Schools* showed 68 per cent of the group polled to be
in opposition to the practice, not only on financial grounds, but also on
the ground that it violated the principle of separation of church and
state.[108] So the seemingly endless deadlock continued.

Significant Court Decisions and Their Aftermath

The difficult and much disputed question of the boundary line
between church and state in the American school system has come in
the twentieth century to involve a number of issues besides the one of
public financial support. While these problems may not be of the same
immediate impact as the aforementioned, neither are they purely subsidiary; some of them, indeed, go to the heart of the question of what
constitutes true "separation" in the relationships of institutions of religion and the public school. Here the ambivalence of the position of
the Protestant Christian majority, desiring on the one hand a rigid
separation of public schools from overt denominational control but at
the same time wishing to ensure that these same schools not be "Godless" (from a Protestant point of view, at any rate), created a number
of perplexing problems. Thus the interesting situation resulted that, on
some of these less fundamental church-state issues, the Protestant-
"secular humanist" alliance, which had blocked direct public financial
aid for parochial schools, held firm and thereby won some additional
signal victories, while on others it wavered. The situation was further
complicated by the fact that the multidenominational structure which
was American Protestantism, riven as it was by Modernist-Fundamen-
talist divisions, by no means spoke with one voice on these questions.
   A practice which in many states aroused the opposition of both
Protestants and secular humanists was the employment by local school

[107] *New York Times*, December 4, 1962, p. 40
[108] *School and Society* (September 22, 1962), p. 282.

boards of persons wearing a religious garb as teachers in public schools. By the 1950's, 16 states permitted this practice, but it was under heavy fire, and 22 states forbade it. The development of this kind of situation was usually due to a twentieth-century version of the earlier Lowell and Poughkeepsie plans, involving "cooperation" between a local parochial school and the public education authorities in a community or neighborhood whose population was heavily Catholic. In defense of the practice, it was claimed that the wearing of religious garb did *not* necessarily mean that the individual in question was giving sectarian instruction, and that under the Bill of Rights a teacher could not be barred from employment in the public schools because of views or observances required by his religion. This, indeed, is the interpretation which might be placed upon a school law enacted in 1932 in New York State. The courts of the state, however, had dissented earlier from such a view of the matter. In the case of *O'Connor v. Hendrivk* (1906), the New York State Supreme Court had ruled that teachers in religious garb *could* be excluded from the public schools because such garb did in fact exercise a sectarian influence:

> There can be little doubt that the effect of the costume worn by these Sisters of St. Joseph at all times in the presence of their pupils would be to inspire respect if not sympathy for the religious denomination to which they so manifestly belong. To this extent the influence was sectarian, even if it did not amount to the teaching of denominational doctrine.

In 1910 the Pennsylvania Supreme Court rendered a somewhat similar decision, holding that exclusion of a religiously garbed teacher from the public schools would not disqualify that individual from employment because of religious sentiments. Such a law "is directed against acts, not beliefs, and only against acts of the teacher while engaged in the performance of his or her duties as teachers." This issue continued in subsequent years to be disputed, and adjudicated on the local and state level; the Supreme Court made no ruling on the question.[109]

Another practice which provoked criticism by some Protestant and many secular educational leaders was the granting of credit within public school systems for religious instruction. By mid-twentieth century 10 states were permitting voluntary religious instruction by church teachers inside public schools, and a drive was on in many communities

---

[109] Johnson and Yost, *Separation of Church and State*, pp. 115-18; Mason, *Church-State Relationships in Connecticut*, pp. 264-65; Stokes, *Church and State in the United States*, II, p. 721.

to have official credit awarded for the completion of such courses. These programs had been introduced as a result of pressures exerted by ministerial associations and other clerical groups. Proponents usually suggested that an interfaith committee administer the instruction based on the Douay, King James, and Jewish versions of the Bible.[110] Commenting on such projects, Alvin W. Johnson observed:

> If the state is to grant scholastic credit for religious instruction given under the control of the interfaith committee, . . . then it is difficult to say on what ground it can refuse similar credit for religious instruction given by leaders of paganism, Mormonism, Christian Science, spiritualism, Swedenborgianism, Buddhism, or Brahmanism. These religions exist in America, and many of them are educating their followers and children in their own religious institutions and at their own expense. . . .

Johnson warned that any seemingly mild and innocent program for supposedly "interfaith" religious instruction in public schools could end ultimately with ecclesiastical and political coercion and the teaching of religion by the state.[111]

An even more controversial problem was posed by the requirement of compulsory Bible readings in the public schools. In some cases this practice was coupled with the required singing of hymns and recitation of prayers, particularly the Lord's Prayer. In an age of compulsory school attendance legislation, the question arose as to whether the inclusion of such mandatory readings and ceremonies in response to pressures from organized religious groups did not violate rights of conscience and the spirit of separation of church and state. In the nineteenth century Roman Catholics had been the leading opponents of compulsory Bible readings in public schools, maintaining that selections from the Protestant King James Version read by laymen, without the authoritative interpretation required by their Church, violated the rights of conscience of their children. Many Protestant groups were just as firm at that time in demanding that the existing program of Bible readings remain in the schools. In the twentieth century many communities with a Catholic majority authorized Biblical readings from the Douay version and Catholic opposition to the practice lessened. The brunt of the campaign against such a program in public schools was thereupon left to be carried on by some Protestant groups, practically all Jewish groups, many secular-humanist organizations, and civil liberties groups.

[110] Stokes, *op. cit.*, p. 720.
[111] Johnson and Yost, *op. cit.*, pp. 98-99.

During the nineteenth century only one state, Massachusetts, passed a statute (enacted in 1826) requiring Bible readings in all public schools within its jurisdiction. Many American school systems did in fact require such readings during those years, but the problem was then handled on a local basis. In the early twentieth century vigorous lobbying activities of the new Fundamentalist movement in Protestantism and the new friendliness in certain states of the Roman Catholic church toward a Bible reading program, properly policed from its point of view, interjected a novel element into the situation. Permissive, local option was no longer thought to be adequate. By 1950, 13 states specifically required daily Bible readings at all opening exercises in all public schools. Twenty-four other states authorized local communities to institute such a mandatory program.[112]

In the course of time, several actions alleging unconstitutionality and challenging the mandatory Bible reading statutes were brought in state courts. The resultant rulings sometimes upheld but more often invalidated these laws.[113] Some representative judicial rulings on this problem may help us to clarify the points at issue.

In 1902 the Nebraska Supreme Court declared that a reading of the Bible in public school was constitutional:

> The Iliad may be read in the schools without indicating a belief in the Olympic divinities, and the Koran may be read without teaching the Moslem faith. Why may not the Bible also be read without indoctrinating children in the creed or dogma of any sect? Its contents are largely historical and moral; its language is unequaled in purity and elegance; its style has never been surpassed. Among the classics of our literature it stands pre-eminent. The fact that the King James translation may be used to inculcate sectarian doctrines affords no presumption that it will be so used. . . .[114]

A similar mode of reasoning was used by the Supreme Court of Kentucky in 1910 when it rejected a Catholic complaint against readings from the King James Version of the Bible:

> That the Bible, or any particular edition, has been adopted by one or more denominations as authentic, or by them asserted to be inspired, cannot make it a sectarian book. The book itself, to be sectarian, must show that it teaches the peculiar dogmas of a sect as such, and not alone that it is so comprehensive as to include them by the partial interpretation of

---

[112] Stokes, *op. cit.*, p. 721; Johnson and Yost, *op. cit.*, pp. 33-35.
[113] Johnson and Yost, *op. cit.*, pp. 68-72.
[114] *State* v. *School*, 91 N.W. 846 (1902).

its adherents. . . . The history of a religion including its teachings and claim of authority, as, for example, the writing of Confucius or Mohammed, might be profitably studied. Why may not also the wisdom of Solomon and the life of Christ? . . .[115]

A very different point of view, however, was expressed by the Ohio Supreme Court in 1872 when it unanimously upheld the refusal of the Cincinnati Board of Education to permit Bible readings in the public schools of that city:

> Legal Christianity is a solecism, a contradiction of terms. When Christianity asks the aid of government beyond mere impartial protection, it denies itself. Its laws are divine, and not human. Its essential interests lie beyond the reach and range of human governments. United with government, religion never rises above the merest superstition; united with religion, government never rises above the merest despotism; and all history shows us that the more widely and completely they are separated, the better it is for both.[116]

In a case in Minnesota in 1927 the court ruled in favor of Bible readings, but the minority decision made it a special point to note these difficult aspects of the situation:

> To require the Jewish children to read the New Testament which extols Christ as the Messiah is to tell them that their religious teachings at home are untrue. . . .
> The Catholic people do not believe it right to have a Bible read to their children in the absence of the light of construction placed thereon by their Church. Are these people to be content to have a Bible read which substantially ignores the doctrines of purgatory, which is one of their vital beliefs? On the contrary, may a Catholic school board have the Catholic version of the Bible read disclosing the theory of purgatory as indicated in the Book of Maccabees, and not interfere with the "rights of conscience" of Protestants? . . .[117]

Finally, when the Wisconsin Supreme Court in 1890 unanimously ruled that Bible readings in public schools were unconstitutional, it stated:

> When we remember that wise and good men have struggled and agonized through the centuries to find the correct interpretation of the

[115] *Hackett v. Brooksville*, 120 Ky. 608 (1910); 87 S.W. 792 (1910).

[116] *Board of Education of Cincinnati v. Minor et al.*, 23 Ohio 211 (1872).

[117] *Kaplan v. Independent School District of Virginia, Minnesota, et al.*, 214 N.W. 18 (1927).

scriptures, employing to that end all the resources of great intellectual power, profound scholarship, and exalted spiritual attainment, and yet with such widely divergent results; and, further, that the realtors conscientiously believe that their church furnishes them means, and the only means, of correct and infallible interpretation, we can scarcely say their conscientious scruples against the reading of any version of the Bible, unaccompanied by such interpretation, are entitled to no consideration.[118]

Unitarian minister Rev. Joseph H. Crooker may have hit upon the nub of the matter when he wrote in 1903 that the Bible as literature, to be read as literature, had the same place in the public schools as Shakespeare or Homer. To read Job in those schools was just as legitimate as to read Hamlet, "if it be read just as Hamlet is read." But the Bible, he continued, had no place in American public schools as an authoritative statement of religious ideas or as a means of worship. To use Bible-reading in the public schools for religious instruction, viewing it "as the infallible Word of God, as the supernatural source of divine truth, as the supreme and final authority respecting all ideas and beliefs concerning God, duty, and destiny" would be to violate the American idea of freedom. The public schools might very well teach the life of Jesus, as they teach the life of Caesar; what they could not teach were the religious dogmas which had clustered about the life of Jesus. Were the state to do the latter, it would perforce be adopting a religion.[119]

Another strong Protestant pronouncement against compulsory Bible readings in public schools was issued by the Baptist General Association of Virginia which in 1942 memorialized the state legislature while protesting against a proposal for such a law. The Virginia Baptists declared that, in their view, the Bible was distinctly a religious book, and a proper reading of it was an act of worship which could not rightfully be enforced by law. Moreover, there were many versions of the Bible, and reading from any one edition would be looked upon by some as reading from a sectarian book in which they did not believe. The proposal in question apparently did not contemplate study of the Bible as great literature, the memorial continued, because it limited the compulsory reading to five verses, prohibited comment, and excused pupils, upon written request, from attendance upon the reading. The Virginia Baptists thereupon concluded:

[118] *State* v. *District Board of School District No. 8 of Edgerton,* 44 N.W. 967 (1890).

[119] Crooker, *Religious Freedom in American Education,* pp. 55-61.

Baptists in this state would suffer no direct injury from the proposed law, for the Bible which would be read in the schools is the version which the Baptists use; but the Baptists of Virginia know historically what discrimination against their religion means. . . .

This matter seems trivial to some who argue that the compelling of our teachers to read five verses of the Bible each day involves an infringement of their right so infinitesimally small that the law may well disregard it; but to say the least, such a law would be a piece of petty pilfering of the rights of the minority sects, which would make us none the richer, but would brand us as offenders against the sacred rights of others, and render us easy marks for retaliation when circumstances are reversed.[120]

Alvin W. Johnson calls our attention to the fact that while the desire to have the Bible read as part of every morning exercise in public schools might, in the view of many, be argued to be a commendable one, it nevertheless remained a fact that a sectarian religious motive prompted that desire. "If this were not true, why not read the Talmud, the Koran, or Confucius? They are also rich in moral training." [121]

During all of these years the Supreme Court of the United States studiously avoided ruling on the constitutionality of such local and state legislation. By 1959 and 1960, however, the ideological climate of the country had clearly changed. A series of actions were now launched in lower federal courts in order to bring about a clear-cut finding by the highest tribunal.[122] In two epoch-making decisions, rendered respectively in June, 1962, and June, 1963, the high court finally spoke, making it unmistakably clear that all religious practices of the type we have been describing in public schools were wholly and flagrantly in conflict with the United States Constitution.

In the 1962 decision the Court ruled by a six to one vote that any requirement of a public school teacher to lead her pupils in prayer was unconstitutional. "It is no part of the business of government to compose official prayers for any group of American people to recite as part of a religious program carried on by government," said Justice Hugo L. Black, speaking for the majority. It did not matter that the prayer was denominationally neutral, Black declared, or that it was voluntary for public school pupils to recite it. "When the power, prestige, and financial support of government is placed behind a particular religious belief," he noted, "the indirect coercive pressure upon religious minori-

---

[120] Stokes, *Church and State in the United States*, II, pp. 569-70.

[121] Alvin W. Johnson and Frank Yost, *Separation of Church and State*, p. 72.

[122] *New York Times*, September 23, 1959; November 1, 1960; November 2, 1960; *Christian Science Monitor*, October 22, 1960, p. 3; October 25, 1960, p. 5.

ties to conform to the prevailing officially approved religion is plain."

A storm of vituperation directed at the Supreme Court swept the nation following announcement of the decision. Politicians, clergymen, newspaper columnists all pitched in. A C.B.S. television commentator reported that the press reaction of the time showed that "demagoguery superseded discernment or discretion." [123] Clearly the Court had struck a sensitive nerve. Southern Congressmen, in particular, were loud in their demands for curbs on the "Warren Court" and called for constitutional amendments to overrule its decisions. Cardinal Spellman sprang to the barricades once again and stated a dominant reaction in Roman Catholic circles when he linked the New York Prayer case[124] with opposition to federal aid to parochial schools. This he viewed as a "two-pronged attack on the American way of life." According to the Cardinal, what was happening was a drive "to take God out of the public school and to force the child out of the private school." Bishop James A. Pike of the Protestant Episcopal Diocese of California agreed with the Cardinal's viewpoint. The Bishop told the Senate Judiciary Committee that the Supreme Court's decision had "distorted the meaning of the First Amendment." [125]

As time passed, however, more and more clergymen and church publications, particularly Protestant ones, came to accept the Court's position and praise its stand. "In our view the Supreme Court has rendered a service of the greatest importance," declared the *Christian Century*, "to true religion as well as to the integrity of a democratic state." [126] *Presbyterian Life*, the official publication of the 3,260,000-member United Presbyterian Church, warned its readers to "keep their shirts on." An editorial in its August 15, 1962, issue pointed out that "all the Supreme Court has declared against is the use of government-prescribed set prayers in public schools. Taking the prayer in question as a typical sample of the genus, we're inclined to think their findings are right." About the same time a group of 46 Protestant clergymen

[123] *The Nation* (July 14, 1962), p. 3.

[124] The Supreme Court's ruling specifically invalidated a New York Board of Regents recommendation calling for the recital of a 22-word, general, nondenominational prayer to "Almighty God" at the start of each school day. The case had been brought by the American Civil Liberties Union in the name of five parents of New York school children, including two members of the Jewish faith, a Unitarian, a member of the Society for Ethical Culture, and one nonbeliever. See *Salt Lake City Tribune*, June 26, 1962, pp. 1-2; *Civil Liberties*, No. 200 (American Civil Liberties Union, September 1962).

[125] *New York Times*, August 3, 1962, p. 7.

[126] *Civil Liberties* (September 1962).

and laymen, headed by Professor Joseph M. Swomley of the St. Paul, Minnesota, School of Theology (Methodist-oriented) issued a public statement endorsing and supporting the Supreme Court decision. In justification of their position, the signers noted that prayers used in public schools were bound to be offensive to some individuals and groups in the American pluralistic society, and that the responsibility both for religious education and worship belonged to the home, the church, and the synagogue.[127]

Nevertheless school boards across the land continued to evade the 1962 ruling by resorting to a variety of stratagems. The main pretext for these evasions was the argument that the Court had not yet banned school prayers as such; it had only banned the New York Regents prayer and any similar prayer "officially" drafted by government officials at any level. Therefore the Corporation Counsel of the District of Columbia was prompted to insist late in August, 1962, that the Bible and the Lord's Prayer, not being "official," could be constitutionally read or recited at opening public school sessions.[128] This reasoning was followed in the schools of the federal district and in many other school systems during the 1962-63 sessions. The Massachusetts Commissioner of Education authorized the Cambridge public school system, and all others in the state, to continue daily Bible readings, as required by state law, on the ground that the New York case "held unconstitutional only the voluntary recitation of a prayer which was composed by a public authority, namely, the Board of Regents." [129]

Such ruses, to be sure, were not always successful. When the School Board of Hicksville, New York, required public school students in that community to recite as a prayer the fourth verse of the American national anthem (which contains the words, "In God we trust"), the New York Commissioner of Education disallowed the practice. The Commissioner's reasoning in this instance was that the anthem, although written by Francis Scott Key and not by the Hicksville Board of Education, had been adopted by the Board specifically to be used as a prayer in school proceedings, thus making it official and hence unconstitutional.[130]

New York was the only state, however, where school practices were

---

[127] *New York Times*, August 13, 1962, p. 37.
[128] *Boston Globe*, August 29, 1962, p. 15.
[129] *Chronicle and Sun* (Cambridge, Massachusetts), September 6, 1962, p. 1.
[130] *New York Times*, August 30, 1962, p. 1; *Boston Globe*, August 30, 1962, p. 32.

substantially changed as a result of the 1962 decision.[131] The Supreme Court accordingly came to the conclusion that yet another ruling would be necessary to clear up all ambiguities. When cases originating in Pennsylvania and Maryland involving Bible readings and prayer recitations in public schools reached its docket, the Court felt that it finally had an excellent opportunity to make its position unequivocal. On June 17, 1963, by an eight to one vote, it spoke to the nation. In uncompromising terms it outlawed all religious exercises, prayers, or other practices of this nature in public schools as being in violation of the Constitution. Associate Justice, Tom C. Clark, a Presbyterian, read the opinion of the majority. Concurring opinions were entered by Associate Justices William J. Brennan, Jr., a Catholic, Arthur Goldberg, a Jew, and William O. Douglas, a Presbyterian. Associate Justice John M. Harlan, also a Presbyterian, joined in Goldberg's concurring opinion. "In the light of the history of the First Amendment and of our cases interpreting and applying its requirements," wrote Justice Clark, "we hold that the practices at issue and the laws requiring them are unconstitutional under the establishment clause, as applied to the states through the Fourteenth Amendment." The Justice continued with the observation that "the place of religion in our society is an exalted one, achieved through a long tradition of reliance on the home, the church, and the inviolable citadel of the individual heart and mind." But he added this important caution: "We have come to recognize through bitter experience that it is not within the power of government to invade that citadel, whether its purpose or effect be to aid or oppose, to advance or retard. In the relationship between man and religion, the state is firmly committed to a position of neutrality." [132]

Much wider support for the Court's attitude came this time from members of the clergy, Catholic as well as Protestant and Jewish.[133] The General Assembly of the United Presbyterian Church voted, even before the Court's decision was officially announced, to approve the banning of such traditional practices as Bible readings and prayers in public schools, religious observances or displays on public property, and Sunday closing laws.[134] Congressional reaction, at least at first, was

[131] *New York Times*, September 26, 1962, pp. 1, 40.

[132] *New York Herald Tribune*, June 18, 1963, p. 1.

[133] *Boston Globe*, June 18, 1963, p. 4; *Christian Science Monitor*, June 18, 1963 pp. 1-2.

[134] *New York Times*, May 22, 1963, p. 1.

somewhat less violent than in the previous year. Press reaction, too, was not as hostile as earlier.[135] Arthur Krock, veteran Washington correspondent of the *New York Times,* saw the Supreme Court's decision as a means of carrying into the twentieth century Thomas Jefferson's original understanding of the intent of the First Amendment and his idea that children of public school age were not sufficiently mature for forced stimulation to "religious inquiries." [136]

Closely related issues continued to perplex the courts and agitate the public in this era. The one that brought about the deepest splits, at least temporarily, between secular-humanist groups and organized Protestantism, and also within Protestantism itself, was that of "released time." The released time movement, which began in Gary, Indiana, in the early 1920's, called for the dismissal of public school pupils during regular school hours so that they might receive "voluntary" religious instruction from representatives of their own faith, sometimes in the public school building itself, but more frequently outside the school's premises. The practice spread rapidly from community to community as ministerial associations endorsed it, and by mid-century the great majority of the states had given it legal authorization in one form or another.[137] As the movement developed, Roman Catholic opinion concurred that it was a valuable means of "religious education of elementary school children not attending Catholic schools." The National Catholic Welfare Conference favored the plan, and in 1947 Archbishop McNicholas praised it.[138] Secular-minded educational leaders, on the other hand, were generally hostile to "released time," and many Jewish groups were cool to it. Among Protestants, however, there was a divided mind on this important question. The rigid "separationists," as Leo Pfeffer called them, joined with the "secularists" in opposing released time as representing a dangerous breach in the wall dividing church from state. To support such a program would be equivalent to "playing the Catholics' game." [139] A much larger group of Protestants disagreed with this stand, however. More worried about the menace of "secularism" and "irreligion" than about any advantage the Roman Catholic

---

[135] *Boston Herald,* June 18, 1963, p. 22; *Christian Science Monitor,* June 18, 1963, p. 15; *New York Herald Tribune,* June 18, 1963, p. 18.

[136] *Boston Herald,* June 18, 1963, p. 23.

[137] Johnson and Yost, *Separation of Church and State,* pp. 74-76; Stokes, *Church and State in the United States,* II, p. 720.

[138] Stokes, *op. cit.,* p. 545; Mason, *Church-State Relationships in Connecticut,* pp. 278-81.

[139] Pfeffer, *Creeds in Competition,* p. 74.

Church might win from such a religious education program, they supported "released time" in public schools.

One leading Protestant organizational proponent was the International Council of Religious Education. Its frankly sectarian motivation influenced its acceptance of the released time policy:

> The weekday church school is an essential part of the church's educational program, carried on under the direction of a local church or of several churches in a community associated in a Council of Religious Education, or Council of Churches and its Department of Religious Education.[140]

The National Council of Churches also issued from time to time statements upholding this general proposition.[141]

The constitutionality of released time practices remained somewhat indeterminate as state courts gave varying rulings on the matter.[142] The main trend of these decisions ran favorably to the practice until 1948 when the Supreme Court of the United States undertook to rule on the issue. In that year, by an overwhelming majority of eight to one, the nation's highest tribunal declared unconstitutional an interdenominational released time program conducted gratuitously in Champaign, Illinois, in the local public school buildings. Mrs. Vashti McCollum, wife of a University of Illinois professor, brought suit against the program on the ground that she was a "rationalist" and objected to religious instruction being given to her ten-year-old son in a tax-supported school, the practice of which was a violation of the First and Fourteenth Amendments of the Federal Constitution.[143] Those who supported the Champaign system argued that the 30 minute religion classes once a week were purely voluntary and were available only when the parents consented, that they constituted an act of "public welfare," and that the program as set up was designed to foster tolerance rather than intolerance. Separate briefs opposing the constitutionality of Champaign's released time plan were filed by the General Conference of

---

[140] *The Weekday Church School* (International Council of Religious Education, 1940).

[141] Johnson and Yost, *op. cit.*, pp. 77-81.

[142] Note the contrast between *Stein* v. *Brown*, 211 New York 822 and *Peoples* v. *Graves*, 219 New York 187.

[143] Her suit was backed by the Chicago Civil Liberties Committee and the American Civil Liberties Union, and the brief was signed by distinguished lawyers from seven states.

Seventh Day Adventists, the Joint Baptist Conference on Public Relations, and the Synagogue Council of America.[144]

Announcing the decision of the high court in this momentous McCollum case was Justice Hugo Black. Black stated that the facts

> showed the use of tax-supported property for religious instruction and the close cooperation between the school authorities and the religious council in promoting religious education. The operation of the state's compulsory education system thus assists and is integrated with the program of religious instruction carried on by separate religious sects. Pupils compelled by law to go to school for secular education are released in part from their legal duty upon the condition that they attend the religious classes. This is beyond all question a utilization of the tax-established and tax-supported public school system to aid religious groups to spread their faith. And it falls squarely under the ban of the First Amendment (made applicable to the states by the Fourteenth) as we interpreted it in *Everson* v. *Board of Education*, . . .

Justice Black further pointed out:

> Here not only are the state's tax-supported public school buildings used for the dissemination of religious doctrines. The state also affords sectarian groups an invaluable aid in that it helps to provide pupils for their religious classes through use of the state's compulsory public school machinery. This is not separation of church and state.[145]

In a concurring opinion, Justice Frankfurter called attention to the interesting circumstance at Champaign that "while a child can go to any of the religious classes offered, a particular sect wishing a teacher for its devotees requires the permission of the school superintendent who in turn will determine whether or not it is practical for said group to teach in said school system." Frankfurter further suggested that:

> If it were merely a question of enabling a child to obtain religious instruction with a receptive mind, the thirty or forty-five minutes could readily be found on Saturday or Sunday. If that were all, Champaign might have drawn upon the French system, known in its American manifestation as "dismissed time," whereby one school day is shortened to allow all children to go where they please, leaving those who so desire to go to a religious school.[146]

---

[144] Stokes, *Church and State in the United States*, II, pp. 515-17.
[145] 333 U.S. 203 (1948).
[146] *Ibid.*

The lone dissenter in this case, Justice Stanley Reed, argued that the constitutional prohibition of an "establishment of religion" did not rule out "every friendly gesture between church and state." It was not, in his opinion, an "absolute" prohibition. Many instances of close association of church and state had developed in American society, such as the required attendance at chapel of cadets at West Point and midshipmen at Annapolis. Reed held that, "This Court cannot be too cautious in upsetting practices embedded in our society by many years of experience. A state is entitled to have great leeway in its legislation when dealing with the important social problems of its population." [147]

The McCollum decision was hailed by some, heatedly denounced by others. The *Christian Century* and many Baptist leaders joined Unitarians, Jews, civil liberties crusaders, and secular-humanists in praising it as a landmark in the development of American religious freedom. Leaders of the National Education Association declared that "dismissed time" rather than "released time" would now be the only constitutional method whereby public school children could secure religious training.[148] Under this system, students were simply dismissed early one day a week and there was no accompanying attendance check "on whether they improve the shining hour in the local church, movie house, or poolroom." [149] In addition, Dr. Stokes called attention to the fact that the Court's decision did not rule out "the objective sudy of the history of religion in public schools under public school teachers." [150]

The head of the International Council of Religious Education, the leading Protestant sponsor of released time, expressed disappointment at the decision, but stated that the Protestant churches must now seek clarification of the law, reorganize their week-day systems of education to conform to it, and find unqualifiedly constitutional means to combat secularism.[151] Another Protestant critic of the decision noted that many exceptions were still allowed to the Court's dictum. The high tribunal had labored like a mountain to bring forth a mouse. "And a very puzzling mouse it was. Seldom had such an unbending decision been so flexible." [152] The most severe attacks on the McCollum decision, however, came from Roman Catholic spokesmen. Wilfrid Parsons charged the Court with abandoning judicial procedures in extending

[147] *Ibid.*
[148] Stokes, *op. cit.*, p. 522.
[149] *Time Magazine* (March 22, 1948), p. 81.
[150] Stokes, *op. cit.*, p. 522.
[151] *Ibid.*
[152] Cuninggim, *Freedom's Holy Light*, p. 115.

the "no-establishment" clause of the First Amendment to the states through the Fourteenth Amendment, encroaching upon the rights of localities and regions, and assuming frankly legislative functions.[153] J. M. O'Neill went even further. The American people should either ignore the decision completely, he raged, enact a new constitutional amendment spelling out the true meaning of the First Amendment, or demand that Congress curb the court by removing some of its jurisdiction! [154]

The McCollum decision left the released time situation in a state of flux. Some school systems whose practices differed somewhat from those of Champaign decided to sit tight. In others all released time classes were ordered to be moved away from public school buildings. In still others they were terminated. State courts, also, differed widely in their interpretation of the decision. A New York court held that it applied only to sectarian instruction *inside* public schools, while a St. Louis district court ruled that it invalidated released time classes *outside* the public school premises as well.[155] There was an obvious need for further clarification.

In May, 1952, in the case of *Zorach* v. *Clauson, et al.*, the Supreme Court attempted to furnish such guidance to school systems throughout the country. By a six to three vote the Court upheld a one-hour-a-week "released time" program in New York, which involved the releasing of children from public school classes, on the ground that the religious instruction in this case was given *outside* the school buildings. In addition to location of instruction, there were other differences between the New York and the Champaign systems. In New York no public funds were expended in connection with the released time classes, and the public school officials did not recruit pupils for the religious instruction nor supervise or approve the courses and their teachers. Speaking for the majority, Associate Justice Douglas wrote:

> In the McCollum case, the classrooms were used for religious instruction, and the force of the public school was used to promote that instruction. Here the public schools do no more than accommodate their schedules to a program of outside religious instruction. . . . No one is forced

[153] Wilfrid Parsons, *The First Freedom* (New York: Declan X. McMullen Co., 1948), pp. 177-78.

[154] J. M. O'Neill, *Religion and Education Under the Constitution* (New York: Harper & Row, Publishers, 1949), pp. 266-72.

[15] *Lewis* v. *Spaulding et al.*, 86 New York 682; *Balaza* v. *Board of Education of St. Louis*, #18369, Div. No. 3, Circuit Court, St. Louis, Mo.

to go to the religious classroom, and no religious exercise or instruction is brought to the classrooms of the public schools. A student . . . is left to his own desires as to the manner or time of his religious devotions, if any.

The Constitution does not say that in every and all respects there shall be a separation of church and state. Rather it studiously defines the manner, the specific ways in which there shall be no concert or union or dependency one on the other.

That is the common sense of the matter. Otherwise the state and religion would be aliens to each other, hostile, suspicious, and even unfriendly. . . .[156]

One of the dissenting Justices, Hugo Black, stated in his opinion that the Court had intended in the McCollum case to make it "categorically clear" that released time was unconstitutional even if the religious instruction were given *during* school hours *off* public school premises. The only constitutional system was to dismiss *all* public school pupils for a stated period each week. This the New York plan did not do. The effect was, therefore, to "manipulate the compelled classroom hours of the compulsory public school system" in aid of religious instruction. In a separate dissenting opinion, Justice Jackson concluded that the New York released time program was utilizing the public schools "as a temporary jail for students who will not go to church." This meant that the coercive power of the state was being used to aid religious sects in violation of the First Amendment. "The day," Jackson warned, "that this country ceases to be free for irreligion it will cease to be free for religion—except for the sect that can win political power. We start down a rough road when we begin to mix compulsory public education with compulsory godliness." [157]

Many observers who had been critical of the McCollum decision expressed satisfaction with the Zorach ruling and attributed the Court's change in position to the impact of the public criticism which had been directed at it in the years following 1948.[158] A strong argument could be made, however, for the proposition that the Zorach case did not fundamentally repudiate the Court's position in the Everson and McCollum cases. The Justices expressly stated that they still adhered to the McCollum decision and that, under the First Amendment, "Gov-

---

[156] 343 U.S. 306.
[157] *Ibid.*
[158] F. William O'Brien, *Justice Reed and the First Amendment* (Washington, D.C.: Georgetown University Press. 1958), pp. 178-79; Cuninggim, *Freedom's Holy Light*, pp. 116-17, 144-45; F. Ernest Johnson, ed., *American Education and Religion* (New York: Institute for Religious and Social Studies, 1952), p. 188.

ernment may not finance religious groups nor undertake religious instruction." [159] Indeed, one Catholic critic of the Court, after a careful study of the opinions in the Zorach case, concluded that the high tribunal had not experienced a change of heart at all.[160] From the opposite side of the ideological fence, *The Nation* belabored the Court for its "clear reversal" of its earlier position.[161]

Much of the force behind the drive for released time programs in the years following World War I seems to have derived from a growing feeling, at least among American Protestants, that the Sunday school was no longer doing the effective job of religious education that it had been designed to do.[162] However, advocates of complete separation between church and state continued to assert that the constitutional prohibition of "an establishment of religion" ruled out "impartial" promotion of religious instruction in public schools by means of released time.[163] Certainly it is difficult to ignore William Torpey's observation that, irrespective of judicial approval or disapproval, such a system was inexpedient for a country which sincerely wished to maintain a complete divorce of sectarianism from its public schools since the result was "possible religious discrimination between the students of different sects, and a denial of equal privileges to the student whose religious society does not provide local training at the same time as the other sects." [164]

How, then, stood the relations of church, state, and public school in the United States as the nation entered the second half of the twentieth century? Very obviously new boundary lines were being spelled out and venerable constitutional traditions were being revitalized and redefined; important principles were being evolved to meet modern situations that could not possibly have been foreseen by the Founding Fathers. In a self-consciously pluralistic society, with Catholics, Protestants, Jews, and secularists all proposing programs for solution of the issue, this work of redefinition—at least as far as the courts were concerned—promised to be an ongoing process. These latest solutions were firmly based upon earlier American precepts of separation of church and state; if anything, the effect of twentieth-century controversy was to

[159] Pfeffer, *Creeds in Competition*, pp. 48-49.
[160] Joseph H. Brady, *Confusion Twice Confounded* (South Orange, N.J.: Seton Hall University Press, 1954), pp. 184-90.
[161] *The Nation* (May 10, 1952), p. 441.
[162] Herbert W. Schneider, *Religion in Twentieth-Century America* (Cambridge, Mass.: Harvard University Press, 1952), pp. 36-39.
[163] Butts, *The American Tradition in Religion and Education*, p. 210.
[164] William G. Torpey, *Judicial Doctrines of Religious Rights in America* (Chapel Hill, N.C.: University of North Carolina Press, 1948), p. 329.

deepen and strengthen attachment to this principle. At the same time, the question of actual implementation remained much disputed.

American Catholics at mid-century were busily engaged in expanding and developing what was probably the most extensive and highly organized system of education in the history of their church. Fourteen per cent of the nation's total elementary and secondary school enrollment by this time was to be found in Catholic schools. In many cities the percentages were much higher: Boston, 30; Buffalo, 40; Pittsburgh, 42; Philadelphia, 39; Chicago, 34; and New York, 26.[165] From an attitude shaped by self-conscious minority-group status and embattled defensiveness, Catholics passed in the mid-twentieth century to a more confident, positive, and assertive posture in defending their parochial schools and in vigorously demanding public support for them.[166] As Monsignor Frederick G. Hochwalt, Director of the Department of Education of the National Catholic Welfare Conference, put it in 1952:

> If one agrees with my first point that parents are to be served, then there would be many kinds of public schools in the United States, each kind serving the needs of parents and the community in which they live. . . . In some other democratic situations public support of religious education is regarded as necessary to *protect* religious freedom and avoid discriminating against parents who want to give their children a religious education. . . .[167]

The new boldness and confidence of the American Catholic community led, as we have seen, to the abandonment of its previous suspicion of religious exercises in public schools (as likely to be predominantly Protestant) and resulted in a strong Catholic drive in many states for the inclusion of religious education programs in public systems.[168] Catholic activism was motivated, as it had been in previous generations, by the conviction that education, to have any real value

---

[165] Neil G. McCluskey, *The Catholic Viewpoint on Education* (Garden City, N.Y.: Doubleday & Company, Inc., 1959), p. 46.

[166] Will Herberg, *Protestant-Catholic-Jew* (Garden City, N.Y.: Doubleday & Company, Inc., 1955), p. 162.

[167] Rt. Rev. Frederick G. Hochwalt, "A Catholic Educator's View," in Johnson, ed., *American Education and Religion*, pp. 72-73.

[168] Herberg, *Protestant-Catholic-Jew*, pp. 248-49; Pfeffer, *Creeds in Competition*, pp. 72-73; Burns and Kohlbrenner, *History of Catholic Education in the United States*, pp. 171-75; Luke E. Ebersole, *Church Lobbying in the Nation's Capital* (New York: The Macmillan Company, 1951), p. 178; Theodore Roemer, *The Catholic Church in the United States*, pp. 372-79; Theodore Maynard, *The Catholic Church and the American Idea* (New York: Appleton-Century-Crofts, Inc., 1953), pp. 230-32.

and meaning for the prospective adult, must be deeply rooted in the precepts and doctrines of the Church. "The child must be seen whole and entire," the American hierarchy proclaimed in 1950. "He must be seen as a citizen of two worlds. He belongs to this world surely, but his first and highest allegiance is to the kingdom of God. From his earliest years he must be taught that his chief significance comes from the fact that he is created by God and is destined for life with God in eternity." [169]

For this reason, many Catholic leaders were profoundly suspicious of the orientation and atmosphere of the public school. They viewed it as shot through, from top to bottom, with religious indifferentism and Godless secularism. They saw the influence of Thorndike, Kilpatrick, and Dewey as being baleful, deepening what they termed the atheism and materialism of the secular, nonsectarian school. Some retained hope that the public school might be, at least in small part, redeemed through the forcing of programs of religious education and religious exercises into it, but they felt that the main reliance for the salvation of their children remained a school system *completely* under Catholic control.[170]

When we note the vigor with which American Catholic spokesmen denounced modern trends in the secular public schools, it is all the more remarkable, as Father Walter Ong has pointed out, that the parochial schools they set up should have come to resemble those very same public schools in so many important respects! Father Ong has taken note here of the same phenomenon which impressed Will Herberg and other perspicacious observers; namely, that Roman Catholicism in the United States was becoming "Americanized" and "bourgeoisified" so that it too, in contrast with traditional and European Catholicism, was "other-directed" (to use David Riesman's term) and embodied such features as a booster-type optimism, coeducation, and sports frenzy, all alien to the medieval church. Much of this "Americanizing" was fostered by the "moving-up" of Catholics from lower-class immigrant

[169] Rev. Raphael Huber, ed., *Our Bishops Speak* (Milwaukee: Bruce Publishing Co., 1952); on this subject, see also Rev. George Schmidt, *The American Priest* (New York: Benziger Bros., Inc., 1919), pp. 44-50; Neil G. McCluskey, *Public Schools and Moral Education* (New York: Columbia University Press, 1958), pp. 268-72; Rev. James Keller, *All God's Children* (Garden City, N.Y.: Doubleday & Company, Inc., 1953), pp. 290-91; Ellis, *American Catholicism*, pp. 110-11.

[170] Louis J. A. Mercier, "The Reaction Against Secularism," and Rev. G. O. O'Connell, "Sources of Secularism," in *Man and Modern Secularism* (New York: National Catholic Alumni Federation, 1940); McCluskey, *The Catholic Viewpoint in Education*.

neighborhoods in urban centers to middle-class suburbs inhabited more and more by professionals and junior executives. Also aiding in the process was the intermarriage of Catholics from different ethnic groups, producing a more "American" type.[171] These developments were bringing forward a new kind of American Catholic and a new kind of parochial school:

> In their educational procedures and aims, more practical and in many ways more successful socially than anything that Catholic or non-Catholic Continental Europe has ever been able to manage, American Catholics exhibit many of the very traits which a mind such as Dewey's set out to deal with and channel. It is of course evident that Catholics could not string along with Dewey's kind of naturalism, which has much in it diametrically opposed to the faith. Still, it is worthy of observation that, faced with their own behavior and the doctrines of Dewey which do something both to explain and to foster this behavior, they have felt called on to focus their attention on what was *wrong* in Dewey rather than to try to assess and assimilate his real contribution to America's understanding of herself.[172]

Father Ong found the American parochial school unique because of its "social and recreational emphasis," which reflected the optimism, busy organizational activity, good fellowship, and "togetherness" of the surrounding nonelitist, mass culture. By way of contrast, European Catholic schools remained "brain factories where isolated individuals are formed on intellectual assembly lines." [173] And, indeed, as one surveys the wide-ranging activities of American parochial schools from the 1930's to the 1960's, one finds ample documentation for this thesis. These schools possessed the truly "American" attributes of twentieth-century popular education: a stress on organized sports; flourishing dramatics; musical groups of all kinds; guidance services and student counseling; Parent-Teacher Associations; yearbooks and other student publications; and student assemblies. This "activity program" within the schools was supplemented by the multifarious undertakings of the Catholic Youth Organization. "Organization Man," Catholic version, got a good start at school. At the same time, the administrative structure of the parochial school system became just as complex, and in many ways just as standardized, as its public school counterpart. And the

---

[171] Herberg, *Protestant-Catholic-Jew*, pp. 160-73, 256-59.
[172] Walter J. Ong, *Frontiers in American Catholicism* (New York: The Macmillan Company, 1957), pp. 106-7.
[173] *Ibid.*, pp. 6-10, 44.

curriculum, with its emphasis on social studies, training for citizenship, and the usual foundational studies, together with an increasing provision for commercial and vocational training, was not remarkably different from the public school's program.[174] Thus we have the paradoxical situation that American Catholics were rejecting the dominant American pattern of public education "on the conscious theoretical level" while at the same time accepting it, with marked enthusiasm, on a subconscious and largely unexamined level.[175]

Not all American Catholics gave their unqualified support to the parochial school approach, although doubtlessly the vast majority did. As far back as 1870, a controversial priest, Father Edward McGlynn of St. Stephen's Church in New York City, had vehemently attacked the idea of separate parochial schools for Catholic children and had firmly upheld the common public school wherein "an infidel, a Jew, or a Mohammedan" would have the same rights as a Catholic.[176] In the 1950's a graduate of Catholic schools wrote in *Commonweal* that "ominous reference to the 'pain of mortal sin' is apparently necessary to keep many of us from choosing the public school or secular college for our children, even where Catholic institutions already exist." The writer, Joseph E. Cunneen, went on to state: "The fact is that in many cases the additional parochial school is a threat to the public school, in terms of both economic and moral support." Such a threat was underlined, in his opinion, "by what looks like Catholic cooperation with groups which, sometimes unintentionally, have served to undermine

[174] Joseph H. Fichter, *Social Relations in the Urban Parish* (Chicago: University of Chicago Press, 1954); *Parochial School, A Sociological Study* (South Bend, Ind.: University of Notre Dame Press, 1958); Brother William Mang, *The Catholic High School Curriculum* (Notre Dame, Ind.: The Ave Maria Press, 1941), pp. 40-54; Sister Mary A. Leary, *Catholic Education in Albany* (Washington, D.C.: Catholic University of America Press, 1957), pp. 344-52; Carl J. Ryan, *The Central Catholic High School* (Washington, D.C.: Catholic University of America Press, 1927), pp. 110-14; Sister Mary Janet, *Catholic Secondary Education* (Washington, D.C.: National Catholic Welfare Conference, 1949); Rev. William Maguire, *Catholic Secondary Education in the Diocese of Brooklyn* (Washington, D.C.: Catholic University of America Press, 1932); Sister Mary Montay, *Historical Development of Catholic Education in Chicago* (Washington, D.C.: Catholic University of America Press, 1953); Norbert M. Shumaker, *The Behavior Problem Child in the Catholic School* (Washington, D.C.: Catholic University of America Press, 1932); Rev. J. O'Dowd, *Standardization and Its Influence* (Washington, D.C.: Catholic Education Press, 1936); Sister M. M. Gross, *Success of Catholic Elementary School Teachers* (Washington, D.C.: Catholic University of America Press, 1933); Sister B. Meyers, *The Education of Sisters* (New York: Sheed & Ward, Inc., 1941).

[175] Ong, *op. cit.*, p. 107.

[176] Schneider, *Religion in Twentieth-Century America*, p. 34; Connors, *Church-State Relationships in New York*, pp. 107-8.

confidence in public schools from Pasadena to Scarsdale." And this was not all, in his opinion:

> We are too fond of saying what a saving our schools are to the American taxpayer. It is undoubtedly true that in a crowded city whose educational facilities are already strained, pupils can be educated more cheaply in a parochial school than in a public school, thanks to the nuns' vow of poverty. Even here the "gift" to the city is not as absolute as we often represent it; the hidden economics involved in paying for the parochial school affects the entire community. There is only so much money. That withdrawn for Catholic schools is being taken out of a potentially common fund. Some economy-minded Catholic members of large city boards of education make non-Catholics understandably skeptical about or boast of a gift to the taxpayer. . . .
>
> . . . If cultural pluralism is an un-American bugaboo in the sense that all doctrine and ideological differences must be ironed out before genuine assimilation can be achieved, then Catholicism, too, is un-American. The editors of such a journal as the *Christian Century*, however, who cannot be considered indifferent to the problem of religious education, have something else in mind when they warn against pluralism.
>
> They are asking whether the common good is not imperiled if distinct and total social groupings are solidified in early and formative years, and if there is a tendency to carry over such groupings unduly even in later years, cutting straight through the social structure. . . . Would it not be more logical for a Catholic child, reared in specifically Catholic institutions from parochial to graduate school, to be drafted into segregated "Catholic" divisions of the army, or serve on a "Catholic" warship or air wing? [177]

A few years earlier, Thomas Sugrue had expressed similar misgivings about the divisive effects of specifically Catholic schools in the pluralistic American culture. He feared that their purpose was to condition young people "to live their lives as part of a Catholic group, separated from other groups, insisting on participation in all the privileges of citizenship but acting only in the interest of their particular group." [178] In any event, for whatever reason or reasons, millions of Catholic children in America continued at mid-century to be sent to public schools, despite the vigorous continuing effort to expand parochial school enrollments; at least one Catholic prelate commented that in the face of this reality "complacency may not be indulged." [179]

[177] J. E. Cunneen, "Catholics and Education," in *Catholicism in America* (New York: Harcourt, Brace & World, Inc., 1953), pp. 146-54.

[178] Thomas Sugrue, *A Catholic Speaks His Mind* (New York: Harper & Row, Publishers, 1951), p. 49.

[179] O'Hara and Purcell, *Archbishop Ireland, Two Appreciations*, p. 8; see also Maury, *The Wars of the Godly*, p. 191.

What of the attitude of non-Catholic groups toward church-state-school problems? American Jews, despite an increasingly important movement following World War II to build up Jewish day schools, remained firmly opposed to any deviation from the most rigid separation of Church and state. Few Jews asked for public funds for their religious schools. As a group conscious of its minority status in a land where various Christian denominations made up the majority, the Jewish segment apparently believed that any weakening of the "wall of separation" would place it at a marked disadvantage, both in public school and in society. As Herberg has aptly noted: "At bottom, this attitude may be traced to the conviction, widely held though rarely articulated, that because the Western Jew achieved emancipation with the secularization of society, he can preserve his free and equal status only so long as culture and society remain secular." [180] It was from this separationist context that Simon Greenberg, Vice-Chancellor of the Jewish Theological Seminary of America, viewed the Everson decision and its implications:

> . . . the Jewish community views with suspicion any action that would put tax-collected funds at the service of privately conducted educational agencies. . . . If transportation to a distant point is provided, why not also provide textbooks to the private school for the study of nonreligious subject matter? And why not pay out of tax-collected funds for instruction in private schools in nonreligious subject matter? . . . Nor are the religious services offered by the armed forces of America through the chaplains in any way comparable to the situation in the public school system. In the first place, the chaplains are serving mature or presumably mature individuals. Second, no denominational services are held at which all must of necessity be present or withdrawal from which is a public act. In the armed forces the religious services are offered under conditions that make their acceptance an absolutely voluntary act on the part of the individual. . . . Under public school auspices the individual starts as a member of a group from which he must differentiate himself publicly, if he is determined to vary from the program planned for the group as a whole. Moreover, he is expected to do so while he is still young and therefore very much under the influence of the pressures of public opinion and group psychology.[181]

[180] Herberg, *Protestant-Catholic-Jew*, p. 255; see also Pfeffer, *Creeds in Competition*, p. 78.

[181] Simon Greenberg, "A Jewish Educator's View," in Johnson, ed., *American Education and Religion*, pp. 43-44, 51-52; see also the similar viewpoint expressed by Philip Jacobson, "A Jewish Viewpoint on Church-State-School Relations," *School and Society*, 89 (May 20, 1961), pp. 242-47.

As the nation entered the second half of the twentieth century, a number of leaders of the Protestant majority, in alliance with various Jewish and secular groups, became more militant than ever before in defending the principle of separation of church and state. As Catholic demands for aid to parochial schools mounted and grew more insistent, some Protestants saw in this development a challenge to the very nature of the American system and even to Protestantism itself. The more militant proceeded to form an organization known as Protestants and Others United for Separation of Church and State. The nonsectarian public school became for them a symbol of their defense against threatened Catholic encroachment. The Albany District Evangelical Conference spoke for most Protestants when in 1938 it asserted:

> The position of all American, as well as Christian, citizens of whatever church body should be clear and decisive. Parochial or religious schools are private schools, and should ask nothing of public treasuries. It may seem insignificant to divert small sums of public money for denominational or sectarian purposes, but experience has shown that beginnings must be resisted. Once the principle of demanding the clear-cut separation of church and state is surrendered the complete usurpation of public money for religious purposes will be inevitable.

The growing corporate strength and organizational assertiveness of Catholicism in America was particularly alarming to Protestantism because the latter had for so long identified itself with American culture and education as a whole. The result was that while as late as 1930 many liberal-minded segments of Protestantism had called for tolerance of Catholicism in the face of Ku Klux Klan bigotry, by 1947 much of the sympathy in these liberal Protestant circles had begun to change to fear of Catholic designs.[182] Protestantism in America came to present "the anomaly of a strong majority group with a growing minority consciousness."[183] Nevertheless Protestants were not of one mind on how to deal with this challenge. While all Protestant groups opposed public aid to sectarian schools, some were willing to concede that the government might contribute to welfare services for pupils in such schools. As a matter of fact, the Federal Council of Churches endorsed this position in 1949. Then, too, some Protestant leaders were so alarmed

---

[182] Luke E. Ebersole, *Church Lobbying in the Nation's Capital*, pp. 173-80; Pfeffer, *op. cit.*, pp. 91-92.
[183] Herberg, *op. cit.*, p. 250.

at what they considered the menace of secularism that they were willing to collaborate with Catholics in sponsoring released time religious education programs in public schools.[184]

This did not remain the position of all major Protestant leaders, however. Equally characteristic, and perhaps more representative of a developing Protestant attitude by the early 1960's was the comment made by the Rev. Dr. Eugene Carson Blake, Stated Clerk of the United Presbyterian Church, on the Supreme Court's school prayer decisions:

> [The decision] . . . underscores our firm belief that religious instruction is the sacred responsibility of the family and the churches. Our church shares the concern of those who are troubled about the moral upbringing of children never touched by the church or the synagogue. Yet we reiterate that religious instruction is not the responsibility of a public institution.
>
> It is of greater importance that the public schools aid in the moral growth of our children by teaching them to respect those with whom they disagree, to oppose the unjust treatment of any human being, and to care about the disenfranchised and distressed.[185]

What pass, then, had the nation arrived at by the seventh decade of the twentieth century? It had evolved a system characterized by absolute freedom of religion with increased attention now to the working out of details and a more precise definition of the rules that were to govern relationships among public institutions of learning, private secular ones, and schools supported by adherents of a particular religious faith. This process of definition involved, in the main, the spelling out of the meaning of the First Amendment to the United States Constitution and its application, through the Fourteenth Amendment, to states and local communities. The resultant position guaranteed the right of private and denominational school systems to exist alongside the public schools, but it excluded the former from any direct assistance from the public treasury. Welfare benefits designed to aid the child rather than the school were found, however, to be exempt from any inherent constitutional ban, though many persons continued to doubt the wisdom of such grants on the grounds of expediency. It became increasingly clear,

---

[184] *Ibid.*, p. 254; Cuninggim, *Freedom's Holy Light*, pp. 126-44; Stokes, *Church and State in the United States*, II, pp. 688; Neil C. Harner, "A Protestant Educator's View," in Johnson, ed., *American Education and Religion*, pp. 88-91.

[185] *New York Herald Tribune*, June 18, 1963, p. 2.

moreover, that compulsory school attendance laws could not constitutionally be utilized by religious groups to foster the giving of religious instruction or the holding of even nondenominational religious exercises *within* public school buildings.

Spokesmen for one of America's great religious groupings have suggested that the pattern of church-state relationships in education as outlined above be replaced by a program they regard as more equitable. This would involve general and impartial state subsidy of all schools, public, private, and parochial, as in certain European countries. Were this to be done, however, it would create many new and serious problems for a multidenominational society such as that of the United States. Comparisons with European systems in this connection can be highly misleading. In many of the countries where state subsidies to denominational schools are paid, a state-supported church exists, or at least there are closer official ties between the general government and various religious organizations than has ever been the case in America since the adoption of the Constitution. There seems to be little justification, at this juncture, for the United States to turn its back on 175 years of history and move in the direction of a state church on the European model.

Other Americans have been alarmed at the rising tide of conscienceless materialism and juvenile delinquency and for this reason have sought to strengthen the religious element in public education by means of compulsory Bible readings and released time programs. But if their aim is sincerely the moral and spiritual uplift of American youth and not sectarian proselytizing, why have many of the programs such people have lobbied through state legislatures and local school boards retained an obvious sectarian flavor? Why have they so clearly infringed upon the rights of conscience (whatever exceptions *in theory* are made possible) of minority religious groups and dissenting individuals? Why, as a matter of fact, must religion be presented to American school children in a denominational guise? Beyond question instruction in man's religious heritage and an appreciation of his spiritual strivings is a vital part of any truly liberal education. How can one claim to be educated who has never been exposed to this essential part of life? For this reason a purely secular school would, in truth, be an imperfect educational institution. Literature, art, architecture, philosophy, human history itself would be robbed of important aspects of meaning if taught with no reference to religion. But why, in an American public school, does such teaching have to be motivated by a spirit, not of open-minded learning, but of sectarian and devotional indoctrination? Is the latter approach truly educative?

Why could not all public schools substitute daily inspirational readings from the holy books and ethical teachings of *all* the world's great religions and philosophic movements for the unconstitutional required Bible readings and prayers? And, in place of released time sectarian programs of questionable constitutionality, why not require that all public schools offer solid, objective, informational courses, available to students who wish to elect them, in the history and principles of the world's great religions and philosophies? If the real objective is to train a child to be religiously literate and cognizant of the role of faith and search for meaning in life, such a program would surely realize that aim splendidly. At the same time, no one's rights of conscience would be infringed upon, and the vital American principle of separation of church and state would be maintained unimpaired. If, however, the purpose is to *indoctrinate* the child with one's own particular set of religious beliefs, the plan stated above would of course not be satisfactory.

The 1963 Supreme Court's decision in the Maryland and Pennsylvania cases stated the problem very well:

> . . . it might well be said that one's education is not complete without a study of comparative religion or the history of religion and its relationship to the advancement of civilization. It certainly may be said that the Bible is worthy of study for its literary and historic qualities. Nothing we have said here indicates that such study of the Bible or of religion when presented objectively as part of a secular program of education, may not be effected consistent with the First Amendment.
>
> But the exercises here do not fall into those categories. They are religious exercises, required by the states in violation of the command of the First Amendment that the government maintain strict neutrality, neither aiding nor opposing religion.
>
> Finally, we cannot accept that the concept of neutrality, which does not permit a state to require a religious exercise even with the consent of the majority of those affected, collides with the majority's right to free exercise of religion. While the free exercise clause clearly prohibits the use of state action to deny the rights of free exercise to anyone, it has never meant that a majority could use the machinery of the state to practice beliefs. . . .[186]

Perhaps the confusion in the mid-century American mind on the role of religion in public education is due not alone to the purposeful

[186] *Boston Globe*, June 18, 1963, p. 4.

lobbying activities of self-interested sectarians but even more to an equating of meaningful religious experience with group conformity. In this respect the other-directed bent of the American mass culture has tended to transform religion itself into just another element in society which brings individuals "together" and makes for a homogeneous, smoothly functioning people. According to this line of reasoning, all programs which would help the school child "adjust" to these desirable norms of the great majority must, *ipso facto*, be accepted without question. Will Herberg reflects this viewpoint when he describes the contemporary American population as divided into three great "melting pots" or religious "pools" which actually work to create unity in diversity. The educational programs sponsored by these three "pools" is seen by him as having a "unifying" function, one which is "not annulled because Catholics have their own schools and Jews attempt to inculcate their children with a loyalty to their 'people.' The same basic values and ideals, the same underlying commitment to the American Way of Life, are promoted by parochial school and public school, by Catholic, Protestant, and Jew, despite the diversity of formal religious creed." This American unity in multiplicity was thus seen as being fostered by all three of these great historic faiths, which are defined by Herberg as "religions of democracy." [187]

A prescient commentator on the American Catholic scene described the deep impress that the contemporary mass culture has made upon this particular "pool" of the national culture. Unlike European Catholicism, which in its educational system had still a strong intellectualist and individual emphasis, the American Church was strongly dominated by a social emphasis, constantly reflecting aspects of "the American's way of keeping 'feelers' out among his fellow men and measuring himself by them." It found its most useful entry into American life to be "the spirit of camaraderie or good-fellowship of the classless society." A certain type of personality was created by such a highly industrialized culture—an organization man:

> The social and recreational activities in the Catholic parish in the United States—from baseball teams to sewing clubs, from bowling leagues to religious study circles—come into being, at the expense of great effort on the part of priests and laymen, because of the group consciousness which is so much a part of the American way of life. . . . Americans go

[187] Herberg, *Protestant-Catholic-Jew*, p. 258.

through life in a froth of "organizations," and if the Church does not become present in terms of such organizations, she is not very effectively present at all.[188]

Given this American reality where religious devotion itself began to take on some of the coloration of expected and accepted organizational response, the question arises whether so-called "voluntary" religious programs in public schools really afforded freedom of choice to the individual child. In an age of conformity, the social pressures upon the youngster who wished to "belong" might be so strong as to vitiate any such right, however adequate it might seem to be in theory. In a case in 1960 involving religious observances in the public schools of Miami, Florida, a succession of social scientists testified that merely calling a program voluntary did not make it so. Dr. Baker M. Hindman of the University of Miami told the court that social pressures were quite strong in such a situation. "Compulsion to go along with the group is frequently much stronger than parental action or anything else," he said. Dr. Michael Gilbert, a Miami psychiatrist, testified that such psychological compulsion is greatest in its impact upon young children. Dr. Granville Fisher, Professor of Psychology at the University of Miami, declared that a child who asked to be excused during a religious program in school faced social pressures "which are more inimical to his welfare than if he did attend." [189]

Perhaps America could develop a more truly religious life and her schools could help engender a deeper spiritual experience in more people if all mechanical and superficial means of fostering religiosity by statute or by organizational pressures as a form of "togetherness" were abandoned. Then, instead of forced conformity through chanted school prayers and pledges as yet another "nice" means of "adjusting" the young to presumably high and elevated national norms, individuals might find greater freedom to grow in true spiritual awareness and to work out their religious destiny in the only way it has ever been meaningful, namely, in terms of authentic personal experience. To be sure, this is not the way of the "organization man," but then it never has been.

[188] Ong, *Frontiers in American Catholicism*, pp. 10-11.
[189] *New York Times*, November 1, 1960, p. 21.

CHAPTER SEVEN

May 17, 1954

The high-ceilinged chamber of the United States Supreme Court was jammed with people. Every available seat was taken. At the front behind a long mahogany bench sat the nine justices; in back of them were rich velour hangings; at the other end of the room were stout, massive-looking doors; all about stood imposing marble columns. In this impressive setting, the spectators sat quiet and tense this 17th of May, 1954. It was 12:52 P.M., and Chief Justice of the United States Earl Warren reached for a printed document on his desk and began to read. His voice was calm but firm. The eight Associate Justices, the spectators in the crowded visitors' section, the reporters in the press gallery strained to catch every word. Departing from custom, the Court had not handed out advance copies of its opinion to newsmen. But it was not long after Warren commenced reading that everyone present realized that this was going to be it—this was the long awaited "Decision Monday." Across the nation and around the world a bulletin flashed over Associated Press wires: "Chief Justice Warren today began reading the Supreme Court's decision in the public school segregation cases. The Court's ruling could not be determined immediately."

To the hard-working journalists whose assignment it was to cover the Supreme Court, the whole procedure seemed unusual. The segregation cases had first come to the Court in 1952 on appeal from rulings of lower federal courts. On December 9 and 10, 1952, arguments had been heard by the high tribunal, but the justices had been unable to reach a decision. They had thereupon ordered the cases to be reargued in the present court term. The result was that they had heard the cases for a second time on December 7 and 8 of the previous year. Since that time, each decision day had been greeted by an anxious crowd of spectators expectantly awaiting the ruling, as was true of this May 17th. If the decision were coming down, however, none but the justices knew. The reporters had been told: "It looks like another quiet day." Three minor decisions were announced and the men in the press section were beginning to believe the prediction when Banning Whittington, the Court's information officer, began putting on his coat. "Reading of the segregation decisions is about to begin in the court room," he announced. "You will get the opinions up there." The court room was one floor up from the press room, reached by a long flight of marble steps. Mr. Whittington led a headlong, frantic exodus, which reached the court room just as Chief Justice Warren had begun to read.[1]

By 1:20 P.M. Warren had finished, and the Court's decision was clear and unmistakable. Racial segregation in public schools anywhere in the United States was null and void because it violated the Constitution. On this fundamental question the Court was unanimous, to the surprise of many. Justice Robert H. Jackson, who had suffered a mild heart attack on March 30, had left the hospital on the week end preceding the court session to be with his fellow-justices on this history-making occasion as if to underline the single-mindedness and determination of the high tribunal.[2]

The Segregation Issue

The dramatic events of that memorable day climaxed a drive for equality of educational opportunity which dated back at least as far as Civil War times. The sudden emancipation of 3,500,000 illiterate Negro slaves had confronted the United States with the most difficult educational task in its history. Seeking to cope with it were northern

---

[1] *New York Times*, May 18, 1954, p. 14.
[2] *Ibid.*, *Time Magazine* (May 24, 1954), p. 12.

philanthropic organizations, the United States Freedmen's Bureau, and the reconstructed governments of the southern states.

The dimensions of the problem are vividly illustrated by the boyhood experiences of a slave destined in later years to attain eminence as a college president in Alabama.[3] This educator, William H. Councill, recalled that he lived during the war years in a little log cabin with Aunt Phillis, a noted "conjure woman." She was the young lad's whole school and primary course of study. From her he heard "tales of ghosts, Brer Rabbitt, Brer Fox, Brer Bear, and Mr. Terrapin." She carried him to "Saturday night dances on the adjoining plantation, where to the music of the gourd banjo, by a sputtering grease lamp, we patted and danced 'till broad day light in the morning.'" She took him to the slave "meeting" where she was regarded as having almost supernatural powers. And at night, through a hole in the torn quilt, the wide-eyed youngster used to steal a glance at Aunt Phillis, by the ghostly glare of dying embers, down on her knees, talking to her two little red "Father" and "Mother" conjure bags, and reading future events by their whirling, circling motion.[4]

It was a long, rocky road up from slavery. The mother of the famous Negro educator, Booker T. Washington, was a plantation cook; his father he never knew, although he was told that he was a white man from a nearby plantation. Though nearly penniless, Washington made an overland trip to Hampton Institute, overcoming heartbreaking obstacles along the way, and passed his entrance examination—the cleaning of a room—with flying colors.[5] His hard struggles were by no means unique among the colored people of his generation. Ezekial Ezra Smith, born a slave, eventually became principal of the Fayetteville (North Carolina) Normal School and, still later, Minister to Liberia. His first regular job in Wilmington, North Carolina, was one of making barrel staves in a turpentine factory. His pay was 25 cents a day. Somehow or other he was able to save enough to cover tuition and costs necessary to enter Shaw Collegiate Institute at Raleigh.[6]

[3] At the Agricultural and Mechanical College for Negroes, Normal, Alabama.

[4] William H. Councill, *Synopsis of Three Addresses Delivered at the Chautauqua Assembly at Waterloo, Iowa, . . . Spirit Lake, Iowa, . . . and at State Normal School of Iowa at Cedar Falls . . . 1900* (Normal, Alabama, 1900).

[5] Samuel R. Spencer, Jr. *Booker T. Washington and the Negro's Place in American Life* (Boston: Little, Brown & Co., 1955), pp. 21-25.

[6] N. C. Newbold, *Five North Carolina Negro Educators* (Chapel Hill, N.C.: University of North Carolina Press, 1939), pp. 91-92; 120-121. Mature laborers in the 1870's rarely earned more than 50 cents a day in that part of the South, while farm hands earned considerably less.

Ex nihilio nihil fit. These freedmen were growing up in a region that had never developed a real interest in public education. Traditional southern allergy to taxation made the common school unpopular in *ante bellum* times because it would require state or local imposts. During the Reconstruction era state-supported public school systems were introduced for the first time. With the "Thermidorean Reaction" of 1876, the white "Redeemers" of the South stated their intention of continuing these schools. Nevertheless they cut school appropriations to the bone and decreased the average length of the school term by more than 20 per cent. The 100-day term, the highest average of Reconstruction times, was not to be reached again until 1900.[7]

The result was the continuance of a high illiteracy rate and a fearful educational lag. "I see in the South millions of unlettered children," Senator James Z. George of Mississippi said in 1884. "I see in the South, wasted and desolated by war, an inability to educate them." [8] Efforts to improve the situation by means of federal aid to education proposed by New Hampshire's Senator Henry W. Blair in the 1880's became enmeshed in a tangled skein of sectional suspicion, partisan striving, and feuding over the tariff issue.[9]

Not all of the South's educational troubles were financial, however. Walter Hines Page reported at the turn of the century a conversation in a gentlemen's club in North Carolina that revealed in bold relief the attitude of southern white people toward the whole question of education for Negroes. Page had reported hearing a local Negro schoolboy translate and construe a passage of Xenophon. "Teach 'em Greek!," exclaimed an old Judge. "Now a nigger could learn the Greek alphabet by rote, but he could never intelligently construe a passage from any Greek writer—impossible!" Page then told the Judge that he had just heard the recitation in question himself. "Read it? Understand it? Was black? A black man teaching him? I beg your pardon, but do you read Greek yourself?" Reassured on this point too, the sceptical old gentleman at last replied, with a show of traditional courtesy, "Sir, I do not for a moment doubt your word. I know you think the nigger read

[7] C. Vann Woodward, *Origins of the New South, 1877-1913* (Baton Rouge, La.: Louisiana State University Press, 1951), pp. 61-62.

[8] *Congressional Record* (48th Congress, 1st Session [Washington, D.C., April 2, 1884]), p. 2514.

[9] Gordon Canfield Lee, *The Struggle for Federal Aid* (New York: Teachers College (Columbia) Press, 1949), pp. 134-35, 158-59, 164-66; Woodward, *op. cit.*, p. 64.

Greek; but you were deceived. I shouldn't believe it if I saw it with my own eyes and heard it with my own ears." [10]

The truth is that to many white southerners the education of Negroes symbolized the elevation of the colored race to a status inconsistent with the role they were supposed to play in the southern social system. In the early 1890's a northern visitor asked the public librarian in a southern town whether Negroes could borrow books. The latter replied, "Oh, no, the colored people don't come here. . . . We don't believe in Social Equality, you know." [11] Forty years later a white school teacher in Mississippi, who prided herself on being moderately "liberal" in her attitude toward Negroes, told an interviewer from the North, "No matter how much education you give them, a million years from now a nigger will still be a nigger in the South." [12] The intervening years had apparently brought about very little change in southern attitudes. As Horace Mann Bond pointed out, to many whites the literary education of a mule was no more absurd than teaching Negroes to read and to write. "Muleteers may love their beasts, but they do not try to teach them the alphabet." [13]

This viewpoint is put into stark relief by a character in one of Ellen Glasgow's novels when he tells a talented young Negro:

> "I am glad to have a good report of you, Parry, but I hope you won't let your head get chock-full of tomfool ideas about education. Your race doesn't need lawyers. There are too many white lawyers already, and if any of you get into trouble that's not your fault, your white friends are always ready to help you out. The best thing you can do is to turn your hand to some suitable work. There's room for a good waiter or porter, or you might find a job as a postman, though that's less easy, I imagine, than it used to be. But take my advice and don't get fancy ideas in your head. There's too much education, anyway. Too much foolishness out of books and too little old-fashioned religion." He cocked a suspicious eye over his paper. "You go to church regularly, I hope."

[10] Walter Hines Page, *The School That Built a Town* (New York: Harper & Row, Publishers, 1952), pp. 97-98. In an article, "The Rebuilding of Old Commonwealths," which originally appeared in the *Atlantic Monthly* in May, 1902, Page adds: "Such are the baffling facts of a sparse population and of a self-satisfied life that lingers past its day."

[11] Lillie B. C. Wyman, "Angelina W. Grimke's Drama of Rachel and the Lynching Evil," *Journal of Negro History* (April 1921), pp. 8-9.

[12] Hortense Powdermaker, *After Freedom, A Cultural Study* (New York: The Viking Press, Inc., 1939), pp. 300-303.

[13] Horace Mann Bond, *The Education of the Negro* (Englewood Cliffs, N.J.: Prentice-Hall, Inc., 1934), pp. 45-46.

Parry did not reply. He merely stood there, in a kind of downcast immobility, while the animation drained slowly out of his face and figure, and even out of the new blue cap which hung, limp as a rag, in his relaxed grasp.[14]

The tenaciously held conviction that Negroes need not be educated beyond the rudiments was one of the few propositions upon which southern whites of all classes could agree.[15] Nevertheless a few prominent Southern leaders began in the early twentieth century a campaign to convince their fellow citizens that Negro education should be improved. On May 24, 1912, a University Commission on Southern Race Questions was organized at Nashville, Tennessee, under the leadership of Dr. James H. Dillard, an official of both the Slater and Jeanes Funds. Pitching its appeal primarily to college-educated opinion, the Commission published an "Open Letter" in 1916, noting that "it is axiomatic that a developed plant, animal, or man is more valuable than the undeveloped. . . . The inadequate provision for the education of the Negro is more than an injustice to him; it is an injury to the white man. The South can not realize its destiny if one third of its population is undeveloped and inefficient." [16]

Such views made disappointingly slow headway with the majority of whites. While separate schools for the two races were insisted upon as a *sine qua non*, equality of facilities was realized only in theory. In 1921 southern Negroes, constituting 26 per cent of the region's population, received less than 10 per cent of its school funds.[17] And this differential became greater rather than less as the years passed. The southern "Educational Renaissance" during the period 1900 to 1940 was evidently accomplished, at least in part, at the expense of Negro education. By 1940 the Southern states were spending on the average $58 for each white school child as against $18 for each Negro child.[18]

[14] Ellen Glasgow, *In This Our Life* (New York: Harcourt, Brace & World, Inc., 1941), pp. 124-25.

[15] Louis R. Harlan, *Separate and Unequal* (Chapel Hill, N.C.: University of North Carolina Press, 1958); "J. L. M. Curry to Robert C. Winthrop, September 1, 1886" (J. L. M. Curry Papers, Library of Congress), as quoted in Woodward, *Origins of the New South*, p. 64.

[16] Josiah Morse, "University Commission on Southern Race Questions," *South Atlantic Quarterly*, 19 (October 1920), pp. 302-6. See the similar argument presented by southern sociologist W. D. Weatherford, in *Negro Life in the South* (New York: Association Press, 1911), pp. 174-75.

[17] Robert R. Moton, *The Negro of Today* (Tuskegee Normal and Industrial Institute, 1921), p. 11.

[18] E. Franklin Frazier, *The Negro in the United States* (New York: Macmillan, 1957), p. 436.

The emergence by this time of many costly new educational services such as visual aids and laboratory equipment still further reduced the percentage of public funds available to Negro schools.[19] In 1943 some Southern counties were actually spending more for their white children on bus transportation alone than for all school purposes for Negro children! [20]

Such conditions, unhappily, were not limited to any one section of the South. A student of Texas public education in the mid-1930's found ample evidence for his proposition that the Texas school system was essentially a white system with Negro education incidental to it.[21] In Gainesville, Georgia, Negro primary school children of the World War I era were crowded together three or four in seats intended only for two, and desks were packed so closely together as to leave almost no aisle space.[22] A visiting educator from the British African colony of Rhodesia in 1932 was astounded to learn that 63.8 per cent of all Negro schools in the South were one-teacher institutions. Everywhere he went he found malnutrition and ignorance of the most elemental facts of hygiene.[23] Gunnar Myrdal, a few years later, went into many one-room, one-teacher Negro schools in the South where he "hardly believed his eyes and his ears," so primitive were conditions and so "bottomless" was the ignorance of the pupils. Poorly trained, poorly paid Negro school teachers were seeking to cope with the situation as best they could, but their efforts, given the conditions, proved largely unavailing.[24]

This state of affairs did not just happen; it was carefully planned and controlled. School funds were consciously and purposefully diverted from Negro children to whites, especially in "Black Belt" counties— i.e., those with a large Negro majority. Expedients were generally found in these areas permitting appropriation to the white minority of the state aid which was forthcoming for the education of all children. In

[19] Horace Mann Bond, *Education of the Negro*, pp. 170-71.
[20] Commission on Interracial Cooperation, *Understanding Our Neighbors* (Atlanta, 1943), p. 23.
[21] William R. Davis, *Development and Present Status of Negro Education in Texas* (New York: Teachers College, Columbia University, 1934), p. 137.
[22] Ruth Reed, *Negro Women of Gainesville, Georgia* (Athens, Ga.: University of Georgia Press, 1921), pp. 41-42.
[23] W. H. Seaton, *Schools in Transition* (New York: Carnegie Corporation, 1932), pp. 14-17.
[24] Gunnar Myrdal, *An American Dilemma* (New York: Harper & Row, Publishers, 1944), pp. 902-3. "Negro teachers on all levels are dependent on the white community leaders. This dependence is particularly strong in the case of elementary school teachers in rural districts. Their salaries are low, and their security as to tenure almost nothing," p. 880.

some cases, these diverted state funds were sufficient in themselves to support the white schools without the necessity for additional local appropriations.[25]

Discrimination of this kind on the county level produced astounding disparities. In 1939-40 Russell County, Alabama, spent on its white schools $67.62 per child and on its Negro schools $3.66; Lowndes County in the same state spent $89.03 per white and $5.12 per Negro; De Soto Parish, Louisiana, $87.31 and $8.53; and St. John Parish, Louisiana, $67.37 and $7.33.[26]

Jim Crow marched hand in hand with unequal school opportunity. Racial segregation in the public schools of the South became entrenched as early as Reconstruction times, long before the official redemption of the region from the carpetbaggers.[27] And the segregation principle was ultimately applied to nonwhite other races than the Negro, winning the approval of the United States Supreme Court in the case of *Gong Lum* v. *Rice* (1927).[28] As a matter of fact, racial segregation in the schools had never been limited to the South. It had existed in many northern communities long before the abolition of slavery, and its practice continued to be the norm in certain northern and western areas as late as World War II.[29]

School segregation was a prominent factor in southern public education because it was the one aspect which was believed essential to implement the values basic to the southern way of life. Explaining the *rationale* of this policy, novelist Thomas Nelson Page argued in 1904 that the Negro race was fundamentally too immoral and too lacking in self-discipline to make any progress up the ladder of civilization. The two races would continue to interact much as they had before; the

---

[25] Harlan, *Separate and Unequal*, pp. 256-59; Bond, *The Education of the Negro*, pp. 114-15; Rayford W. Logan, *The Negro in American Life* (New York: The Dial Press, Inc., 1954), p. 286.

[26] *Understanding Our Neighbors* (Atlanta, Ga.: Commission on Interracial Cooperation, 1943), p. 23.

[27] C. Vann Woodward, *The Strange Career of Jim Crow* (New York: Oxford University Press, 1955), p. 15. For the congressional reaction to this problem during these early years, see Alfred H. Kelly, "The Congressional Controversy Over School Segregation, 1867-1875," *American Historical Review*, LXIV (April 1959), pp. 537-63; and for an early experiment in southern school desegregation, see Louis R. Harlan, "Desegregation in New Orleans Public Schools During Reconstruction," *American Historical Review*, LXVII (April 1962), pp. 663-75.

[28] Charles S. Mangum, *Legal Status of the Negro* (Chapel Hill, N.C.: University of North Carolina Press, 1940), pp. 82-85.

[29] Robin Williams and Margaret W. Ryan, *Schools in Transition* (Chapel Hill, N.C.: University of North Carolina Press, 1954).

racial "traits, instincts, and forces which have governed and propelled them since the dawn of history will in all human probability still control and propel them so long as they exist as races." [30]

White supremacy demanded not only separate *and unequal* public schools but also the exclusion of Negro citizens from the ballot. Up to about 1895 the latter aim was realized mainly by informal means, which were not always very thorough or consistent. From 1895 to 1910, however, white control of the vote was institutionalized by what one observer has called the "Southern Counterrevolution." The Fifteenth Amendment was effectively nullified by a series of constitutional revisions and intricate legal devices. Partly this turn of events represented white reaction to increased Negro participation in politics during the Populist-Conservative battles of the Nineties. Partly it reflected northern quiescence on the race question, demonstrated by the failure of Henry Cabot Lodge's federal election bill in 1890. Then, too, all over the world a Kiplingesque white imperialism was expanding at the expense of colored peoples and the idea of Caucasian race superiority was at flood tide.[31]

Some Negro leaders continued to hope for a fairer deal on both schooling and suffrage. When a disfranchisement bill was under consideration in North Carolina in 1900, P. W. Moore, principal of the Elizabeth City Normal School for the Colored Race, told a white friend that such an amendment "will be a blessing in disguise to my race. . . . Our leaders are now subjected to the hectoring of the illiterate of our race. . . . With the white man's recognized sense of justice, your leaders will hasten to prepare all men, irrespective of race, to exercise the rights of suffrage intelligently." [32] But high expectations such as these were soon dashed to the ground. "Understanding" clauses, "Grandfather" clauses, and the like were adopted in state after state

[30] Thomas Nelson Page, *The Negro* (New York: Charles Scribner's Sons, 1904), pp. 74-84, 94-98, 116-17, 158-59, 286. Another southern novelist of this period, George W. Cable, thoroughly disagreed with this viewpoint, and said the only question was whether the Negro would be given "that full measure of an American citizen's public rights, civil and political." Cable, however, succeeded only in provoking a storm of protest in the South and settled ultimately in Northampton, Massachusetts. Alva W. Taylor, *A Southerner Looks at Discrimination* (New York: International Publishers, 1946), pp. 7-12, 29-33, 40-45.

[31] William G. Carleton, "Introduction," in H. D. Price, *The Negro and Southern Politics* (New York: New York University Press, 1957); C. Vann Woodward, *The Strange Career of Jim Crow* (New York: Oxford University Press, 1955), pp. 42-45, 56-61.

[32] N. C. Newbold, *Five North Carolina Negro Educators* (Chapel Hill, N.C.: University of North Carolina Press), pp. 111-12.

so that Negro voters, educated or not, would be barred from the polls while masses of white illiterates were admitted as voters.[33]

A cry of protest came from Booker T. Washington, who pointed out that such a shabby trick was bound to devaluate in the public mind the importance of authentic educational achievement. In an open letter to the Louisiana constitutional convention of 1898, Washington stated: "No state in the South can make a law that will provide an opportunity or temptation for an ignorant white man to vote and withhold the same opportunity from an ignorant colored man, without injuring both men." [34] A few southern white leaders agreed with Washington's indictment.[35] But the majority seem to have agreed with Clark Howell who, while campaigning for the governorship of Georgia in 1906, demagogically warned against educated Negroes: "Whenever the nigger learns his *haec, hoc,* he right away forgets all about Gee-Whoa-Buck!" [36] Senator Vardaman of Mississippi seemed to be articulating the ruling sentiment south of the Mason-Dixon line when he proclaimed: "I am just as much opposed to Booker Washington as a voter . . . as I am to the cocoanut-headed, chocolate-colored, typical little coon, Andy Dotson, who blacks my shoes every morning."

Indeed, one delegate to the Virginia Constitutional Convention of 1901-2 wanted specific assurances that the new suffrage tests would not somehow or other enfranchise the "new-time" Negro—"your reader, your writer, your loafer, your voter, your ginger-cake school graduate, with a diploma of side whiskers and beaver hat, pocket pistols, brass knucks, and bicycle." [37] Seeking to quiet such fears, the chairman of the Virginia convention's suffrage committee made it clear that his purpose was to disfranchise all Negroes, whether literate or not, and to sacrifice no potential white voter, no matter how illiterate. To accommodate this proposal, an "understanding" clause had to be included in the proposed constitution. This was necessary because, *unfortunately,*

    [33] William A. Mabry, "Disfranchisement of the Negro in Mississippi," *Journal of Southern History,* IV (August 1938); *idem,* "Ben Tillman Disfranchised the Negro," *South Atlantic Quarterly* (April 1938); *idem,* "White Supremacy and the North Carolina Suffrage Amendment," *North Carolina Historical Review* (January 1936).

    [34] Booker T. Washington, *Open Letter to the Louisiana Constitutional Convention* (Tuskegee, Alabama, 1900?).

    [35] William A. MacCorkle, *The Negro and the Intelligence and Property Franchise* (Cincinnati, Ohio: Robert Clarke Co., 1900), pp. 15-19; Mabry, *North Carolina Historical Review* (January 1936), p. 23.

    [36] Dewey W. Grantham, Jr., "Georgia Politics and the Disfranchisement of the Negro," *Georgia Historical Quarterly* (March 1948), pp. 6-7.

    [37] Paul Lewinson, *Race, Class, and Party* (New York: Oxford University Press, Inc., 1932), pp. 84-85.

illiteracy was fast disappearing among the colored population of Virginia. The chairman saw this development as posing a "threat" to the state. But he solemnly assured the delegates: "I expect the examination with which the black man will be confronted to be inspired by the same spirit that inspires every man upon this floor and in this convention. *I do not expect an impartial administration of this clause.*" [38]

Booker T. Washington and W. E. B. DuBois

"The actual sight of a first-class house that a Negro has built is ten times more potent than pages of discussion about a house that he ought to build, or perhaps could build. . . . The individual who can do something that the world wants done will, in the end, make his way regardless of race." [39] The words were those of Booker T. Washington, ex-slave, President of Tuskegee Institute, and most widely publicized Negro educator of the late nineteenth and early twentieth centuries. Washington personified an approach to the education of the southern Negro which stressed industrial training, accepted segregated schools, and preached collaboration with the white South. [40] He was, however, by no means unique in upholding these propositions. Among his Negro contemporaries there were many, like William H. Councill, who followed his basic strategy. [41] And in the years that followed Washington's death, other Negro spokesmen arose who professed ideas very similar to those he had held. [42]

For the general public, however, Booker T. Washington remained the best-known Negro exponent of the industrial education approach. After the publication of his *Story of My Life and Work* in 1900, and his *Up from Slavery* a year later, tens of thousands of readers knew of

[38] Kirk H. Porter, *A History of Suffrage in the United States* (Chicago: University of Chicago Press, 1918), pp. 216-19. Italics are mine.

[39] Booker T. Washington, *Up from Slavery* (Garden City, N.Y.: Doubleday & Company, Inc., 1901), pp. 154-55.

[40] August Meier, "The Beginning of Industrial Education in Negro Schools," *The Midwest Journal*, VII (Spring, 1955).

[41] William H. Councill, *Synopsis of Three Addresses; Negro Development in the South* (Philadelphia, Southern Industrial Convention, 1901), pp. 2-5, 9-10; "The American Negro—An Answer," *Publications of the Southern Historical Association*. Vol. 6. January, 1902.

[42] Robert Russa Moton, *What the Negro Thinks* (Garden City, N.Y.: Doubleday & Company, Inc., 1929); Joseph Winthrop Holley, *You Can't Build a Chimney from the Top* (New York: William-Frederick Press, 1948); *Education and the Segregation Issue* (New York: William-Frederick Press, 1955).

his progress from a humble slave cabin in Virginia to the educational leadership of his people. The story had interest, suspense, and best of all, a happy ending. It enabled Americans to take satisfaction in the Horatio Alger-like rise of an ex-slave from rags to world fame by dint of hard work and zealous dedication to the larger good.

Washington's writings, after the fashion of Dr. Samuel Smiles, sing a long drawn-out hymn of praise to the virtues of industry, thrift, utility, and enterprise. Most influential in shaping his outlook was General Samuel Chapman Armstrong, founder of Hampton Institute in Virginia. For Armstrong industrial education furnished the means whereby the Negro masses could be uplifted economically. Since at the same time the Negroes were to give up their demands for political rights or anything smacking of "social equality," Armstrong had ingeniously fashioned a platform broad enough for southern whites, northern philanthropists, and some Negroes to stand upon. Booker T. Washington was the General's outstanding disciple.[43]

Washington's residence for a time in Washington, D.C., while he was doing graduate work, confirmed an already existing prejudice against training that stressed only the liberal arts and not practicality. He disliked the young Negro men-about-town he saw in the nation's capital who would spend half a week's salary on a buggy to ride up and down Pennsylvania Avenue on Sundays. Negro government workers who could not support themselves decently on the respectable salary of $100 a month aroused his contempt.[44]

Again and again in later years Washington expressed disdain for "people who call themselves 'the Intellectuals' [who] understand theories, but . . . do not understand things." [45] Negro graduates of liberal arts colleges who knew nothing of the actual conditions existing in the South were useless to their race and to their country. "There is no room in this country, and never has been, for the class of people who are merely gentlemen, and . . . the time is coming when there will be no room in any country . . . for people, in other words, who are not fitted to perform some definite service for the country or the community in which they live." [46] Equally reprehensible, in Washington's eyes, were professional race leaders "who make a business of keeping

[43] Meier, *The Midwest Journal*, VII, pp. 22-42.
[44] Samuel R. Spencer, Jr., *Booker T. Washington and the Negro's Place in American Life* (Boston: Little, Brown & Co., 1955), p. 41.
[45] Booker T. Washington, *My Larger Education* (Garden City, N.Y.: Doubleday & Company, Inc., 1911), pp. 120-21.
[46] *Ibid.*, pp. 299-301.

the troubles, the wrongs, and the hardships of the Negro race before the public" in order that they might make a good living from this state of affairs.[47]

In his widely publicized address before the Atlanta Cotton States Exposition in 1895, Washington presented an educational program which was essentially the old Hampton Institute plan, refurbished after a careful study of Henry W. Grady's influential blueprint for a "New" industrial South.[48] The Negro was to "prove himself" to the white community by becoming an efficient producer, capable of standing on his own two feet economically. To do so, he would have to concentrate on industrial and agricultural training, not abstract liberal arts. He also should, for the present, call off his crusade for equal rights and seek instead to *earn* acceptance by making himself indispensable to the white South.[49]

Repeatedly, in books, articles, and speeches, Washington hammered away at the same themes. Proud that he had never formally studied pedagogy, he instinctively favored pragmatic methods of teaching. "We wanted to teach them," he wrote of Tuskegee, "to study actual things instead of mere books alone." [50] The southern white man would come to support Negro education "provided it can be shown that this education has actually benefited and helped in some practical way the masses of the Negro people with whom the white man in the South comes most in contact." [51] Successful brick-making at Tuskegee had been a particularly gratifying triumph because it had shown the white residents of the neighborhood that the education of the Negro was not making him worthless, that Tuskegee was adding something to the wealth and comfort of the community. "As the people came to us to buy bricks, we got acquainted with them; they traded with us and we with them. Our business interests became intermingled. We had something which they wanted; they had something which we wanted." [52]

[47] *Ibid.*, pp. 118-19.
[48] Oliver C. Cox, "New Crisis in Leadership Among Negroes," *Journal of Negro Education*, XIX (Fall, 1950), p. 460.
[49] Spencer, Jr., *op. cit.*, pp. 50-51, 103-6.
[50] Washington, *Up from Slavery*, p. 126; see also *My Larger Education*, pp. 128-30. H. B. Frissell, Principal of Hampton Institute in 1905, characterized Washington's program as being the very embodiment of the "Learning by Doing" principle which John Dewey had announced six years before in his *School and Society: see From Servitude to Service* (Chicago, 1905), pp. 136-37.
[51] Washington, *My Larger Education*, p. 303.
[52] Washington, *Up from Slavery*, p. 153. On this theme see also Booker T. Washington, *The Story of My Life and Work* (Atlanta, Ga.: J. L. Nichols, 1900), pp. 232-34.

A stocky man, light yellow of skin, arose at a Boston church meeting in 1905. A shock of "close-curled black hair" covered his head and his eyes burned like live coals. "Mr. Washington," he called out in a clear, strongly Harvard-accented voice, "Mr. Washington, will you please explain to this audience just what your stand. . . ." The speaker got no further. Police rushed at him from all sides, seized him, and carried him away, struggling, to jail.[53] The questioner was William Monroe Trotter, Phi Beta Kappa graduate of Harvard College. His father, Register of Deeds for the District of Columbia under President Grover Cleveland, had accumulated a comfortable competence and had been able to give the young man every educational advantage. The incident just described had occurred one hot July evening in 1905 when Booker T. Washington had come to Boston to speak on the Negro question. Trotter and some like-minded associates, the very kind of "intellectuals" Washington despised, were present for the express purpose of heckling the eminent visitor from Tuskegee. The police had been alerted, however, and had moved swiftly to prevent any interruption of the meeting.[54]

The Boston disturbance dramatized the discontent with Booker T. Washington's leadership which had been rising among influential groups of American Negroes even before 1905. This hostility was most virulent among Negro intellectuals. Members of "the talented tenth," as W. E. B. DuBois called them, charged that Washington's claim to be leader of the Negro people was spurious. They saw him rather as a selfish and power-mad collaborator with the white South in upholding a system of unfair discrimination against the Negro.[55]

Particularly resented was the tremendous power the Tuskegee educator had come to wield over the Negro press and, through his influential connections with white educational foundations, over institutions of learning. Things had come to such a pass, W. E. B. DuBois recalled, that when any Negro complained or advocated a new course of action, he was silenced with the remark that Mr. Washington would not agree with this. Irritated young Negro intellectuals had reached the

[53] W. E. B. DuBois, *Mansart Builds a School* (New York: Mainstream Publishers, 1959), p. 65.

[54] W. E. B. DuBois, *Mansart Builds a School* (New York: Mainstream Publishers, 1959), pp. 65-66; idem, *The Ordeal of Mansart* (New York: Mainstream Publishers, 1957), pp. 303-4; Spencer, Jr., *Booker T. Washington*, pp. 139-46.

[55] Oliver C. Cox, "The Leadership of Booker T. Washington," *Social Forces*, XXX (October 1951), pp. 93-95; for a picture of a southern Negro educator in Washington's time who had a somewhat more militant outlook, see William J. Walls, *Joseph Charles Price, Educator and Race Leader* (Boston: Christopher Publishing House, 1943).

point where they were ready to explode: "I don't care a damn what Booker Washington thinks! This is what I think, and I *have a right to think*." [56]

In 1901 Monroe Trotter and another Boston Negro, George Forbes, began publishing *The Guardian*, a newspaper which lashed into Washington unmercifully as a collaborationist and a defeatist. Two years later, DuBois published a widely discussed collection of papers entitled *The Souls of Black Folk*, in which he questioned Washington's "counsels of submission" and "unnecessarily narrow" educational programs. [57] For the next 12 years DuBois was to be Washington's "self-appointed gadfly." [58] It would be difficult to find a person more different from Washington in antecedents and training. DuBois was northern-born, educated at Fisk, the University of Berlin, and Harvard (where he earned a doctorate); he was a proud, dignified person, full of fire, dedicated to the intellectual's life but ready to forsake the ivory tower in order to battle uncompromisingly for equality and justice. This young professor from Atlanta University soon became the leader of the whole body of articulate Negro opinion which was coming to challenge the ex-slave's influence. [59]

The arrest of Trotter in 1905 was the signal for an angry protest by members of DuBois's group. Meeting in Niagara Falls, Canada, they adopted an eight-point platform which demanded full civil rights for every American, abolition of all caste distinctions based on color, and "recognition of the highest and best human training as the monopoly of no class or race." [60] It was not long before a group of whites deeply interested in race relations joined hands with the "Niagara Movement." In August, 1908, a terrible race riot broke out in Springfield, Illinois, Abraham Lincoln's home city. William E. Walling, wealthy southern-born settlement house worker and Socialist, was so revolted by the depressing symbolism of this event that he joined with Mary Ovington, a young Radcliffe graduate and social worker among the Negroes of New York City in a call for a new organization that would defend human rights against such outrages. The movement soon attracted the powerful

[56] W. E. B. DuBois, *Dusk of Dawn* (New York: Harcourt, Brace & World, Inc., 1940), p. 75.

[57] W. E. B. DuBois, *The Souls of Black Folk* (New York: The Blue Heron Press, 1953), p. 44.

[58] Samuel R. Spencer, Jr., *Booker T. Washington*, p. 151.

[59] Francis L. Broderick, *W. E. B. DuBois: Negro Leader in a Time of Crisis* (Stanford, Calif.: Stanford University Press, 1959), pp. 50-89; Cox, *Journal of Negro Education*, XIX, pp. 461-63; DuBois, *Dusk of Dawn*, pp. 10-68, 70-81.

[60] DuBois, *Dusk of Dawn*, pp. 86-87.

support of Oswald Garrison Villard, grandson of the great abolitionist William Lloyd Garrison, and editor of the *New York Evening Post*. All informal gatherings on the one hundredth anniversary of Lincoln's birth launched upon its career the organization which soon came to be known as The National Association for the Advancement of Colored People.

From the first, extremists like Monroe Trotter, suspicious of the purposes of any white-initiated organization, refused to have anything to do with the NAACP. Negro followers of Booker T. Washington also carefully disassociated themselves from its activities. When, however, DuBois joined the Association's staff in 1910 as Director of Publicity and Research and editor of the fiery periodical *The Crisis*, most of the promoters of the "Niagara Movement" went over to it. Strong support for the NAACP was soon forthcoming from members of the Negro professional and business classes in all parts of the nation.[61]

The launching of this militant new organization in the race relations field meant that henceforth the ideas of people like DuBois would play an increasingly important role. And specifically what was DuBois's concept of Negro education? It was based, above all, on the assumption that "no group or nation which seeks advancement and true development can despise or neglect the power of well-trained minds" and the conviction that "this power of intellectual leadership must be given to the talented tenth among American Negroes before this race can seriously be asked to assume the responsibility of dispelling its own ignorance." [62] Placing the main emphasis on utilitarian training was therefore held to be ill-advised and shortsighted. While popular education should be encouraged and industrial training, in its proper place, was important, the essential element in Negro progress was high-quality professional and liberal arts training for future leaders of the race. This last must never be slighted, surrendered, or bartered-away.[63]

This viewpoint was the position not only of DuBois or the other members of the "Niagara Movement" but also of the majority of spokesmen for the Negro liberal-arts colleges of the land, including such re-

[61] Daniel W. Wynn, *NAACP* vs. *Negro Protest* (New York: Exposition Press, 1955), pp. 34-35, 47-55; Mary W. Ovington, *The Walls Came Tumbling Down* (New York: Harcourt, Brace & World, Inc., 1947), pp. 102-11; Flint Kellogg, "Villard and the NAACP," *The Nation* (February 14, 1959), pp. 137-40; DuBois, *The Ordeal of Mansart*, pp. 302-16; *idem, Mansart Builds a School*, pp. 65-73.

[62] W. E. B. DuBois, *Training of Negroes for Social Power* (Atlanta, Ga.: Atlanta University Press, n.d.), pp. 7-8; Broderick, *W. E. B. DuBois*, p. 51.

[63] Spencer, Jr., *Booker T. Washington*, pp. 155-56.

spected institutions as Howard, Atlanta, and Fisk.[64] In 1903 Professor W. S. Scarborough of Wilberforce College in Ohio, reflecting these views, conceded that it was necessary to know how to earn one's living but noted there were finer feelings in human life which had no market value but which nevertheless had to be kept alive. When a mass of people were to be lifted from a lower to a higher plane, one had to deal in the final analysis with individual people, not a race in the mass. The Negro intellectual would face a wall of utilitarian ignorance and maliciousness, but he must continue nevertheless to strive unceasingly, uncomplainingly, placing "ambitions and longings on the altar." [65]

The High Court's Decision and Its Aftermath

In 1922 Charles Garland, a wealthy young man interested in humanitarian causes, set up the American Fund for Public Service. One of the major objectives of the Fund was to improve conditions of life for the American Negro. To this end a coordinated legal campaign against every form of segregation and discrimination was planned. Eventually an agreement was worked out with the NAACP to put the drive into operation in the educational and other fields.[66] In carrying forward this work, the most active of the NAACP's subdivisions was its National Legal Committee. Beginning in the early 1930's, the Committee instituted a series of legal actions designed to bring about equalization of salaries between Negro and white teachers in the South. In one Maryland county white janitors in white schools were shown to be averaging $100 more a year than Negro high school teachers. Facts such as these presented in the decisive case of *Alston* v. *School Board of City of Norfolk* led to a ruling by Judge John J. Parker of the United States Circuit of Appeals on June 18, 1940, wiping out all salary inequalities as contrary to the federal Constitution. The Supreme Court refused to reverse this decision.[67]

[64] H. B. Frissell, *From Servitude to Service*, (Chicago, 1905), pp. 15-19.

[65] W. S. Scarborough, *The Educated Negro and His Mission* (Washington, D.C.: The American Negro Academy Press, 1903), pp. 9-11.

[66] Herbert Hill and Jack Greenberg, *A Citizen's Guide to Desegregation* (Boston: Beacon Press, 1955), pp. 56-58.

[67] *Teachers Salaries in Black and White* (New York: NAACP, 1941); Wynn, *op. cit.*, p. 95; Walter White, *A Man Called White* (New York: The Viking Press, Inc., 1948), pp. 163-65.

In attacking racial segregation of students in the public schools, the Legal Committee faced a more difficult task. In 1896 the Supreme Court had construed the Fourteenth Amendment in such a way as to sanction segregation. In *Plessy* v. *Ferguson* the Court majority held that the sole object of the Fourteenth Amendment was to secure "absolute equality of the two races before the law." State-enforced segregation did not necessarily stamp Negroes with a badge of inferiority so long as the facilities furnished were *equal to those from which they were excluded.* "The case reduces itself to a question whether the statute of Louisiana is a reasonable regulation," stated the Supreme Court, "and in respect to this, there must be a large discretion on the part of the legislature." [68]

It is particularly interesting that the Court, in its argument that the Louisiana statute was "reasonable" and based upon existing traditions and usages of the American people, cited various school segregation laws as evidence for its conclusion. The justices paid special attention to the 1849 decision in the case of *Roberts* v. *City of Boston* in which the Massachusetts Supreme Judicial Court had overruled Charles Sumner's contention that enforced separation could never be equal because it implied inferiority. The Massachusetts court had upheld school segregation on a separate but equal basis. [69]

The *Plessy* v. *Ferguson* precedent was cited again and again in subsequent years by lower courts in upholding school segregation statutes in various states. At the same time the Supreme Court itself for the next 40 years permitted the 1896 decision which originally had been directed only to the question of public transportation to become the *de facto* constitutional rule of public education. This it did by refusing to rule on the constitutionality of segregated schools themselves, thus implying, by its own inaction, that the *Plessy* v. *Ferguson* principle applied to them also. Only three times during this 40-year span did the school question come directly before the Court—*Cummings* v. *Board of Education* (1899); *Berea College* v. *Kentucky* (1908); *Gong*

---

[68] Albert Blaustein and Clarence Ferguson, *Desegregation and the Law* (New Brunswick, N.J.: Rutgers University Press, 1957), pp. 95-98. The case arose as a result of a Louisiana statute requiring racial segregation in railroad coaches. The sole dissenter was Justice John Marshall Harlan, who declared, "Our constitution is color blind, and neither knows nor tolerates classes among citizens."

[69] Leonard W. Levy and Harlan B. Phillips, "The Roberts Case; Source of the 'Separate but Equal' Doctrine," *American Historical Review*, 56 (April 1951), pp. 510-17.

Lum v. *Rice* (1927)—and in all three cases a direct ruling on school segregation was carefully avoided.[70]

NAACP lawyers, considering ways and means in the mid-1930's of reversing these rulings, abandoned an earlier plan which had contemplated the filing of a large number of taxpayers' suits demanding absolute equality of facilities in elementary schooling.[71] Instead, a new strategy was adopted which involved a campaign to eliminate segregation in graduate and professional schools, especially law schools. It was felt that inequality at this level in the South could be easily demonstrated, that duplication of facilities for advanced work would be prohibitively expensive, and that judges would most probably be appreciative above all else of the need for good legal education. It was hoped that important precedents could be established by this line of attack which would lead to an eventual general desegregation.[72]

It was not long before the new approach began to pay dividends. The Supreme Court in 1938 overruled a state's exclusion of a Negro from the all-white law school at its publicly supported university.[73] It must either establish law school facilities for Negroes "substantially equal to those which the state there afforded for persons of the white race" or else admit Negroes to the already existing school.[74] Ten years later the Court ordered the immediate admission of a Negro applicant to the University of Oklahoma Law School.[75] The nine justices unanimously found this action to be necessary "forthwith" since no provision had been made for Negro legal education either within the state or outside.[76] In 1950 came two more sweeping decisions. On the same day, June 5, the Court aimed two heavy blows at the wall of separation between the races in higher education. In *Sweatt* v. *Painter* it ruled that a hastily established Texas law school for Negroes did not meet the requirement of equal treatment not only in various tangible criteria but also in "those qualities which are incapable of objective measurement but which make for greatness in a law school." In *McLaurin* v. *Okla-*

[70] Albert Blaustein and Clarence Ferguson, *Desegregation and the Law*, pp. 100-103; Herbert Hill and Jack Greenberg, *A Citizen's Guide to Desegregation*, pp. 50-52.

[71] It had at first been hoped that such suits, if successful, would create such an economic burden that the states would be forced eventually to abandon segregation.

[72] Herbert Hill and Jack Greenberg, *A Citizen's Guide to Desegregation*, pp. 56-59.

[73] *Missouri ex rel. Gaines* v. *Canada* (1938).

[74] Walter White, *A Man Called White*, pp. 144-145.

[75] *Sipuel* v. *Board of Education* (1948).

[76] Albert Blaustein and Clarence Ferguson, *Desegregation and the Law*, pp. 109-110.

homa the justices found that even though a Negro graduate student had been admitted to the University of Oklahoma, he still did not enjoy the equality guaranteed by the Fourteenth Amendment so long as he was segregated in the library, the cafeteria, and even in classrooms. "Such restrictions," they felt, "impair and inhibit his ability to study, engage in discussions and exchange views with other students, and, in general, to learn his profession." [77]

Clearly this was a different court from the one which had rendered the *Plessy v. Ferguson* decision. Its new mood reflected a changed atmosphere in the country and, to a limited extent, even in the South. By the middle of the twentieth century a movement was under way which some historians have chosen to call the "Second Reconstruction." Unlike the original Reconstruction period, this later wave of social change was producing a more thoroughgoing and permanent revolution in southern life. Many developments combined to produce these fateful results—New Deal social and economic legislation, the movement of large Negro populations to northern and western cities, the quickening industrialization of the South, the defeat of Nazism with its "master race" ideology in a life-and-death struggle involving all of America, the anti-imperialist uprising of colored nations all over the world against white domination, and, finally, the competition of Communist nations with the United States for the hearts and minds of men everywhere. The American Southland was too much an integral part of one of the world's major power centers to be able to isolate itself from the "cold war" battlefront and continue unchallenged with traditional racial policies as the Union of South Africa was attempting to do. Recognizing these realities, proponents of the "Second Reconstruction" could well paraphrase Voltaire and say: "If Marx had never existed, we should have had to invent him." [78]

One of the most noteworthy fruits of the "Second Reconstruction" was the ending of racial segregation, by Presidential directive, in all branches of the federal government, including all offices, military bases, housing developments, and federal-run schools in the southern states. Also of immense significance was the return of a considerable number of southern Negro voters to the ballot box. A series of federal court

[77] Ward W. Keesecker, "Recent Federal Court Decisions Affecting Education," *School Life* (October 1950); Woodward, *The Strange Career of Jim Crow*, pp. 130-35.

[78] James W. Vander Zanden, "Foundations of the Second Reconstruction," *School and Society* (May 7, 1960), p. 229; William G. Carleton. "Introduction," in Price, *The Negro and Southern Politics*, pp. xiv-xvii.

decisions between 1941 and 1953 outlawed the last of the barriers which southern "white-supremacy" advocates had erected to keep the Negro out of politics, namely, the "white primary." [79] Important as were these changes, southern *mores* were not revolutionized overnight. Racial segregation continued to be the norm at lunch counters, in hotels, in residential areas, and on transportation systems, although these practices came under increasingly heavy fire. In the area of public education, a major question still remained in the 1950's for the Supreme Court to decide, a question which it had for more than 50 years been disinclined to consider. *Was separation itself inherently unequal?* Should the Court agree to rule on this question, one of the most momentous judicial decisions in American history would be in the making.

Encouraged by its successes in the Sweatt and McLaurin cases, the NAACP Legal Committee levied an all-out campaign to destroy the remaining citadels of segregation in public education. The Committee decided to appeal to the Supreme Court not one but several cases on the elementary and secondary school level which had arisen in various localities—South Carolina, Kansas, Delaware, Virginia, and the District of Columbia. Noting that the Court's 1950 decisions had been based to an important extent upon intangible factors in segregated education such as the psychological and sociological influences that fostered feelings of inequality, the NAACP lawyers decided to introduce the testimony of a number of social scientists and educational specialists who could present evidence on the harmful effects of segregation *per se.* Ultimately more than 40 experts testified before the Supreme Court in this connection and their testimony filled nearly four volumes.[80]

In reaching its decision on May 17, 1954, the Court decided to rule on the four state cases before it in one consolidated opinion.[81] While they were "premised on different facts and different local conditions," it was noted that "a common legal question justifies their consideration together." The District of Columbia case, involving as it did federal law, was considered in a separate opinion rendered at the same time.[82]

---

[79] C. Vann Woodward, *Strange Career of Jim Crow*, pp. 124-139; Henry L. Moon, *Balance of Power* (Garden City, N.Y.: Doubleday & Co., 1948), pp. 178-198; Harry Ashmore, *The Negro and the Schools* (Chapel Hill: University of North Carolina Press, 1954), pp. 48-49, 136-138.

[80] Herbert Hill and Jack Greenberg, A *Citizen's Guide to Desegregation*, pp. 78-102.

[81] These cases were *Brown v. Board of Education; Briggs v. Elliott; Davis v. County School Board; Gebhart v. Belton*—347 U.S. 483.

[82] *Bolling v. Sharpe*, 347 U.S. 497.

The Court's decision was remarkable for a number of reasons. For one thing, its opinion outlawing racial segregation, one of the most significant issues ever to come before it, was one of the briefest and most succinct ever rendered in a major case. Moreover, the unanimity of the Court was noteworthy. Justices leaning to a states' rights interpretation of constitutional questions joined in this instance with upholders of federal supremacy on the one proposition that racial school segregation anywhere was unconstitutional. The equal protection clause of the Fourteenth Amendment was violated by such state practices, said the unanimous Court. Furthermore, the due process clause of the Fifth Amendment (which has no equal protection clause) was seen as being violated by similar practices existing under the federal government in the District of Columbia. More important, the nine justices implied that even if these amendments did not specifically apply to the cases at issue, the Constitution would outlaw school segregation anyway because the latter was "not reasonably related to any proper government objective." Thus 58 years after his lone dissent a unanimous Court had come to accept Justice John M. Harlan's famous contention that "the Constitution is color blind." [83]

Most remarkable of all, perhaps, was the extent to which the Court based its decision on the primacy of the general welfare as well as on purely legal considerations. "To separate them [Negro children] from others of similar age and qualifications solely because of their race," said Chief Justice Warren in stating the Court's opinion, "generates a feeling of inferiority as to their status in the community that may affect their hearts and minds in a way unlikely ever to be undone." The Court appeared to be notably impressed with the testimony of the social scientists on the adverse effects of discrimination on personality development. Such findings seemingly confirmed, in its opinion, that, even with equal school buildings and other physical facilities, segregated Negro school children would receive a substantially inferior education.

In arriving at this conclusion, the Court took into account with noteworthy realism the place of the public school in American life, not in 1868 when the Fourteenth Amendment was adopted, nor even in 1896 when *Plessy* v. *Ferguson* was written, but in the modern age of mass education when it had become a powerful acculturating mechanism as well as an institution for multi-purpose training:

[83] *Brown* v. *Board of Education*, 347 U.S. 483; *Bolling* v. *Sharpe*, 347 U.S. 497; *N.Y. Times*, May 18, 1954, pp. 14, 28.

. . . Compulsory school attendance laws and the great expenditures for education both demonstrate our recognition of the importance of education to our democratic society. It is required in the performance of our most basic public responsibilities, even service in the armed forces. It is the very foundation of good citizenship. Today it is a principal instrument in awakening the child to cultural values, in preparing him for later professional training, and in helping him to adjust normally to his environment. In these days, it is doubtful that any child may reasonably be expected to succeed in life if he is denied the opportunity of an education. Such an opportunity, where the state has undertaken to provide it, is a right which must be made available to all on equal terms.[84]

James Reston of the *New York Times* called attention to the fact that, by adopting this line of reasoning, the Court was by implication accepting the late Justice Benjamin N. Cardozo's thesis that "the final cause of law is the welfare of society." The noted liberal jurist had further written: "When the social needs demand one settlement rather than another, there are times when we must bend symmetry, ignore history, and sacrifice custom in the pursuit of other and larger ends." [85] By sustaining the findings of experts in psychology, psychiatry, sociology, anthropology, and education in a case whose importance ranked with such classic decisions as *Marbury* v. *Madison, McCulloch* v. *Maryland,* and *Dred Scott* v. *Sanford,* the Court testified to Justice Cardozo's prescience as a prophet.

There still remained the vital question of a *modus operandi.* How and when would school segregation actually be outlawed? The Court decided to deal with this thorny problem by the method of gradualism. It ordered that rearguments be heard at its next term to determine how its sweeping decision was to be applied. The cases would be restored to the docket, Chief Justice Warren said, "in order that we may have the full assistance of the parties in formulating decrees."

On May 31, 1955, a little more than a year after its first decision, the Court announced its policy on implementation. Again its finding was unanimous. The states were to make "a prompt and reasonable start" toward ending racial segregation in their public school systems. Negroes were to be admitted to nonsegregated public schools "with all deliberate speed." The Court was careful, however, to set no particular deadline or time limit. Its formula for securing compliance with its ruling was flexible. Three-judge Federal District Courts were to pass

[84] *Brown v. Board of Education,* 347 U.S. 483.
[85] As quoted in *New York Times,* May 18, 1954, p. 14.

upon the adequacy of enforcement procedures. This approach was held
to be desirable "because of their proximity to local conditions and the
possible need for further hearings." Full consideration was to be accorded to the complexities involved in local situations:

> To that end, the courts may consider problems related to administra-
> tion, arising from the physical condition of the school plant, the school
> transportation system, personnel, revision of school districts and attend-
> ance areas into compact units to achieve a system of determining ad-
> mission to the public schools on a nonracial basis, and revision of local
> laws and regulations which may be necessary in solving the foregoing
> problems.

The Court warned, however, against any attempt to frustrate its judgment by causing unreasonable or unnecessary delays. Compliance with
the ruling was to begin promptly. It must be carried out in "a systematic and effective manner" and "with good faith." [86] The nine
justices had thereby adopted a middle-of-the-road position on enforcement, rejecting equally the demands of NAACP spokesmen that a
specific deadline of a year be set for complete compliance and the
wishes of the legal representatives of the southern states that implementation be postponed indefinitely.

The Court's decision affected 40 per cent of the nation's public school
enrollment, or 8,200,000 white and 2,530,000 Negro children resident
in 17 states and the District of Columbia, which in 1954 were still
maintaining segregated public schools by law. Sixteen other states specifically prohibited segregation in public schools, 11 had no specific laws
on the matter, and 4 authorized local option.[87] In any event, desegregation moved very slowly in the affected areas. Four years after the Court's
decision a New York Times survey found that in only 792 school districts out of a total of 8,832 segregated districts had any action been
taken in the direction of racial integration. And all but 15 of these
desegregated districts were in so-called "border" states.[88] In April, 1960,
it was reported that only 6 per cent—or 180,000—of the total Negro
children enrolled in the South's public schools were actually attending
classes with white students. Again nearly all of these integrated schools
were to be found in "border" states such as Missouri, Maryland, West
Virginia, Delaware, Kentucky, Oklahoma, and Texas. Forty-six per cent

[86] Brown v. Board of Education, 347 U.S. 483.
[87] U.S. News & World Report, May 28, 1954, p. 22; New York Times, May 18,
1954, p. 21.
[88] New York Times, September 7, 1958, p. 47.

of the total Negro school enrollment of the South, or 1,391,921, was
to be found in 5 states of the Deep South which continued to maintain
complete segregation—Alabama, Georgia, Louisiana, Mississippi, and
South Carolina.[89] A year later the Civil Rights Commission reported
that the number of new school districts annually integrating their children was dropping sharply and that, even in these, the number of Negro
children affected was so small as to be "no more than a minimal
token." [90] In September, 1962, the situation had hardly improved. Out
of 2,265 southern school districts having a mixed population, only 243
—or just over 10 per cent—had begun actual rather than theoretical
desegregation. In 3 states—Alabama, Mississippi, and South Carolina—
not one school or college had been desegregated.[91] Furthermore, in
many southern and border zone cities population movements following
the 1954 decision had brought about what amounted to a "resegrega-
tion." As a result, several cities by the early Sixties had totally or heavily
Negro schools, while their suburbs now had all-white schools. In St.
Louis, Missouri, and Baltimore, Maryland, for example, school officials
noted that there was now more actual segregation than had existed
before 1954.[92]

Some progress had been made nevertheless. In Little Rock, Arkansas,
a plan to admit a small group of Negro students to the city's high
schools resulted in riots which finally led President Eisenhower to call
up the National Guard. Integration was thereupon put into effect and
by the fall of 1962, 78 Negro children were enrolled in the city's high
schools and junior high schools. To be sure, this number was small for
a total school population of 10,000, but it did mark a significant
change.[93] In addition, there were a few stormy weeks in November
and December, 1960, when it seemed that a new "Battle of New
Orleans" was raging as a consequence of the effort to introduce, under
a federal court order, Negro school children into the first grade of the
city's hitherto segregated public schools.[94] Two years later, however, a
New York Times correspondent was able to report that desegregation
was finally being accepted in that agitated city "as a fact of life." [95]

[89] *Christian Science Monitor*, April 4, 1960, p. 3.
[90] *New York Times*, September 26, 1961, p. 36M.
[91] *Ibid.*, September 11, 1962, p. 32C; *Saturday Review of Literature*, September 15, 1962, p. 64.
[92] Worcester (Mass.) *Daily Telegram*, November 24, 1961, p. 7.
[93] *New York Times*, August 31, 1961, p. 1; April 7, 1962, p. 12; August 7, 1962, p. 1.
[94] *Ibid.*, September 11, 1962, p. 32C.
[95] *Ibid.*

In early 1961 an effort to admit two Negro students to the University of Georgia was similarly greeted with mob rioting, but the important fact is that they were finally admitted. When a parallel attempt was made in September, 1962, to admit a Negro student James Meredith to the University of Mississippi (under a federal court order) a pitched battle broke out in the town of Oxford, Mississippi, between a pro-segregation mob and federal troops and marshals. The newspapers described the event as "the bloodiest clash between federal troops and southerners since the Civil War," but Meredith was finally enrolled and stayed to get his degree.[96]

The slowness of the white South to comply with the Supreme Court's desegregation ruling indicated to one British observer that no final comprehensive solution of the race question—"America's anomaly and agony"—was in sight. Legislation could not be the final answer because it was "a question of changing men's hearts and no certain way of doing that has yet been found in any democracy." [97] Professor Arthur L. Harding of Southern Methodist University spotlighted this dilemma in a statement at a National Conference on Christianity and the Law. Court enforcement of school integration reminded Harding of the federal police efforts that failed to carry out the prohibition features of the Volstead Act. "It is extremely hard to change the thinking of a body of people overnight by a court decree," he pointed out.[98] Emphasizing these same difficulties, the Episcopal Bishop of Little Rock, Arkansas, noted that "the southerner has a lot to adjust to, but condemnation will not quicken his transformation." Attitudes toward the Negro had been deeply ingrained for generations. When racial pride appeared to be threatened by an assertive, organized people who had never before had the temerity to make demands, southerners instinctively moved to protect themselves.[99]

It was increasingly obvious that every kind of legal device would be resorted to by these southerners to delay the end of segregated schools. What the Supreme Court decision actually accomplished in its immediate effects was to "give a green light" to communities of the

[96] *Ibid.*, September 25, 1962, p. 1; September 28, 1962, p. 1; October 2, 1962, p. 1; *Boston Globe*, October 1, 1962, p. 1; October 2, 1962, p. 1.

[97] Patrick O'Donovan (of the London *Observer*), in *Courier* (Champaign-Urbana, Ill.), June 27, 1960, p. 19.

[98] *New York Times*, September 9, 1958, p. 24.

[99] Robert R. Brown, *Bigger Than Little Rock* (Greenwich, Conn.: The Seabury Press, 1958), pp. 18-19.

"border" South with relatively mild race problems to go ahead and desegregate, thus providing "showcases" which it was hoped would encourage similar action in other areas of the 17-state region in the future. It was precisely in those localities where the number of Negroes was smallest that there was the least opposition to court-enforced integration. And it was in rural areas of the southern "black belt," where the incidence of Negroes to the white population was highest, that the most violent opposition to any change in the *status quo* appeared.[100] George Peabody College for Teachers, Nashville, Tennessee, pointed out that even the end of *legal* school segregation in southern urban centers, to which more and more Negroes were repairing, would not necessarily mean a violent revolution in the southern social structure. De facto segregation, based upon the segregated pattern of living conditions in the various urban neighborhoods, would continue to be the case in such cities, as in many Northern cities.[101]

Perhaps the greatest significance of the *Brown* v. *Board of Education* decision was its indication of a greater sensitivity to the world's opinion of American race relations on the part of the highest organs of the federal government. Even before World War I, W.E.B. DuBois was writing prophetically that "the problem of the twentieth century is the problem of the color line." [102] Mrs. Eleanor Roosevelt sized up the problem in 1959 by posing a portentous question: "If we cannot solve our difficulties and remove segregation from our country, why should it be possible to attract the colored peoples of the world to our philosophy, to our form of government, to our way of life . . . ?" [103] It was doubtless no coincidence that within an hour of the announcement of the segregation decision in May, 1954, the "Voice of America" was broadcasting news of this event to the world via short wave in 34 languages.[104]

Elaborating on this important aspect of the decision, Allison Davis,

---

[100] Wilma Dykeman and James Stokely, *Neither Black Nor White* (New York: Holt, Rinehart & Winston, 1957), pp. 176-179; Arthur S. Miller, *Racial Discrimination and Private Education* (Chapel Hill: University of North Carolina Press, 1957), pp. 125-126.

[101] *New York Times*, May 18, 1954, p. 14; June 1, 1955, p. 29; *Saturday Review of Literature*, September 15, 1962, p. 64.

[102] W.E.B. DuBois, "Atlanta University," in *From Slavery to Servitude*, pp. 195-97.

[103] Eleanor Roosevelt, "Segregation," *The Educational Forum*, XXIV (November 1959), pp. 5-6.

[104] *New York Times*, May 18, 1954, p. 1.

a member of the Committee on Human Development of the University of Chicago, noted:

> It makes clear to the colored peoples of Japan, Africa, India, and Indonesia, as well as to the European colonial powers, that the United States is not defending a color hierarchy in the world but is defending a democratic political system which is proving itself efficient.
>
> When this decision is implemented, it will result in a tremendous increase in the fund of ability and skill available to our country. Outnumbered as we are, the survival of the United States seems to depend upon its developing the ability of millions of our citizens whose capacities have been crippled by segregation.[105]

The response of the American people to the most important Supreme Court decision of the "Second Reconstruction" is significant not only for what it tells us about the race problem in mid-twentieth century America, but also for what it reveals of basic American attitudes toward education and its role in society. Neither the militant advocates of immediate integration nor the stubborn upholders of segregated schools were disposed to accept any concept of discrimination which would be based on individual excellence and on that criterion alone. The NAACP, in the course of its long battle for equal rights for Negroes in education and in all other areas of American life, faced the necessity of creating a solid front of colored citizens.[106] In so doing, it had perforce ended by making sweeping demands for acceptance of the race *as a mass and as a nonsegregated unit.* Its main demand was *not* for selection of students and segregation of school classes on the basis of individual talent and ability, irrespective of race. While W.E.B. DuBois, in formulating a NAACP appeal to the United Nations in 1947, pitched his argument mainly on the injustice of discrimination against the individual of "wealth, training, and character" solely because of color of skin, Walter White, Executive Secretary of NAACP, apparently expressed a more widely held attitude in 1955 when he professed skepticism of the application of qualitative standards of selection to either white or Negro children for admission to tax-supported schools.[107] As NAACP-sponsored movements got under way by the beginning of 1963 in more than 60 northern and western cities to force "redistricting," it became clear that Negro spokesmen were demanding acceptance or

[105] *New York Times,* May 18, 1954, p. 18.
[106] *Appeal to the World* (New York: NAACP, 1947), pp. 1-2.
[107] *Ibid.,* p. 12; Walter White, *How Far the Promised Land?* (New York: The Viking Press, Inc., 1955), p. 55.

rejection on a group and purely race-determined basis rather than on an individual one. The white society of the country, however, was on the whole not eager to offer either type of acceptance to the Negro.

Leading white educators both in the North and the South expressed concern over the lowering of academic standards that might result from the sudden admission to schools, under integration procedures, of large groups of Negro children who were retarded academically because of handicapping home conditions or prior inadequate school facilities. Few of these educators, however, would be quoted as demanding selectivity in admission to a particular grade of instruction on a purely intellectual basis or homogeneous grouping of intellectually handicapped children, white and black, in special classes. Indeed, it was frequently stated with confidence that academically backward children would be stimulated to higher levels of achievement by being "integrated" with those more advanced in their schoolwork and by being given more effective teaching.[108]

It soon became clear that the many "pupil placement" laws passed by southern states after 1954 were not a genuine effort to assign children to schools on the basis of individual ability and potential. If fairly administered, such laws would not have resulted in the admission of many southern Negro children to higher grades, but they would also have excluded large numbers of academically retarded white children. And this the white South was clearly not prepared to do. So "pupil placement," far from being the doorway to equality of opportunity on the basis of individual excellence which a true Jeffersonian spirit would have required, turned out to be just another desperate maneuver to maintain "white supremacy" and segregated inequality.[109]

The bare fact seems to be that both sides of the segregation controversy reflected in their attitudes the mass conformity, group-pressured, increasingly "other-directed" nature of mid-century American society. Ironically, insofar as any white opponents of integration were

[108] Bonita H. Valien, *The St. Louis Story* (New York: Anti-Defamation League, 1956), p. 67; Carl F. Hansen, *Miracle of Social Adjustment* (New York: Anti-Defamation League, 1957), pp. 68-69; Omer Carmichael, *The Louisville Story* (New York: Simon and Schuster, Inc., 1957), pp. 89-92, 140-43; Bond, *The Education of the Negro*, pp. 302-3, 330-31, Sarah Thurmond, "Comparison of Intelligence of Twelve-Year-Old Negro Children," *Phelps-Stokes Studies*, No. 12 (1933), pp. 36-39; *School and Society* (May 7, 1960), pp. 240-42; *Christian Science Monitor*, December 23, 1959, p. 22; March 23, 1960, p. 3; April 4, 1960, p. 3.

[109] Don Shoemaker, ed., *With All Deliberate Speed* (New York: Harper & Row, Publishers, 1957), pp. 12-13, 136-40, 192-93; Albert Blaustein and Clarence Ferguson, *Desegregation and the Law*, pp. 252-55.

pressured into acquiescing in its implementation, this reluctant adjustment was linked to the very national passion for conformity which was blindly stamping out dissent of all kinds. The basic social trend was the leveling of all barriers—individual, group, class, racial, sectional, and local—and the achievement of an integrated mass society. Some now maintained that it was part of the price exacted by "togetherness," by conformity to the nation's new "other-directed" norms, and proposed that previously existing barriers of discrimination and segregation be leveled. It was now more "respectable" than in the past to do so, and various localities and regions were expected to conform. Besides, it was argued, such action was necessary to show the Communists and the peoples of Asia and Africa how democratic Americans really were. And in the midst of the life-and-death struggle of the "cold war," who could resist such noble aims?

Moreover the American democratic outlook, which ever since the middle of the nineteenth century had been more Jacksonian and equalitarian in orientation than Jeffersonian and selective, furnished an ideal seed-bed in which such conformist tendencies could sprout under the cumulative impact of modern machine technology and standardization. In this setting it was perfectly understandable that both the NAACP leadership and the white segregationist politicians of the South would be reluctant to give articulate public support to the concept of an *elite* based on excellence. Nor in dealing with the segregation problem would many American educational leaders publicly propose solutions which would involve setting individually gifted children apart, irrespective of race, in homogeneous groupings of their own. Segregation based upon intellectual excellence apparently was abhorrent to American opinion.

Many of the findings of Gunnar Myrdal in his exploration of American Negro attitudes toward education strengthen this conclusion. It appears that many Negro Americans, in common with other Americans, had come to accept a basically materialist, "cash value" concept of education. Under this profoundly nonintellectual interpretation, education was mainly valuable in terms of what it "paid off" on the market in economic and social returns.[110] Under these circumstances, there would of course be no effective support for the concept of selective excellence. The latter program would welcome equality of education opportunity primarily as a means of producing a "natural aristocracy" whose worth would be measured neither in bank accounts nor family

[110] Gunnar Myrdal, *An American Dilemma*, p. 884.

connections (basic values of American materialism) but in inherent intellectual merit.[111]

There is yet a deeper question. Can education *per se, of any type,* solve the American race problem? Kardiner and Ovesey, after extensive study of the effects of multiple discriminations upon the American Negro's personality, say no. They maintain that Negro self-esteem cannot be retrieved nor Negro self-hatred destroyed by any surface rearrangements of a school program unless the main aspects of the surrounding society are significantly changed. The American Negro needs not just education, but re-integration. "There is only one way that the products of oppression can be dissolved, and that is to stop the oppression." [112]

This brings us back to the basic question of how to affect what is deep in the hearts of men, perhaps even what is embedded in their subconscious. Many years ago the Negro poet James Weldon Johnson suggested a way in which education, while not necessarily furnishing a final solution, might help to improve American race relations. "What the greater part of white America merely *thinks* about us," he wrote, "is an influential factor in making *our actual condition* what it is." [113] Thus it might be the white man, even more than the Negro, who needs education. Even more than a merely mechanical and superficial "integration" of heterogeneous and intellectually unclassified school populations, a thoughtful and systematic re-education of the American white majority, coupled with a selective segregation of students on the basis of talent and intellectual ability alone, might afford real hope of finding a way out of American democracy's oldest and gravest dilemma.

[111] For an interesting discussion of this problem, see Horace Mann Bond, *The Search for Talent* (Cambridge, Mass.: Harvard University Press, 1959).

[112] Abram Kardiner and Lionel Ovesey, *The Mark of Oppression: A Psychosocial Study of the American Negro* (New York: W. W. Norton & Company, Inc., 1951), p. 387.

[113] James Weldon Johnson, *Negro Americans, What Now?* (New York: Viking Press, 1938), pp. 52-53.

CHAPTER EIGHT

Evaluations of American
Education by Foreigners

Some of the most penetrating commentaries upon American civilization and upon America's system of schooling have been written by outsiders. It is no accident that the observations of Tocqueville and Bryce quickly attained the status of classics in their sharp delineation of our way of life. Such foreign commentaries often tell us a great deal, not only about what appeared to the visitor to be unique and distinctive in the American pattern, but also what his dominant objects of concern were and what the frame of reference was with which he approached his observations.

1900-1920

Suppose, first of all, that we consider what foreign visitors during the early twentieth century had to say about the American commitment to universal public education. Although noting certain of the problems basic to attaining such an ambitious goal, the foreign observers, on the whole, heartily approved of the effort. The members of the highly publicized English Mosely Educational Commission, who came to America in 1902-3, professed to be deeply impressed by the "absolute belief in the value of education" which it had discovered in the United States. Furthermore, the British experts were convinced that "during the last quarter of a century education has had a powerful and far-reaching influence; and it cannot be doubted that, in the future, it will become more and more the cause of industrial and commercial progress and of national well-being." [1]

Another British observer Sara Burstall noted as a result of a tour of American schools in 1908 that Americans consciously aimed to educate the mass of the people, while Britain centered primarily on the leaders. She was favorably impressed with the fact that "the public elementary school there is historically the common school used by all sections of the people, common to all; and not, as historically with us, a school originally founded by benevolent persons and societies for the children of the poor." From one point of view this was "an element of strength," wrote Miss Burstall, but from another it was a weakness. For under the American system "nothing is done to select these [the exceptionally able pupils] at an early age when they show promise on particular lines, to develop them and train them thus to high scholarship." The result, said the author, was that Americans did not get work of as high a standard as the British "at the top of their schools." [2]

Much more uncritical in its fulsome praise of the democratic tendencies inherent in the American system of mass education was a book published in 1910 by British visitor Georgette Bowden-Smith. Only the public common school as it had developed in America, she insisted, could in modern times "discharge the task of universalizing the benefits of civilization." Furthermore, she rhapsodized:

> This whole-hearted faith in the School Catholic [sic] is one of the most striking and inspiring features of American life. It finds expression in such works as Professor Dewey's *School and the Child* and *School and Society*. It underlies the broad and admirable treatment of educational questions by such men as Dr. Murray Butler and Dr. Stanley Hall. It keeps before the eyes of educationists an ever-growing ideal towards which the School must approximate—an ideal which will only be realized as the private institution, with its sectional class spirit or its proprietary profit, disappears, and the true School Universal takes its place, to educate each individual up to the limits of his capabilities, to give to each and all that training which the State, as declaring the common will, decrees.[3]

[1] *Joint Report* (Mosely Educational Commission to the United States, October-December, 1903 [London: Cooperative Printing Society, Ltd., 1904]), p. xxiii.

[2] Sara A. Burstall, *Impressions of American Education in 1908* (London: Longmans, Green & Company, Ltd., 1909), pp. 20-27, 42-44.

[3] A. Georgette Bowden-Smith, *An English Student's Wander-Year* (London: Edward Arnold Publishers, Ltd., 1910), pp. 286-87.

This favorable attitude toward American common schools was shared by an Australian visitor in 1908, Frank Tate, as it was by a French observer in 1906, Charles Wagner.[4] Not so lavish in his praise of the system but more objective and critical in his observations was German psychologist Hugo Münsterberg, an instructor at Harvard for a number of years.[5] One member of a German educational mission to the United States in 1906 noted with approval that "all schools from the kindergarten to the university are attended by all classes of people, that in all schools instruction is gratuitous, and that, except as to the colored race in the South, there is no distinction of race or nationality in the attendance." Another member of the same group approved "the fact that the elementary school is open to rich and poor alike, as a mutual spur to greater effort on the part of both, and as a preventive of class hatred." He further felt that the extension of such common instruction to the fifteen-year-old group could not "but be beneficial to the great mass of the people." [6]

Presenting a much more adverse view was Louis Klemm who, in a study published in 1911 comparing American and German education, asserted that American public schools wasted much more time than their German counterparts. Mistakenly the American public tended "to regard school as a hospital for all the failings of society, for all the defects and deficiencies in the state, as well as for all ailments of the community." The time available for regular school work, as a consequence, was shrinking lamentably and in many instances instruction had deteriorated from real work to a kind of play.[7]

Yet another implication of American democratic education was noted by a Latin-American visitor Alberto Gutierrez, who wrote in 1904 of his travels in the United States. This Chilean pointed out that general and universal schooling in America had been able to blunt somewhat the impact of class conflict. Since the American working classes had more knowledge and organizational power (as a result of the common schools) with which to wring salary and other concessions from capitalists and employers, they were not, for this very reason, as likely as

[4] Frank Tate, *Preliminary Report of the Director of Education* (Melbourne, Australia: Education Department of Victoria, 1908), p. 34; Charles Wagner, *My Impressions of America* (New York: McClure, Phillips & Co., 1906), pp. 160-61.

[5] Hugo Münsterberg, *The Americans* (New York: McClure, Phillips & Co., 1904).

[6] William N. Hailman, *German Views of American Education* (U.S. Bureau of Education Bulletin No. 2 [Washington, D.C., 1906]).

[7] Louis R. Klemm, *Public Education in Germany and in the United States* (Boston: Richard G. Badger, 1911), pp. 30-32.

their counterparts in Europe and Latin America to turn upon the upper classes in a violent explosion of blind fury and social revolution.[8]

A prominent phase of the work of the American "School Universal" that attracted the attention of observers from abroad was its "Americanizing" and acculturating function, particularly as it pertained to the children of recently arrived immigrants. As Professor Klemm saw it, "The common school of the United States is a crucible in which the heterogeneous elements that land on our shores are to be fused into a homogeneous mass, into a people the component elements of which are no longer engaged in constant strife over love of country and aims of life, over language and mode of thought, but rather are striving in friendly emulation toward a common goal under conditions that are, to all intents and purposes, similar." [9]

Some foreign visitors found that the American public school was successfully performing its assimilative task; others were not so sure. Charles Wagner was most favorably impressed by the ways in which American schools were taking immigrant youth and adjusting them to a new culture.[10] Miss Bowden-Smith felt that in these respects the work of the public schools in the great American cities was "unique." Nowhere else, she reported, did "the State, through its schools, make such careful provision for the thorough assimilation of the immigrant and for his initiation into the institutions and standards of his chosen land." [11]

Another English sojourner in the States was not quite as sanguine as Miss Bowden-Smith with respect to the long-range results of the school "Americanization" campaign. H. G. Wells expressed serious doubts that America, by such means, "is going to assimilate all that she is taking in now; much more do I doubt that she will assimilate the still greater inflow of the coming years." Wells was willing to concede that America "will . . . impose upon them a bare use of the English language and give them votes and certain patriotic persuasions, but I believe that if things go on as they are going the great mass of them will remain a very low lower class—will remain largely illiterate, industrialized peasants." [12] Louis Klemm took a similarly dim view of

[8] Alberto Gutierrez, *Notas e impresiones de los Estados Unidos* (Santiago de Chile: Imprenta Cervantes, 1904).

[9] Klemm, *Public Education in Germany and in the United States*, p. 11.

[10] Wagner, *My Impressions of America*, pp. 104-5.

[11] Bowden-Smith, *An English Student's Wander-Year*, pp. 294-97.

[12] H. G. Wells, *The Future in America* (New York: Harper & Row, Publishers, 1906), pp. 142-43.

the American utilization of the public school as an acculturating device. This development, to his mind, explained why American schools were "incapable of producing the excellent results secured by German schools." The great numbers of children of Slavic and South European immigrant parentage were so radically different in culture and outlook from the native "Germanic" stock that in many localities they offered almost insurmountable difficulties to the teacher and constituted "an irremediable cause of the poor results attained by public education." [13]

One aspect of American public education which was noticed, and not too favorably, by Miss Burstall was its high degree of standardization. Despite the prominence of local administrative agencies, she detected a rigidity and uniformity in the public schools from one end of the country to the other. "Such are the attempts," she wrote, "to standardize individuals as if they were pieces of a watch or a locomotive, and the despotism of the official, so that the teacher has no freedom of initiative, and the best men tend to go out of teaching." [14]

Another feature which displeased the visiting Englishwoman was the thoroughgoing secularism of American public schools. She felt that the secular solution adopted by the United States in order to cope with the "difficulties and anomalies" inherent in "a free and heterogeneous modern community" was the easy way out, but not the best way. Much better, in her opinion, was the system in Great Britain where "simple religious education" was "given in all types of English public schools, in one form or another, which satisfies a deep instinct of the nation." [15] The German schoolmen who visited America in 1906 also noticed that the public schools of the country were independent of every church. They stressed the significance, however, of a closely related phenomenon which Miss Burstall had not taken into account. Some churches, they observed, "maintain also their own schools from the elementary grades to the university, competing with the public institutions; for the Americans have, indeed, the idea of compulsory education, but not that of compulsory schools." [16]

Equally favorable was most of the foreign comment on the American pattern of free public secondary education. The Mosely Educational Commission was firmly convinced that because of this tuition-free system in America, "the organization of secondary education on a broad

---

[13] Klemm, *op. cit.*, pp. 9-12.
[14] Burstall, *Impressions of American Education in 1908*, pp. 5-6, 290-92.
[15] *Ibid.*, pp. 286-89.
[16] Hailman, *German Views of American Education.*

and liberal basis and as part of the public school system results in a better prepared class of students entering the higher institutions than is generally the case in England." [17] Robert Blair, a member of that Commission, was greatly impressed by this fact too. Britain, he wrote in 1904, lacked the fundamental basis for a national system of education which the Americans already possessed; it lacked awareness of the fact "that education is that possession of the aristocracy which democracy most needs and can most readily obtain." [18] E. S. A. Robson came to believe that "the success [in America] of the universities, the schools of technology, and the training colleges for teachers depends upon the efficiency of the high schools." Furthermore he was of the opinion that "until such a public system of education is put into operation in England the lack of adequate preparation will continue to compel the Universities to waste the first year of study on what is really secondary school work." [19]

Miss Burstall too was ready to award an accolade to the American system of free secondary schools. These schools had a better, because more systematized, curriculum than their English counterparts, and they certainly made it possible "for every type of student to receive higher education." She was particularly struck by the way opportunity was provided in these American institutions for the education of women and girls.[20] To Frank Tate, similarly, the development of free public high schools in the United States during the preceding 50 years was nothing less than phenomenal. In Australia, he asserted, such educational opportunities were not as easy to obtain since "at the time of writing, the continuation schools for the training of junior teachers in Victoria are being closely watched by the Association of Private Secondary Teachers for fear that a boy or girl should manage to get a cheap secondary education under the cloak of becoming a teacher." [21]

A dissenting vote on American secondary education, however, was cast by the French educator Gustave Lanson in a book published in 1912. Admitting that he had not been able to make extensive investigations of high schools during his short visit to America, Lanson nevertheless derived an impression from observing their students that such institutions were inferior in many ways to French lycées. These students

[17] *Joint Report*, Mosely Educational Commission.

[18] Robert Blair, *Some Features of American Education* (Dublin: Alexander Thom & Co., 1904), p. 31.

[19] Robson, *op. cit.*, p. 46.

[20] Burstall, *op. cit.*, pp. 30-31, 295-96.

[21] Tate, *op. cit.*, p. 34.

lagged behind their French counterparts and completed a comparable secondary course at a much older age. The Americans were undoubtedly well trained in moral and civic virtues, but they did not emerge, like the French, truly "cultured" persons with a harmoniously developed intellect and outlook.[22]

Another unique tendency in American education quickly noted by foreigners was the broad opportunity for instruction made available to women either through coeducation or through separate institutions for girls. Señor Gutierrez saw this trend as the reflection of the revolutionary tendencies of American social democracy which was elevating the masses of both sexes, improving their competencies, and leaving to the Old World the twin evils of ignorant, degraded working classes and dictatorial militarisms.[23] Other commentators from abroad, however, did not agree with him that the development of woman's education in America was in every respect an unalloyed blessing. Although Sara Burstall was willing to concede that in many ways American women had greater educational advantages than their English sisters, largely because of the prevalence in the New World of coeducation, she insisted that in the actual structure of American education—as teachers, administrators, and school board members—women in the United States played a much less important role at the time of her writing than they did in Britain.[24] Another negative opinion on the subject was introduced by Dr. Kuypers, a member of the German educational mission of 1906. The Herr Doktor was willing to admit that coeducation as it had developed in America demonstrated moral advantages which exceeded possible dangers and had led to an unaffected relationship between boys and girls in the presence of others. He felt, however, that such a system should not extend to children older than twelve, because after that age boys and girls required different materials and methods of instruction. Furthermore, Dr. Kuypers believed that boys over twelve should be instructed principally by men, which was less and less coming to be the case in the United States.[25]

One aspect of the American educational system which was praised almost universally by foreign observers during these years was its superb physical equipment. E. S. A. Robson of Manchester, England, wrote in 1905 that "in the larger cities the public schools are fine handsome

[22] Gustave Lanson, *Trois Mois d'Enseignement aux États-Unis* (Paris: Libraire Hachette et Cie., 1912), pp. 95-99.

[23] Gutierrez, *Notas e impresiones*, pp. 290-91.

[24] Burstall, *Impressions of American Education in 1908*, pp. 258-75.

[25] Hailman, *German Views of American Education*.

buildings of four or five storeys in height, fitted with modern improvements, including dual desks, heated cloak rooms, gymnasia and shower baths." [26] Dr. Dunker of the German educational delegation of 1906 alluded with much approval to the care given in America to sanitation in the construction and equipment of schoolhouses and to instruction in hygiene. "We have seen nothing like these," he said, "in any German school and urgently recommend its imitation." [27] The visiting Australian Frank Tate marveled that a people reputed to be so business-like and practical should spend money so liberally upon education of all grades. "In every part of the United States that I visited," he wrote, "I found the free public schools occupying the best buildings with the finest architecture, the most luxurious furnishing, with all appointments such as lighting and ventilation as perfect as modern science can make them." [28] Sara Burstall found many practical devices in American schools which, she believed, the English might well borrow. The use of secretaries, the employment of card catalogues, the simultaneous bell-signal system, the superior school furniture, the splendid gymnasium equipment, the trained school librarians all attested in her opinion to the American genius for "excellent business organization" and the successful utilization of "various labour-saving devices." [29]

The opportunity in American secondary education providing for vocational and technical training was approved of by a number of visitors from overseas in the early twentieth century. The Mosely Educational Commission, sent over with the specific mission of determining whether America's industrial progress was due to her system of technological training, was much struck by our system of practical education. As the chairman of the Commission put it, "My observations lead me to believe that the average American boy when he leaves school is infinitely better fitted for his vocation and struggle in life than the English boy, and in consequence there are in the United States a smaller proportion of 'failures' and fewer who slide downhill and eventually join the pauper, criminal, or 'submerged tenth' class." The American experience in this field, he concluded, had much to teach the British, particularly with respect to the implementation of the new English Education Act of 1902.[30] For his part, Robert Blair received the strong impression

[26] E. S. A. Robson, *Report of a Visit to American Educational Institutions* (Manchester: Sherratt & Hughes, 1905), pp. 10-11.

[27] Hailman, *op. cit.*

[28] Frank Tate, *Preliminary Report*, pp. 33-34.

[29] Burstall, *op. cit.*, pp. 292-93.

[30] *Joint Report*, Mosely Educational Commission, pp. vi-x.

"that the future industries and commerce of America are being directly and profoundly affected by the schools of today." The British plan of training leaders for industry, thought Blair, was "distinctly inferior to the American," largely because the former did not have as close a link as the latter between technical schools on one hand and commercial and industrial organizations on the other.[31]

Similarly impressed with the American movement of industrial education was Sarah Burstall. She found it "outstanding," however, for a somewhat different reason. What she liked was the absence of conscious class distinction in the American system. Britain, she felt, had developed a much too rigid "two-track" system. "We specialize too much; we do not value, because we do not realize, the effect of a liberal education in helping people to do their ordinary work in the world." Miss Burstall felt that Britain might well profit from the American example in this area and demand more firmly than was presently done "a good general education as a condition before technical training begins." [32]

A Latin-American observer Benjamin E. del Castillo was also notably enthusiastic about American provisions at this time for practical training. American education, he wrote in 1910, was specifically dedicated to building up the industrial greatness and general well-being of the country. Every youth was expected to be useful and to make some positive contribution to the national welfare. There was a pleasant absence in the United States of the type of foppish young rich man, so well known in South America, whose only means of coping with boredom was to throw money away. North American altruism and practicality would never permit such waste of potential. The ideal of "Yankee" education was to produce the trained, tireless, dedicated worker.[33]

Not all foreign comment on American technical education was unreservedly favorable, however. In 1917 the French observer Victor Cambon stated that while technological education on the college and university level, and even in certain urban technical high schools, was very well developed, provision for specialized training in the lower grades and in continuation schools serving the great mass of the workers was inferior to that found in Switzerland and Germany.[34] Writing about this subject a few years earlier, Miss Bowden-Smith had reached similar

---

[31] Blair, *Some Features of American Education*, pp. 66-75.

[32] Burstall, *op. cit.*, pp. 248-50, 299-300.

[33] Benjamin E. del Castillo, *Dos Américas* (Valencia: F. Sempere y Compañia, 1910), pp. 45-47.

[34] Victor Cambon, *États-Unis, France* (Paris: Pierre Roger et Cie., 1917), pp. 75-76.

conclusions. She found American urban schools to be limited by "the same inadequate provision for technical training which besets the educationists of older countries." In many communities neither enough time nor money was available to make specialized training meaningful in secondary schools. However, a number of American educators were aware of the problem, she reported, and were seeking to remedy these deficiencies.[35]

Monsieur Cambon also made reference to a characteristic of the structure of American educational administration which was noticed, sometimes favorably, sometimes unfavorably, not only by a number of his fellow-countrymen, but by many other twentieth-century visitors from abroad. "The federal government," he wrote, "ignores education. . . . One quickly sees in Washington a library with a rich collection serving public instruction, but this institution contents itself with publishing reports and statistics; it has little influence on popular education." [36]

Interesting, too, to many foreign visitors was the extracurricular life which was developing in most American schools. The Mosely Commission, somewhat surprisingly, concluded that competitive sports did not "form anything like so important a part of the everyday life of the schoolboy . . . as is the case here [in Britain] and not nearly so much time is devoted to them." [37] In 1908 Saint-André de Lignereux, on the other hand, was struck by the integral part which organized sports played in the life of the American boy and girl. Furthermore, he was impressed by the fervent way in which American school children participated in clubs and extracurricular organizations of all types—althletic, journalistic, muscial, and photographic. These the children somehow were able to organize by themselves, manage by themselves, even finance by themselves.[38] This same strain of busy independence and easy self-reliance in the extracurricular field was noted by Miss Burstall too, who observed that in American public high schools "teachers are not so much *in* things, games and societies as with us [the English]; the pupils run their societies themselves." [39]

Lastly many of the foreign observers asked, what were the end results

[35] Bowden-Smith, *An English Student's Wander-Year*, pp. 288-92.
[36] Cambon, *États-Unis, France*, p. 76. This quotation was translated by the author from the original French text.
[37] *Joint Report*, Mosely Educational Commission, p. xiii.
[38] Saint-André de Lignereux, *L'Amérique au XXth Siècle* (Paris: Librairie Illustrée, 1908), pp. 158-59.
[39] Burstall, *op. cit.*, pp. 66-67.

of the American system of instruction as they viewed it in action? Its accomplishment obviously could be seen reflected in the products it turned out; namely, the young people of America. Here most of the visitors' comment was commendatory. An exception to this viewpoint were the remarks directed by Louis Klemm to a German audience. An overfeminized teaching staff, he asserted, was allowing American children to grow up undisciplined and ignorant of distinctions between good and evil. A cult of the child had developed in which it was even considered appropriate for children of fourteen to choose their own studies! In Klemm's view all this was errant nonsense.[40]

Somewhat more complimentary, although tinged with gentle irony, was the comment of Arnold Bennett, the renowned British novelist. In a work published in 1912, Bennett reported on the amazing sight he had witnessed during a visit to America. This phenomenon was a group of high school children coming out into the street of a residential suburb:

> It was a great and impressive sight; it was a delightful sight. They were so sure of themselves, the maids particularly; so interested in themselves, so happy, so eager, so convinced (without any conceit) that their importance transcended all other importances, so gently pitiful toward men and women of forty-five, and so positive that the main function of elders was to pay school fees, that I was thrilled thereby. . . . I had never seen anything like it. I immediately desired to visit schools. Profoundly ignorant of educational methods and with a strong distaste for teaching, I yet wanted to know and understand all about education in America in one moment—the education that produced that superb stride and carriage in the street! [41]

After due investigation Bennett hit upon what he believed was the explanation: The American child was the center of a kind of national worship and was duly appreciative of that fact. "A child is not a fool," he reminded his readers. "A child is almost always uncannily shrewd. And when it sees a splendid palace provided for it, when it sees money being showered upon hygienic devices for its comfort, even upon trifles for its distraction, when it sees brains all bent on discovering the best, nicest ways of dealing with its instincts, when it sees itself the center of a magnificent pageant, ritual, devotion, almost worship, it naturally lifts its chin, puts its shoulders back, steps out with a spring, and

[40] Klemm, *Public Education in Germany and in the United States*, pp. 33-41.
[41] Arnold Bennett, *Your United States* (New York: Harper & Row, Publishers, 1912), p. 149.

glances down confidently upon the whole world." Under these circumstances, Bennett asked, who wouldn't? [42]

The "air of triumphant liberty" which the American school child carried about with him was equally impressive to Saint-André de Lignereux.[43] "That each pupil should be a somebody," added another Frenchman, Charles Wagner, "[should] be conscious of his dignity, take upon himself the responsibility for his acts, and preside over the republic within him—this is the aim toward which [American] education is directed." [44]

The same self-reliance and independence was construed as an end-product of American education by some of Arnold Bennett's fellow-countrymen. Miss Burstall declared that "nothing is more remarkable or more puzzling to an English teacher than the good discipline and the absence of any elaborate system of rules and penalties in an American school." Such a situation was possible, she maintained, because Americans *believed* in education much more than the English and because American boys and girls in school were "quieter, steadier, and more self-reliant and hard-working than the corresponding types in England." [45] Equally laudatory was the report by the Mosely Commission. "What struck me," wrote the chairman, "in going through the public schools, whether primary or college, of the United States was the success attained in making the scholars self-reliant, in bringing out their individual qualities, and [in] teaching them to reason." [46] This, then, was the keynote of American public education which made the deepest impression upon early twentieth-century visitors from abroad.

1920-1945

During the years between the end of World War I and the end of World War II, observations with respect to education in the United States continued to be published by visitors from abroad. A salient aspect still fascinating to the foreign traveler was the deep-seated democratic character of the American public schools. This phenomenon was much more pronounced in America, in their opinion, than in their re-

[42] *Ibid.*, pp. 152-53.
[43] Lignereux, *op. cit.*, pp. 155-57.
[44] Wagner, *My Impressions of America*, pp. 168-69.
[45] Burstall, *op. cit.*, pp. 24-25, 34-35.
[46] *Joint Report*, Mosely Educational Commission, p. viii.

spective homelands. A Chinese observer Chien-Hsun-li pointed out in 1927 that the development of the school system in America had been the precise opposite of what it was in China. In America schools had grown naturally from the people—from the bottom upwards; in China, they had been imposed by the central government on the local districts, and had thus developed from the top down.[47]

Another visitor from the East wrote in 1920 that it was almost impossible not to be struck by the democratic spirit which permeated the whole of school life in America. "It is indeed," Dr. Sudhindra Bose of India reported, "something more than a mere vague, elusive spirit. You can almost feel it, touch it—it is so vital, so real. This wholesome American democracy finds a living expression in the absolute equality which exists among students." According to Bose, it was a common thing in America to see "the boy whose father owns a thousand acres of land and has a big red automobile treated by school-mates and teachers just like the ragged urchin by his side, whose father is the 'hired man' of the rich man." [48]

The same theme was stressed by two visiting Australian educators in 1930. "The conscious aim in many of the more advanced schools in America," they wrote, "is to introduce into the schoolroom as many as possible of the elements of a democratic society." As a result, they observed, "the whole life of the school is conceived as a training in citizenship." [49]

Two Argentinian wayfarers agreed with this view of American schools. In 1939 Señor Enrique Gil, lawyer, university professor, and publicist, wrote a pamphlet explaining why he sent his son to the United States to be educated. He did so, according to this version, because the young man would receive an excellent preparation for undertaking public responsibilities, with good character training to boot.[50] Dr. Edmundo Correas, President of the University de Cuyo in Mendoza was pleased to note three years later that the American's approach to democracy was a sound and realistic one which was reflected in his schools. "Democracy is not numerical equality," he wrote, "but hierarchy and choice.

[47] Chien-Hsun-li, *Some Phases of Popular Control of Education in the United States* (Shanghai: The Commercial Press, Ltd., 1927), pp. 208-13.

[48] Sudhindra Bose, *Fifteen Years in America* (Calcutta: Kar, Majumder & Co., 1920), pp. 70-71.

[49] K. S. Cunningham and G. E. Phillips, *Some Aspects of Education in the U.S.A.* (Melbourne: Melbourne University Press, 1930), pp. 36-37.

[50] Enrique Gil, *Por que envíe a mi hijo a una escuela de los Estados Unidos* (Buenos Aires: Publicaciones del Instituto Cultural Argentino-Norte Americano, 1939), pp. 12-13.

A fool may be a king, a dictator, or a demagogue, but never a true democrat." Correas added that this was "known by all United States children, and practised by its people." Capability was the common regulator of all offices in America; voters in many states were asked to read and write correctly, and even to comment intelligently on the Constitution. Furthermore, perjury was rare and would not be covered up by others. Whereas in Latin America such dishonest conduct would be reckoned as good comradeship, in the United States it would be accounted treasonable and disloyal. Finally, North Americans were much more likely than Latins to hand out praise and demonstrate appreciation for their fellows. They were not purely negative or bitterly antagonistic. They were "proud of their country and its people . . . always on the lookout for talent. . . ." [51]

Some observers hastened to inform their readers that, because of its very dedication to the ambitious task of molding a democratic nation, the American school system might not in some respects always be able to match the high intellectual standards attained in the more selective schools of the Old World. In 1934 the Australian Frank Tate warned:

> The visitor accustomed to high standards of proficiency in arithmetic in Australian primary schools may . . . be tempted to speak slightingly of American schools, in which, deliberately and after searching inquiry, less emphasis is put upon this subject in order to give more time and attention to subjects deemed to be of greater value at that stage. Or, when one comes from a country where an aristocratic tradition in regard to higher education is followed, it is easy to condemn the lower standards of American secondary schools and university colleges, and to make merry over some of the subjects included in their courses.

But, Tate was careful to add, it should be kept in mind that "in the one case higher education is the privilege of an *elite* carefully prepared for entrance to the new field, while in the other an attempt is made to bring secondary and higher education within the grasp of the many." [52]

A visiting Cambridge University professor referred to the same reality when he remarked in 1943 that if American education were to be judged primarily as a means of formal instruction, it would be both "overrated and underrated." It would be overrated if one went just by the amazing enrollment figures; it would be underrated if qualitative comparisons

---

[51] Edmundo Correas, *Public Instruction in the United States of America* (Mendoza, Argentina: Universidad Nacional de Cuyo, 1942), pp. 4-8.

[52] Frank Tate, "Introduction," in Kenneth S. Cunningham, *Educational Observations and Reflections* (Melbourne: Melbourne University Press, 1934), pp. v-vi.

were made between the academic standards of most American schools and good Western European schools. But Professor Brogan warned his readers not to judge the American students harshly on the basis of their academic accomplishment. The point to remember, he emphasized, was that in the American cultural context, schools were doing far more than simply "instructing" children. In America, the public schools were assimilating and "Americanizing" immigrants, helping to acculturate migrants to the cities from rural districts, seeking to create a high level of mass democratic citizenship. The schools therefore had to let these children "instruct each other in how to live in America. . . . They have to learn a common language, common habits, common tolerances, a common political and national faith." And, Brogan added, "they do!" This striving on the part of a highly diversified, heterogeneous people for *e pluribus unum* explained to this British observer the high premium put in many American schools upon nonintellectual, extracurricular "activities." [53] The same strenuous loyalty to school, student society, and classmates, which Brogan noted as playing such a large part in "Americanization by ritual," equally impressed Garcia Guijarro as quite notable when he visited the United States in 1913. The cult of "Alma Mater" and the deep religious fervour of the "pledge to the flag," when recited in unison by a large group of school children in their classroom, seemed to this onlooker from Spain to be a most meaningful manifestation of the North American people's culture and cast of mind.[54]

As in the earlier period, the foreign visitors professed to be dazzled by the rich resources in terms of physical equipment which American schools had at their disposal. To Dr. Correas, this equipment was nothing less than "marvellous . . . attractive, varied, sumptuous and complete, like a fairy world." American classrooms looked to him "like luxurious reception rooms. . . . Learning is no longer difficult, students may learn at a glance." [55] Howard Whitehouse, a leading British educator who had visited the United States during the early 1920's, praised America's provision for school children. "No money appears to be grudged on school buildings, school equipment," he told a conference of teachers in England. "You have only to see these equipments—swimming baths, shower baths, and practical workrooms—attached to ele-

[53] D. W. Brogan, *The American Character* (New York: Alfred A. Knopf, Inc., 1944), pp. 135-41.
[54] L. Garcia Guijarro, *Notas Americanas* (Madrid: Fontanet, 1913), pp. 112-20.
[55] Correas, *Public Instruction in the U.S.A.*, pp. 5-6.

mentary schools to realize how true this is." [56] Frank Tate stated flatly that "nowhere in the world" would the visiting Australian "find more magnificently equipped schools. . . . There is, indeed, a good chance that he may be carried off his feet by admiration of some of the schools which appear to him to be the last word in school provision." [57]

There were other special aspects of the American educational order which during these years attracted foreign praise. Dr. Bose from India liked the fact that America did not permit church creeds or dogmas to be intruded into its public schools. He also was most favorably impressed by the American system of practical and vocational training, a system which he felt could well serve as the model for a reorganization of excessively classicist Indian schools.[58] A visiting New Zealand high school principal J. E. Strachan agreed in 1940 that American trade schools were performing a vital function, one which was appreciated by the young people themselves. "The young people were demanding to be educated," he noted. "Why? To get on, to succeed, to make money, to avoid the grinding worry and shame of material poverty, and so to attain power, social status, self-respect." [59]

Two visiting Australian schoolmen declared in 1930 that the United States had probably done more than any other country to establish a profession and science of education. American scholars were fast building up an impressive body of professional knowledge dealing with problems of learning. And such findings, they reported, were immediately applied as generally as possible in actual classroom work in the schools. This sprang from an American "desire to make education touch life at as many points as possible, to prevent the development of an artificial antithesis between school life and 'real' life." The Australians were particularly interested in the provisions many American schools made for guidance counselors and pronounced this arrangement to be so obviously valuable "that it would appear to be well worth while to consider seriously the possibility of making a commencement with the system in some of the large centres of population in Australia." [60]

[56] J. Howard Whitehouse and G. P. Gooch, *Wider Aspects of Education* (Cambridge, England: Cambridge University Press, 1924), p. 43.

[57] Tate, "Introduction," in Cunningham, *op. cit.*, pp. vi-vii.

[58] Bose, *Fifteen Years in America*, pp. 72-79.

[59] J. E. Strachan, *New Zealand Observer* (New York: Columbia University Press, 1940), p. 106.

[60] Cunningham and Phillips, *Some Aspects of Education in the United States*, pp. 38-39, 75-76; Cunningham, *Educational Observations and Reflections*, pp. 19-20.

Not all comments from abroad during this period were favorable to American education, however. Charles Bastide, a French visitor, remarked in 1921 that secondary education was the weak point in the American school system. Its course of study, he insisted, was not as rich in intellectual content as that of the French *lycées*, its teaching staff, on the whole, not as well prepared, its work, in too many places, mediocre or worse, and the line of demarcation between it and the higher learning not as well marked as in France.[61] The German Count Hermann Keyserling professed to see serious weaknesses in the American school system as it existed in 1927. The country was dangerously overfeminized, he declared, and the resultant infantilism, passivity, and childishness was reflected in its schools with their "kindergarten complex."[62] Somewhat more gentle in his critique, the Australian observer Kenneth S. Cunningham wondered whether America's "besetting sin" was not a craze for publicity. This carried over into the schools, he very much feared. Too often American young people were encouraged to believe that the surest sign of success was to "get into the news." Too much of this kind of hoopla accompanied the election of officers for student organizations and the holding of athletic meets and competitions. Thoughtful educators, he felt, should seek to cut down on such overemphasis.[63]

1945 to the Present

Following World War II, a number of additional commentaries on American education were published by foreigners. One question which interested outside observers during the Fifties and Sixties was that of the status of the American school teacher and his relations with his charges and their parents. A most informative work *Exchange Teacher*, published in 1960, shed considerable light on this picture. This book was edited by Philip Goodhart, a Conservative Member of Parliament, on behalf of the Bow Group, an organization of young Conservatives who frequently conducted social and political studies, and was based on a compilation of the opinions of 67 British teachers

[61] Charles Bastide, *Les Écoles et Les Universités* (Paris: La Renaissance du Livre, 1921), pp. 2-5.
[62] Hermann Keyserling, *America Set Free* (London: Jonathan Cape, 1930), pp. 270-89, 421-23.
[63] Cunningham, *op. cit.*, pp. 17-19.

and 38 American ones who returned to their respective countries in 1958 after a tour of duty as exchange teachers.[64]

The great majority of the British teachers reported that teacher-pupil relationships in America were much more informal, relaxed, and friendly than in their own country. They clearly enjoyed the difference, particularly in the primary schools, although a number of the British teachers were somewhat unsettled by the fact that the amount of respect shown by American pupils seemed to be based wholly on the particular instructor's personality. As one of the visiting English put it, "one had to act as a sort of maiden aunt." [65]

Many British teachers expressed surprise at the degree to which American parents participated in the education of their children through such organizations as Parent-Teacher Associations. Although the majority of the exchange teachers were ready to concede that American parents tended to be more interested and helpful in school affairs than their counterparts in Great Britain, a number were critical of parental interference. Reported one British teacher: "The Parent-Teacher Association was very powerful in my part of America. The principal had to keep on their right side to get financial help for new extras required for the school. So he gave in to their policy. . . . They were allowed freely to criticize the work and methods of the professional teachers. This horrified me." [66]

On a visit to the United States in 1959 Geoffrey Lloyd, the British Minister of Education, arrived at conclusions on teacher-pupil relationships in America which closely resembled those of the exchange teachers. Teachers and pupils in American high schools, he found, had a "first-class, a charming relationship." And he added: "Your boys and girls seem to possess more self-confidence and are less inhibited than the students in our schools, but they are very much alike." [67] Times had not changed: Arnold Bennett had noted the same phenomenon nearly 50 years before!

One aspect of the American teacher's working environment which greatly interested the visiting British was the disciplinary situation in New World classrooms. Here the majority of the British exchangers found that American school discipline compared well with anything they had known. "It was an easy discipline," one teacher reported,

[64] Philip Goodhart, *Exchange Teacher* (London: Conservative Political Centre, 1960), pp. 6-7.
[65] *Ibid.*, pp. 22-23.
[66] *Ibid.*, pp. 24-26.
[67] *New York Times*, February 28, 1959, p. 21.

"and accepting this, I think it was better, not one student showing me the slightest impertinence." It is important to keep in mind in connection with these findings one fact which editor Goodhart frankly acknowledged in his Introduction—the British teachers seem to have been purposely assigned to a picked, above-average group of American schools. None were sent to "Blackboard Jungle" areas.[68]

Another phase of the life of the teacher in the United States which was carefully noted by the British was the great burden of paper work and other administrative duties, much heavier than on the other side of the Atlantic. Too much school time, many of them felt, was taken up with nonteaching duties. Mr. Goodhart, in compiling the British teachers' responses on this point, wondered why it was that American teachers, in a largely nonselective system, "should spend so much more time preparing reports and keeping records of their children than British teachers do in a selective system." He slyly hazarded the guess that the reason he had gotten only 38 responses to his questionnaire from American exchange teachers as against 67 from British ones was that the former "were probably snowed under by the amount of paper work that seems to be required in American schools." [69]

As in the earlier periods we have surveyed, one feature of the American school system that the British exchange teachers generally agreed could be imported to greatest advantage into their own country was the splendid equipment and physical facilities which were lavished on so many schools in the United States. "Ten times more equipment," wrote one British teacher, was the "aspect of American education I would most like to see adopted here." Another pointed out that:

> The extremely good reading textbooks that were provided at grade levels would be of great help. Their adequate library supplies and the films, slides, and records that were provided all helped to make teaching easier and more interesting.[70]

Perhaps the most important problem of American education which the British survey and other foreign studies commented upon was that of the intellectual quality of schooling given in the United States. The general conclusion of the British exchange teachers of 1958 was that American school children were at least two years behind their British

[68] Goodhart, *op. cit.*, pp. 7-8, 27-29.
[69] *Ibid.*, pp. 6, 34-36.
[70] *Ibid.*, pp. 39-40.

counterparts in most academic subjects, even though they did have more poise and inventiveness than British children and a much greater facility for oral expression. The most consistent academic deficiency among their American pupils, in the opinion of the British teachers, was in mathematics, particularly in the earlier grades. Following closely on the heels of this lag were shortcomings in English grammar, writing, reading, and spelling.[71]

The British teachers believed that there was not enough separation of brighter pupils from the less bright in American schools and too much bias in favor of the mediocre student. Furthermore, they said they believed that not enough demands were made on students in America—particularly the bright ones—and that in many cases school was simply too easy. Interestingly enough, the American exchange teachers in Britain, whose opinions were surveyed as part of the same investigation, were in general agreement that the British did more for their better students than United States schools did, but in so doing they neglected their mediocre and slow ones.[72]

A number of observers from abroad agreed with the findings of the British exchange teachers on the much mooted question of intellectual quality. John Garrett, headmaster of the Grammar School in Bristol, England, came to the United States in 1952 as a Smith-Mundt Fellow in Education and one year later recorded in the *Atlantic Monthly* his conclusions on American secondary education. He seriously questioned whether education in the United States was calculated to produce an *elite* of leaders of high intelligence. There was too much emphasis upon social adjustment and not enough upon intellectual development. "Young Americans," he remarked, "are certainly kept less at the stretch than young Britishers," adding that "At eighteen, Americans are intellectually anything from eight months to two years behind our young people, and at the universities they have to make up two years of education which in England they would have done at school."

It was difficult for Garrett to resist the conclusion that "in the modern American school the snail's pace becomes the school's pace." Perhaps this was due, he speculated, to the fact that Americans were afraid "tensions" might result from allowing the clever child to outpace the dull. But what, he asked, of the frustration and boredom that must inevitably be the lot of the able child who was held back? Garrett summed up his critique by quoting with at least partial approval the

[71] *Ibid.*, pp. 17-19.
[72] *Ibid.*, pp. 19-21.

remark made to him by an American teacher after a year of exchange in Britain: "Your system produces snobs, ours slobs." [73]

A number of French visitors to the American schools of mid-century agreed with these conclusions. In 1947 Antoinette Gommes found an absence of intellectual discipline, of adequate preparation for advanced work, and of the critical or analytical spirit. These deficiencies stood out even more starkly in mind because she had first of all praised warmly the teacher-training, extracurricular life, social consciousness of educators and the provision for student health which she had found in America.[74] Four years later André Potier recalled as his main impression after a stint of teaching in the United States (at the college level, to be sure) that the main preoccupation of American schools was to produce "good mixers." [75]

The eminent French scholar and novelist André Maurois, setting down for an American periodical in 1961 his reasoned conclusions as to the differences between the schools of his country and those of the United States, found their dissimilarities in essence to amount to the following: "In America, where education is meant to be essentially democratic, all school children, whatever their I.Q.s, are treated about the same way." Maurois continued:

> I heard American teachers say, "Let us beware of being ostensibly partial to brilliant minds; slow-witted pupils might then acquire an inferiority complex." Their unconfessed desire is that the bottom boy should feel equal to the head boy. In some extreme cases a dunce may be told to stay in the same grade for a second year, but an American educator doesn't take such a decision without reluctance. The child might feel humiliated. The less gifted child is given easier work suitable to his interests and abilities.[76]

A fact-finding survey sponsored by the *Saturday Evening Post* in 1960 presented statistics that tended to bear out many of the conclusions about American schools reached by foreign commentators. The *Post* utilized the Gallup Poll to research 4142 children in five nations —the United States, England, France, West Germany, and Norway.

[73] John Garrett, "Do American Schools Educate?" *Atlantic Monthly*, 191 (February 1953), pp. 70-71.

[74] Antoinette Gommes, A *Travers Les Écoles d'Amèrique* (Paris: Les Presses d'Ile de France, 1947), pp. 189-90.

[75] André Potier, *Un Français a l'École Américaine* (Paris: Amiot, Dumont, 1951), pp. 266-67.

[76] André Maurois, "A Frenchman Appraises U.S. Schools," *Saturday Review of Literature*, 44 (April 15, 1961), p. 54.

The sample employed was divided equally by sex and age—half were boys, half girls, half were ten years old, half fourteen. Attempts were made also to utilize correct proportions of students from poor homes and rich ones, from public, sectarian, and private schools. Both the dull and bright children, the gifted and retarded, were included. In addition, scores achieved by more than 800 children in each of the five countries on an identical test covering geography, arithmetic, science, and the identification of world-famous men were compiled. Finally, interviewers tabulated reports on such matters as homework, school and parental discipline, teaching methods, outside pupil activities, and attitudes toward education in all five countries.[77]

While the findings of surveys based on such a small statistical sample as the Gallup Poll have to be appraised with great caution, the general conclusions that resulted from this particular study are most interesting. As compared to the European child of identical age, the American youngster was found to:

Spend less time in classroom work during an actual school year;

Do much less homework (except for the English child);

Give more trouble to his teachers;

Read fewer books;

Memorize poorest of all;

Spend more time watching television (except for the English child) and telephoning;

Write fewer essays;

Be high in science, lowest in knowledge of world-famous men, poor in geography, and low in arithmetic.[78]

Perceptive foreign observers professed to find the explanation for the unevenness of American educational achievement in the excessive tenderness toward mediocrity which had developed as a result of the country's deep commitment to democracy. They also added that other valuable clues could be discovered in the broad nationalizing objectives set for American schools by historical imperative and even present in the very administrative framework of the United States, itself a product

[77] George Gallup and Evan Hill, "Is European Education Better Than Ours?" *Saturday Evening Post*, 233 (December 24, 1960), pp. 59-76.
[78] *Ibid.*, p. 63.

of a distinctive line of historical development. Thus Philip Goodhart quoted with approval an article from the American magazine *Time* which attributed the "oddly uneven" quality of public schools in the United States to excessive local control. "Compared to Europe's state-run systems," this article asserted, "U.S. schools seem an anarchist's brainchild." This critique further asserted:

> With their genius for decentralization the Constitution's writers left education in the laps of the states, which handed it over to local communities. Today nearly all responsibility is vested in 198,108 members of 49,477 school boards. The schools they command reflect vastly different standards. The teachers they hire receive grossly varying salaries. The results range from splendid to shameful.

Mr. Goodhart hastened to add, to set the record straight, that there was also "more than a touch of anarchy in the British system," but that nevertheless England had a number of unifying features in its schools such as a government Inspectorate and national standard examinations (notably, the famous "eleven-plus") not present in America.[79]

André Maurois commented on the same issue when he suggested how astonished a visiting Frenchman would be to be informed "that there is no uniform program, that in many places a student himself chooses, from a vast catalogue, the subjects he wishes to study, as he would make his own menu in a cafeteria. . . ." How is that possible, the visiting Frenchman would ask. "Does not the Ministry of Education in Washington determine the programs of exams for the whole country? When he is then told that Washington has nothing to do with education except for statistics and that the subsidies of the federal government are given through the states, his astonishment increases." Not so in France, Maurois reminded his readers! Whether a young man studied in Paris or Caen or Aix he had to study the same subjects, and his diploma had the same value as any other French diploma. Meanwhile the high school years had been a permanent ordeal by examination. Every week there was a test in subjects such as French composition, history, and mathematics, and each pupil was told his position on the list. The bottom ones would not go on to the next grade. Nor was this all:

> Every year a General Competition takes place between all French lycées [high schools]. The best pupils of each lycée write on the same day on

[79] Goodhart, *Exchange Teacher*, pp. 6-7.

the same themes a French composition, a Latin version, an essay on philosophy, etc. The prizes are solemnly handed over, at the Sorbonne, by the President of the French Republic. On that day Napoleon's dream comes true and it often happens that small provincial towns outrank Paris.[80]

Was such a unified system better than the American variegated one? Maurois conceded that, superior or not, the French plan would never work in the United States.

> You cannot impose on Mississippi a type of university that suits Massachusetts. Between populations, traditions, and needs, the differences are too wide. America is a continent. Moreover one cannot compare the American system, whose object is to give the same education to all children, with the French system, which, after each cycle, requires a successful examination before allowing the pupil to proceed. As to superior education, in France it is intended for a small intellectual elite.[81]

The nub of the problem, according to Sir Geoffrey Crowther, chairman of Britain's Central Advisory Council for Education in 1960, was that educational systems of Western European countries like England aimed for depth, while that of the United States aimed for breadth. In both cases these purposes were shaped by history. "In America," wrote Sir Geoffrey, "you have always been very conscious of the need to build up a new society. You have wanted to construct something bigger, richer, better than you have." The circumstances in which the Americans lived and worked practically dictated that education would have to serve important social purposes.

> It has been regarded as an instrument by which society can build its own future. From its nature, it has inescapably been concerned with the rank and file of the people. Its chief concern for many generations has been to do something to the masses—and I think the word is *to*, not *for*— in the interests of the American dream.

By way of contrast, continued Sir Geoffrey, an old, settled European country such as England had not been as conscious of a necessity to build a new society. As a matter of fact, it had a fully developed society with which it was on the whole fairly well satisfied. Hence English education had been designed primarily for maintenance, with improve-

---

[80] André Maurois, "A Frenchman Appraises U.S. Schools," *Saturday Review of Literature*, p. 54.
[81] *Ibid.*, p. 54.

ment coming second. Hence also the strong note of selectivity in British education. Post-primary education, in this context, had always been thought of as a privilege, not something that must be given to the multitude in the national interest. Such a system did not necessarily exclude the poor boy, the writer pointed out. "There is no such thing as working your way through college in England. We do not need a National Merit Scholarship scheme because we have one already. Nor is this a recent thing." Mid-century national educational reforms were expanding educational opportunity in Britain, but by no means eliminating the basic principle of qualitative selectivity. For these valid historical reasons, Sir Geoffrey concluded:

> Nonselection—if that is the opposite of selection—as it is practiced in America is totally unknown in England. By nonselection I mean the principle of treating all children alike, allowing them to sort themselves out by their choice of courses, by what they find easy and difficult, or by their varying ambitions—with counseling assistance, no doubt, but without any compulsory segregation. I am sure that your system seems as odd to us as ours does to you.[82]

[82] Sir Geoffrey Crowther, "English and American Education, Depth versus Breadth," *Atlantic Monthly* (April 1960), pp. 37-42.

CHAPTER NINE

The "Cold War" Among American Educators

The Australian Kenneth S. Cunningham noted as one of the most pleasing aspects of American education "a desire to face the facts, to exchange opinions without prejudice, and to enquire into underlying principles." In illustrating this tendency he recalled that "the severest and most searching criticisms of American education come from within rather than without." [1] And indeed as one reviews the comments that have been penned on the development of twentieth-century American education by foreigners and by natives, one immediately realizes that, by and large, the criticisms by Americans themselves have been much more severe. This difference may be partly due to gentlemanly restraint in that the foreigners may have felt themselves to be much more obliged to bow to courtesy in making remarks about another land than would be true of the natives. It may also be due, as Robert M. Hutchins suggests, to the circumstance that many of the visiting foreign scholars toured mainly the great universities, the largest, best equipped city school systems, and the most spectacular laboratories, thus having little opportunity to witness personally the poorer conditions of the hinterland.[2] Or Charles William Eliot may have come closest to the explana-

[1] Kenneth S. Cunningham, *Educational Observations and Reflections* (Melbourne, Australia: Melbourne University Press, 1934).

[2] Robert M. Hutchins, *Some Observations on American Education* (Cambridge, England: Cambridge University Press, 1956), pp. xii-xiii.

tion when in 1903 he wrote that the American people were perhaps "too impatient for peerless fruitage from the slow-growing tree of liberty; we all expect sudden miracles of material and moral welfare—we get only a slow development and a halting progress." [3] Whatever the reasons, the difference in tone between foreign and domestic commentaries on American education is notable.

Since World War II marks an important watershed in the history of American education, let us use it as a dividing line to sort out the earlier American comments on educational trends from the later ones. If we take a close look, then, at the viewpoints expressed before 1945, the main impression we carry away with us is a negative one. For a variety of reasons those Americans who were taking the time and trouble to formulate a reasoned critique of their country's educational system during the first four decades of the twentieth century found much to condemn, little to praise.

Neil E. Stevens, for example, writing in 1912 about American "educational advertising" in the *School Review*, complained that too many schools were encouraging extracurricular activities which they nevertheless realized were useless or harmful. They did so, he charged, as a form of educational advertising—an attempt to attain the interest and approval of the parents of their students. Since many of these parents had not themselves received a liberal education, they could hardly be expected to know what it was. It was essential for the school, Stevens insisted, to enlighten such parents as to what a true education really was.[4]

At the close of World War I Charles W. Eliot professed to see a number of deficiencies in American education which had been spotlighted by the events of 1917 and 1918. Continuing illiteracy, disclosed by the Armed Forces draft, seemed to point to a need for federal aid to education. The prevalence of bodily defects and physical ailments among American youth underlined the importance of better school health programs and physical training. The lesson that the war had taught of the crucial importance of industrial technology and productive agriculture in modern times meant that in the school curriculum more stress should be placed on applied and practical sciences, and that these subjects should be taught by more effective, more concrete

---

[3] Charles W. Eliot, *More Money for the Public Schools* (Garden City, N.Y.: Doubleday & Company, Inc., 1903), pp. 56-57.
[4] Neil E. Stevens, "Educational Advertising," *School Review*, 20 (November 1912), pp. 577-79.

methods. The necessary time could be secured for these new subjects by more closely correlating traditional ones such as history and geography, or government, economics, and sociology. Finally, Eliot declared, the war had shown that modern youth needed to be given a greater sense of obligation, of personal and individual duty to community and country. Every secondary school should seek to give instruction in "cooperative enterprises in which young people can take part for the benefit of the community." Workers must *want* to be punctual, orderly, and efficient. Youth must develop an "enjoyable aquiescence" in discipline. The school could cultivate this badly needed spirit by fostering singing in parts, band concerts, orchestra, folk dancing, gymnastic exhibitions, the performance of plays, and team play in sports.[5]

In 1924 veteran "muckraker" Upton Sinclair followed up an exposé of conditions in the nation's colleges with *The Goslings,* a bitter condemnation of the nation's public school administrators as the sycophants and hirelings of intriguing politicians and "vested greed." From a militantly socialist point of view, Sinclair related at length how self-seeking interests manipulated the schools for their own profit while "ten thousand fancy-salaried administrators of education" hid these goings-on from the public and told "their seven hundred thousand teacher-geese and their twenty-three million goslings that this is the greatest, the grandest, the most beautiful and most Christian country that God ever created." [6]

In 1927 came another home-grown attack on the American school system, but this time from the vantage point of intellectual elitism. In that year Abraham Flexner charged that Americans did not really value education, but merely the diffusion of educational opportunity to the widest possible extent. This they did not understand to be true learning but only the prolongation of youth. Intellectuals and scholars had no real status in the country. Flexner could only conclude that "abundance of opportunities to go to school and college can therefore be in part interpreted as meaning that we value comradeship, fun, sport, in a word—happiness, at an easy, unproductive, nonenergized level." [7]

This critique must be read against the background of the rise of mass education, particularly on the secondary school level, in the years fol-

[5] Charles W. Eliot, *Defects in American Education Revealed by the War, An Address* (New York: League for Political Education, 1919), pp. 1-12.
[6] Upton Sinclair, *The Goslings* (Pasadena, California: Upton Sinclair, 1924), p. 442.
[7] Abraham Flexner, *Do Americans Really Value Education?* (Cambridge, Mass.: Harvard University Press, 1927), p. 8.

lowing World War I. Two other observers during these years entered dissents much like Flexner's. President Nicholas Murray Butler of Columbia University gave it as his opinion in 1929 that the form and content of American public school education had gone "distinctly backward" rather than having kept pace with the "astounding advances that have been made on the administrative and material side." This gloomy state of affairs Butler attributed to the replacement of true philosophy with "shallow and contradictory substitutes." The result was that "we are now actually invited and urged to take as our model for the education of the American child, the cow, which grazes lazily in the pasture and munches what pleases the eye and seems likely to fill the stomach." [8]

A similar point of view was advanced in 1932 by Albert Jay Nock. He argued in a persuasive little book that America had once, in the time of Thomas Jefferson, possessed a meaningful educational system which, like that of Continental Europe, tended "primarily towards salvaging the educable person, seining him out of the general ruck, and making something of him." Such a system was not "hamstrung by any insane pseudo-equalitarian and pseudo-democratic notions." It was based squarely on the idea "that educable persons are relatively few, that their social value is great, that they are accordingly precious and should be enabled to make the most of themselves." Such an approach would do reasonably well by the ineducable too, the author insisted, but it would foster no sentimentalist or romantic view of their capacities. It would in no case "go through the specious and immoral pretense of educating them," as modern American schools were doing, nor would it pretend that when it had finished "processing a proverbially refractory raw material, the product is a silk purse or anything in the least like a silk purse." [9]

With the coming of the Great Depression of the 1930's, the attention of many students of American education shifted back once again to the social role of the school. What Lawrence Cremin has called the "Veblenian critique of American education" had already been advanced by Upton Sinclair in his previously cited diatribe; by Thorstein Veblen himself (*The Higher Learning in America*); by Harold Stearns; by John Kirkpatrick (*The American College and Its Rulers*); and, perhaps most

---

[8] Nicholas Murray Butler, *Changes of a Quarter Century* (New York, 1929), pp. 8-11.

[9] Albert Jay Nock, *The Theory of Education in the United States* (New York: Harcourt, Brace & World, Inc., 1932), pp. 150-52.

consistently, by Professor George S. Counts of Teachers College, Columbia University.[10] A dissatisfied critic like Counts bitterly objected to the class bias in American school board membership and demanded that the school come to grips with contemporary industrial reality and eschew mere superficiality. This kind of thinking led in 1933 to the publication of an influential volume, *The Educational Frontier*, edited by William H. Kilpatrick and contributed to by John L. Childs, Boyd H. Bode, V. T. Thayer, John Dewey and others. The authors demanded that the American school curriculum be drastically changed to inform the public about the "facts" of modern industrial civilization. They also called for changes in the country's system of school administration so that the actual teachers and students in the schools would play a more important role in managing the institutions of which they were a part.[11]

While "socially conscious" commentaries such as *The Educational Frontier* were a far cry from the kind of blanket indictment of the schools, and even of educational progressives, which authentic American Left-Wingers were making at this time,[12] frantic conservatives saw the former as blatantly "red." Typical of this approach was the nearly hysterical attack which Bessie Burchett in 1941 directed against such American proponents of progressive education as Harold Rugg and John Dewey (gratuitously throwing in Charles A. Beard for good measure). The "Social Studies" program advocated in the schools by such worthies, in the opinion of Miss Burchett, was helping to prepare for the day of world revolution. Worst of all, she declared, in teacher-training institutions from coast to coast prospective members of the profession were taught to revere such subversive professors.[13]

Continuing to use World War II as a road marker in reviewing twentieth-century critiques of modern American education by Americans, we discover that some of the most searching and influential analyses ap-

[10] See Lawrence A. Cremin, *The Transformation of the School* (New York: Alfred A. Knopf, Inc., 1962), pp. 224-27; for an example, see George S. Counts, *The American Road to Culture* (New York: The John Day Company, Inc., 1930), pp. 12-19, 79-91, 138-40.

[11] William H. Kilpatrick, ed., *The Educational Frontier* (New York: The Century Co., 1933).

[12] For example, note the comment in Rex David, *Schools and the Crisis* (New York: International Publishing Co., 1934): "Their 'liberal' leaders have made genuine advances in developing methods and materials to protect and develop the children in their care. But their support comes from private schools and wealthy communities. They are as weak and supine in the struggle against attacks on the public schools as the NEA and the state associations" (p. 33).

[13] Bessie R. Burchett, *Education for Destruction* (Philadelphia: Published by the Author, 1941), pp. 110-11, 120-21, 130-31.

peared in the years following 1945. Americans, for a number of reasons, began to subject their schools to what amounted to an agonizing reappraisal (see Chap. 5). Published explanations of what was wrong (and very occasionally even what was right) with American education now became more numerous and more voluminous than at any other time in the century. Even before Sputnik sped into space in 1957, the clamor of criticism, by and large condemnatory in nature, had grown to vociferous dimensions.

A problem which moved increasingly to the forefront of public discussion during these years was that of the adequacy of American teacher training. Many critics seemed to agree with I. Peggy Moses who declared that American teachers were poor because the kind of preparation they received in teachers colleges stifled intellectual curiosity and ignored intellectual values.[14] Agreeing with this indictment was a retired high school teacher who wrote to the *New Republic* that "the intellectually superior teacher is an anomaly." For, she continued,

> He cannot remain intellectually superior and do the job required of him. For his job is not primarily to teach. It is to keep a roomful of youngsters busy and interested, to sponsor their clubs, their sports, their social activities; to keep records of their attendance and achievements. . . . He must carry out the edicts handed down from above, follow courses of study which neither he nor they created. . . . He must enforce the authority of the state legislature, the local school board, and the even more local school administrators and faculty. . . .[15]

Springing to the defense of the teachers colleges, William Heard Kilpatrick, the grand old man of progressive education, joined the journalistic debate and even wrote a special article for the *New Republic* defending the "New Education." "Any implication that the colleges of education are headed in the wrong direction," he stated, "seems unjustified." The only valid criticism that Kilpatrick could conceive of in connection with these institutions was that the task they were undertaking was a relatively new one. This situation, he conceded, might have resulted in some initial inadequacies. "One hundred years or even two hundred years is too short a time within which to reconstruct a system strongly entrenched for two thousand years." [16]

[14] I. Peggy Moses, "Why We Have Poor Teachers," *New Republic* (September 14, 1953), p. 7-8.
[15] Edith Sprague Field, "Do We have Poor Teachers?", *New Republic* (October 5, 1953), p. 15.
[16] William Heard Kilpatrick, "What We Want of Our Teachers," *New Republic* (December 21, 1953), pp. 9-14.

Another vocal American spokesman was Dr. Robert M. Hutchins, former President of the University of Chicago and leading critic of progressive education, who took a dimmer view of matters than Dr. Kilpatrick. In a little book which appeared in 1956, Hutchins re-emphasized all the charges which had been made by Miss Moses. "The education of teachers has not been good," he said. "Neither is their financial or social position." Low salaries, insecure tenure, lack of professional solidarity, intellectual status, or prestige explained, in his view, why school teaching had failed to attract a large proportion of the abler youth of the country.[17]

Echoing this stand, Arnold A. Rogow wrote a year later in *The Nation* that the American educational "malaise" was not primarily due to lack of money or equipment but to the lack of interest on the part of the American public in things intellectual or in any way nonconforming. "In essence," he asserted, "the community wants the schools to present basic, factual information, not the questioning of institutions and values." It insists, he added,

> on adjustment rather than individuality. Additionally, it wants its teachers to be unquestioning and noncritical, and to live easily with community customs and mores. It *expects* them to read the *Reader's Digest* and *Life*. And no matter what salary it pays its teachers, the community is not willing to accord the teaching profession the status, independence, and respect it accords most of the other professions.

The result of this situation, Rogow pointed out, was that in study after study education majors in American universities were recording the lowest aptitude scores of any group of students engaged in graduate work. Obviously many of these future teachers of America were *less* intelligent or well-informed than their brighter students were likely to be.[18]

Adlai E. Stevenson, twice candidate on the Democratic ticket for the Presidency of the United States, added his voice in 1959 to the growing chorus of dissatisfaction with teacher-training methods. Making the keynote address at the annual convention of the National School Boards Association, Stevenson said that it was about time America acknowledged "the unhappy fact that our schools of education and teachers colleges in the main live in isolation from the sources of in-

[17] Robert M. Hutchins, *Some Observations on American Education*, pp. 86-87.
[18] Arnold A. Rogow, "The Educational Malaise," *The Nation* (January 26, 1957), pp. 71-74.

tellectual ferment in the great universities." In his opinion there had been too much emphasis on how to teach a child, rather than what to teach. Stress on solid content must be restored in the preparation of American teachers.[19]

One of the organizations most critical of mid-twentieth-century methods of teacher-training was the Council for Basic Education, a body created in part as a result of the ferment generated by Arthur Bestor's controversial books of the Fifties. James Koerner, a vocal critic of American teacher preparation, became president of the Council and was commissioned by it to make a detailed study of the problem. In 1963, after two years of work, Koerner's study was published in book form under the title of *The Miseducation of American Teachers*. The author was sharply critical of teacher-training institutions, stating flatly that all "the remaining teachers colleges in the United States should be shut down or converted to general purpose institutions." Many teachers colleges which had relabeled themselves general colleges had, in his view, "moved too slowly in strengthening the faculty and in changing the nature" of their programs. Thus they were guilty of "misleading students, parents, and the general public." While upholding the importance of instructing future teachers in methods of teaching, Koerner contended that many methods courses suffered from a lack of good teaching methods on the part of the professors of education themselves. He further indicted practice teaching as it was conducted in many places as being inadequately supervised. To document these contentions, Koerner presented a series of classroom case histories to his readers. In American higher education in general, and in teacher preparation in particular, he concluded, it would be salutary if education could be purged of "low standards, poor teaching, hucksterism, the proliferation of courses and empire-building." [20]

Promising to have great influence ultimately on American patterns of teacher education was another in the series of notable "Conant Reports." Published in 1963, this newest disquisition, *The Education of American Teachers*, stirred up widespread discussion among educators, administrators, and interested laymen. After a two-year study of teacher-training procedures, including visits to some 77 colleges and 16 state departments of education, Conant and his staff came to the conclusion that there was, as often charged by critics of public education, an

[19] *New York Times*, January 27, 1959, p. 25.
[20] James D. Koerner, *The Miseducation of American Teachers* (Boston: Houghton Mifflin Company, 1963); see also *idem*, "Can Our Teachers Read and Write?" *Harper's Magazine*, 209 (November 1954).

"establishment" which tightly controlled the field. This comprised an interlocking directorate of professional educators located in state offices of education, graduate schools of education, and the National Education Association. While Conant conceded that the existence of such a group was not in itself an unusual circumstance (some definite and clearly identifiable body of persons had to, after all, assume responsibility for the operation of the public schools), he did feel that it was excessively rigid in its response to proposals for change. "I think it must be said," wrote Conant, "that in almost every state the establishment is overly defensive; it views any proposal for change as a threat and assumes that any critic intends to enlarge its difficulties and responsibilities while simultaneously undermining its ability to bear them. In short, there is too much resentment of outside criticism and too little effort toward vigorous internal criticism. In some instances I found the establishment's rigidity frightening." [21]

In order to introduce more flexibility in the field of teacher training, Conant's major proposal contemplated shifting the responsibility for such programs from the various state departments of education to the approximately 1,150 American colleges and universities which educated teachers. The state under this plan would require only that each prospective teacher be a college graduate who had demonstrated competence during a period of practice teaching in a public school approved by the state's authorities. There the candidate would have been supervised by selected public school teachers and by a "clinical professor of education" from his college. This prescribed practice-teaching program would last approximately half a semester, but aside from that each college was to be free to plan whatever new programs for teacher training it wished to introduce. The only other requirement would be that each college authorized by the public authorities to grant teaching certificates testify that "the institution *as a whole* considers the person adequately prepared to teach in a designated field and grade level." The purpose of this provision was to make certain that responsibility for effective teacher training was placed on the entire faculty involved. In this way professors in the liberal arts as well as those in professional education would have to assume an active role in teacher education. Neither side would be able to stand aloof and blame the other for any inadequacies which arose.[22]

Attracting even more comment than teacher training during the post-

[21] James Bryant Conant, *The Education of American Teachers* (New York: McGraw-Hill Book Company, 1963).
[22] *Ibid.*

World War II years was the evolution of the modern public high school. Some observers were pleased by the shape this institution was assuming, while others held serious reservations. Harl Douglass, who approved of the trend, wrote in 1956 that it was inevitable that the pattern of secondary education would reflect the changes which had occurred by the middle of the century in its student constituency. A much greater proportion of young people of high school age were attending and completing high school than ever before. And, said Douglass, a new type of adolescent had emerged. The interests of young people "have become so closely associated with the richer and more thrilling leisure activities open to them that the chances of success in designing a curriculum that is attractive to adolescents are not as great as formerly, except when the curriculum and teaching are more closely adapted to these interests."

Vigorously defending the life-adjustment approach to secondary education (the *Cardinal Principles Report* of 1918 he described as the "Magna Charta" of the modern high school curriculum), Douglass insisted that America was entering an epoch when individualistic virtues would be of less and less relevance and that, accordingly, "youth of today must possess another set of virtues, based upon the cooperative character of their age." The necessity for a revised high school curriculum in view of this situation was plain for all to see. Modern and "functional" theories, i.e., life-adjustment concepts, would increasingly dominate the procedures of the American secondary school. The old exclusivist college-preparatory orientation was dead, Douglass was happy to report. The only enemies of this line of development, in his opinion, were opponents of freedom of thought in public education and "intellectuals interested only in the book education of the very bright youngster." But the good sense of the American public had led it to repudiate all sabotaging attacks of this nature. "Improvement of secondary education goes steadily forward." [23]

Looking at developments from the other side of the pedagogical fence, Robert M. Hutchins found the intellectual quality of the American high school definitely to be deteriorating by the mid-fifties. The pressure toward "automatic promotion" was now such that the units above had difficulty in rejecting the graduates of the unit below. This meant that the high schools were blithely graduating great numbers of students who could not read, could not spell, could not build correct

[23] Harl Douglass, ed., *The High School Curriculum* (New York: The Ronald Press Company, 1956), pp. 2-9.

sentences. And, even more remarkable, many of these semi-literates were gaining admission to colleges and in some cases, no better prepared for intellectual work, going on to graduate school! [24]

Historian Henry Steele Commager, viewing trends in the high school with an equally jaundiced eye, complained in 1957 about the dominance of life-adjustment concepts. High schools had a duty as agents of social development, he argued, "to resist, rather than yield to, community pressures." If each generation of young were merely to be fitted to the existing order of things, Americans would end up, not with a dynamic society, but with a "Byzantine" type of civilization. While schools were a part of society, they should not, in Commager's opinion, be a complete mirror of society. They should offer "not a repetition of experience but a challenge to, and an extension of, experience." They should not be tranquilizers "but a conscience for society." All this potential, Commager warned, would be wasted if community reverence for the fetish of adaptation, adjustment, and conformity was yielded to without a fight.[25]

Seeking a mean between the preceding two extremes was former President of Harvard University Dr. James Bryant Conant, who, after his return from serving as ambassador to West Germany, began in 1957 a series of studies of American public schools for the Carnegie Corporation. In 1959 Conant published the first fruit of his extensive investigations, a volume entitled *The American High School Today*. The work approved of the basic direction of public secondary education in the United States but made a number of specific suggestions for improvement. Conant argued that the American "comprehensive" high school was a characteristic product of American society and had "come into being because of our economic history and our devotion to the ideals of equality of opportunity and equality of status." He was not one who felt that the highly selective system of European pre-university schools was superior to the American pattern, believing that there was too great a waste of potential talent where less than 20 per cent of youth were able to pursue a secondary education and an even smaller percentage went on to the university.

Having visited some 55 public high schools, Conant found their condition generally good and was of the opinion that most of the

---

[24] Hutchins, *Some Observations on American Education*, pp. 79-83.
[25] Henry Steele Commager, "A Historian Looks at the American High School," in Francis S. Chase and Harold Anderson, eds., *The High School in a New Era* (Chicago: University of Chicago Press, 1958), pp. 8-10.

schools which were unsatisfactory for one or more reasons could be made acceptable "by relatively minor changes." Academically talented students, he believed, were not working hard enough and were not being sufficiently challenged. Able boys were too often neglecting non-scientific subjects, while able girls were finding it too easy to neglect scientific ones. Small high schools were unable to maintain economically the range of offerings needed for an adequate program. As specific remedies, Conant suggested a drastic reduction in the number of small high schools through district reorganization; less emphasis on basketball, football, marching bands, and the like; individualized programs for every student instead of a few separate curriculum "tracks"; at least one year of required mathematics and one year of science for all; grouping of the students by ability, subject by subject; more highly diversified programs so that marketable skills could be developed; expanded programs for the academically talented; and special provision such as the Advanced Placement program for the highly gifted.[26]

Conant's report was greeted with criticism from both ends of the educational spectrum. One group charged that he was essentially a "whitewasher," guilty of servility to the established pattern. His remarks were nothing new; he was offering "first aid" rather than necessary basic reform. Others challenged his right to generalize his own individual subjective judgments into a program for "reform" of all American high schools. He was too obsessed with the quantitative time allotments devoted to subject matter subdivisions in the high school curriculum, they said. Concentrating on specifics, he had articulated no meaningful educational philosophy. He had too much of a Puritanical obsession with the magical efficacy of hard work *per se*. Defenders of Conant, on the other hand, praised what they regarded as the essential simplicity of his proposals and his rejection of extremes. His very pragmatism was his strength, they declared. He had "the scientist's capacity to tackle a great mass of facts, shake them down and refine them so that an opinion and a line of action emerges." [27]

Marvin Mayer, interested in the comparison between American schooling and western European education, questioned Conant's whole approach. How, he asked, could one recommend high school programs in terms of so many "years" to be taken in a particular subject when

---

[26] James B. Conant, *The American High School Today* (New York: McGraw-Hill Book Company, 1959), pp. 2-6, 40-63.

[27] Stephen M. Corey, "The Conant Report on the American High School," *The Educational Forum* (November 1959), pp. 7-9.

there was no uniformity in American secondary education which would guarantee a minimum amount of learning in all schools within a stated period of time? On the whole, Mayer took a much less enthusiastic view of the American high school than did Conant. To Mayer it appeared to be "a monstrously inefficient operation. . . . Teaching methods and the technology of education are astonishingly ill-developed." Nevertheless Mayer felt that American high school students were working hard. The problem, he declared, was more one of wasted effort and wasted time than lack of effort.[28]

Mayer also questioned Conant's sharp distinction between the rigid selectivity of European secondary education and the contrasting "comprehensiveness" of the American version. He conceded that in Britain, for example, secondary education was based upon a process not so much of selection as elimination. But he went on to ask whether the English system which had developed since World War II was not in a real sense more democratic than the American. "In the United States, the quality of education which a child receives is strongly influenced at all times by the social status of his parents. Children of middle-class people elect the academic program in the high school and often continue to college, regardless of any native deficiencies in talent for academic work. . . . In England, . . . a child's schooling is influenced almost entirely by his individual talents—as measured, of course, by tests. The English grammar school has a rigidly maintained 'I.Q. cut-off point,' below which nobody, whatever his parents do for a living, may be admitted to secondary education." [29]

As a further illustration that "the notion that European school systems select and American school systems take everybody" was pure "mythology," Mayer pointed out that the task performed by such selective examinations as the "eleven plus" in England was accomplished in the United States "through the mechanism of the elective system, especially at entrance to the ninth grade." The only difference from the European system, he argued, was that Americans "will try to put at least half the kids in a junior high school into an academic program and let them find out 'on the job' whether or not they can handle it." Thus, in his view, "despite all the printed propaganda," the aim was "not to *avoid* selection but to make the selection in the most equitable and even charitable way." In any event, Mayer was certain that the

---

[28] Marvin Mayer, *The Schools* (New York: Harper & Row, Publishers, 1961), pp. 320-24.

[29] *Ibid.*, pp. 140-47.

"general" and "business" programs which great numbers of children were electing in American high schools were "not secondary education at all—they are postprimary education very similar in most respects to the *cours de fin d'etudes* in France, the secondary modern school in Britain, and the continuation folk school in Finland."

The tyranny of "Carnegie Units" over the secondary school curriculum only re-enforced for Mayer what he believed was the real weakness in the American high school—the national obsession with the "all-around" student. "Only in the United States," he wrote plaintively, "is it believed that an 'A' student is 'A' in everything, or that 'academically talented' children should spread themselves thin through secondary education (and even through the first two years of college, under the new 'general education' programs) by swallowing an equal bite of every intellectual goody in the school showcase." Why, he asked, must American educators take the ideal of Renaissance Man as their model? Logically, since there were no European-style national examinations imposed on the American high school and hence no need "to construct false fronts," one would expect to find its program "studded with courses for beginning specialists." But such was not the case. The result of such curricular comprehensiveness was "that combination of glibness and shallowness which is so glowingly rewarded on the College Board examinations—and then so bitterly condemned the next year by the college freshman, who complains that his high school never taught him 'how to study' or 'how to think.' " [30]

According to Marvin Mayer, the worst crisis through which the American high school passed during the 1950's was the deterioration of its vocationally oriented segment. "Blue collar" jobs considerably decreased in number during these years while average income increased and more and more parents began to think of college for their children. As a result the quality of children on the vocational track dropped until it came to reflect *only the bottom third* of the intelligence distribution. It was to the many ramifications of this and related problems that Dr. Conant and his research associates directed attention in another one of their major reports *Slums and Suburbs*, published in 1961. Conant agreed with Mayer's facts with respect to the decline and retrogradation of vocational schools, particularly those located in the slum sections of great metropolitan areas. "Social dynamite" was building up in such neighborhoods, the report disclosed, because of the large number of unemployed, out-of-school youth, especially in Negro slums.

[30] *Ibid.*, pp. 287-90, 327-30.

In some neighborhoods of this type "over half of the boys between 16 and 21 are out of school and out of work." [31]

What was to be done? Conant presented a series of specific proposals which he felt could alleviate the situation. Other critics before him had either found that the problem of the slum school in modern America could not easily be made to yield to any pat formula[32] or, as in the case of Miss Joan Dunn, had concluded that it was magnified by the persistent effort to apply a philosophy of education—child-centered progressivism—which was ludicrously unworkable in an urban slum setting.[33] Conant, however, was willing to step in where others had feared to tread. His plan included the development of "meaningful" courses for youth with less than average ability. "To this end," he recommended, "consideration should be given by every school and community to the expansion of work-study programs for slow students, and to the provision of at least an auto mechanics shop for boys in every high school in the metropolitan areas." In addition, he proposed to hold the public schools responsible for both the educational and vocational guidance of all out-of-school youths until they reached the age of twenty-one. Finally, he warned that Americans must make improvement of slum-area high schools a high priority task and must for this purpose spend more money on them, upgrade their programs, and probably pay specially trained teachers in them more than the staff members of schools in high income areas.[34]

A particularly revealing aspect of Conant's *Slums and Suburbs* report was that it did not stress the unifying theme of democratic "comprehensiveness" to the extent that had been true in his earlier reports. Instead a new note was sounded, one which brought his position a little closer to those who in the Forties and Fifties had been making a radical critique of the "life-adjustment," "secondary and post-secondary education-for-all" point of view. Having closely studied "education for all" in slum high schools and suburban high schools, Dr. Conant had now come to realize that "dramatic contrasts" existed between them. "The contrast in the money available to the schools in a wealthy suburb and to the schools in a large city," he wrote, "jolts one's notions of the

[31] James B. Conant, *Slums and Suburbs* (New York: McGraw-Hill Book Company, 1961), pp. 41-47, 145-47.

[32] Charles Calitri, *Strike Heaven on the Face* (New York: Crown Publications, Inc., 1958); Evan Hunter, *Blackboard Jungle* (New York: Simon and Schuster, Inc., 1954).

[33] Joan Dunn, *Retreat from Learning* (New York: David McKay Co., Inc., 1955).

[34] Conant, *Slums and Suburbs*, pp. 144-46.

meaning of equality of opportunity." Clearly a program which might be suitable for one kind of high school constituency might be wasted on another. Indeed, under certain circumstances, he was now convinced, it would be ridiculous to expect a certain segment of youth to pursue high school studies with profit. It was impossible, he said, even to talk about education "without specifying the kinds of homes from which the pupils came." Or, to put it another way," to speak eloquently about raising standards is of little help unless one specifies what kinds of schools one is considering and defines accurately what is meant by the words 'academic standards.' " [35]

Granted that these differences did exist in the public schools, what suggestions did Conant have to make with respect to schools in wealthy suburbs? Here the important thing to do, he indicated, was to check the unreasonable but aspiring ambitions of parents whose children lacked qualifications for college. As a related move, Conant favored greatly extending the junior college idea to take enrollment pressure off four-year colleges. He also advocated making admission to graduate and professional schools contingent upon passage of an examination that would test "wide and solid academic education." Such a requirement at the last rung of the educational ladder would, in his opinion, stiffen standards all the way down the line. Finally, in the well-financed suburban high schools, he believed it to be both possible and desirable "to create a climate of opinion that will encourage bright students to elect the kind of wide program that is required of students in the Bronx High School of Science," a school considered by Dr. Conant to be the most highly selective secondary school, public or private, in the United States.[36]

In general, American critics were vocal not only about high schools, but also about a host of other aspects of the schools in the post-World War II years. As we have already indicated, they were more inclined to find fault than to heap praise. Increasingly, too, their spleen was vented on modern and progressivist trends in curriculum and methodology. Lawrence Cremin calls the resultant furor "the most vigorous, searching, and fundamental attack on progressive education since the beginning of the movement." [37] Some of this criticism emanated from local taxpayers groups or national lobbying groups of a marked "rightist"

[35] *Ibid.*, pp. 5-21.
[36] *Ibid.*, pp. 46-51, 110-16, 134-46.
[37] Cremin, *The Transformation of the School*, pp. 339-43; for another review of the postwar critical onslaught, see V. T. Thayer, *The Role of the School in American Society* (New York: Dodd, Mead & Co., 1960), pp. 315-50.

orientation like Allan Zoll's National Council for American Education. However, much of it was advanced by public-spirited citizens with no particular axe to grind.

In 1949 two nonpolitical commentaries appeared. The first of these, Bernard I. Bell's *Crisis in Education*, frankly sought "to point out not the virtues of American education, which are considerable, but rather its faults." Reverend Bell was doubtful that "any improvement worth mentioning can come to our society as long as educators are wholly the obedient servants of the Common Man." What was needed, he felt, was better teacher training, more adequate financial support of the schools, less political interference, smaller classes, and less waste of the student's time. America must attempt more consistently and consciously than it had done thus far to seek out and cultivate superior brain power. In connection with this basic intellectualist purpose, wrote Bell, "the schools should refuse to assume burdens properly parental; they have quite enough to do without that." American public education, he concluded, lacked above all else a fundamental purpose, and to attain such it would have to teach moral values or in a broad sense "religion," if one preferred the latter term. Only then could the nation's culture attain a meaningful unity and direction.[38]

The second of these works, Mortimer Smith's *And Madly Teach*, paralleled Bell's criticisms in many respects but made a much sharper attack than the latter upon educational administrators and professors of education. In Smith's opinion, these worthies were responsible for the low intellectual quality of American schooling. Their anti-intellectualism, however, only reflected the fundamental outlook of the culture and for this reason, he remarked sardonically, was immensely popular. While public schoolmen were boasting that they were "freeing the child's personality" by doing away with academic authoritarianism, they were meanwhile exalting a new authority, the authority of the social mass. In so doing, they were helping to produce automatons ripe for exploitation by unscrupulous political demagogues, newspaper publishers, movie producers, and the like. Anticipating the later sociological formulations of William Whyte, Jr., and David Riesman, Smith observed:

> In the contemporary spiritual atmosphere of American society, and of the schools as part of that society, the public schoolman is admirably

[38] Bernard I. Bell, *Crisis in Education* (New York: McGraw-Hill, Inc., 1949), pp. 200-228.

fitted to the job. He is giving the customers what they want: Did not a recent nationwide survey reveal that 71,000 high school students think the first aim of education is How to Earn a Living? Why should he risk his job and his reputation by going against the trend? His own schooling emphasized social, not individual, considerations and inculcated in him a respect for majority opinion and the ideas and ideals of the collective. He can only be suspicious of true education, intellectualism, culture, and individualism. These call for qualities that are inimical to herd ideals: such qualities as independence, personal responsibility, personal conviction, and moral judgment.[39]

In 1953 an acidulous critique of many trends in American public education was produced by former school board member Albert Lynd. In this strongly worded volume, Lynd spelled out quite as vividly as Smith the responsibility of vested interests among the professional "Educationists" for the intellectual demoralization of American schools. Although the progressive education movement was singled out by the author as lending itself admirably to the generation of "oceans of piffle" in the classroom, he conceded that "quackery" in the schools was not necessarily "related to any particular theory or technique of education." Rather he felt that it was "a product of Educationism itself as a self-aggrandizing enterprise." Ironically, Lynd pointed out, these same "Educationists" were demanding absolute immunity from lay criticism as a group of professionals. Any disagreement with their precepts, whatever they might be, immediately labeled one as an "enemy of the public schools." Such a position, Lynd remarked, amounted to an "insistence that a professional enterprise may not be honestly criticized without the sanction of its operators." He then continued:

> The temptation offered to Educationists to inflate their course offerings to meet the demand of a market rigged by themselves is the heart of the quackery problem. . . . The Education lobby is usually well organized. Upstate lawmakers are easily impressed by the academic trappings of its spokesmen, by their specious identification of Education with education, and by their insinuation that their opponents are "enemies of the public schools" and therefore enemies of our children. . . .[40]

Proposing remedies for the situation, Lynd suggested that laymen become better informed on educational problems and play a more ac-

---

[39] Mortimer Smith, *And Madly Teach* (Chicago: Henry Regnery Co., 1949), p. 82; see also pp. 78-81, 91-94.

[40] Albert Lynd, *Quackery in the Public Schools* (Boston: Little, Brown & Co., 1953), pp. 266-68.

tive role, particularly on local school boards, in determining basic educational policy. If this were possible, he was somewhat more confident than Smith that the advocates of pragmatism, progressivism, and the empire-building interests of the "Educationist's" lobby would not have their way so easily. As a first step, Lynd felt that citizens should strongly support increased salaries for public school teachers. Yet he conceded that better pay would not automatically attract better minds to the American teaching profession. It was further necessary, along with the higher salary scales, for the citizenry and their school board to exercise vigilance over the quality of persons employed. Nevertheless he noted that, human nature being what it was, better talent would be attracted to a career in teaching if it came to be known that it was compensated at least as well as some of the other professions. And once this happened, there would be improvement all along the line because "joker courses could not be offered to sharp-witted students." Very soon "the most absurd offerings [of the Education faculties] would die on the vine." [41]

Much more widely discussed than the disquisitions of Smith, Bell, or Lynd were the observations of a professor of history at the University of Illinois. In 1952 Professor Arthur E. Bestor submitted a series of resolutions to the Council of the American Historical Association deploring "the growth of anti-intellectualist conceptions of education among important groups of school administrators and educational theorists" and calling upon the Association to join with other learned societies in creating a commission of scholars to scrutinize programs of teacher training, systems of teacher certification, and the structure of educational administration with the aim of preserving and strengthening "disciplined intellectual training in the schools." While not endorsing Bestor's resolution, the historians' ruling council in December, 1952, voted cautiously to authorize its incoming president to appoint a committee to formulate a statement of policy on the subject and "to approach the other learned societies and professional educators on the subject of a common position relative to the problem." [42]

Bestor further enunciated his views in a series of strongly worded articles which appeared in the *American Scholar, Scientific Monthly,* the *AAUP Bulletin,* and the *New Republic.* Then, in 1953 he brought his commentaries together in one explosive volume *Educational Waste-*

[41] *Ibid.,* pp. 256-57; see also pp. 258-82.
[42] "Resolutions Concerning Public Education," *School and Society* (January 31, 1953), pp. 68-70.

lands. Belaboring the baleful influence in the public schools of what he termed an "interlocking directorate" of educationists, he noted that "the acumen that is necessary to manage the organizational details of such an enterprise successfully is not precisely the same as the knowledge and discernment that are necessary to determine the intellectual content of programs that are conducted within these well-ordered school buildings." Once recognized scholars had furnished indispensable counsel to schoolmen with respect to the main subject-matter areas, but now this was no longer the case. The life-adjustment philosophy of the professional "educationalists" now ruled the school curriculum and was robbing it of meaningful content. As a result, anti-intellectualism was rife and true learning was all but submerged. His conclusion was rather grim:

> Across the educational world today stretches an iron curtain which the professional educationists are busily fashioning. Behind it, in slave-labor camps, are the classroom teachers, whose only hope of rescue is from without. . . . American intellectual life is threatened because the first 12 years of formal schooling in the United States are putting education more and more completely under the policy-making control of a new breed of educator who has no real place in it—who does not respect and is not respected by—the world of scientists, scholars, and professionals.[43]

Two years later Bestor increased his onslaught with a new volume *The Restoration of Learning.* This latest publication restated and expanded the professor's argument and presented a long-range program for reformation. It was a scandal, he asserted, that after "nine full years of formal schooling a student need not be expected to read his mother tongue or to know the multiplication table." What American public schools should seek to produce, said Bestor, was the disciplined mind, a mind which had attained command of written English, foreign languages, mathematics, and methods of abstract reasoning. Such intellectual abilities were required "not merely as prerequisites for advanced study, but also and especially for intelligent participation in the private and public affairs of a world where decisions must be made on the basis of informed and accurate thinking about science, about economics, about history and politics." The kind of training which was becoming increasingly predominant in American schools, namely, vocational and life-adjustment education, led not to liberation but to servile depend-

---

[43] Arthur E. Bestor, *Educational Wastelands* (Urbana, Ill.: University of Illinois Press, 1953), p. 121; see also pp. 95-118.

ence. Originality, reason, and common sense were ignored, while formulas, tricks-of-the-trade, and "glorified baby-sitting" were at the forefront. Far from upholding democracy in education, Bestor declared, such an approach revealed "a contemptuous lack of faith" in the contemporary age of universal schooling and "in the native good sense of the common man." And who were the villains? Bestor insisted once again that by accepting "the unfounded pretensions of so-called professors of education, we have permitted the content of public school instruction to be determined by a narrow group of specialists in pedagogy. We have permitted them, moreover, to sever all real connection between the public schools and the great world of science and learning." [44]

What was to be done? Bestor's blueprint centered upon the key proposition that qualified scholars in the liberal arts should reassert, with the backing of the general public, an effective control over the content of courses in the public schools and the training of teachers in those schools. The degrees of Master of Education and Doctor of Education should be reorganized and made to rest upon a much larger amount of liberal arts work than was currently the case. Professors of Education would be confined to presentation of the techniques of pedagogy and would be replaced by subject-matter specialists in the various arts and science fields. For example, courses in the teaching of mathematics would be handled by the department of mathematics. In addition, professors of the liberal arts would exercise vigilance over the accrediting of secondary schools and colleges and would work to do away with the methods-oriented teacher certification requirements which the interlocking educationist directorate had succeeded in writing into the legislative codes of the several states. In this connection, Bestor suggested that a national commission of educators, scholars, and citizens be set up to formulate new norms of teacher certification which would be more flexible than existing ones with respect to course work in pedagogy and more demanding in terms of basic subject-matter preparation.[45]

Bestor's two provocative books created a veritable storm of controversy in American education. Praised by like-minded individuals such as Smith and Lynd, his proposals were, nevertheless, attacked in the *Saturday Review of Literature* by Professor Maurice Ahrens of the Uni-

---

[44] Arthur E. Bestor, *The Restoration of Learning* (New York: Alfred A. Knopf, Inc., 1955).
[45] *Ibid.*

versity of Florida's school of education as based on a "stacked" selection
of sources, marred by sweeping generalizations without supporting data,
unenlightened by visits to actual public school classrooms, and, in general, "impractical, unrealistic, and fantastic." [46] V. T. Thayer maintained in 1960 that Bestor's remedy was "the familiar one of avoiding
the evils of one extreme by rebounding violently to another." [47] And
Lawrence Cremin pointed out the great reversal which had occurred
here. "Whereas Joseph Mayer Rice in the Nineties had called upon
the public to reform the schools by creating a new class of professionals
who would manage education according to scientific principles, Bestor
was now calling upon that same public to undo the damage of the
professionals by returning the schools to the arts and science professors." [48] In any event, Bestor's arguments made a considerable impact
upon the thinking of members of liberal arts faculties in various colleges and universities as well as on the general public. And in 1956 a
Council of Basic Education was established to advance his ideas.

As the battle between critics and defenders of existing practices in
the schools waxed hotter and hotter, some observers sought to appraise
the situation from a middle ground between the two extremes, which
they felt would give an opportunity for a more balanced and realistic
analysis of American education at mid-century. One such commentator
was sociologist David Riesman, who in a little book of essays published
in 1957 noted that the evil results attributed by critics like Bestor and
Smith to the progressive education movement and the life-adjustment
philosophy of the "educationists" had deeper and more complex reasons. Essentially, Riesman contended, these problems arose as a consequence of "the dilemmas of democratic education itself." And as a
result, he added, they could *not* be "simply . . . willed away if only one
could restore the classical curriculum and discover an elite to administer
. . . it." For one thing that the Bestors and Smiths forgot, said Riesman, was that the progressive educators did not intend originally to
dilute the intellectuality of the schools, but to add to it. They were
educational pioneers, seeking to break down the entrenched prejudices
and apathies of hidebound educational administrators. Men like Dewey
wanted to utilize "emotional and group-anchored life" for the support
of intellect, not for the destruction of it. Thus progressivism "in its

---

[46] Maurice R. Ahrens, "Redeeming American Education? No," *Saturday Review
of Literature* (1955), p. 31.
[47] Thayer, *The Role of the School in American Society.*
[48] Cremin, *The Transformation of the School*, p. 346.

original impetus was counter-cyclical; it was an all-out attack on the Colonel Blimps of the school world, on cruelty and one-sidedness, on uniformity of curriculum and pacing." [49]

But what went wrong with the progressive ideal? Riesman believed that "something of a short circuit in the communication of ideas" occurred. Originally performing an emancipating function in a "restricted and constrictive home and school setting," by mid-century so-called Progressive education had very often "become simply an excuse for friendly torpor, far from the aims of the movement's founders." Instead of being a liberating movement, it had now hardened into a series of formulas and catch-words which were repeated mechanically with less and less real meaning. Worse, its true purport was twisted and distorted to justify the abandonment of serious content courses. In other words,

> progressive education now serves in many prosperous communities to deprive the more studious of challenges they could well endure and profit from and to give their teachers a high-minded excuse for being distracted from devotion to their subjects, in exchange for devotion to cultivating an harmonious and democratic classroom atmosphere.[50]

The important point, according to Riesman, was that this outcome could not justly be laid at the door of progressive education *per se*. Rather one must keep in mind the altered context in which progressive education attempted to function, most particularly the situation created by mass education through the immense increase in the number of American youth who attended high school. Under these circumstances many crimes were committed in the name of progressive education. That movement was used as an excuse to drop serious study of content and to come to terms with the lowest common denominator in the new mass clientele which overwhelmed the schools. Children were encouraged, in a new context of American family life, to gain a precocious social poise and "adjustment" at the expense of ordered and disciplined intellectual development. But, Riesman asked, was the culprit here the authentic and original progressive education approach or the mass culture itself? The pendulum had swung far enough, he concluded, in the direction of developing the social capabilities and *savoir faire* of American young people. What seemed to be needed now in the schools was

---

[49] David Riesman, *Constraint and Variety in American Education* (Garden City, N.Y.: Doubleday & Company, Inc., 1958), pp. 143-50.

[50] *Ibid.*, p. 129.

a new "counter-cyclical" policy, one which would stress the importance of intellectual values. Many American schools, seeking to make
up for deficiencies of earlier days, were giving their youngsters what
amounted to a post-graduate course in social relations "when what
they most need is something very different, namely, protection for certain long-term intellectual and humanistic interests that are momentarily
under pressure and apt to be squeezed out." [51]

Even more middle-of-the-road was an overview of American schools
published in the same year that Bestor's dynamite-laden treatise appeared. This was Paul Woodring's *Let's Talk Sense about Our Schools*.
Woodring, then a professor of psychology at the Western Washington
College of Education, argued that much of the public criticism directed
at American schoolmen was inconsistent. The critics were demanding
more emphasis upon the fundamentals, but they had failed to decide
among themselves what *was* fundamental. Americans generally had an
almost too exalted conception of the powers of formal schooling. As
a result, they made exaggerated and contradictory demands upon the
public schools. While insisting upon the right of every youth to a
high school education, they "have inconsistently blamed the teachers
for the lowering of academic standards which inevitably resulted. They
have asked the schools to eliminate fads and frills. At the same time
they have formed themselves into very powerful pressure groups which
insist that the local high school maintain a winning football team and
a marching band." [52]

It was Woodring's main contention that American public schools
in 1953 were "neither so bad as some critics have said nor so good as
our publicity agents make them appear." The worst problem, in his
opinion, was the confused thinking about education in America, the
lack of a coherent philosophy. As for the teachers' roles,

> The best thing about contemporary education is that a great many class-
> room teachers ignore the gobbledy-gook and the pedaguese and go right
> ahead and do a sensible job of teaching. If one visits the classrooms instead
> of reading the journals, he may well conclude that the schools are not so
> bad after all. It all depends on which classroom you visit.[53]

The successful launching of Sputnik I into space by Soviet Russia
in the fall of 1957 introduced, as we have seen, a new note of urgency

[51] *Ibid.*, pp. 143-74.
[52] Paul Woodring, *Let's Talk Sense about Our Schools* (New York: McGraw-
Hill Book Company, 1953).
[53] *Ibid.*, p. 197.

into the analyses of schools made by American writers (see Chap. 5). The voices raised at this time all agreed that American education could not afford to rest on its laurels, that it must institute drastic and sweeping changes if it was to meet the challenges of the hour.

Some of the most perceptive writing on these problems came from the pen of Myron Lieberman, a rigorous and thoughtful critic of the structure of American public education. In previous years commentators such as Bell, Lynd, Smith, Bestor, and even Conant had aimed their evaluations at the general public, holding that informed laymen could, through community action, bring about necessary changes in American schools. Lieberman's approach was entirely different. In two controversial books and also in articles in leading magazines, he argued that interference by the public would harm the schools more than it would help them and that American education could only be improved by the building up of a powerful, highly organized teaching profession.

In his first compendious work *Education As a Profession*, which appeared in 1956, Lieberman flatly stated that: "A genuine profession of education would not accept *any* lay determination, either local, state, or federal, of what to teach and how to teach it." [54] In his next important work *The Future of Public Education*, he attributed whatever ineffectiveness existed in American schools to the "anachronistic and dysfunctional power structure" of public education. Contributing to this weakness, in his opinion, was the lack of real power of such organizations as the National Education Association, the American Federation of Teachers, and the American Association of University Professors. Another principal villain in Lieberman's estimation was the continuing American "myth" of the necessity for preserving local control of public schools. He was certain that "local control of education has clearly outlived its usefulness . . . and must give way to a system of educational controls in which local communities play ceremonial rather than policy-making roles."

At the end of the volume the author listed a number of propositions which, if put into effect, would in his view vitalize and improve American public education. The essence of his proposal was the building up of stronger national organizations of teachers which would displace existing professional bodies in the field. These new associations would be bolstered by compulsory membership provisions and financed by high dues collected by a check-off system. They would come to have

[54] Myron Lieberman, *Education As a Profession* (Englewood Cliffs, N.J.: Prentice-Hall, Inc., 1956).

more power over the schools than local supervisory boards of laymen. They would control entry into the teaching profession and set national qualitative standards for teacher training and certification. They would also be in a position to enforce a standard national teaching contract on local employing authorities. This contract would maintain conditions of employment and prerequisites for advancement on a uniformly high professional level.[55]

Particularly interesting in this concluding section was Lieberman's denial of the traditional concept that in America the schools had always been close to the people. Public education in the mid-twentieth century, was not at all in the mainstream of American life. To prove this thesis, he cited the fact that elections to school boards usually attracted a smaller turnout than elections to any other public office. Furthermore, he said, few, if any, of the leading persons working in the field of public education ever became nationally known personalities. In addition, no great American newspaper had a daily interpretive column on the subject of schools and their problems. In general, Lieberman noted, the facts indicated a widespread public indifference to the schools despite all the brave talk about American grass-roots concern with public education.[56]

In spite of the appearance of Lieberman's pleas for more professionalism, the drive for reform of the schools by laymen had by no means spent its force in the post-Sputnik period. Symbolizing this continuing crusade, there now came forward one of the nation's most renowned and articulate citizens to battle for the cause, the "father" of the atomic-powered submarine, Admiral Hyman Rickover, USN. The Admiral's interest in promoting educational reform went back at least as far as 1947, when he began a long and frustrating search for technical personnel to join the Navy's atomic reactor program. Finding few critical, probing minds among the thousands of well-educated young Americans who were considered for membership in the program, Rickover began to investigate conditions in the nation's schools in an effort to find an explanation for this deficiency. Increasingly he was drawn to a position which was very much like that of Professor Bestor's Council on Basic Education. Because of a real gift for dramatic, searing language and a talent for attracting national publicity, Rickover managed in time to

[55] Myron Lieberman, *The Future of Public Education* (Chicago, Ill.: University of Chicago Press, 1960), pp. 272-83. See also *idem*, "Four Myths Cripple Our Schools," *The Nation* (February 28, 1959), pp. 179-85; *idem*, "Education for Tomorrow: 67 Theses," *School and Society* (January 16, 1960), pp. 34-38.

[56] Lieberman, *The Future of Public Education*, pp. 283-85.

get under the hide of many of the nation's educational administrators and professors of education more thoroughly than Bestor had ever done. The Admiral even came to be seriously mentioned at one time as a possible candidate for United States Commissioner of Education.[57]

Rickover, equally with Bestor, felt that professional administrators had had a noisome effect upon American schools, but because of the Admiral's frustrating experiences with Navy and industrial bureaucracy, he was able to view the problem in a much broader context. The trouble, as he saw it, was not only with educational administrators of the "interlocking directorate," but with *all* the pompous, semi-educated, "practical," stuffed-shirt type administrators of an overly bureaucratized, increasingly conformist age. Speaking at an anniversary dinner for the Roosevelt Hospital in New York City, Rickover declared on October 29, 1959, that the United States was handicapped in its scientific race with Russia by "overadministration." Medical doctors, he pointed out, had been able to retain their high professional standing because they would "never submit to orders from a layman" on how to diagnose a disease or treat a patient. But, he said, this was not true of professional men in government agencies or in public schools. "Good professional people," he asserted, "have a high I.Q. that puts them in the top 1 or 2 per cent of our population; in bureaucracies, they are commonly the subordinates of men of substantially lower intellect."

This situation was most marked in the United States, he continued, because periodically the passionate American belief in the equality of man "deteriorates into egalitarianism and hostility to all that is excellent." Furthermore, he noted,

> The administrative head of a large bureaucracy is the nearest equivalent we have to an absolute monarch—something of an anachronism in a democratic society. He runs his bureaucracy in an authoritarian manner; he expects unquestioning obedience from his subordinates, even in matters in which they are expert and he is ignorant; he tolerates no criticism of his organization from within or from without.
>
> This excessive power of administration is a consequence of our respect for concrete things . . . and our disrespect for things of the intellect, for the highly endowed and rigorously educated professional expert whose only capital is his excellent mind.

This state of affairs very definitely prevailed in the world of education as in other areas of American culture, Rickover said. Public education

[57] *New York Times,* September 13, 1962, p. 23.

was in his opinion a "high bureaucracy dominated by all sorts of non-teaching people—people trained as administrators, athletes, guidance counselors, public relations men, sociologists, and what have you."

Rickover presented his solution to remedy these conditions in *Education and Freedom*, a book which appeared in 1959, the same year as the above-mentioned speech. First of all, he emphasized, Americans must realize that their public schools had accomplished their original priority tasks of "Americanization" and acculturation. "This job is finished. The schools must now tackle a different job. They must concentrate on bringing the intellectual powers of each child to the highest possible level. Even the average child now needs almost as good an education as the average middle- and upper-class child used to get in the college-preparatory schools." And how was this to be done? Here the Admiral brought forward a proposal which he had been supporting publicly for two years or more. Private organizations in the fields of labor and industry and the great foundations should sponsor on an experimental basis the founding of approximately 25 demonstration high schools in various parts of the country. They would be frankly elitist schools, aiming to provide superior free education to the academically talented. Admission and promotion would be on the basis of intellectual merit only. Students would be encouraged to accelerate and complete their total secondary program in four years instead of the present six. The teaching staff in these demonstration schools would be of uniformly high intellectual calibre and would have no extra curricular assignments. "The schools would be scholastic institutions, so social activities would be kept at a minimum." Furthermore, these institutions were to achieve a ratio of at least 1 teacher for every 20 pupils.

The aim of the demonstration schools, wrote Rickover, would be to show that a broad liberal-arts education could be obtained in America by academically talented students in no more than 14 years. Also, unlike Conant, the Admiral believed that it would be a positive advantage to "remove the serious students from the atmosphere of trivialities and easy school life to one where everyone is concerned with matters of the intellect. . . . The students would be no more one-sided 'oddballs' than are the students at Eton or in the academic secondary schools of Europe." The program could be started at once by private subsidy, he noted, and would produce "in the quickest possible time professionals trained in the humanities as well as in the sciences and mathematics." It was Rickover's hope that at the end of a trial period of perhaps five years, the demonstration high schools would have proved their worth so unmistakably that local communities would then be anxious to take them over and operate them as public institutions, while maintaining the already-established high standards.[58]

Like Bestor and Lieberman, Admiral Rickover was greatly impressed with the need for establishing high national standards for American student and teacher competence. For this reason he elaborated in *Education and Freedom* upon a suggestion which came to him originally from the Council on Basic Education. According to this plan a special board would be set up on a voluntary, constitutional basis to introduce uniform standards into American education. A private agency in the form of a national council of scholars, financed by the colleges, universities, and educational foundations, would establish national standards for the high school diploma and for the scholastic competence of teachers. "High schools accepting this standard would receive council accreditation, somewhat on the order of the accreditation given medical schools and hospitals. Teachers would receive a special certificate if they completed the requisite course of studies." [59]

To prove his point that a separate system of highly selective public schools with a liberal arts orientation was not incompatible with a free, federated, democratic society, Rickover turned in 1962 to the example of Switzerland. In *Swiss Schools and Ours: Why Theirs are Better*, the Admiral observed that the Swiss managed more successfully than the Americans to maintain a whole spectrum of public education for all levels of their people, not just university-bound children, and that the Swiss second and third levels were sometimes qualitatively better than the American top levels. Moreover, Swiss universities (which were all public, low tuition, and academically excellent, with ten times more Nobel prize winners on a per capita basis than the United States) constituted the keystone of all Swiss education and set national scholastic standards which either directly or indirectly affected all other levels of schooling in the country. In Switzerland, too, the teacher had a much higher status than in America. In the latter country, wrote Rickover, "ex-athletic coaches are often made school principals, on occasion even college presidents, incredible as this may seem. . . . Because we have always been much more impressed with practical than with learned

---

[58] Hyman G. Rickover, *Education and Freedom* (New York: E. P. Dutton & Co., Inc., 1959), pp. 208-15.
[59] *Ibid.*, pp. 216-18.

men, we habitually subordinate the latter to the former, even in enterprises devoted to learning." [60]

In May of 1962 the peppery Admiral went as a witness before the Committee on Appropriations of the U.S. House of Representatives to make yet another slashing attack upon what he might very well have labeled the "Boost-the-Boob" movement in American education. Schools in the United States should be teaching more English, mathematics, history, and science, he told the Committee, instead of "how to be likeable, lovable, and datable." American public schools had a built-in bias against the very bright because of the current emphasis on life-adjustment and social leveling. American education, to his way of thinking, moved "at the snail's pace of the child of average ability, average motivation, average home background." He recommended that the country adopt some of the practices characteristic of the British school system. This would include separate types of high schools for children of different ability levels and also standard examinations on basic subjects to be taken by students seeking nationally recognized accreditation. The latter system, Rickover pointed out, would help citizens judge objectively the performance of their local schools and would end much guesswork by college admission officials and prospective employers. "It surely is not federal tyranny," he said, "to ask that a diploma give an honest description of what the holder has accomplished scholastically. The ordinary person is just as much in need of help when he tries to judge a school or a diploma as when he looks at a cut of meat or a bottle of medicine." Rickover suggested that the existing College Entrance Examination Board tests might be expanded and, with the aid of public funds, used as the basis for the broader national certification and testing he proposed. The resultant program would be something like the English General Certification of Education or other national tests of this nature given in European countries. To oversee the machinery for such a testing program Congress might well sponsor the setting up of "a small committee of eminent, trustworthy, intelligent, and broadly educated men to keep American education under close scrutiny." Such a committee could uphold standards, keep duplication to a minimum, and support worthwhile educational projects. Rickover felt it would be comparable to the English Universities Grants Committee, a body which dispensed government funds but which had no

[60] Hyman G. Rickover, *Swiss Schools and Ours: Why Theirs are Better* (Boston: Atlantic-Little, Brown & Co., 1962).

power to interfere with the autonomy of British universities. The Admiral restated the essential argument presented before the Congressional Committee in a characteristically outspoken book which was published in 1963 entitled *American Education—A National Failure.*[61]

That Rickover's arguments were finding their mark in the nation's apprehensive post-Sputnik mood was indicated when the national certification proposal was publicly endorsed by United States Commissioner of Education Francis Keppel.[62] And, as we have already seen, Congressional concern with the necessity of up-grading the nation's intellectual standards was manifested as early as 1958 in the proceedings that led to the passage of the National Defense Education Act.[63] Sometimes, to be sure, the new Congressional enthusiasm for knowledge seemed to be rather uncertainly directed. Thus, in February, 1962, Senator Mike Mansfield reported that Senate subcommittee aides who distributed a questionnaire to a group of Marines to test their knowledge of communism asked the latter, among other things, to identify one "Ming-Se-tung." A Marine major asked his subcommittee interrogators whether "you don't mean 'Mao-tse-tung' (Chairman of the Chinese Communist Party)." The major was told: "We mean 'Ming.' " A sergeant who brought up the same point after completing the questionnaire was told: "We put that in to test you." Somewhat less ludicrous was the complaint of Dean William C. Warren of Columbia University's School of Law in 1957 that "the inability of college graduates who come to us to read and write is a malady of epidemic proportions." It was one of Dean Warren's frequently recurring dreams that some day his professional school would find applicants for admission who possessed "some ability to write grammatical and reasonably literate English prose" free from the "misspellings, the solecisms, and the abuse of language." [64]

In 1958, a group of 42 of America's most distinguished citizens and educators published a significant report entitled *The Pursuit of Excel-*

---

[61] Hyman G. Rickover, *American Education—A National Failure: The Problem of Our Schools and What We Can Learn From England* (New York: E. P. Dutton & Co., Inc., 1963). Admiral Rickover's testimony, though given on May 16, was not made public by the House Committee until September 2, 1962.

[62] *New York Times*, April 8, 1963, p. 21.

[63] *Collection of Excerpts and Bibliography* (Senate Document No. 109, 85th Congress, 2nd Session [Washington, D.C., 1958]).

[64] "Illiteracy of Law School Applicants," *School and Society* (March 2, 1957), p. 76.

lence[65] for the Rockefeller Brothers Fund. The report called attention to the nub of the educational problem with which embattled crusaders such as Bestor and Rickover were concerned. "By insisting that 'equality' means an exactly similar exposure to education, regardless of the variations in interest and capacity of the student, we are in fact inflicting a subtle but serious form of inequality upon our young people." Such a state of affairs, the Rockefeller Brothers panel insisted, was not in any way a necessary or an inevitable by-product of democracy. What democracy required as a *sine qua non* was equality of *opportunity*, but it did not demand as an inherent part of its basic structure that a people limit "the development of individual excellence in exchange for a uniformity of external treatment." Yet this is just what "the entire educational spectrum" in America was doing, declared the report. "Too many of our school systems have evolved into a lock step under which all young people start off together at the age of six and march forward one grade per year. Because many educators reject the idea of grouping by ability, the ablest students are often exposed to educational programs whose content is too thin and whose pace is too slow to challenge their abilities." [66]

[65] Among the notable educators and scholars who participated in the drafting of this report were John W. Gardner, President of the Carnegie Foundation, Fred M. Hechinger, educational journalist, J. Douglas Brown, Dean of Faculty, Princeton University, Philip Coombs, Director of Research, Fund for the Advancement of Education, Dael Wolfle, executive officer, American Association for the Advancement of Science, sociologist David Riesman, and economist Eli Ginzberg.
[66] *The Pursuit of Excellence*, Rockefeller Brothers Fund, Inc. (Garden City, New York: Doubleday & Company, Inc., 1958), pp. 12-15.

CHAPTER TEN

The School in the Making of Modern America

Much of what has been said thus far brings into sharp relief the fact that American education has acquired its basic direction from American democracy. This fixed course, as James B. Conant has said, was not very different at the midpoint of the twentieth century from what it had been at the beginning of the century.[1] If anything, the basic patterns were re-enforced by new developments, such as the vastly increased percentage of American youth now enrolled in high schools and colleges.

The necessity for mass education became apparent not only for America but for Europe and the whole world when, in the nineteenth century, industrialization and the scientific revolution began to transform ways of living. As we have seen, the response to the times by the settled, somewhat less mobile, European cultures was different from the American approach. Educational standards were more uniform than in America, and a frank differentiation between those going on for university and professional education and those going into a trade or industry was made at a much earlier age than in the United States. Americans, lacking a leisure class of feudal origins and possessing a pioneering society which had always frowned on the "idler" and dilet-

---

[1] James B. Conant, *The American High School Today* (New York: McGraw-Hill, Inc., 1959), p. 6.

tante, preferred to make a different kind of adjustment to industrialism and mass culture.[2] But the mere newness and rawness of the country is not enough to explain its deep-seated equalitarian commitment, a fact which becomes clear when we compare its schools with those, say, of New Zealand, Australia, or any of the Latin American republics.[3] Obviously there is a deep motivation in the American situation which goes beyond the mere exigencies of a new society or the favoring circumstances of a fluid social order.

One aspect which, as we have seen, played a particularly vital role in the United States was that of the "melting pot." Millions of immigrants and their children, representing practically every country of the world, had to be "Americanized" and molded to a common United States culture and citizenship. Public education was the chosen vehicle to accomplish this herculean task. Important, too, was the fact that, ever since the Revolution, Americans had been moving toward a definition of their political society that increasingly became an all-inclusive democratic one. By the middle of the nineteenth century this concept had triumphed in the form of universal suffrage and Jacksonian equalitarianism, reflecting concomitant realities in the socio-economic living patterns of the aggressive pioneering population. The logical educational counterpart was universal schooling aiming at a totally literate and responsible citizenry. When a "Second American Revolution" occurred after 1865 and made the New World democracy into a giant industrial-urban power, important new functions could be assigned to the people's schools. Machine power for the first time in history made it possible for all men to have leisure in which to seek the mental development that in earlier ages would have been an impossibility. The nation had now acquired the enormous wealth which made it more than merely theoretically possible to provide genuine education for all. The interests of humanitarians, social reformers, and labor leaders coincided at this point in demanding the raising of the school drop-out age and the replacement of traditional industrial apprenticeship patterns by a compulsory school attendance system. The proponents were able to rationalize this as an attempt, in the modern industrial age, to improve the conditions of human life, and particularly child life, by "welfare state" action. It was re-enforced by earlier American commitments to the

[2] See the interesting argument in Robert M. Hutchins, *Some Observations on American Education* (Cambridge, England: Cambridge University Press, 1956), esp. pp. 17-20.

[3] James B. Conant, *Education and Liberty* (Cambridge, Mass.: Harvard University Press, 1953), pp. 4-23.

unique value of every human person, derived from the combined impact of the country's twin Christian and rationalist-Enlightenment heritages. But the important point here is that the American people, as they entered the twentieth century, had reached a stage in their growth as a wealth-producing society where they could actually *afford* the luxury of maintaining a longer period of formalized schooling for *all* their children, even including their adolescents. What had previously been mere high-sounding theory could now be translated by national prosperity into operational fact.

In this kind of cultural context, it is not surprising that from time to time voices were heard in the land proclaiming not only that all American children must be formally educated on a more or less equal plane, but also that if any child had to drop out of school for academic reasons, this was a reflection on the school and not on the child. Moreover, the child must not be made to "feel bad" because of failure. This type of argument was to many twentieth-century Americans no *reductio ad absurdum*. To a number of progressive, "democratic"-minded educational theorists and administrators it seemed a most reasonable, almost irrefutable proposition. The famous Committee on the Reorganization of Secondary Education endorsed this position in its influential "Cardinal Principles" report.[4] And other American educational leaders independently articulated substantially the same ideas.

Dr. Luther H. Gulick, noted physical educationist, expressed the prevailing mood very well in 1910 when he wrote: "It is less expensive and more humane to give special help to a child so that he may be promoted than it is to degrade him with all the loss to the individual, the school, and the community which is involved." It was a national scandal, Gulick declared, that 250,000 school children in the United States had during the preceding year dropped out of school or failed to graduate. This situation could not be tolerated, he warned, because "the whole theory of democracy is based on the theory that the voters shall be intelligent." [5] Dr. Gulick had written a year earlier that the American public school could not consider itself to be a success if it merely trained the intellects of the individual pupils. Americans must also become group-directed. The pupil must "become trained to take his place and help on the whole social mechanism. He must become ad-

[4] *Cardinal Principles of Secondary Education*, Committee on the Reorganization of Secondary Education (U.S. Bureau of Education Bulletin No. 35 [Washington, D.C., 1918]), pp. 29-30.
[5] Luther H. Gulick, "Why 250,000 Children Quit School," *World's Work* (August 1910), pp. 1-5, 26-27.

justed to that harness of traditions which carries the results of our racial experiences and be prepared to take his place in maintaining the new race experiences of democracy, or self-group control." [6]

Returning to the theme of drop-outs, Gulick declared that teachers in America must become more flexible in defining the standards for promotion to the next school grade. Actually, all that should be asked for was the attainment of sufficient knowledge and skill to permit the next grade's work to be understood. And, according to Gulick, this involved in most years "only a fraction of the whole work covered." But, he continued,

> The objection raised is that this means lowering the standards. A high standard is one which secures the best and most effective and successful work from the pupil. Those standards are vicious and low which promote failure and discouragement. . . . A man teaching boys to jump, who would put the stick at such a height that a considerable number failed and stopped trying, would not be regarded as maintaining high standards. It is his business to teach boys to jump—not to discourage them so that they will leave the field.[7]

In the years that followed, particularly those after World War I, the fondest hopes of men like Gulick and the authors of the "Cardinal Principles" report were realized. Education for all, in the broadest sense of that term, became an actuality in America. The full effects of a rigorously enforced and vastly expanded compulsory attendance system began to be felt, and the public school became an all-important "socializing" and "acculturating" device. The "comprehensive," mass-enrollment public high school, seeking to unite in one and the same institution both the intellectual and the practical and aiming to do the best it could for each pupil, became a characteristic landmark of the American educational landscape. Where there had been only 519,250 students enrolled in such schools in 1900, by 1928 this total had already reached the amazing figure of 4,217,300.[8] More than any other aspect of American public education, the newly triumphant high school seemed to symbolize dramatically the nation's continuing faith in universal education and its determination to make the latter even more

[6] Luther H. Gulick, *Children of the Century* (New York: Russell Sage Foundation, 1909), p. 8.

[7] Gulick, *World's Work* (August 1910), pp. 26-27.

[8] I. L. Kandel, *History of Secondary Education* (Boston: Houghton Mifflin Company, 1930), pp. 482-83.

all-inconclusive than before, covering the needs of a great variety of interest groups and the widest possible range of ability levels.[9]

All of this was an inevitable reflection in the realm of education of the emergence in twentieth-century America of a mass culture which in turn was the product of an urban-industrial, mass-production society. Observers such as Valentine, Riesman, Packard, and Whyte have already delineated at length for us the sociological characteristics of the new era. Ernest Van den Haag sums them up as including "increased income, mobility, and leisure, more equally distributed; increased egalitarianism, communication, and education; more specialization and less scope for individuality in work." Explaining what he meant more fully, he pointed out that mass production aimed necessarily to please an average of tastes and, while catering to all to some extent, could not satisfy any individual taste fully. Furthermore, he noted, "The mass of men dislikes and always has disliked learning and art. It wishes to be distracted from life rather than to have it revealed; to be comforted by traditional (possibly happy and sentimental) tropes, rather than to be upset by new ones." Finally, this commentator observed another portentous social phenomenon stemming from an inherent gesellschaft orientation: "As a result of the high psychological and economic costs of individuality and privacy, gregariousness has become internalized. People fear solitude and unpopularity; popular approval becomes the only moral and aesthetic standard most people recognize." [10]

Developments such as these, it should be emphasized, were not limited, in the modern industrial age, to the North American culture. Thoughtful students of twentieth-century civilization, such as the Spaniard Ortega y Gasset and the Briton George Orwell, have called attention to the standardizing and group-dictated conforming patterns which have arisen necessarily as a consequence of the rise of the masses in the modern industrial matrix.[11] Such powerful influences were bound to affect concepts of schooling in Europe as well as in the United States,

[9] See the interesting discussion in David H. Russell, *Problems and Trends in American Education* (Brisbane, Australia: University of Queensland, 1960), pp. 5-12.

[10] Ernest Van den Haag, "A Dissent from the Consensual Society," in Norman Jacobs, ed., *Culture for the Millions* (Princeton, N.J.: D. Van Nostrand Co., Inc., 1959).

[11] See José Ortega y Gasset, *The Revolt of the Masses* (New York: W. W. Norton & Company, Inc., 1932); George Orwell, *Animal Farm* (New York: Harcourt, Brace & World, Inc., 1946); *idem*, *1984* (New York: Harcourt, Brace & World, Inc., 1949).

although in the former area they were somewhat slower to manifest themselves since the resistance offered by an older, settled, more traditional culture was stronger than in the New World. Although the idea of a general education for *all* continued as late as the 1950's to be considered ridiculous by many schoolmen in western Europe,[12] there were increasing signs that winds of change were beginning to sweep through that part of the world. By 1961 ambitious plans were being formulated in Britain to double the number of young people attending its colleges and universities during the succeeding ten years.[13] And a conference in 1958 of educators from 26 north European and Mediterranean countries agreed that a European secondary school "revolution," due to technical change and the pressures of population increase, was under way. Traditional classic courses were going to be broadened and a wider clientele served by the schools.[14] Soviet delegates at the conference boasted that their country had already attained these objectives, and indeed, a speech by Premier Nikita S. Khrushchev to the 13th Komsomol Congress on April 15, 1958, indicated that Soviet Russia had decided to reorganize its secondary school program on a new, more "practical," all-inclusive basis that would stress education for all rather than preparation for universities and other higher educational institutions.[15]

The historical imperative which was operating in these times seems clear. But what, we may ask, was its deeper meaning? What was the ultimate value of democratic education as it had developed in twentieth-century America? As we have noted, Americans have been among the most severe critics of American schools. In the years following World War II much of this fire was concentrated on so-called "life-adjustment" and "progressive" education. But it does not appear that many of the critics saw the problem in appropriate historical perspective or, for that matter, went to the heart of the subject in arriving at their conclusions. For example, the questions of the value of a child-centered curriculum, vocational training, or what contemporary jargon called "education for life" were hardly new ones or peculiar to America or even peculiar to the twentieth century. Perhaps what was involved was the degree to which they were seriously discussed or implemented.

---

[12] James B. Conant, "An American Looks at European Education," in Francis S. Chase and Harold Anderson, eds., *The High School in a New Era* (Chicago: University of Chicago Press, 1958), pp. 26-27.

[13] *Christian Science Monitor*, May 26, 1961.

[14] *School and Society* (December 20, 1958), pp. 460-61.

[15] Nikita S. Khrushchev, "Educating Active and Conscious Builders of a Communist Society," *School and Society* (February 14, 1959), pp. 65-67.

Then, too, the semantics of the situation added to the confusion. One astute observer has pointed out that education has always been under the control of what might be termed "professional educationists," no less in the medieval university than in the modern American high school. Furthermore, "educationists" of earlier times were involved to a surprisingly large extent in studying and teaching the arts of communication or social skills. As mass society emerged, the problem of effective communication and attendant social interrelationships of course enlarged and became exceedingly complex, but its basic nature remained the same.[16]

In any case, there were those who, surveying the American educational scene in the early 1960's, refused to pronounce progressive education dead and buried. "The basic questions which men like John Dewey, William Heard Kilpatrick, George Counts, and Boyd H. Bode raised are inescapable questions," wrote William Van Til in the *Saturday Review of Literature.* "To these probing and fundamental questions, matters of organization and technique while important, are necessarily subordinate." [17] Nevertheless, the crescendo of condemnation which was leveled at American schools during the post-1945 era did succeed in focusing public attention on some organizational weaknesses which were symptomatic of deeper failings under the surface. Most important in this connection was the total lack of national standards of pupil or teacher competence. This was the point at which Bestor, Lieberman, and Rickover all hammered away, and it was this portion of their argument which seemed to make the most lasting impression. In April, 1963, the United States Commissioner of Education, Francis Keppel, termed national scholastic standards "an obviously sensible" goal that "would be useful to parents, to schools, and to everybody else." In thus endorsing greater uniformity and standardization on a permissive basis, Keppel made it clear, however, that he believed great care must be taken to preserve the flexibility which American schools already possessed. And here he was spotlighting a very difficult question, indeed. Could the United States (a much larger, more diverse nation than Switzerland, Britain, or France) upgrade its schools intellectually and at the same time avoid stifling bureaucratization, excessive conformism, pedagogic "red-tape" and "Big Brotherism"? Or would the

[16] See the interesting discussion by Rev. Walter J. Ong, "Educationists and the Tradition of Learning," *Journal of Higher Education* (February 1958), pp. 59-70.
[17] William Van Til, "Is Progressive Education Obsolete?" *Saturday Review of Literature* (February 17, 1962), pp. 56-59.

frantic national effort to re-establish meaningful academic standards
open the door wide for the loss of whatever freedom and individuality
remained?

There is still another question: What does it profit a society to
maintain a system of popular schools for all? M. A. Foster argued in
1925 that democratic education, American style, did, in fact, "pay" the
community. This writer, a statistician in the United States Bureau of
Education, presented data which in his opinion proved the case that
public education returned a measurable dividend because those states
having highest per capita incomes and the lowest illiteracy rates among
native whites were those which had spent the most for education 10 or
20 years before.[18] Other students of the problem demurred. H. F. Clark,
writing in the *Journal of Educational Research* in 1928, pointed out
that if supply and demand factors were taken into account, it might
very well be that so much of a particular kind of education could be
supplied in a society that it would *not* produce an economic return.
The marginal net return would be less in such a situation because some
people of the particular grade or level of ability involved could be
better employed in other channels. For this reason, Clark maintained
that it was a waste of time to speak of education paying or not paying.
Certain kinds of schooling in definite amounts might or might not
"pay" economically. It all depended on the *kind* of schooling. One
variety paid for itself, while the other had to be "paid for" out of the
social surplus.[19]

Other perplexities in the theory and practice of education for all
were noted. Leonard J. Vanden Bergh wrote in 1929 that after a lengthy
study of the administration of California's compulsory education law,
he could only conclude that it was actually contributing to juvenile
delinquency. Children were required to attend school through age sixteen, but the attendance division had the right to grant part-time work
permits. Many intractable older boys were violating the law, and the
writer asserted that "teeth" could not be put into it because vote-seeking
politicians did not want to offend doting parents by putting habitual
delinquents in jail or in special schools.[20] John L. Tildsley, speaking of
the "mounting waste" of the secondary school, stated in 1936 that the

[18] M. A. Foster, *Education Pays the State* (U.S. Bureau of Education Bulletin
No. 33 [Washington, D.C., 1925]).

[19] H. F. Clark, "Some Economic Consequences of Education," *Journal of Educational Research* (November 1928), pp. 279-80.

[20] Leonard J. Vanden Bergh, *Public Schools vs Delinquent Youth* (Los Angeles:
Clark Publishing Co., 1929), pp. 124-29, 174-77.

assumption that "the high school is the best place for all American boys and girls of ages twelve to eighteen" needed "to be demonstrated rather than taken for granted." Tildsley believed that only the upper streams of ability levels should "be directed into schools labeled high schools." The lowest stream or streams, he recommended, should "be deflected into continuation schools of an entirely different character, with teachers on an elementary school schedule." He further wanted to do away "with large buildings, with huge organizations, with everything that operates to prevent education in the high school from becoming an individual process." [21]

Basic to any evaluation of American popular education is the question of its role in the improvement of society. Could democracy's schools really build a new social order? Robert S. Lynd, sociologist and author of the celebrated "Middletown" study, doubted that this could be done. If major changes were required in order to cope with pressing problems in twentieth-century American culture, Lynd felt that it was "impossible to rely primarily upon popular education to effect such changes." He remarked that "this amounts to saying that one cannot get an operation performed by setting out to teach the masses about appendicitis." Lynd concluded that when fundamental changes in the cultural structure were urgently needed, they could only be brought about if well-established specialists and scholars in the social sciences courageously assumed leadership and pointed the way to reform.[22]

It was also rather doubtful, despite the almost-religious dedication of the American people to education for all, whether their public schools were training the bulk of the leaders of American society. A study in 1958 of the data listed in *Who's Who in America* revealed that private schools predominated in terms of the *proportion* of their graduates listed. On this basis, the over-all ratio in *Who's Who* amounted to six private school graduates for each public high school graduate. In the case of ten of the most famous private schools, the ratio was much higher—39 to 1! [23]

Data such as the above emphasizes the crucial challenge to American democratic education posed by the ruling concept in the public schools that potential leaders of the country must be trained within an

[21] John L. Tildsley, *Mounting Waste of the Secondary School* (Cambridge, Mass.: Harvard University Press, 1936), pp. 10-12, 87-89.

[22] Robert S. Lynd, *Knowledge for What?* (Princeton, N.J.: Princeton University Press, 1939), pp. 8-11, 236-50.

[23] Cedric A. Larson, *Sixty Years of American Eminence* (New York: McDowell, Obolensky, 1958), pp. 247-52.

education-for-all framework. Going even further, a question pondered by many modern eugenicists arises to haunt those who place their faith in popular education for individual and social improvability. How far, in actual fact, is man in the mass improvable, even educable? Can the school build a new social order which will produce a "new man," or must there *first* be the "new man"?

Perhaps the leading American educational spokesman in the early decades of the twentieth century for what might be called the "eugenicist" point of view was the measurement specialist, Edward L. Thorndike. The facts did not in his opinion "support the promises of educational evangelists that, if all the children for a generation or two had enough education of the right sort, they would be healthy, wealthy, and wise, living in peace and amity, free from vulgarity and meanness, busy with noble thoughts and deeds." If one had been "nourished by the hope of reforming the world in short order by extending schooling to all to age 21 (or 61, for that matter), he will be disappointed to find that the quantity and quality of a state's schooling in 1900 caused less than 20 per cent of its welfare status in comparison with other states in 1930." It was Thorndike's estimate that differences in home life and training accounted for less than a fifth of the variation among individuals in I.Q.[24] While conceding that free popular education was "one of the finest and most beneficent" institutions that had been developed to help improve human welfare, Thorndike believed that such a tool could only produce meaningful results if a systematic eugenics program of selective breeding was put into effect in connection with the human stock which was to be educated. To tell the American public anything else was to mislead it grievously, he wrote. "What is more contemptible than an ignorant educational reformer (or conservative) selling his wares to a trustful public, taking a profit from spreading guesses and lies!" [25]

Thorndike's data suggested to him that the much-vaunted equality of opportunity that America's system of mass schooling was seeking to provide had in fact "no equalising effect in so easily alterable a trait as rapidity in addition," and little power over such traits as energy, stability, or intellectuality. Long before a child began his schooling, and even before he was born, his potential for work and achievement was determined by hereditary factors. To Thorndike this meant that the only

---

[24] Edward L. Thorndike, *Education As Cause and As Symptom* (New York: The Macmillan Company, 1939), pp. 66-69.
[25] *Ibid.*, pp. 70-71.

true panacea for man's ills was selective breeding for superior intellect and character. "Any method of selective breeding, then, which increases the productivity of intellectually or morally good stock over that of poor stock, will improve man, with one possible added requirement—that breeding should be for fertility as well. . . ." Thorndike labored under no illusions that it would be easy to persuade mankind to accept a eugenic method of race improvement. But he hoped that some day ethics and religion would, in combination, teach man to want it. "It is a noble thing," he remarked, "that human reason, bred of a myriad unreasoned happenings, and driven forth into life by whips made aeons ago with no thought of man's higher wants, can yet turn back to understand man's birth, survey his journey, chart and steer his future course, and free him from barriers without any defects within. Until the last removable impediment in man's own nature dies childless, human reason will not rest." [26]

Supplementing Thorndike's analysis, Professor Ernst Mayr, director of Harvard University's Museum of Comparative Zoology, reported in 1963 that the brain size of man had increased up to Neanderthal times, some 100,000 years ago, but had not grown appreciably since then. Indeed, Mayr found no evidence of any *biological* improvement in man in at least the last 30,000 years. Man's brain grew originally because of his need to communicate and solve the new problem of speech, said the scientist. Intellectually superior specimens in those early days tended to be the leaders and produced more children than the average or below-average members of the tribe. These superior types had a reproductive advantage and were better adapted for survival. But this had not been true in modern times. A few superior individuals could now help the average and below average to enjoy a better standard of living and to survive and breed. The result was, as Sir Julian Huxley had also pointed out, that "man's genetic nature (spiritual and intellectual) has degenerated and is still doing so." The only solution, Mayr said bluntly, was planned mating and production of offspring by the intellectually superior. This latter-day endorsement of Thorndike's eugenicist position was also advocated by Dr. Hans Muller, Nobel prize-winning scientist of Indiana University.[27]

What, we may ask, could the schools of a democratic society, what

[26] E. L. Thorndike, "Eugenics: With Special Reference to Intellect and Character," in *Eugenics: Twelve University Lectures* (New York: Dodd, Mead & Co., 1914), pp. 322-30, 339-42.

[27] Ernst Mayr, *Animal Species and Evolution* (Cambridge, Mass.: Harvard University Press, 1963).

could the schools of *any* society, do to bring about fundamental improvement of the human breed? Perhaps very little, and if so, Americans obviously had been misleading themselves and living in a fool's paradise of great educational expectations. On the other hand, possibly a great deal could be done by the school, if only to produce the kind of leadership needed to take the first steps in the direction of race improvement and the type of intelligently informed public opinion which would be essential to support such efforts. Here, again, Edward L. Thorndike made some rather astute observations. Speaking at a scholarly conference in 1938, he stated that even if psychology should discover the perfect means for selecting the best leaders and even if educational science was able to fit them best to "maximize" the welfare of humanity, it would still be doubtful that mankind would let them do it. History has shown, he contended, that mankind has been "careless and perverse in its treatment of the good leaders who have emerged." Because of this, able leaders have often been obliged to advertise and promote themselves in order to entice and wheedle mankind into welfare. Often, too, instead of able leaders, the situation has bred "fighting propagandists, charlatans, demagogues." A change of human hearts and habits was necessary. "The change of heart that is necessary," Thorndike observed, "is from a trust in luck and miracles and a fondness for whom and what makes one feel comfortable to a courageous acceptance of the real world and a resolute and loyal allegiance to genuine experts wherever they may be found." For this reason, he concluded, the proper education of leaders was not enough; it would have to be paralleled by the proper education of followers, followers who would learn to discriminate in choosing responsible leadership and to trust expert knowledge.[28]

But could this be done by a democratic system of popular schooling, dedicated in an age of the emergence of the masses to education for all? Why not? As the Rockefeller Brothers report of 1958 pointed out, there is no inherent clash in a democratic society such as that of twentieth-century America between equality of opportunity and the pursuit of excellence. An "education for all" society could, if it so chose, embrace the concept of appreciation of many kinds of achievement, of many varieties of excellence. Carried out to its full implications, the con-

---

[28] Edward L. Thorndike, "How Should a Democratic People Select Leaders," in I. L. Kandel, Leta S. Hollingworth, and E. L. Thorndike, *How Should a Democratic People Provide for the Selection and Training of Leaders in the Various Walks of Life* (New York: Columbia (Teachers College) University Press, 1938), pp. 34-41.

scious acceptance of such a principle would make possible, for the first time in human history, the realization of Thorndike's dream of *both* an educated leadership *and* a discriminating followership, with meaningful social and race improvement as the ultimate consequence.[29]

Professor R. M. Harper of the University of Alabama noted in the *Scientific Monthly* in 1920 that in any historic society, whatever its system of economics or government, there has always been a tiny minority of talents "whose chief occupation is adding to the sum of human knowledge, or writing or doing things that have not been said or done before, such as investigators, explorers, inventors, scientists, poets, novelists, humorists, cartoonists, composers, artists, 'empire builders'. . . ." It is on this small class, Professor Harper asserted, "constituting (in the United States) something like one ten-thousandth of the total population, that the progress of civilization mainly depends." [30] The very fact that the *Pursuit of Excellence* report was published in 1958 showed that important leaders of the American nation were becoming convinced that the actual survival of American democracy depended, first, on the cultivation of such a creative segment and, second, on the development of an appreciation among the masses of the people of the vital contributions such talents were capable of making. Such an appreciation of excellence in a modern democratic setting would be basically different from the ancient classical concept. The latter distinguished free men as a caste from slaves and limited "liberal" or "liberating" education to a tiny minority, while training slaves, serfs, manual workers, and artisans in keeping with their future socio-economic functions. The American implementation of the search for excellence would be based on a fundamental commitment to the education of everyone to the limit of his possibilities. Every man would be given a chance to develop as a man. Through a system of equality of opportunity, it was hoped, a mass appreciation of trained excellence would emerge. From such an educational structure would come the realization of Thomas Jefferson's dream of a "natural aristocracy" as democracy's leadership. But this would be a modern "natural aristocracy" attuned to the new

[29] See Charles W. Eliot, "Survey of the Condition of American Education," in *Twentieth Century Club*, University Lectures, 1901-1902 (Boston: J. P. Schults, 1901); in *More Money for the Public Schools* (New York: Doubleday & Company, Inc., 1903), pp. 57-63, Eliot specifies a number of developments which he believed proved that American popular education had, up to that time, positively improved the quality of national life, had promoted intelligence, and diffused more widely a sound mental training.

[30] R. M. Harper, "Graphic Method of Measuring Civilization," *Scientific Monthly* (March 1920), pp. 292-305.

needs of an industrial, scientific democracy, to the rise of the masses, to the impact of universal and instantaneous communication, to the human possession of hitherto undreamed sources of knowledge and power.

The *Pursuit of Excellence* report put this concept very strongly when it asserted that:

> . . . on its [America's] ability to solve this problem rests its fate as a free people. In a free society an undiscovered talent, a wasted individual skill, a misapplied human ability is a threat to that people's capacity to survive. Hence a free nation's search for talent is always a critical aspect of its national existence. . . . Society as a whole must come to the aid of the individual—finding ways to identify him as a unique person, and to place him alongside his fellow men in ways which will not inhibit and destroy his individuality. By its educational system, its public and private institutional practices, and perhaps most importantly, by its attitude toward the creative person, a free society can actively insure its own constant invigoration.[31]

Although stated in somewhat different language, the preceding concept does not really seem to be at variance with John Dewey's hope for the cultivation of significant problem-solving capacity in the people's schools and the application of purposeful trained intelligence to the task of social engineering and the reconstruction of the nation's life.

Robert M. Hutchins has pointed out that the goals of American democratic education are right if democracy itself is right.[32] From the time of Franklin and Jefferson to the time of national soul-searching in the mid-twentieth-centry era of "Cold War," the American people have refused to believe that the idea of a fair chance for every person to develop his capacities to the uttermost and an equal chance for all to compete for society's positions of creative leadership is just a dream. As long as they retain this faith there is a good chance that they will realize it. And if they so succeed, that success will in itself be a challenge to them to improve upon, perfect, and strengthen a truly unique educational heritage.

[31] *The Pursuit of Excellence*, Rockefeller Brothers Fund, Inc. (Garden City, N.Y.: Doubleday & Company, Inc., 1958).

[32] Hutchins, *Some Observations on American Education*, p. 22.

Index